One Night, Two Teams

One Night, Two Teams

*Alabama vs. USC and the
Game That Changed a Nation*

Steven Travers

TAYLOR TRADE PUBLISHING
Lanham • New York • Boulder • Toronto • Plymouth, UK

Published by Taylor Trade Publishing
An imprint of The Rowman & Littlefield Publishing Group, Inc.
4501 Forbes Boulevard, Suite 200, Lanham, Maryland 20706

Estover Road, Plymouth PL6 7PY, United Kingdom

Distributed by NATIONAL BOOK NETWORK

Library of Congress Cataloging-in-Publication Data
Travers, Steven.
   One night, two teams : Alabama vs. USC and the game that changed a nation / Steven Travers. — 1st Taylor Trade Pub. ed.
      p. cm.
   Includes bibliographical references and index.
   ISBN-13: 978-1-58979-370-5 (cloth : alk. paper)
   ISBN-10: 1-58979-370-6 (cloth : alk. paper)
   1. University of Alabama—Football—History—20th century. 2. Alabama Crimson Tide (Football team)—History—20th century. 3. University of Southern California—Football—History—20th century. 4. Southern California Trojans (Football team)—History—20th century. 5. College sports—Social aspects—United States. 6. Discrimination in sports—United States. 7. Sports rivalries—United States. I. Title.

GV958.U513T73 2007
796.332'630973—dc22

                                                                2007006435

♾™ The paper used in this publication meets the minimum requirements of American National Standard for Information Sciences—Permanence of Paper for Printed Library Materials, ANSI/NISO Z39.48-1992.
Manufactured in the United States of America.

This book is dedicated to the Greek concept of Platonic justice
and to the universal ideals of the Lord Jesus Christ,
because these principles have made America the greatest country
in the history of mankind.

I don' need ta know history, I know now.
—*Charles Barkley*

Those who do not remember the past are condemned to relive it.
—*Santayana*

Res ipsa loquitur.
The thing speaks for itself (i.e., the thing stands on its own).

Ye shall know the truth, and the truth shall make you free.
—*Jesus Christ, the Gospel According to John*

Contents

Foreword

Winston Groom

By the late 1960s, University of Alabama football coach Paul "Bear" Bryant had seen the handwriting on the wall. Sometimes on Friday nights before a college game, he'd go to high school contests (many still played between predominantly black schools) and marvel at the size, speed, and athletic abilities of some of the black players. But there were no black players on Bryant's football teams.

A few of the Southeastern Conference schools, Kentucky and Vanderbilt, for instance, had a few black players, but none of the old-line Deep South colleges such as Alabama, even though the school was integrated and blacks were already playing basketball there.

But Bryant was a canny enough politician to know that, with racial tensions running high as they were (this was the heyday of the civil rights movement), any black player who came to the university would have a large, glaring spotlight shining on him.

Schools cannot choose who their fans are going to be, Bryant knew—and there were probably some racists, maybe more than a few, among Alabama's. Therefore, he concluded that the first black football player or players he recruited would need to be exceptional—actually, more than exceptional. Bryant knew that only in this way would the player gain immediate and unconditional acceptance and not have his youthful ego pounded into the ground by the screaming of seventy thousand mostly white football fans if he happened to throw five interceptions on a bad Saturday afternoon.

Bryant had been quietly trying to recruit blacks of exceptional caliber but had been unsuccessful. During depositions for a lawsuit that had been brought against the university, Bryant said that all the star blacks he spoke with did not want to attend the university, which only six years earlier had to be forcibly integrated. They wanted to go to schools such as USC or Michigan—places where they believed they would feel more welcome.

Finally the breakthrough came, but in the most disagreeable fashion— a stunning home-game loss to Southern Cal in 1970, in which two black players, Sam Cunningham and Clarence Davis, ran all over the famed Crimson Tide. And to make it even more embarrassing, Davis was from Birmingham, Alabama, then the site of 'Bama's premier home games.

With this humiliating defeat staring everyone in the face, Bryant now felt safe enough to begin recruiting black players big time and out in the open. Soon he signed Wilbur Jackson, who led the Tide to a shared national championship in 1973, and the race barrier was broken forever at the University of Alabama.

In this book, *One Night, Two Teams*, USC graduate Steve Travers tells us all about the exciting and remarkable football contest that changed not only the way the game is played but also the way Southern whites look at their black brethren—and therefore changed the nation.

Winston Groom is an Alabama graduate who was acquainted with coach Paul "Bear" Bryant. He is the author of The Crimson Tide: An Illustrated History of Football at the University of Alabama. *He also wrote* Forrest Gump, *as well as fourteen other books.*

Acknowledgments

A book like this is the product of many things coming together, and I would like to hereby acknowledge some people. I would like to first thank agent Craig Wiley. You would not be reading this without his efforts. Also, thank you to Taylor Trade, a division of Rowman & Littlefield Publishers, Inc.; my editor, Rick Rinehart; and his assistant, Dulcie Wilcox. Further thanks to production editor Alden Perkins, along with Katherine Smith, Jen Linck, Jenni Brewer, Sabrina Sicard, and Lauren Pogue.

This book has already been featured in two documentaries, one on Paul "Bear" Bryant and another, *Tackling Segregation*, both by College Sports Television, a division of CBS. Thanks to Bridget Dungan, Meredith DePaolo, and everybody over at CSTV. Thanks to my late uncle, Col. Charles Travers, who graciously allowed the film crew into his home to conduct interviews.

The subject of this book is also being made into a major motion picture. I would like to extend my thanks to Kerry McCluggage, USC '74, of Allumination/Craftsman Films for believing in our project. This would not have occurred without the vision of my "producing partners," legendary Trojan Anthony Davis and my good friend Jim Starr. Furthermore, it was the great efforts of Lloyd Robinson of Suite A Management in Beverly Hills that turned the whole idea into reality. The aforementioned Craig Wiley and Rick Rinehart also deserve kudos for helping untangle the thicket of book and movie rights to the satisfaction of all.

Thank you also to Professor Dan Durbin of the USC Annenberg School of Communications for inviting me to be the guest speaker in his

"Sports, Culture and Society" class when the subject of this book was a featured topic. Thank you so much to the other panelists that day: Craig Fertig, Willie Brown, Manfred Moore, Dave Brown, George Follett, and Rod McNeill. Thanks also to Dr. Patricia Dean and Professor Ken Sereno of the Annenberg School. Thank you also to Peter Miller of PMA Literary and Film Management, Inc. in New York City.

Thank you so much to the USC Bookstore and USC Collections at the South Coast Plaza in Orange County for rolling out the red carpet for me.

I want to thank former Trojan football player John Papadakis, who once called me "a true USC historian and a loyal Trojan!" To Sam "Bam" Cunningham and Allan Graf: thank you. Further thanks to Mark Houska and Petros Papadakis of Fox Sports and movie producer and attorney David Dizenfeld, USC '71.

I wish to thank former University of Southern California sports information director (SID) Jim Perry, who also coauthored legendary Trojan football coach John McKay's successful 1970s autobiography, *McKay: A Coach's Story*. Perry has been an institution for years at Heritage Hall. He was the SID when I worked alongside Tim Tessalone during my brief student internship in the USC sports information office. My gratitude goes out to Tim, who after succeeding Perry has maintained the high standards that Jim set for the office. A further shout-out to Jason Pommier and Paul Goldberg of USC's football media relations, plus Chris Huston, who has helped me many times over the years.

Thank you to the University of Alabama sports information office, in particular Barry Allen and Larry White. Also, thank you to Jan Adams at the Paul W. Bryant Museum, and particularly Ken Gaddy. Thanks go to Winston Groom, author of *Forrest Gump*.

I extend my gratitude to former *L.A. Times* sportswriters Jeff Prugh and Dwight Chapin, two real pros; to current USC beat writer Gary Klein; and to former *Times* sports editor Bill Dwyre. I also thank the widow of the great Jim Murray, Linda McCoy-Murray; Tony McEwing; and Gene Collier of the *Pittsburgh Post-Gazette*. Thank you to Allen Barra and Keith Dunnavant, who have written extensively on Bear Bryant and Alabama football.

I thank USC head football coach Pete Carroll, who has stated that I am "the next great USC historian, in the tradition of Jim Murray, John Hall, and Mal Florence," and also wrote that "the Trojan Family needs your work!" Coach Carroll and I went to the same suburban California high school. I grew up hearing stories about Carroll, who was a classmate of comic actor Robin Williams. Thanks also to others in that circle, who include Skip Corsini, Jim Peters, Bill Peters, Bob Troppmann, Ken Flower, Phil Roark, and Jess Payan.

Coach Carroll's former assistant, Mark Jackson, and USC athletic director Mike Garrett are in line for acknowledgments, as is Dennis Slutak. Thank you to others in the Trojan family: Jen Noriega, Teresa Verbeck, Chad Kreuter, Dave Lawn, Mike Gillespie, Irene Puentes, Danielle Martinez-Galvan, and former Trojan basketball coach Jim Saia.

I also wish to mention Dale Komai, Bruce Seltzer, Joe Enloe, Brad Wong, Melanie Neff, Lindsay Lautz, Melanie Pedrick, Rob Pedrick, Jamie McGinley, Dr. Keith Matsuoka, Kathy Yaffe, Red Smith, Chuck Lamb, Rene Lamb, Mark Gonzalez, Jim Restrich, Shannon Abraham, Marni Lovrich, Cynthia Christian, Nick Rasich, and everybody else with the USC Alumni Association. Thanks to Barry LeBrock of Fox Sports, John Wooden, Dave Daniel, Joe Jares and Matt Derringer of *USC Report*, Loel Schrader and Steve Bisheff, Gary Paskiewitz of www.wearesc.com, Andy Bark of *Student Sports*, Bob Rowher of the *L.A. Times*, the late Sam Skinner and Kathy Pfrommer of the *Oakland Tribune*, John Underwood, Wayne Fontes, Dennis Fitzpatrick, Donavon McNabb, Joe Gibbs, the Washington Redskins, Joe Gibbs Racing, Charlie Evans, Rod Sherman of the Trojan Fantasy Camp, Rich Burg, Stu Zanville, Craig Long and the Oakland Raiders, Frank Jordan, Paul McDonald, Rob Fukuzaki, Dave Smith, Pete Arbogast, 710/KSPN, Fred Wallin, Harvey Hyde, Chuck Hayes, Sharon Gould of the Eagle Rock High School Alumni Association, San Clemente High School, Charlie Weaver, the Detroit Lions, Richmond High School athletic director Roy Rogers, Arizona Western Junior College, Ray Butcher, Jimmy Jones, the Harrisburg Boys Club, Joe Namath, the African American Registry, Ken Hall, Mal Moore, Ken Stabler, Kim Bush, Simon & Schuster, Nancy Covington and Mike Neemah of Mississippi State University, Vigor High School, Suzanne Dowling and Chris Bryant of the University of Alabama media relations department, Alabama Booksmith, the University of Alabama Press, Reid Drinkard, Fred Kirsch of the New England Patriots, Mr. and Mrs. Hannah of Albertville, Alabama, the San Francisco 49ers, the Pittsburgh Steelers, Gene Upshaw and the NFL Players Association, the K Club, the University of Alabama Alumni Association, Richmond Flowers Jr., the University of Tennessee sports information office, Jeff Dubinsky of ESPN Classic, Liz Kennedy and Jose Eskenazi of USC, Daniel Hopper and the Department of Intercollegiate Athletics at the University of Alabama, former University of Alabama head football coach Mike Shula, John

Sciarra, John Robinson, J. K. McKay, Pat Haden, Art Spander, Don Andersen, Mike Walden, Tom Kelly, Dave Levy, Rod Martin, Johnny Musso, B. Green of the Paul W. Bryant Museum, Shirley Ito and Wayne Wilson of the Amateur Athletic Foundation of Los Angeles, and Howard Schnellenberger.

Additional thanks to Clarence Davis, Sam Dickerson, the late, great Bud "the Steamer" Furillo, Clem Gryska, John Vella, Dr. Culpepper Clark, Jack Rutledge, John Hannah, Christ Vagotis, Scott Hunter, Wilbur Jackson, Sylvester Croom, Wendell Hudson, and John Mitchell.

I would like to make special mention of three extraordinary Trojans, who not only gave tirelessly their time, intellect, memory, and support but also formed a bond of Christian fellowship with me: Dave Brown and Manfred Moore, who were as mentioned on the panel with me at the Annenberg School of Communications, as well as the beautiful, gracious Charles "Tree" Young. God bless you, and I honestly mean this: I love all of you dearly.

I would like to remember the late Tody Smith and to thank his brother, football Hall of Famer Bubba Smith.

I also thank Cherie Kerr, Earle Self, and Bruce H. Franklin, plus Neal McCready and Randy Kennedy of the *Mobile Press-Register*. Thanks also to the National Collegiate Athletic Association.

Since this book is largely about the University of Southern California, I want to thank everybody in the extended Trojan family. As it is often said, "You are a Bruin for four years but a Trojan for life!" These are true words. In that spirit, thanks to the late John McKay and the late Marv Goux, who granted me interviews shortly before their respective passings. Thank you also to Goux's lovely widow, Mrs. Patricia Goux; his daughter Linda (whom I had a class with at USC); and his granddaughter Kara (who created the inspiring phrase "Win one for the Goux," at his memorial service).

I would like to extend my gratitude to the past and present pastors, as well as all of my fellow members, at Christ Lutheran Church.

My most sincere thank-yous are reserved for the end. This includes my parents, who gave me encouragement and support, as they always do; and my sweet daughter, Elizabeth Travers. No acknowledgments are complete without naming my cousin Bill Friedrichs and his wife, Jean, whose great help and support over the years can never really be repaid. I also want to thank eight close friends. Kevin McCormack and Terry and Cecile Marks are true Trojans. Jake Downey roots for the Bruins but possesses the nobility of a Trojan. Mike McDowd and Don Rasmussen have provided fellowship over the years. Bradley Cole (who comes from a true USC family) and I go back a long way. Alex Jacobs helped with research.

Finally, my biggest thank-you is reserved for my Lord and Savior Jesus Christ, who is the source of all that is good, decent, and true!

Author's Note

> The truth, when witnessed in an American arena,
> is never misunderstood.
>
> —*Former USC football player John Papadakis*

The above statement by John Papadakis is one the former Trojan linebacker has made many times in interviews and in public settings such as banquets. It succinctly tells the story (perhaps the only time John has ever been succinct) of what happened on the night of September 12, 1970, at Legion Field in Birmingham, Alabama. It describes perfectly the practicality of a football game and the spirituality that accompanied it.

When I set out to write this book, it was my intention to view this story as one primarily driven by Christianity. In interviewing many people on both sides—USC and Alabama, liberal and conservative, Christian and non-Christian—I posed this question and heard varied answers and interpretations on my theory. At the end of the day, I continue to hold to the belief that Christianity propelled the transformation of the American South and therefore lies at the heart of this tale of sports, race, politics, and religion.

It is necessary to briefly tell my story in order to put my opinions in perspective. I was baptized Lutheran but not raised in the church. I attended public schools. When I was a senior in high school, a classmate whose name I have forgotten but whose kind face I will never forget saw me sitting on a bench, eating lunch by myself. He asked if he could tell me about the Lord Jesus Christ. I said yes, and I accepted the Lord then and there. I did not immediately become a "good Christian" or regular church-goer. I continue to this day to be a flawed, sinful man; but every year since then, my faith has grown stronger and my sins perhaps a little weaker. It is extremely important, at least in my case, to understand that I am not perfect because I am a Christian but that I need Christianity precisely because I am so imperfect!

When I was in college, I attended a basketball game and heard the Athletes in Action Christians talk about Jesus at halftime. The experience was an epiphany for me. Several of my baseball teammates who competed with me for playing time also expressed their benevolent Christian love to me. This opened my eyes. Many of my friends were Catholic, and I occasionally attended Mass with them, which I always found fascinating. After I pitched and won my first professional baseball game in the St. Louis Cardinals organization, I was the last to leave the clubhouse because I had to ice my arm afterward. Walking back to the hotel by myself through the quiet streets of a small Tennessee town, I had an emotional "conversation" with my Savior. I thanked Him for seeing me through to my goal in life, which was, up until then, to play baseball at the professional level.

Over the years, my achievements were matched by my failures. I came to recognize that becoming a millionaire baseball star was not God's plan for me. Other priorities, such as fatherhood and the realization that the "plan" for me was to make use of my intellect and passion for writing, became self-evident. Throughout it all, I understood through Christ the nobility of struggle, thanking Him for what I had and realizing that what I did not have was a test of my faith over which I would prevail. At the heart of it all is the desire that, despite my selfish nature, I want to *do good*! I pray that in writing this book I have done that.

The relationship of sports and race is another theme of this work, and again I have to start from my own perspective. I was born in California and raised in an affluent, almost entirely white suburb. Since I was a good athlete, I was part of a team that ventured past the narrow boundaries of our community. I earned a scholarship to play ball in college, where I further expanded my worldview. I played collegiate summer ball in Canada and the Midwest. I traveled and had teammates from different places and backgrounds, and I was a better man for it.

As a minor league baseball player, I traveled all over the South and the Rocky Mountains. My teammates and opponents were blacks from inner cities and the rural South; Dominicans and other Latinos, many of whom did not speak English; and young men from every educational, socioeconomic, and geographical background. Friendships and common understandings were formed. Baseball provided two essential things: travel with real-life experience that cannot be taught in a classroom, and a truly level playing field. Sports may be the fairest, most egalitarian occupation there is. Between the white lines, your talent and desire are all you have. You fail and succeed based strictly on these factors.

In trying to make sense of sports and religion in the Alabama of 1970, I discovered that integration succeeded for the same reason that America succeeds: the trident of religious morality, democratic freedom, and market capitalism. Those who take the cynical view that the South—specifically the University of Alabama—allowed blacks to play football only because their alumni wanted to win games are partly right. Those who see integration as America's political promises finally being kept are also partly right. As they say, the Lord works in mysterious ways.

As a former professional athlete, I developed rapport with the ex-players and coaches I interviewed, a connection few writers ever get to make. The experience was not only enjoyable but also inspiring. Most anybody who has ever gone to high school or college has seen star athletes receive special treatment. The fact is, many popular athletes—especially males who play football, basketball, or baseball in high school, college, and especially professionally—often physically bully others, think of sex as their birthright, and have no idea that the world does not revolve around them. There are exceptions to this, but anybody in the sports media knows this stereotype is rooted in truth that extends across racial lines. I can make this observation because it describes me as a young man.

The athletes and coaches I interviewed were at the very top of their professions in the late 1960s and early 1970s. These were legendary head coaches, prized assistants, and first-rate scholarship blue-chippers playing at two of the best Division I programs in America, in the height of their glory. Many of these athletes went on to star in the NFL. Some were All-Pro, even in the Hall of Fame. The very best of the best.

Though this book revolves around a game, the nuts and bolts of that game—statistics, performance—take a backseat to the important issues that revolved around its larger meaning: civil rights, politics, social change, religion, and race.

My interviews were not centered on game performance. Instead, I challenged these men to address these very issues. The results were inspiring.

Thirty-seven years after the game, these men are no longer star athletes. The world does not revolve around them anymore, and they know it. Instead, they are political scientists, philosophers, lawyers, financial advisers, teachers, coaches, and husbands. Some are Christians; others are antireligious. Some of these former popular athletes are now divorced men who discovered that the girls who were their "birthright" at twenty no longer saw luster in them at fifty-five. Some are fathers struggling to impart wisdom to children who are just like they had once been.

Now these physically intimidating men, men of massive power and brutal strength, recall the event in the soft light of historical analysis, religious conviction, and personal relationships, which transcend the sport they played.

Something happens to people between the ages of eighteen and thirty in America: a natural maturation process often turns twenty-something unimpressives into responsible citizens a decade or so later. I found men tempered by life, by marketplace capitalism, by unfairness, by experience, and by this great nation we live in. Almost to a man, they are better off for having experienced the 1970 USC-Alabama game and for living in the United States in the succeeding years. All of them would state that sports have been a positive influence in their lives. They have unique perspectives on the effects of that game—racially, morally and personally.

I am a graduate of the University of Southern California, so I have heard the story of this game from the Trojan perspective. In this book, I was determined to give both sides a fair shake. I was struck by the differences between the perceptions of whites and blacks, USC and Alabama. I was also struck by the similarities brought about by the shared experiences of football in America. I am also happy to report that I could not detect one single case of even slightly latent or residual racism from a single Southerner I spoke to. Conversely, with perhaps one small exception, the black players from USC harbored no ill will. Furthermore, I am here to report that, after I did the research, Alabama coach Paul "Bear" Bryant emerges in my view as a true hero of the civil rights movement. His counterpart, USC coach John McKay, was a modern Moses of progressivism in their profession. I spoke to some who disagree with this analysis, and I report their opinions using their own words.

Although I'm a USC graduate, I hope I do not demonstrate bias in my writing. The fact is that my favorite team is the good ol' U.S. of A. That's right, I root for America.

I welcome feedback—positive and negative—from Trojan and Crimson Tide fans. I welcome the opinions of all college football fans, political pundits, religious theorists, and the like. My opinions are mine. I have well-thought-out reasons for them, and I offer them with respect. Please offer yours in the same manner.

Steven Travers
USCSTEVE1@aol.com
(415) 455-5971

Introduction

Segregation was the law. It was a violent time then.

—*Former University of Alabama player and coach Sylvester Croom*

In 1787, the Founding Fathers hammered out the U.S. Constitution. Written in part by Southern slaveholders, the document spoke to that "peculiar institution." The Founders wanted to end the practice of slavery, but they needed the South's agrarian economy to grow the young country. The compromise was that slavery would remain, but after around 1800, no more slaves would be imported from Africa. The theory was that over time, the existing slaves would die of old age, and the South would incrementally change its workforce according to capitalistic principles.

Slave importation was eventually stopped, but the plan "failed" because American slaves were clothed, fed, housed, treated medically, Christianized, and allowed to marry and have families that were sometimes kept together. Instead of "dying off," the slaves grew in population, becoming a vital force in the Southern farm economy. Then, out of America's Puritan Christian ethic grew the increasingly powerful abolitionist movement. Slavery was the driving issue behind the Civil War. When that war ended, so did the legal practice of slavery.

What followed was a century of hatred and recrimination. After Abraham Lincoln's assassination, the Reconstruction was botched. The Ku Klux Klan rose in "righteous indignation." For another century, Southern blacks lived a life of de facto slavery, confined by Jim Crow laws to a segregated world of "whites" and "colored" drinking fountains, bathrooms,

1

restaurants, hotels, and, of course, schools. These laws were legitimized by the Democratic Party, which dominated Southern politics and supported the sordid practice.

The pride of the South was its colleges, ranging from venerable private institutions such as Vanderbilt to public colleges such as Alabama and Mississippi. No black man or woman dared enter these hallowed halls.

After World War II, the U.S. Army desegregated. In 1954, the Supreme Court's *Brown v. Board of Education* decision ruled that segregation of public high schools (and by extension, at least in theory, colleges) according to race was illegal. President Dwight Eisenhower understood the Southern mind-set. He pursued an incremental approach to civil rights. Still, he attempted to bring forth legislation that would ensure black voting rights and other freedoms. Southern Democrats blocked his efforts.

In 1963, Vivian Malone and James Hood entered the University of Alabama, becoming the first blacks to do so. Governor George Wallace countered their entrance. Wallace made his celebrated "stand" and his infamous "segregation today, segregation forever" speech. A similar incident occurred at the University of Mississippi, where a courageous African American named James Meredith braved hatred to pursue higher education.

Black civil rights leader Dr. Martin Luther King Jr. had begun the bold practice of staging marches, sit-ins, and demonstrations in the heart of Dixie. He led the 1955–1956 boycott of the Montgomery bus lines. In 1963, he wrote "Letter from a Birmingham Jail" following a large-scale protest in that city. In the same year, he led the March on Washington, where he made his famed "I have a dream" speech in front of the Lincoln Memorial. He won the Nobel Peace Prize.

In 1964, King fought for black voter registration by leading the Freedom March from Selma to Montgomery, Alabama. He was jailed. His supporters, white and black, met with violence. Blood filled the streets. King insisted on maintaining the movement, in the tradition of Mahatma Gandhi, as one of nonviolent revolution.

President John Kennedy made tentative steps toward legal integration. When he was murdered in 1963, an unlikely torchbearer emerged. President Lyndon Johnson, from Texas, ushered in the Civil Rights Act of 1964 and the Voting Rights Act of 1965. The South was still widely Democratic and opposed it widely. Republicans, however, stepped up and helped pass the law.

At the 1968 Mexico City Olympics, African American athletes Tommie Smith and John Carlos finished first and third in the 200-meter dash. They raised black-gloved fists during "The Star-Spangled Banner." Both were suspended and thrown out of the Olympic Village. Both athletes had been approached by African American Berkeley sociologist Dr. Harry Edwards in an effort to boycott the Games. Many black athletes, including UCLA basketball All-American Lew Alcindor (later renamed Kareem Abdul-Jabbar), joined the boycott.

In 1968, Richard Nixon began the tightrope act that helped transform Southern politics. He formed a delicate coalition of Republicans and supporters of Wallace who wanted their vote to count. His "Southern strategy" resulted in his election to the presidency. Eventually, this provided the impetus the Grand Old Party needed to husband Dixie back into the mainstream.

* * *

In 1892 William Henry Lewis became the first black football player at Harvard. He was a two-time All-American.

Fritz Pollard, a black man, played in the 1916 Rose Bowl for Brown and made All-American. The *New York Times* described him as "a player of such brilliancy as illuminated the gridiron about every half dozen years."

Another African American, Paul Robeson, played at Rutgers in the 1920s. He later became a controversial singer, actor, and mouthpiece for Communism, apparently until a visit to the USSR opened his eyes to the evils of it, leading to a reported deathbed reversal.

In the late 1950s and 1960s, blacks made enormous strides in college football. Syracuse stars Jim Brown and Ernie Davis made their marks. Occasionally, Southern teams played integrated squads in bowl games, always with controversy and fan resistance. These contests were almost never south of the Mason-Dixon Line. Great black athletes from the South and East filled out college rosters in the Pacific 8 and Big 10 Conferences. Michigan State played the famous 1966 "game of the century" versus Notre Dame with a black quarterback, Jimmy Raye, and an All-American black defensive end named Bubba Smith, who hailed from Texas.

In 1966, basketball coach Don Haskins fielded an all-black starting five at Texas Western University (now the University of Texas–El Paso). He took Texas Western all the way to the NCAA tournament. His opponent was legendary coach Adolph Rupp, whose Kentucky team dominated the pre-UCLA and John Wooden era but was now finding itself left behind. When Haskins's team won, the "old order" was upended. Rupp has been portrayed as a racist. To put it more kindly, he was a man of a certain time and place.

Birmingham, Alabama, was nicknamed "Bombingham" after the 1963 bombing of the 16th Street Baptist Church. Four little black girls lost their lives. Condoleezza Rice, who would become the secretary of state, was growing up in Birmingham at the time and knew one of the girls.

It was "acts like these set Alabama apart in its savagery in the eyes of the country," Chris McNair, the father of the youngest bombing victim, was quoted saying by writer Don Yaeger.

University of Alabama football coach Paul "Bear" Bryant and members of the board of trustees had been in Bear's second-story office in a building on the corner, where they witnessed Alabama governor George Wallace's infamous "stand in the schoolhouse door," which occurred in Tuscaloosa the same year as the bombings.

Bryant was the child of sharecroppers. His nickname, "Bear," came from his teenage years when he wrestled a black bear at a local fair in rural Arkansas.

"Bryant literally *is* the American dream," said Taylor Watson, curator of the Paul W. Bryant Museum. "He understood that it all involved hard work."

"Coach Bryant saw no difference between black kids and white kids," said Allen Barra, author of *The Last Coach: A Life of Paul "Bear" Bryant*. "I think this goes back to his youth growing up in Morro Bottom."

Indeed, Bryant had been raised on the "wrong side of the tracks," as the saying goes, but in 1963 he was seen as part of the white establishment. If at this point in his life he saw "no difference" between the races, he was not somebody counted on as an ally by black folks.

He had been a star end opposite Don Hutson, playing in the 1935 Rose Bowl. He coached at Maryland, Kentucky, and Texas A&M before returning to 'Bama in 1958.

In 1959, Alabama faced Penn State in the Liberty Bowl. Bryant was criticized for facing an integrated Nittany Lion team with five blacks. Local "citizens' groups" in Tuscaloosa objected. Alabama lost the game, 7–0.

During the next eleven years, there was little improvement in racial opportunity for athletes in the South. Wake Forest brought in a token black player. Lester McClain was a black wingback at Tennessee from 1968 to 1970. But state laws precluded segregation in certain cases.

Richmond Flowers Sr. became a foil for Governor Wallace's segregationist views. As Alabama's attorney general, he prosecuted the KKK. But when he ran for governor against Wallace's wife, Cornelia (who ran because her husband faced term limits), he was badly beaten. His son, Richmond Flowers Jr., was known as the "fastest white boy alive." An Alabama prep track and football star, he engendered more hatred for the family by spurning the University of Alabama in favor of Tennessee.

"I really wanted to get out of Alabama and get it behind me," sportswriter Don Yaeger quoted Flowers as saying. After starring at Tennessee, Flowers embarked on a pro career starting with the Dallas Cowboys.

Still, Bryant did not share the racist views of many of his fellow Alabamians. He knew that through education would come understanding. He had seen it in his own life.

Wallace was a political chameleon. He originally campaigned for black votes in the style of Earl and Huey Long, the demagogic Louisiana political brothers who spurred the "populist" movement during the New Deal. Wallace lost a gubernatorial election to a strict segregationist, John Patterson, in 1958. He vowed never to be "out-n--red again." He became the most strident voice of segregation in the 1960s. Later he decided to change his segregationist stance in anticipation of the 1972 elections. In the meantime, Bryant monitored these issues, as had new university president David Matthews.

"Segregation was the *law*," emphasized former Alabama player, assistant coach, and later Mississippi State head coach Sylvester Croom. "It was a violent time then."

A documentary detailing Bryant's career, aired in the mid-1990s, showed footage purportedly from 1970 or perhaps earlier of Coach Bryant saying blacks did not have the necessary attributes, *at that time*, to play big-time college football in the South.

However, Bryant left himself an out. He based his opinion not solely on black football skills, but on their ability to handle the academic course work. This would indicate that he was concerned about their social treatment and felt that the public schools failed to provide adequate education for them. Bryant, ever the politician, was mainly playing to his base constituency, which was white and segregationist. In truth, he had already taken steps to effectuate change. To those who knew Bryant well, he was never racist. Apparently he put on a different face for his varied friends, associates, and players.

On July 2, 1969, U. W. Clemon, then a Birmingham civil rights lawyer, "inherited" a lawsuit on behalf of eleven black people against Bryant and the University of Alabama, specifically with regard to the school's lack of athletic scholarship offers to African Americans. One year later Bryant testified, "Three or four years ago we began looking in the state and this was prior to the time when they started blacks and whites playing one another. And our thinking was that [if] any good ones came along, we certainly didn't want them to get away, and if we wanted to start, we wanted to start with Alabama boys."

Bryant kept a list of the best players, which he protected for fear of "Auburn knowing who we are after." Clemon stated that while taking Bryant's deposition, he did not sense that the man was a racist. He said he had taken the depositions of many racists and had a "feel" for such a thing. Bryant noted several black prospects in the state, but he matter-of-factly noted that each had "gotten away," recruited by another program, lost for one reason or another in the way that any blue-chipper might be scooped up by a rival. The deposition listed some ninety-three pages of these kinds of incidents—lack of academic qualifications, lost to Grambling, family said no, plucked up by a Western program . . .

The case was dismissed, but oddly both sides had made their point. The game versus USC was by that time scheduled for a couple months away. Wilbur Jackson was in school, John Mitchell would soon be recruited, and the times they were a-changin'.

Bryant had won national championships in the preceding decade. He coached two of the game's most popular personalities, Joe Namath and Kenny Stabler. He knew how to harness these kinds of players.

"In the South, of course, being on the wrong side of slavery has a tough memory," said Taylor Watson in the 2006 College Sports Television documentary *Tackling Segregation*. "It was hard to forget about the politics of race in the South. . . . Alabama doesn't have a lot to be proud of, but Alabama football was something we could be proud of."

They *were* proud, but the fact that he won with all-white teams perpetuated racist notions.

"And there were avowed racists roaming this land, and they could all point to the all-white team of Alabama as vindication for their theory that you don't have to have integration, integration won't work, and we can do it without getting blacks involved," stated Clemon.

But the racial makeup of Bryant's teams posed problems despite their success on the field of play. In 1966, the Stabler-led Tide ran the table, finishing undefeated with a 34–7 victory over Nebraska in the Sugar Bowl. Despite this, they finished third in the national rankings. Notre Dame and

Michigan State had tied each other, and neither went to a bowl, yet they both finished ahead of Alabama.

"When it comes right down to it, many people have speculated that sportswriters and the wire service polls were biased against Alabama" is the "official" history according to the Paul W. Bryant Museum column on the 1966 season. "After all, this was the Alabama of George Wallace, 'Bull' Connor's police dogs and fire hoses, and the Montgomery bus boycotts among other things."

"I suppose," Bryant said of the 1966 snub, "by then, the voters were tired of seeing us up there, and hearing Bryant brag on his quick little boys."

On November 19, 1961, Jim Murray of the *Los Angeles Times* wrote that Birmingham was "the place where when they say 'Evening Dress,' they mean a bed sheet with eyeholes." Alabama needed to integrate before they were considered a "legitimate national champion," which they were that season. They also needed to play north of the Mason-Dixon Line, a fact accentuated because, due to a scheduling conflict, they had filled their open date in 1966 with Louisiana Tech, which impressed nobody.

Alabama should "change the lyrics [of 'Dixie'] ever so slightly like 'do the folks keep segregatin'—till I cai'nt win no polls. . . . Old Bear is tired of winning the magnolia championship. He wants to play some modern football," Murray wrote after the 1966 polls were released.

The 1966 poll snub has been attributed to revulsion over Alabama politics, but there are other factors. In 1964, the Tide "won" an illegitimate national championship when the Associated Press awarded it to them, but their subsequent 21–17 loss to Texas in the Orange Bowl has led historians to revise that year's real winner to the deserving Razorbacks of Arkansas. Bryant was right in assessing that the voters were indeed "tired" of seeing Alabama win it all, and the 1966 vote was also a "correction" of the flawed 1964 "national championship."

Furthermore, the all-white 1969 Texas Longhorns would—with the imprimatur of President Richard Nixon's "blessing"—win the national championship over Joe Paterno's unbeaten integrated Penn State Nittany Lions, so the argument that social pathos entirely dominated the 1966 polls is not fully accurate. The "Catholic vote" favoring Notre Dame was at least as prevalent a factor.

However, after Ken Stabler's departure, 'Bama declined in the late 1960s, barely maintaining a winning record. Schools with black players—USC, UCLA, Penn State, Ohio State, and Michigan—were among the dominant programs of the era. The Southeastern Conference was not mediocre, but they were not the top league.

Bryant knew that if anybody *could* integrate college football in Alabama, he was the man. He and a minority of others in the South began to see that if he wanted to continue his winning ways, then black athletes needed to be brought in.

"Negro players in the Southeastern Conference games are coming," read an enlarged, highlighted text in a major article quoting Bryant in a 1965 edition of *Look* magazine. "We're not recruiting Negro athletes; that's a policy decision for others to make," the coach added.

Behind the scenes, it was around this very time that Bryant was getting to know John McKay, whom he spent time with at a summer high school football camp in California run by a coach named Bob Troppmann. It was at those camps where the seeds of the 1970 game and integration were being discussed.

"We probably didn't know at the time that segregation had lost its hold because it had been a way of life for so long," said Dr. David Mathews, a professor at Alabama in the 1960s and eventually university president.

Furthermore, Bryant knew his team was not going to be strong in 1970. Some have questioned whether the 1970 USC-Alabama game was scheduled specifically to integrate the Bear's program.

"In order to regain national prestige, Bryant knew he needed to beat national powers," stated Allen Barra. "Southern Cal was perfect. They were already there. They had Heisman Trophy winners. He and John McKay were friends."

"I have no question in my mind that it was all planned by Coach Bryant," said Croom.

"Sports are a vehicle for change in this country, because you're looking at heroes," said Barra. "You're looking at black men and white men with their arms around each other, cheering."

"We realized we needed bigger, stronger, faster players," said Pat Dye, an assistant on Bryant's staff in 1970. "And the majority of bigger, stronger, faster players were black."

"I think it was coming, and Coach Bryant was allowing it to happen, slowly," said All-American lineman John Hannah. "I wouldn't be surprised that in the back of his mind, he saw the success of Southern Cal's stellar African American athletes and saw this as an opportunity."

"It was just another game to me at first," said USC's Charles Young. "But the closer we got to the game, you began to realize the ramifications of the game. We were going not on the fields of Gettysburg, but we were going on the *Legion* Field. What was transpiring was two different cultures, two different ideologies, and it had to be demonstrated on that playing field so Bear Bryant can get done what he wanted to get done. So he took it to a stage. What better stage than a football field?"

"We can't beat them this year but we can beat them next year," said Bryant, indicating that he was spinning perhaps two or three records at the same time. He had scheduled not just a 1970 game at Legion Field but also a follow-up game at the L.A. Coliseum for 1971.

One Night, Two Teams tells the story of how two legendary coaches made the most of a football game played on September 12, 1970. It's the story of one night, two teams, and the game that changed a nation.

The book gives an account of the game from the perspective of each team as well as from a journalistic standpoint. These chapters also tell the overall story, based on interviews with many characters and observers of the era, as well as the independent study of history. This is not the kind of revisionism that so many college students are subjected to. Instead, the *true* story is told. This book uses a football game as a metaphor for a changing America, tying the events before, during, and after September 12, 1970, with what Ronald Reagan used to colorfully describe as the "sweep of history."

To understand the present, we must understand the past. This is the template that describes how we came to be what we are. Desegregation did not occur in a vacuum. It was the result of three thousand years of philosophy. The heavyweights of Western civilization are responsible, despite revisionism, for the successes of America. Those heavyweights—Plato, Lincoln, Gandhi, Dr. King, and most importantly Jesus Christ—are given their just due in this unique work, which appeals to both history buffs and football fans.

What happened that Saturday in 1970 can be described as a tipping point; all the events leading up to the game made it happen, and all subsequent events flow from it. The game was only part of the larger context of civil rights in America, but it remains perhaps the starkest evidence, and impetus, of change.

CHAPTER One

The Agenda

Segregation now. Segregation forever.
—*Alabama governor George Wallace, 1963*

It was the beginning of the long, hot summer of 1963. Everybody had an agenda.

In Washington, D.C., President John F. Kennedy had an agenda. Dr. Martin Luther King Jr., that year's Nobel Peace Prize winner, organized the March on Washington, in 1963, demanding equal rights for all Americans.

"I have a dream," King told the assembled multitudes at the Washington Mall. The dream was that America would "live up to its creed" and that black people be judged "not by the color of their skin, but by the content of their character."

JFK had gone back and forth on this subject one year earlier, when James Meredith needed federal troops to open the doors to the University of Mississippi. Governor Ross Barnett, who by virtue of his membership in the Democratic Party was theoretically a political ally of Kennedy's, fought the president tooth and nail, albeit in the dulcet, gentlemanly tones of Southern propriety. It was enough to make Kennedy want to jump through the roof, if only his aching back would allow such dexterity.

Dr. King had an agenda. His national—and growing international—popularity was increasing by leaps and bounds. He had political capital and was willing to spend every dime of it. He would give Kennedy just so much leeway, because the two men knew that they owed each other. In 1960, when King was jailed in Birmingham, Alabama, Republican presidential candidate Richard Nixon, fearing white backlash, declined to come to his aid. Kennedy courageously did help to organize Dr. King's release, engendering the thanks of Coretta Scott King, the skeptical political favor of Martin Luther King, and the loss of support for Nixon of the black icon and former baseball star Jackie Robinson.

In the closest election up to that time, the "Birmingham jail" incident was a big deal in the black precincts of Cook County, Chicago, where the election ultimately was decided. It may well have given JFK the position he sat in now. He knew it. So too did King, Harry Belafonte, and the other black leaders and celebrities who were hounding Attorney General Robert Kennedy, the president's front man on civil rights. But Kennedy knew what Nixon had known three years earlier, which was that if he got too heavily into this issue, it would create Southern enmity. Fence-mending trips to the South, including one to Vice President Lyndon Johnson's home state of Texas, were in the planning stages.

Alabama governor George Corley Wallace had an agenda. An old-style Southern populist in the tradition of Earl and Huey Long, he had reached out with the hand of racial moderation in 1958, only to be beaten in that year's gubernatorial campaign by John Patterson. Wallace adamantly declared he would "never be out-n--red again."

Four years later, his campaign theme could be summed up by the phrase "segregation now, segregation forever," infamous words he uttered at his inaugural on January 14, 1963. He was elected, and he was popular. Now, as the freshman class at the University of Alabama prepared to enroll for the fall semester of 1963, Wallace's agenda was to *appear* to stand up to Kennedy and the federal government. They were using the nine-year-old *Brown v. Board of Education* Supreme Court case as precedent to do at 'Bama what they had done at Central High School in Little Rock, Arkansas, and at Ole Miss.

Wallace marched to the front of the administration building and "blocked" it so that two black students could not enter and enroll in college. A curious mix of 'Bama state troopers, students, and faculty lolled about in the semi-insolent Southern manner that old black-and-white film clips demonstrate from that era. It was as if they wanted to get their way and look like there was never a doubt about it—a smug smile, a dangling cigarette, a splatter of tobacco juice for good measure.

Vivian Malone and James Hood had an agenda. Yes, sure, they wanted a college education, but amid this circus the sheepskin diploma of the University of Alabama was not first and foremost on their minds. They were hoping their federal escorts would protect them, not turn on them. They did not want to be shot, or roughed up, or spit upon. They wanted sanity.

University of Alabama football coach Paul "Bear" Bryant and president Frank Rose had agendas, too. Along with members of the board of trustees, they stood in the window of Bear's second-story office, a building on the corner, where they were witnessing history. For better or for worse.

President Rose was a friend and ally of Jack Kennedy's. He found himself walking a tightrope. The Democrats ushered the South into the modern era. Franklin Roosevelt's works programs of the 1930s, particularly the creation of the Tennessee Valley Authority, made it possible for new generations of Southerners to pursue higher education at institutions such as the one he now presided over.

But 'Bama was a state university. His boss was the firebrand two stories below making the stand in the schoolhouse door—the man with the bushy eyebrows, the former amateur pugilist, the man *L.A. Times* reporter Jeff Prugh called "America's merchant of venom."

Bryant was the child of sharecroppers. His nickname, "Bear," came from his teenage years when he wrestled a black bear at a local fair in rural Arkansas. He had befriended a black kid and almost gotten thrown into jail with him as a result of a youthful prank. He had served in the Navy, managed a blues band. He had been a star end opposite Don Hutson, playing in the 1935 Rose Bowl. He had tried to integrate the football programs at Maryland, Kentucky, and Texas A&M. At A&M, he was told the "last" thing that would ever happen at College Station would be integration.

"Waal," drawled the Bear, "*last's* where we'll finish then."

He was, despite his impossible-to-understand Southern mumble, a worldly man who, like Lyndon Johnson, sympathized with the plight of minorities because he too had come from the wrong side of the tracks.

When his 1959 team faced integrated Penn State in the Liberty Bowl, local "citizens' groups" (read: the KKK) in Tuscaloosa objected. But in 1961, Bryant won a national championship. When you do that in Alabama you can walk on water, which Bryant did in Coca-Cola billboards along the Alabama highways. To top that off, he landed the most blue chip of all blue-chip recruits, a hotshot with bedroom eyes from Beaver Falls,

Pennsylvania, named Joe Willie Namath. Namath, a junior that fall, created quite a stir by making quiet solo visits to the black neighborhoods of Tuscaloosa, where he *mingled* with the local citizenry.

"He looks like a cool jazz singer," thought a black youth with an agenda, too. Sylvester Croom, growing up in those black neighborhoods, had football aspirations of his own. He dared not dream of playing for the Crimson Tide. But Namath was so . . . cool.

Maybe . . . just maybe. . . .

So, everybody had an agenda.

Enter Nicholas Katzenbach, assistant to Attorney General Kennedy. Oh yes, he had an agenda, too. He wanted justice done, and he wanted it done without violence.

Aha. Nonviolence. At last, a crossroads in which all politics, which as former House Speaker Tip O'Neill famously put it, is local. On that day, the American political scene was indeed localized to the campus of the University of Alabama in Tuscaloosa. Indeed, all the players in this Shakespearean drama wanted to *avoid violence.*

Dr. King figured that out a long time ago. He studied Mahatma Gandhi, how he had forged Indian independence. Passive resistance. *Satyagraha.* The delicate art of putting your morality on the other guy, of making his crimes against you crimes he was committing *against himself.* Dr. King saw in his approach a morality attached not just to his cause but also to his "enemies," whom he did not see as his enemies but as his brothers. In the Christian South, Dr. King saw humanity where so many others saw hatred, violence, and ignorance. So, too, did Bear Bryant.

"When people are ignorant," the Arkansas "hillbilly" said, "you don't condemn 'em, you teach 'em."

So it was that all the Bard's players were in place when Katzenbach arrived with a solution that would, at least for the time being, meet the agendas of President Kennedy, Martin Luther King Jr., Governor George Wallace, Vivian Malone, James Hood, Bear Bryant, Frank Rose, and Sylvester Croom.

Katzenbach, he of the Kennedy school of "back-room deals"—the Boston politics of "Old Man Joe" and "Honey Fitz" that their children had learned so well—made a back-room deal with Wallace.

"Governor," Katzenbach told him, "you don't want a riot, I don't want a riot. TV cameras are here. But you've got your constituency. Here's what we're gonna do. We're gonna enroll Malone and Hood the day before. Then we're gonna send them to the administration building. You can make your speech and say what you have to say. We won't be using troops to enforce anything, but you can look like you stood up to the federal government."

George Wallace knew a good deal when he had no other choice in the matter. It was a Henry Kissinger–style offer, a triangulation, which Kissinger learned in his studies of post-Napoleonic Europe. A face-saver. The two men shook on it. It was not until Jeff Prugh, now covering Southern politics for the Atlanta bureau of the *Los Angeles Times*, uncovered this political maneuver that it became publicly known in 1978.

But Bear Bryant found out about it. Nothing got past him. This was a man who made his living orchestrating organized mayhem, but in a world gone mad, a world of riots, police dogs, and rubber hoses, he wanted nothing more than to accomplish the important tasks at hand *smoothly*. Like a baby's cheek.

Other Voices: Alabama Football Fans

These are e-mails and postings culled from Alabama football websites and in response to e-mail inquiries I made as part of my research around the winter of 2004–2005. At the time, rumors of a book and possibly a movie about the 1970 USC-Alabama game were prevalent.

Earle Self usually posts as "TIDE-HSV." He is an administrator on the Tidefans.com website.

I declared against segregation in 1955, when I was a sophomore in high school. I've seen a lot change in the South since then. The *Huntsville Times* has an intern from England who came to write about the remaining vestiges of segregation in the South. He wrote a column in the *Times* confessing he couldn't find any in Huntsville. (Of course it remains, but remember—he's English). Much later in my life, I found that, of my great-grandfathers, both Alabama natives, one had fought in the Union Army, and the other was a member of the Union League—had all his property confiscated by the Confederate government of Alabama. He sued to get it back, and continued his suit after the Civil War. The defense of the new government (same people, pretty much) was that the taking had been done by an illegal government, and the present one wasn't responsible.

As trivia, you might be interested to know that Coach Bryant detested the nickname "Bear," although he was not above using it in advertising. Younger 'Bama fans sometimes call him "Bear," but that just tells me their age. Those of us who were around as fans and grads at that time refer to him as "Coach Bryant." His contemporaries in coaching referred to him as "the Bear," if they used the nickname at all. Even when I hear it used innocently and ignorantly, it still irritates me—I can't help it. I do have friends who played under him around that time. I'll check with them and see what they remember.

ROLL TIDE ROLL!!!!!

Originally posted by TommyMac

My guess is that this will be just another movie painting the South in the worst possible light. Southerners will be generally portrayed as ignorant, crude, ugly, backward, unwashed racists. On the other hand, the Southern Cal contingent will be cast as all that is good about the human race. They benevolently condescend to teach us the errors of our ways in a noble attempt to bring us into the twentieth century.

In other words, more of the same old tripe from Hollywood. . . .

. . . I hope they do Coach Bryant's legacy right and not make him out to be the bad guy. He would have integrated the Alabama football program a lot sooner had it been up to him.

The other thing I'm sure they'll not cover is the fact that the very next year Alabama went out to Los Angeles with pretty much the same white boys and beat USC on their home turf. It was the unveiling of our wishbone running attack used throughout the 1970s.

Let me quote Coach Bryant: "I'm just a simple plowhand from Arkansas, but I've learned over the years how to hold a team together, how to lift some men up, how to calm others down, until finally they've got one heartbeat, together, a team."

> He take his'n and beat your'n and take your'n and beat his'n. (Bum Phillips on coach Paul "Bear" Bryant)

Originally posted by Ramah Jamah (www.al.com/alabamafootball/i...ear/ story6.html)

"Is it true that Coach Bryant brought Sam Cunningham in to the Alabama locker room after that game?" The former 'Bama players say no.

Let's face it, there's a lot of prejudice against Alabama, and a lot of people dislike Coach Bryant and a lot of people dislike Alabama just because they know we don't back down to anyone. "We don't take anybody lightly and no one takes us lightly, and we like it that way." (Defensive tackle Warren Lyles on his frustration with the poll's lack of respect for Alabama early in the 1979 season. From the book *A Time of Champions* by Steve Townsend.)

. . . Well, if he tells the story right on the Alabama side, at least it will set the record straight about the single colored-ness of Coach Bryant's roster at the time not being as he wanted it.

E-mail from Bruce H. Franklin

In your tagline you said that you were working on a book about the 1970 USC-Alabama game. I hope you mention the 1955 Navy-Mississippi Sugar Bowl and have a lot about the 1956 Pitt-Georgia Tech Sugar Bowl; both were true segregation busters. The former was the first major game in the South where there was not segregated seating because Navy had distributed its tickets without racial consideration and the bowl honored that, and the latter is the first major game in the South with an African American (Pitt's Bobby Grier) player starting for one of the teams. After that game Louisiana passed a law not allowing integrated play, but the damage was done and that law was struck down by the Supreme Court later on. That game is practically a book in itself—and the role of the Sugar Bowl was huge in both drawing attention to segregation and (reluctantly at first) helping to eliminate it.

There are, I understand, a bunch of games such as that USC-Texas one; for your argument, the ones to look for are in Alabama (as you are doing), Mississippi, Louisiana, and Georgia, where Jim Crow laws were strongest. The Sugar Bowl, being the premier college game in the South at the time, had a national significance that other games did not. Until the Pitt game, teams from the North who played in the game would either not bring their black players or agree not to suit them up. The other game to check from the period outside of these states is the Cotton Bowl. Again, because of its national stature, that bowl had some problems with segregation early on. I agree with you that college football was more important to desegregation than is generally known.

Other Voices: Art Spander

Art Spander is part of the "Jim Murray generation" of educated sportswriters who looked beyond the "hits, runs, and errors," writing about the games and the people who play them with a social pathos. He has been in the business for the better part of forty-five years and offers special insight into the events of the 1960s and the aftermath of a chaotic period in American history.

I grew up in Los Angeles and graduated from UCLA. At UCLA I worked in their sports information department. From 1960 to 1961, I served in the Army. When I got out I went to work for the old *Santa Monica Evening Outlook*. I got my break at the *San Francisco Chronicle* and was there from 1965 until 1979, and I was with them in 1970 when this game was played. I moved on to the Hearst-owned *San Francisco Examiner* and eventually moved across the bay to the *Oakland Tribune*, which is now part of the Alameda Newspaper Group, where I'm as active today as I ever was.

In the Bay Area, everybody knew a guy named Sam Skinner. There's a plaque honoring Sam in the SBC Park press box. Sam was from San Francisco, but he was a prominent African American writer who knew all the angles and was especially in tune with sports events that played to an African American angle. He passed away in the mid-1990s, but Sam was a guy who talked about and wrote about that 1970 USC-Alabama game. To the extent that this game passed through the public consciousness, but was revived and recognized for its importance, it was African American sportswriters like Sam who played a big role in this. But Sam was a friend of many, white and black. For instance, when Dan Fouts was at St. Ignatius High School in San Francisco, he was not getting recruited by big schools. Sam arranged for him to get a scholarship at the University of Oregon, and they remained close all the remaining years.

I don't believe he and I ever talked about this game, but I know that because of the importance of the game toward integration, Sam was on top of it and its historical importance. My wife was his travel agent, we were friends away from work, but I don't know specifically his take on that game. But over the years, as black athletes and sportswriters progressed, as the racial situation improved, you'd see Sam at games, all over the Bay Area, at luncheons, at the Bay Area Sports Hall of Fame banquets, and his reputation as a pioneering black member of the media was increasingly evident.

I covered USC and UCLA. I knew everybody. I knew John McKay very well. I knew guys who played at both schools. I knew all the SIDs, Jim Perry, everybody.

McKay had a real personality. He was good friends with and had a lot of respect from Paul "Bear" Bryant. This is what I've heard, unless you really knew Bryant, and he had been at Texas A&M, then Alabama; he was not antiblack. Society down there was. In 1967, I was the golf writer for the *Chronicle*. I went to the Masters in Augusta for the first time, and they had this golf writer's tournament the weekend before the Masters. The whole idea was for the Northeastern writers to go to Augusta and get acclimated to the place and be charmed by the Southern hospitality. I get off the plane, and the paper reads, "USC Signs First Black Player." I'm like, huh? USC down there is the University of South Carolina. But this article told me the times were changing.

I don't think Bryant per se was against blacks, but you got the sense of what was going on in Alabama, which was particularly racist. The people running things were. As you moved down from the Mason-Dixon Line, North Carolina was better than South Carolina, which was better than Georgia. Then there was Alabama and Mississippi. Medgar Evers had been shot, and all that stuff was going on. I don't know if Bryant actually connected with McKay in terms of "planning" this game in order to change society, but McKay respected Bear. Bryant knew McKay well, and I think Bryant was looking to get the blacks who left the South. J. C. Caroline left for Illinois. Bubba Smith and those guys made Michigan State a powerhouse, and Bubba's brother went to USC. I was at UCLA with Mel Farr; I think he was from down there somewhere. The point is, they were losing great athletes to the Midwest and the West.

Can I say that Bryant was a liberal progressive? No, but he also was a realist. Whether Bryant set it up, I don't know, but by Sam Cunningham having that great game and supposedly Bryant saying, "We gotta get people like that or we gonna lose," well, that speaks for itself.

Jim Murray wrote a lot about this issue. He had a real social conscience. I met him in 1959 when he was with *Sports Illustrated*. I picked him up, I was the student SID at UCLA, and I took him to some football players for interviews, then I got to know him well.

Jim and I were very good friends. He was a great guy and a fantastic writer. He once wrote that Alabama was "the King of the Caucasians." There was debate about Alabama winning the national championship one year, and Jim influenced the votes by emphasizing that Alabama didn't have blacks and didn't play teams with blacks. There was a lot of stuff in the papers about that. I can't say for certain, but I think Murray got involved in this whole debate, but when I heard that Sam Cunningham "integrated" Alabama football, then all the South, well Jim influenced these events.

When you look at basketball teams, they're all black, but none of them are old enough to remember that when Walt Hazzard was at UCLA in 1963 and '64, he could not stay in the same hotel with his team in Houston. Kids today would have no clue as to what it was like.

Unless you do a lot of reading, but nobody reads anymore. Oscar Robertson and Jerry West are the same age. I see Oscar at the Final Four, and I say, "I know how good you were," and he says nobody reads anymore. TV is so dominant, it's what happened last night, not twenty or thirty years ago. Kids today, it's the same thing; it's hard to believe forty years ago there were no blacks playing in the South. Texas teams were just starting to integrate. Alabama's first guy was Wilbur Jackson, who went to the 49ers. That was a huge story.

The modern black athlete doesn't know any of this. In 1997 there was a ceremony honoring the fiftieth anniversary of Jackie Robinson entering the Major Leagues. I thought it was wonderful that blacks in 1997, who knew very little about him, unless their fathers told them about what he did, were able to be part of that, but he's not as acclaimed today as he was at that moment.

I covered West and Elgin Baylor. He was Michael Jordan playing a different game, averaging thirty points and nineteen rebounds. The thing is, he was great but almost forgotten. I digress, but the 49ers in 1996 announced their fiftieth anniversary team. They asked us to get involved. I said you can't have one team; kids today all just know Joe Montana, Dwight Clark, and Ronnie Lott, as great as they were, but I know they had guys like Jimmie Johnson, who was there when I was at UCLA. John Brodie was fantastic, but in today's world, unless you're watching *Sports Classic* on ESPN, nobody goes to the history books. Robinson made it so that some blacks never had to understand what had gone on before them. Also, this is like saying, "When we were growing up, we had to walk ten miles to school in the snow," and I know things changed, but it does not matter as much unless they understand how segregated America was. That's why so many blacks rooted for the Dodgers, because of Jackie.

Not to take a knock at USC, but the Trojans were late at integrating until C. R. Roberts. UCLA remained competitive in basketball and football because they brought in lots of blacks. Rafer Johnson and guys like that. They got the best black athletes in southern California.

CHAPTER Two

Platonic Justice

The unexamined life is not worth living.
—*Socrates*

In order to understand change, one must get beyond the physical world. True change comes from inside. It is a change of the hearts and minds. It is a change of the soul.

In order to make sense of the 1970 USC-Alabama football game, and why a seemingly innocuous sporting event became the "tipping point" in the civil rights movement, one must go back to the beginning. The ancient Greeks have been studied backwards and forwards, for good reason. English classical instruction still lists this study in their curricula as "Great."

The search for the American soul begins with Socrates, Plato, and Aristotle. The study of Socrates, Plato, and Aristotle is interesting and begins a trend that threads through history. That trend is to gain understanding in the aftermath of tragedy. It seems that man often does his best thinking when he is desperate to do so. War brings on such desperation. The postmortem of war provides a bounty for philosophical thought, but we also know that such philosophies can be just as dangerous as they are good. Niccolo Machiavelli did his writing in the aftermath of Rome's loss of prestige, much of it brought about by military defeat against the Barbarians. So did Adolf Hitler. To the extent that any "philosophers" existed in the Reconstructionist South, little good came from them in the ensuing one hundred years of Ku Klux Klan terror.

Luckily for us, the Greeks extracted lessons of goodness, not evil, in the disastrous aftermath of the Peloponnesian War. The Peloponnesian War is one that gets a lot of attention. It is studied at West Point. Generals such as Napoleon, George Patton, and Douglas MacArthur extracted lessons from this ancient conflict, fought more than four hundred years prior to the birth of Christ. The reason this battle lives on in memory is because a Greek general named Pericles took the time to analyze the Peloponnesian War in a book called *Funeral Oration*. It was the best seller of its time.

Thucydides, the "first citizen" of Athens, analyzed Pericles' book, which is the beginning of the whole debate on "how we went wrong," to put a modern spin on it. Thucydides then wrote *History of the Peloponnesian War*, detailing Athens's losing battle with Sparta from 431 to 404 BC. Athens's mishandling of power under Pericles' leadership served as the construct on what to avoid in creating a good society. Thucydides had a pessimistic view of human nature, but Plato differed in his assessment.

Athenian democracy gave every male adult citizen a share in direct rule. The assembly met once a month, and there were no other requirements beyond being a male citizen in good standing. Its huge membership was in direct proportion to its restrictions. Women, *metics* (resident aliens), and slaves were not allowed membership, which meant that Athens, a city of 350,000, was ruled by 40,000 of that population. Obviously, considering these numbers, amateurs dominated rule of Athens. It was this absence of professionalism that stuck in Plato's craw. According to some theorists, great and successful social change occurs where Christianity, democracy, and capitalism meet. The first time that trident truly came together was in the formation of America. The Greeks, of course, existed prior to Christianity, although they did adhere to religious morality. But their plebiscites are an example of democracy run amok. The point of combining Christianity, democracy, and capitalism is to demonstrate that if each is left to its own devices, absent any moderating factors, it does just that: runs amok.

Unchecked, organized Christianity, corrupted by power, is subject to the same human failings. An example is the Spanish Inquisition. In the case of capitalism, there are numerous examples of greed, not tempered by morality or public oversight, going too far.

John Papadakis, USC's middle linebacker in 1970 and a man of Greek ancestry, applied Plato's "warrior spirit" to his observations of the historical Trojan football program.

"No team plays the game with the kind of love and enthusiasm of the Trojans," he said. It was this "love and enthusiasm" that carried his team to victory over Alabama. Ironically Troy, a name commonly used to describe USC, was the enemy of the Athenian Greeks. Bear Bryant's Tide, however, could be described as the Spartans, another of Athens's enemies. They were subject to a martinet approach, forced to engage in vicious practice battles in an almost inhuman drill called "the Cage."

"War," said Thucydides, "is a violent teacher." His account was the crux of Plato's and Aristotle's attempt to examine the corrosive nature of humans in search of a good society. The war on the island of Corcyra swept away civilization. People put new emphasis on words and phrases, using them to characterize degenerative deterioration of people's ungovernable passions.

Thucydides found that power operated through greed and personal ambition, the "cause of all evils." This might be the root of the phrase "power corrupts and absolute power corrupts absolutely," for in Thucydides' view power cannot be used for good. It was the search for the good use of power that lies at the heart of Plato's teachings. The contrast is between Thucydides' realism and Plato's idealism. Thucydides did not feel that human nature had much promise, even if exposed to education, once power was allowed to rear its ugly head. Plato said people *can* be taught perfectible humanity. One finds application of these lessons to Abraham Lincoln's incremental approach to slavery. Outlined against the Civil War, he tried to bring a sense of morality into the equation, mixed with practical politics and military necessity. Bear Bryant took the same approach a century later. Bryant made political decisions only when he knew he was strong enough to do so. He was an incrementalist. The morality of his efforts to integrate coexisted with *his* practical necessities of "warfare," which involved maintaining the national standing of his football program.

Socrates lived from 470 to 399 BC and was the leading philosopher in Greece. Many of his teachings were reflected in Plato's writing. Like Jesus of Nazareth some 334 years later, Socrates chose the path of righteous martyrdom. He was given the hemlock that ended his life.

Socrates made an important point in differentiating philosophy from religion when he said that philosophy seeks the truth, while religion claims to possess it. Socrates' truth is dialectical and found through dialogue. Thus, the "Socratic method," which consisted of intense question-and-answer sessions with his students, probing each other for the deepest meaning of things. It was the Socratic method that Papadakis used to engage his black and white teammates in long bull sessions before and after the 1970 Alabama game.

While the Socratic quest for "goodness, beauty, justice, and freedom" has the ring of New Age gibberish, it becomes revolutionary when it is considered that Socrates was not advocating this simply to people in a benign setting. Like Christ he was confronting the power structure at great, and ultimately mortal, danger to himself. In viewing Socrates as the "father" of democracy (with regard to the physician Hippocrates, who influenced the "big three"), one can be quite proud of the origins of our political philosophy. Socrates' willingness to die for what he believed in, even though he had much to lose, influenced the American Founding Fathers, who put their lives on the line, too.

"The unexamined life is not worth living," Socrates declared in a statement that may be elitist. While Socrates said this to explain his "higher obligation" to seek truth, to exhort others to do the same, and like the Hindus, to view as most important the "big questions," the concept that such bravery, intellectual curiosity, and moral righteousness are the requirements of all is far too demanding. Either Socrates is asking this of all people, which is unrealistic, or he is saying that only those with the moral and intellectual compass to take on his challenge are worth being on this earth. If a journalist could interview Socrates, he or she should question this statement, but couch the question in such a way as to give him an out. The statement must be one that he means to pose to himself, not for all. Certainly many people live their lives without thinking these deep thoughts, yet they contribute to the love and beauty of humanity.

In applying Socrates' "unexamined life" philosophy to American civil rights, we see application of this in many cases. Dr. Martin Luther King Jr. was not a major political figure when he decided to insert himself into the debate. Neither were Rosa Parks and the black students who blazed trails at Alabama and Ole Miss. None of these people were "elites," but they decided to apply Socrates' high standards to their own actions, at great risk to themselves.

Plato's *Republic* is the seminal text of the Western philosophical tradition. Plato picked up on Socrates' fundamental issues (malleability of human nature, origins of right conduct, qualifications for exercising political power, reasons for obedience to the law, and mutual obligations in individuals and the state). He did this to be alert to the high purpose and consequence of such an undertaking, his mentor having been put to death for his insightful teachings.

Plato's views differed from Hinduism in that he envisioned the state as an agent of virtue, whereby the Hindus saw it only as a coercive force. Plato must be considered quite the optimist, considering it was the state that executed his friend and teacher. His willingness to still maintain optimism about the state, however, lies at the heart of his ideal world. To succumb to vengeful thoughts because of Socrates would not differentiate Plato from those who committed atrocities at Corcyra, and it was Corcyra and the Peloponnesian War that Plato wanted to learn from in order to make a better world.

At the heart of the state's role are education and the teaching of "right conduct." Current educators differ from this, choosing to legally remove God from the classroom and insisting that teachers are not there to instruct in values or, God forbid, tell children the difference between right and wrong! In *Republic*, Plato pointed out that Socrates' view of "right conduct" was not based on religious theory, which in the end is better. Atheists do not have any excuses.

"Democracy," said Winston Churchill, "is the worst form of government known to man, with the exception of all other forms of government known to man."

But Plato lived some 2,400 years before Churchill and was not privy to all of democracies' alternatives. He knew of military rule and the kind of autocratic power imposed by kings. He lived in a time of slavery and was aware of the dilemma of the ancient Jews in bondage to Egypt. But he never saw Communism or National Socialism. Would a modern Plato have accepted the Churchillian compromise?

Plato's "knowledge" is presented as stages of cognition. The first stage involved uncritical acceptance of the known world. The next stage was a critical examination of society. Next was advancement from opinion to knowledge. Plato said that if man could pursue knowledge of abstract reality as in the study of mathematics and astronomy, why not politics? Finally, he saw a perception of people's humanity, defined as "seeing each other in ourselves."

How does this apply to the 1970 USC-Alabama game? By understanding the nature of truth, which is never misunderstood when it is viewed in an American arena. The fans at Legion Field were observing the truth, which was that black athletes were as good as white athletes, if not better, and that they could coexist as a coordinated, tight-knit, well-disciplined team along with their white teammates and coaches. Football is a game popularized in many ways because people see *themselves* when they watch it. They ask if they could succeed under that kind of pressure. When Sam Cunningham and his team performed in the manner that they did, they began to replace opinion with an entirely different *knowledge*. As it says in our wonderful documents of freedom, "we hold these truths to be self-evident."

Plato uses the "cave allegory" to describe cognition. When man lives in the cave, he fears all outside the cave. Only after leaving the cave to discover the "truth" of life outside its environs does man gain the credentials for leadership in the cave. Plato does ask man to question the truth, for only in so doing does he separate it from illusion. Power is wielded wisely only by those who have "left the cave."

In the pre–cable television, pre-Internet world of the Deep South at that time, many of its citizens had not "left the cave." Coach Bryant, however, had. He had traveled with the Alabama team as a college player. He had managed a blues band and made friendships with blacks, whom he found kinship with because he, too, came from poor beginnings. He had served in the Navy and coached at Texas A&M and Maryland before returning to 'Bama. For the Alabama fans at Legion Field on September 12, 1970, they definitely found themselves "outside the cave."

Other Voices: Bud "the Steamer" Furillo

Bud was truly one of the all-time greats. A native of the Midwest, he came to Los Angeles prior to World War II, and his enthusiastic writings helped put USC, and L.A. sports in general, on the map. Bud was the sports editor at the Los Angeles Herald-Examiner *and later was a radio personality on KABC's* Dodger Talk. *Furillo was a throwback to a time when writers were friends with the players and coaches, not rivals or nuisances. He was also an unabashed fan of the University of Southern California and never cared who knew it. Sadly, Bud—a modern bard— passed from this "mortal coil" in 2006.*

I was at the 1970 USC-Alabama football game, but I don't know what happened in that Alabama locker room. I've heard that story about Bear Bryant telling his team, "This here's what a football player looks like," but I wasn't there to see or hear it. But this is what happened. Bryant wanted to integrate his team. The best way was to get an integrated team down there to prove what was going on. One of his assistants, Jerry Claiborne, said, "'Bam' Cunningham did more for integration in an hour than has been done in the last one hundred years." Holy cow!

I knew Bear very well. He was the best coach ever. At any rate, he wanted McKay to bring his team down there. McKay eased up on him. He could have named the score. It wound up 42–21, but it had been 42–7. John eased up. Sam had a helluva night.

Son of a gun if the next year they beat us 17–10. The wishbone didn't bother McKay as much as Marinovich's dropping that TD pass. [Marv Marinovich, father of Todd, actually played in the early 1960s.]

I never went to the dressing room. I had to write on deadline. I was doing a game story for the *Herald-Examiner*. I brought my son to that game. Maybe Steve Bisheff or Jim Perry was in that room. Maybe Allan Malamud, a favorite of mine who had so much talent, God rest his soul.

Most writers, if they can't knock anybody it's not worth writing about. But this was such a momentous event, and I knew it was going to be. I had a girlfriend down there who was dazzling, God almighty she was pretty. I met her in L.A. and took her to a club with a bunch of 'Bama people, and I told these 'Bama people, "You're gonna get beat." But everybody in Birmingham, they all thought they were gonna win. They had no chance to beat the Trojans, and Bryant *knew* they'd lose.

The reason for this game was Bryant wanted those people to know it was time to integrate. I believe he knew he'd lose and wanted that game to pave the way to change.

I was with Sam Cunningham last year when they inducted me in the USC Hall of Fame. I was so sick with allergies. I saw Sam at the peristyle end of the Coliseum.

John Papadakis had his best game against Joe Theismann in that rainy Notre Dame game. His grandfather, Tom, and I were great buddies. He's got a great Greek restaurant down there in Pedro.

I'll tell you a story about USC. I once took a bus and two streetcars to see a Howard Jones practice in 1940. I lived in Monterey Park. A bus and two streetcars.

That Alabama game was a tipping point; that was it, no question. After that game it was no longer acceptable to prevent integration, and this game did it.

Martin Luther King may be the greatest American, but that football game sure as hell turned Alabama around. Regarding the political fallout since then, well, there aren't many "blue states." California and the

Northeast. I like to think those liberal bastions are also homes of a lot of intelligence. I can't speak for the "red states." As you know, I'm the damnedest liberal *you've* ever known. But W [George W. Bush] is the president, and he's *my* president.

The thing I hated is Democrats hating Bush. The day after the election I stopped hating Bush. He's my president. It's that simple—to think otherwise is almost to be a traitor. I hate the war, I'm ashamed of our being there, I cry for our kids coming back in bags.

I believe the South wanted to do the right thing, but there sure were a lot of holdouts for a long time, but Jeez, I'm so antireligion, maybe I better pass on this. I don't think religion had a damn thing to do with it. I think Martin Luther King was the best American we ever had, but not because of religion.

Jimmy Jones was a leader for USC. So was Ty Hudson, a defensive back.

I never told anybody this, but the McKay-Bryant relationship was so tight. Bear wanted John to replace him at 'Bama. He was gonna go to Tampa Bay; John had it in his hip pocket if he wanted it. The job was his, for more money, more of everything. Hugh Culverhouse at Tampa wanted Bryant for the Buccaneers. McKay was underpaid at USC. We had to fight like hell to get him a swimming pool.

The key, and you are right on, was that the Alabama faithful looked at McKay and knew that he had Bear's respect—it had to carry a lot of weight. They just said, "If it's good enough for the Bear, well it's good enough for us."

Let's get to what I said. I heard different takes on what Claiborne said, but it was something like, "Sam did more in an hour than has been done in the last hundred years." He said it, and I said it, but I'm foggy on it.

Now, you're saying Loel Schrader absolutely says he saw and heard Bryant with Sam, in front of the team, telling them, "This here's what a football player looks like." When you talk about Loel Schrader, this is a guy I have nothing but the utmost respect for. If he said it, you can take it to the bank. Still, Bryant was not the kind of guy to put players on a stool, but the reason for that game was to show those f--ks down there what was going on in football and that it was time to change. I wanna emphasize, McKay *eased up*. McKay, the last time I saw him in the desert, he said, "You're a part of Trojan history." Wow!

As I recall I didn't ride the team bus after that game. We were on the road, and I had to write a quick story. We left right after the game. I used to fly with the team, but that trip I went on a tour.

Other Voices: John Sciarra

John Sciarra was a baseball and football star at Bishop Amat High School, one year behind Pat Haden and J. K. McKay. He grew up spending time around the McKay household and was recruited to USC by coach John McKay. He turned down the Trojans because he had sat behind Haden in high school and had no intention of doing it at USC. An All-American at UCLA, he led the Bruins to a Rose Bowl victory over Ohio State in 1976 and played for the Philadelphia Eagles. Today, he is a successful L.A.-area businessman.

Coach John McKay was a bigger-than-life figure. I gravitated to J. K. McKay and Pat Haden. I took a liking to them, and we became friends, so we'd do things socially together, go over to the McKay house, get something to eat, that kind of thing. The first time I met Coach McKay, I of course knew of his success at USC. I was involved in football at that time; we were the number one team in the state at Bishop Amat. The following year, when I finally took over as the starting quarterback, we repeated that, and I was hoping to get a scholarship. The fact is, even though I had gotten to know J.K. and Pat, and of course visited with the McKay family, I knew Mrs. McKay real well but had not gotten to know Coach McKay real well, but he was always very nice to me. He had a keen sense of humor. He spoke at our high school banquet my senior year, and he had us laughing hysterically at his stories. The way he carried himself, his demeanor, created the kind of respect factor where you had a high opinion of him, yet he was also a very nice man. I never got to know him as a football coach, but I did know him in a football environment, and as I say, he was always polite and nice to me.

He recruited me, and when I went in his office, he said, "We don't need to talk a lot about football, we want you. I gotta tell ya a funny story, though. I know you're fast, I've seen you go one on one with J.K."—which I had done for hours on hours. "I just got a letter from a kid, look at this, this kid's telling me he's run a four-two forty [forty yards in 4.2 seconds]. Let me tell ya something, I coached a lot of guys, and the fastest I ever coached"—this is 1972—"the fastest was Earl McCullough, and he ran four-four. This high school kid says he can run a four-two."

Now, I know I can't run a four-four, but I can get close to four-five.

"The kid's lying," says McKay, laughing. "Obviously we want you, so enjoy your time."

I think stepping back from my personal football perspective, he and Bear Bryant were pioneers in the management and leadership of football.

Looking back and reflecting on certain coaches, when did the head coach job become something of true significance? From the modern perspective, in that era of football, Bryant and McKay were pioneers in that they exemplified a leadership management philosophy, which was to surround themselves with good people. They were more than Xs and Os. They rallied their teams together. McKay was the main guy who brought the position into the modern world, past the strictly physical aspect of sports, but how you made the team. Again, he surrounded himself with great people. Without even looking at the national championships, it was his ability to lead and manage that separated him.

I played football in high school in the late 1960s, early '70s, in college in the early to mid-1970s, pro in the late '70s. These were changing times, and at this point I can try to make some sense of the experience through the prism of football and society. This is an interesting question, because sport has always been something that reflects society during all these times of social change. Obviously, the Vietnam War emerged, and out of that the hippie dissent, protests, drugs were in the forefront. Society was open to what people experienced, to how this other kind of dimension of peace and love and *not* war could affect us. Throw athletics in the mix. There was a book written, I believe, by a pharmacist in San Diego, about the Chargers. It was called *The Nightmare Season*, and it was about the use of drugs in football. I'd sit in the training room in Philadelphia, and I started to read that book. It only took maybe forty-five minutes to read, and it talked about the use of drugs at that time. Players started to look and dress differently, with baggy pants; the African Americans had those big 'fros, *everybody* had long hair, and it was just a cool scene. Looking at society as a whole, a lot of what people were doing were things you couldn't talk about before that. You could talk about the war, the draft, although how that carried over and reflected in sports is hard to decipher. At the end of the day, it's two teams competing with the objective to win. It looks just like today's competition, but the appearance of the players changed with fashions and social mores. From the time I first started until I finished playing seventeen years later, the game was the same, dealing with times and games. So, how athletes would bring their opinion on war is not much different from today, where we face the same issue with Iraq. These times today, rap music is popular; then it was hard rock, psychedelic music, so times are different, but despite social change and certain things evolving, you still gotta compete.

After UCLA, I played two years in Canada. In 1978 I went to the Eagles and played six years, from 1978 to 1983.

I had a lot of black teammates. Looking back now at the late 1970s, many blacks were from the South. Brenard Wilson was from Vanderbilt, Harold Carmichael had gone to Southern. Back then I never got the impression, I never really talked about their experiences with them. Pro football, if you made the team you made the team. Maybe I was out of touch, but everybody was the same to me.

While maybe I can't speak to the idea of blacks coming in, I do think maybe being from California I was looked upon a little differently. Things are more liberal in California. Sure we are, we're looking at things in certain ways. If you're born and raised in the South, then you look at things differently. Call me oblivious or whatever, it's not that I had discussions with blacks who really felt they were dealing with a guy who was a lot different from them, and maybe that's because I was a Californian.

This maybe speaks to the UCLA tradition, now that you bring that up. There was increased black opportunity at UCLA. Some people viewed UCLA as a "Communist" school. I think Angela Davis was on the staff. I don't think of the racial thing as a freethinking liberal thing. I think maybe some have tried to tie that in, but race is something addressed by society, religion, not just liberalism. I recall that UCLA was a platform for saying what you think—just make sure you have a good story to tell and we'll listen. I have spoken with Rafer Johnson, who is a respected African American Olympian, civil rights leader, and man of respect in the L.A. community, but not on this topic

I'm sure there's documentation or books that speak to UCLA's legacy. It's definitely part of the school. UCLA has always been considered more liberal than USC. From our perspective, we thought of ourselves as more open-minded than USC, which we felt was more narrow, more traditional. At UCLA, we get people to open up—let's deal with realism, what's really going on.

I think the rivalry was about some class distinction. Conservatism was slanted toward USC. UCLA was more leftist; that's more of a UCLA stigma, if you will. Obviously, a lot of that has changed, and as I saw the world open up, the dynamics changed. For instance, when USC goes to Alabama, they have African Americans and 'Bama has none. That game was a gateway to African Americans coming in to Southern schools and making a statement. Then you make the comparison, and for me back then, of course you're thinking UCLA is more liberal and USC is more conservative. It's an old-line school. They have that USC way of doing and thinking things, which is success driven, and it's this whole thing about having a big job and making lots of money, but now all of a sudden USC looks pretty liberal compared with Alabama!

It's all about the power to make decisions for yourself. UCLA was more free spirited. It's dynamic here, it's this UCLA-SC rivalry, but the whole comparison is crazy when compared with Alabama.

You know, UCLA has a reputation for going down South, too. We had Southern coaches: Red Sanders, Tommy Prothro, and Pepper Rodgers. Prothro took a team and went to Tennessee. They played the Vols, and after the game he was quoted as saying something like, "Today, I'm not proud to say I'm from the South," because they got jocked by local officials. It was 1969, or maybe 1970. He was there from 1966 to 1971, for sure. But he made it very clear in the paper that he was not proud to be from the South.

Bear Bryant had so much credibility, he was so well liked. Somebody other than Bear might not have been able to pull off the changes that he oversaw. It's not just that he had a lot of wins—it's amazing how much credibility you get when you win—but integration would have been way more difficult if Alabama had not lost that game. It's not just their success that paved the way. They had to explore the changing of the guard and the times, and if you look at Bryant, there were a number of years before he had blacks, but he transitioned, he changed with the times, and if you're talking about leadership in sports, whether it's John Wooden or Bear Bryant, that's the thing people admire the most.

CHAPTER Three

America:
Where Slavery Came to Die

The mystic chords of memory, stretching from every battlefield and
patriot grave to every living heart and hearthstone all over this
broad land, will yet swell the chorus of the Union,
when again touched, as surely they will be,
by the better angels of our nature.

—*President Abraham Lincoln*

The United States of America is the greatest country in the history of humankind, but why? To merely boast such a statement is empty unless it is backed by a solid premise. This is the basis of historical analysis of this nation and how we came to become the most dominant empire in world history.

While America did not achieve its status by pure chance, rather than centering on the concept of the United States as a "Christian nation," we prefer to look at our advancement as the result of a "guiding hand" that defies denomination. Perhaps we were meant not to understand *why* we are the "chosen nation," but rather to focus on the evidence that we are without probing into a spirituality that is beyond our ken.

The first evidence of divine guidance comes during the Revolutionary War, a time in which men with much to lose chose, for reasons more often than not against their personal interests, to put themselves on the line against King George's England. This war could have been lost during many periods, yet somehow fate drove us to victory. To consider the intelligence of the resulting constitution and its lasting importance without believing it was a Godly document is almost impossible.

A recent book by Fareed Zakaria offers some explanation of subsequent American success. Zakaria intertwines Western civilization, embodied by the Christian Church, with capitalism and democracy. The following is excerpted from *The Future of Freedom*:

> Obviously it is an oversimplification to pick a single event to mark the beginnings of a complex historical phenomenon—in this case, the development of human liberty—but stories have to start somewhere. And the rise of the Christian Church is, in my view, the first important source of liberty in the West—and hence the world. It highlights the central theme of this chapter, which is that liberty came to the West centuries before democracy. Liberty led to democracy and not the other way around. It also highlights a paradox that runs through this account: Whatever the deeper structural causes, liberty in the West was born of a series of power struggles. The consequences of these struggles—between church and state, lord and king, Protestant and Catholic, business and the state—embedded themselves in the fabric of Western life, producing greater pressures for individual liberty, particularly in England and, by extension, the United States. (p. 30)

Zakaria, in this excellent book, goes on to point out that within Christianity grew a culture that fostered capitalism, which provided economic freedoms for individuals who no longer were dependent on the state and the monarchy. It is this connection, tying the freedoms of Christianity and capitalism as one, in which the story of Sam Cunningham and the newly integrated South find symmetry. It was capitalism, in part, that pushed integration, for college football by 1970 had been a big money operation for decades.

* * *

The study of slavery gets bogged down in hard moral equations of right and wrong, ignoring the fact that great thinkers such as Plato and Aristotle saw it as natural. They may give credence to an intellectual people, yearning to be free, led by a charismatic leader like Moses who advocates their fleeing from Egyptian bondage. Apparently they view many other forms of the human family to be less worthy of freedom than the Jews escaping to the promised land.

Their views probably do not change very much in a study of the African slave trade. What they would see are white people, skilled, crafty, and smart, in association with blacks who have seemingly made no real evolutionary progress, capturing and selling their own people for profit. They would say these blacks do not have the capacity to "reason," other than amoral self-interest.

Less moral men did justify slavery in later eras by pointing to Aristotle's "natural" views of humankind. In the end, the practice of slavery seems to have survived all theories of science and politics for some 2,220 years. Many religions tolerated it. Judaism-Christianity tolerated it less than all others. In the end run it took a modern version of democracy advocated by Socrates, Plato, and Aristotle, now practiced by a union of sovereign states in a new world, to end the damn thing once and for all. Placed in the middle of the Christian intellectual argument against slavery, one hopes that these three men would have seen the morality of freeing the slaves.

The lack of self-preservation that lies at the heart of our Founding Fathers lies at the heart of America's history. Herein we discern the difference between all other countries and us. While certain diplomats such as Henry Kissinger practiced a European realpolitik, our ultimate purpose has always been one of benevolence. How else to explain that we have achieved unprecedented power so benignly? The United States possesses the ability to dominate all others, to turn the globe into a Pax Americana, to enslave and conquer beyond the realm of all previous conquerors. Can one envision the Romans, Alexander's Greece, the Chinese dynasties, Napoleon, the Soviet Bloc, Imperial Japan, Nazi Germany, even the British Empire, possessing our weapons and our disproportionate strength against the rest of the world, yet also our restraint? What about modern countries such as Iran and China? The question is impertinent in the face of what we know.

So how did we get that way? While the hand of God cannot be discounted, one must consider that timing and the quest for human knowledge have been the weaponry of our good fortune. We had the wonderful hindsight of world history to study in order to determine what mistakes had been made and how to improve on the performance of our predecessors.

* * *

Santayana once said, "Those who do not remember the past are condemned to relive it." America is willing to not only remember the past but, in so doing, also take on the task of shaping a hopeful future.

The overriding American message, for liberals, conservatives, and everybody in between and beyond, is there must be love in our hearts for *everybody*; do not take the politics personally; and in the United States, we are all Americans.

"United we stand," Abe Lincoln once said. "Divided we fall."

Americans like to pat each other on the backs because we got it right where others were off the mark. Our Constitution has lasted well over two hundred years. We managed to effectively end the institution of slavery as a viable trade between legitimate nations. We have fought wars for the right reasons. Instead of plundering the conquered lands for booty, we rebuilt nations and endeared ourselves to grateful millions. We managed to create a political and economic model that defied the previous assumptions of men. Our mistakes are placed in the storefront window, not hidden from view. We study our errors and seek to correct them in a way no country has ever done.

What is important to understand is that the United States has had the great advantage of history, timing, and modern sensibilities guiding its destiny. Imagine how much recorded history had passed, like sands through the hourglass, before the United States came into being. England had crossed the seas, coming upon strange lands filled with mysterious dark-skinned peoples. While the precepts of morality and goodness tell us that the English *should* have treated these populations with respect, it may be too much to expect the English race, faced with their own ignorance, suspicions, and religious view of "pagans," to act in the manner God would intend. The English, imbued with a superior view of themselves, were not advanced enough to welcome nonwhites as equals. Many have tried to blame Christianity for this, but one finds little in the Old Testament (and its modern interpretations), and certainly not in the teachings of Christ Himself, to justify this behavior.

Holding historical people responsible for their acts, using modern knowledge, is a standard that few can live up to. There are exceptions, but they are rare. The American ideal was born from what we knew about the British. Because we were colonists chafing under their authority, it gave us the principles that lie at the heart of our country's foundation. Thank God for it.

This is not to discount our own dark moments. The slavery experience and the Indian Wars, in retrospect, could have been handled much differently. But slavery did not continue, and the Indian experience was not the holocaust it could have been. What other countries in the nineteenth century would have handled the Indian confrontations in a manner substantially different from the United States? A reminder of the Spanish Inquisition offers some perspective. The American West was an unavoidable clash of civilizations.

Mainly, the history of America occurs side by side with enlightened times. The civil rights struggle; women's suffrage; and modern religious, political, economic, and psychological ideas are part of America's growth. The question is worth asking, Has the world grown up because of America, or is America the by-product of a grown-up world? No doubt a little of both.

Western political theory generally falls into three broad areas. The first involves the characteristics of human nature and interaction within society. But what drives human nature? Are we a product of internal or external matter? Does reason or passion drive us? Let us cut to the chase. Are people sinful or good? Violent or nonviolent? Understanding these questions is as fundamentally difficult today as it was in Socrates' time. Further, these essential questions drive public policy today and in our future.

The attempt here is not just to gain some understanding of these tenets of the human animal. The purpose is to apply what we have learned to a study of the unique American character and how that character was embodied in a simple game of football played in 1970. The premise of this treatise is an acknowledgment that in the United States, we have made better and more moral decisions for the public good than any previous power. Still, we have not achieved a perfectly harmonious society. Immoral decisions prefaced the morality that followed that game. Practicality played a large role in the subsequent events. It was not all harmony and serene thoughts.

The quest for harmony goes back several millennia. In order to achieve harmony, leaders must find a balancing act between coercive acts of power and the containment of conflict, as outlined by the laws written by institutions. Is social unity achievable? Is it even what we are looking for? Ah, as Shakespeare once said, there's the rub. This is the nexus of struggle.

What about human rights? The American promise is based on the principle that each person has unalienable rights. Legal theory has over the years ascribed the term "natural law" to this concept. It is brought up a great deal today. Natural law was a major part of the questioning of Supreme Court nominee Clarence Thomas in 1991. When the inevitable debate occurs over *Roe v. Wade*, the abortion decision delivered in 1973, it will be the central theme of this question.

To understand human rights, one must address whether a Creator endows these rights. Americans prefer to think so. The French prefer to believe human rights are bestowed by other humans. The American philosophy requires that leap of faith religious people have made. But many do not take that leap. Furthermore, remember that throughout the ages, many people lived under the rule of *people* who thought *they were gods*. This premise creates further-complicating dilemmas when addressing the question of equality and human rights in the context of social authority.

As somebody once said, the one constant is change. If this is so, should revolutionary thinkers be extolled for endorsing their cataclysmic ideals, or are they just historical conduits of necessity? Inevitable shifting sands of thought? To put it in plain terms, if Socrates, Plato, and Aristotle had not come along, would somebody else have taken their place? Are we dealing with inevitability? If this is the case, one shudders to think that somebody like Adolf Hitler was inevitable.

So the question of dynamics is addressed in the context of moral leadership and inexorable laws of history. The attempt here is to define some kind of absolute truth that exists as obviously in Athenian Greece as in twenty-first-century Iowa. Let us call this what it is: the question of good and evil. To determine a kind of universal, enduring code of ethics is to dispute a premise that makes its way around the modern landscape. This is the idea of moral relativism. Was it okay for Palestinian suicide bombers to blow up fifty Israeli men, women, and children at a shopping mall because Palestine had not achieved independence? Is it okay for the State of Texas to put another human being to death because that person killed another human being? Is it okay for a military commander to order his troops to shoot into a crowd to try to break up a riot that would cause more casualties than those inflicted in order to stop it?

* * *

The American Revolution opened floodgates that had never been truly explored before. The Greeks, the Roman Senate, the Magna Carta, and Oliver Cromwell's England—these were precursors. The Americans created a concept of freedom that was, in essence, "power to the people." It was this power that fueled the French Revolution and the uprisings of nine-teenth-century Europe. Eventually, these events led to Marxism-Leninism. The American ideal was perverted beyond imagination, but it was the power of a popular movement that started in this country that spurred others to think they could do the same. It was the baggage of history in these other nations that caused their revolutions to fail or to become something else.

The United States of America was born and its independence univer-sally recognized. The statesmen of the new country declared that "all men are created equal" and that "government derived their just powers from the consent of the governed." Under Thomas Jefferson, the Virginia Bill of Rights was adopted, with a separation clause between church and state. Freedoms of speech, of assemblage, and of the press were enumerated. Nothing remotely close to it had ever been seen before—not the Magna Carta or any of the writings of Cromwell's England.

The Constitution of the United States, which remains the strongest legal document in the history of the world, is the most copied, adopted, and influential political treatise ever written. Adoption of the Constitution solved the problems of preserving liberty and local autonomy while main-taining strong central control.

General George Washington had been offered a kingship. Some wanted to give him virtual dictatorial powers. The long-held idea that peo-ple wanted security, not freedom, had not completely died. But these ideas were not the popular view of the delegates. They certainly were not the view of the general. Washington was unanimously elected president.

* * *

Plato determined that slavery was a natural result of the human condition, and the British colonial view did not veer far from this concept. These val-ues were thrust upon America. Yet somehow, in four score and seven years, the United States managed to address a thriving institution that had existed for thousands of years and, effectively, end it. This was accom-plished on our shores, using our laws. No foreign power came here, defeated us, and told us what to do. Considering slavery's economic bene-fits in the South, and the cost of the Civil War, the ending of the "peculiar institution" might be the most compelling example of how we changed the politics of self-interest into the politics of better interests. This is a premise meant to cause some controversy and plenty of discussion, always a healthy result of philosophies and critiques.

Most kids grow up loving America and are told all the usual tales of patriotism and valor that make this country the greatest in the world. But there was the blight of slavery. How could a nation that valued freedom so much allow slavery to occur?

In 1997, Steven Spielberg's *Amistad* told the story of a slave-ship rebellion. Slaves bound for the Caribbean overcame the ship's crew, but after drifting at sea were picked up by the United States and brought to America. They stood trial for murder, among other charges, but were declared innocent in a court of law. They were eventually returned as free men to Africa.

As people left the theater, some experienced a strange sensation. They had just watched depictions of Africans shackled and abused on a hellish slave ship, abused and mistreated by racist whites (Europeans on the ship, then Americans). Spielberg no doubt meant such depictions to elicit shame and guilt from the white Americans in the audience. But they did not all feel shame and guilt. Some good, decent Christians who have only love in their hearts for all humankind began to question themselves. Instead of shame and guilt, in fact, they felt pride and patriotism.

As Slim Pickens said in *Blazing Saddles*, "What in the wide, wide world of sports is goin' on here?"

Then they realized that Spielberg, a master filmmaker, had crafted a tale not only of racism but also of patriotism. How could slavery be patriotic? The answer to that question lies in the trial of the slaves. They were declared innocent in an American court of law and allowed to go free. The legal result, however, was not just an isolated kind of event, or the result of a few brave people rising above circumstance to do the right thing. The fact is that it was the result of American laws, as outlined in the U.S. Constitution. The very slaveholders who had kept the "peculiar institution" in 1787 had written a document that had effectively reached some forty years into the future and accomplished what they had "failed" to do the first time.

The story of slavery then opens itself up in its entirety. Undeniable facts became obvious on their faces. The first of these facts is that slavery existed for thousands of years. It not only existed, it thrived. It was a huge part of the economic dynamism of countries and empires for centuries. The Egyptians enslaved the Jews. The Romans enslaved most of the people they conquered. Slavery was never questioned in democratic Athens. Genghis Khan enslaved those unfortunates who fell under his swath. There was scarcely a country in the world that had not benefited from, or at least at some time endorsed, slavery. If not, they had probably suffered from it, too.

England was one of these nations. They came to the New World to establish colonies and brought slaves to do the work. It was not questioned, except by the Christian Americans in the Northeast. They despised the practice and kept it out of their communities. But slavery thrived in the Southern colonies. This was the situation that existed when America came to be.

Now, detractors point out (and they are most reasonable to do so) that the United States did form, and the Constitution was written, allowing for that "peculiar institution" of slavery. Fair enough. But the point is this. Slavery, an institution that thrived throughout human history, continued to thrive at the time of this nation's inception. We declared independence in 1776. We defeated the British in 1781, and the last of their soldiers were gone by 1783. We wrote the Constitution in 1787 and two years later inaugurated our first president. By 1863, a very short time, to use a Reaganesque term, in the "sweep of history," the Emancipation Proclamation was enacted, and the practice was officially illegal.

It would take a while before it was "gone," not just in the legal sense but also in the practical sense, but the first steps had been taken to abolish slavery and to see that it stayed abolished. How? Well, after a terrible struggle, Americans decided it was time for it to be gone. Slavery ended in America. Americans ended it. Repeat: it was ended using American laws written by Americans, not because some foreign power fought us, defeated us, occupied our nation, and told us to end it. And when it ended, it never came back.

This may be a simple premise, but it does not change the fact that this is the simple truth. Yes, there are forms of slavery, sometimes called "white slavery," still in existence. Former Communists in the old Eastern Bloc and in Communist China and throughout Asia formed criminal organizations that have morphed into the "business" of kidnapping and duping women into prostitution. This is little more than slavery. There are black Africans who keep black Christian slaves in Rwanda. But institutionalized slavery, sanctioned by governments and made part and parcel of trade between countries, is no more.

Had America not ended slavery, it seems unlikely that it would have ended throughout the rest of the world in a timely manner. The United States had enormous power, prestige, and influence by the mid-nineteenth century. Many nations would have looked at us and said, in effect, "If they can do it, so can we."

It is true that England and some other countries abolished slavery prior to the Emancipation Proclamation, but at little real cost—at least not in comparison with America. Denied the American colonies after losing the Revolutionary War, the British no longer had the economic benefits of slavery that they previously had. There were slave rebellions against French, English, Spanish, and other colonial authorities in the Caribbean. For the most part, slavery "ended" in these places not out of benevolent politics but through violence inflicted by slaves against former masters.

Furthermore, slavery existed for these European countries on foreign soil, not in their homelands. America was a "white, Christian, Europeanized" nation, "forced" to mature with a huge population of black slaves inherited from its colonial past. It was very easy for Englishmen or Frenchmen, after creating the problem for us in the first place, to take the high road when the issue was not squarely in their midst. Giving up slavery meant giving up something that no longer benefited them. In the American South, slavery was the known culture, and the lifeblood of an agrarian economy. Giving it up offered the prospect of landed aristocracies, the very essence of its political and cultural power base, freely offering to give up their wealth and power. Human nature does not work that way. To the extent that it ever has, it has more in America than anyplace else, but unfortunately it was not to be in the mid-nineteenth-century South. At great cost.

A war was fought over the issue. It was not a war in which the slaves rebelled, fought, and defeated their masters, thus forcing their freedom through the "barrel of a gun." It was a war in which white people were, at least in the light of historical reflection, the "proxies" for the slave cause. They fought to free slaves. Many correctly point out that there were other factors, and there were, but those people who believe the Civil War would have been fought had not Northern political leaders and a large portion of the citizenry believed ending slavery was the moral thing to do are deluding themselves. "States' rights" and secession were just code words for slavery. Economic sanctions applied by the federal government against Southern states were applied *because* of slavery. Over 300,000 white Union Army soldiers died for black people in America, a prospect so far from any possible previous human experience as to be beyond the ken. The notion that a quarter-million Englishmen or Frenchmen would willingly have died for this same cause is a ludicrous concept not even worthy of analysis. What motivated the North to engage in this struggle, to carry it on when things looked bleak, and to sacrifice as they did? To do as they did was far from a normal human reaction. Humans normally act in their self-interest. Most white Northerners had few or no "dogs in the hunt" when it came to Southern slavery.

There seems little logical answer as to why they fought, other than to attribute their motivation to a righteous God inspiring their leaders to write documents and make speeches about freedom. Those documents and speeches seem to have been so divinely inspired as to urge these people to do "divine" things. Can it be compared with the Burning Bush instructing Moses to lead his people to the promised land? The elitist skoffs at such a simpleton's concept. The elitist is wrong to do so.

Racism was alive and well from one end of the world to the other. Had the United States been held up as the "shining example" of why slavery was a worthy practice, there were more than enough people, countries, and leaders who would have been willing to maintain the practice, using America as the example of why they could. The rise of Nazi Germany sixty years after the Emancipation Proclamation shows there were more than enough "cultured" Europeans willing to engage in barbarism if they could be convinced of its justification. Furthermore, if the English, French, and Spanish, for instance, were so much more "moral" than the Americans because they ended a practice that had for all practical purposes been ended "for them"—just a few years before the United States did it *for themselves*—then how come their "great accomplishments" are relegated to little more than Wikipedia searches, while the War Between the States remains the most studied conflict in human history? The answer to that question need not be answered using words herein. Rather, it places itself before our eyes, thus manifesting itself as self-evident truth.

To demand reparations today is ludicrous. The descendants of Union soldiers who died to defeat slavery could ask for reparations. The descendants of the African chiefs who sold other Africans into slavery could ask for reparations. It is just as conceivable (and ludicrous) that the United States could tax the descendants of the slaves because we brought their ancestors here until shortly after the Revolutionary War. This practice stopped, and these descendants now enjoy all the benefits of American citizenship instead of dying in Rwanda, starving in Ethiopia, being imprisoned in Zaire, or experiencing the other regular and sundry horrors of everyday life in Africa.

Slavery most likely would have ended in the United States at some point, even without the Civil War. When? Maybe not until World War I. If this had occurred, the implications for history would have been enormous. Jackie Robinson broke baseball's color line in 1947. *Brown v. Board of Education* and the Little Rock desegregation occurred in the mid-1950s. James Meredith entered the University of Mississippi, providing educational opportunities, in the early 1960s. Martin Luther King's "dream" and the Civil Rights Bill of 1965 turned the tide on racism. Black athletes such as Michael Jordan and Barry Bonds became multimillionaire superstars. Would these events have been pushed back years, decades, had slavery not ended in 1863, "hanging around" until 1900? 1918?

Slavery was evil. Evil slithers and slides around, using lies and justifications. Many of the men who owned slaves were, quite simply, very good men. Some of them were some of the greatest thinkers and contributors to the betterment of society of all times. Yet, slavery "escaped" their moral compass, as it had for Socrates and Plato. To those who believe in such things, the devil used slavery to corrupt greatness. There is nothing the devil cannot lie about, including religion. The fact that men such as Thomas Jefferson and George Washington could own slaves is the greatest proof that the complete man, the real intellectual, the moral seeker, must examine his conscience at the deepest core to find where the devil lurks. Vanity, opportunity, and political justification, to name just a few things, are tools of evil.

Such is our way of explaining how this beautiful country, the land we love and whose history we are so proud of, could do the work of the devil. It is to that same forgiving God that we pray for forgiveness for these occasional forays (and slavery is not our only sin) into darkness. But we put our scandals out front for all to see. We advertise them. We examine them like clinical psychologists. We are not hiders. We do our share of propaganda, but we know that the Big Lie is worse than the Big Confession.

There is the history of humankind. Then came America. The English had instituted slavery prior to the existence of the nation. The practice was with us when we were born. It preceded us. Now we had to deal with it. Washington, Jefferson, and the Founders came up with a plan. The slave states wanted to maintain slavery. In order to maintain the agricultural South, it was agreed to let them join the Union with slavery intact. Slaves were being imported from Africa at that time. The plan was to stop the importation of slaves around the turn of the nineteenth century.

The Founders knew that when the importation of slaves stopped, eventually the existing slaves would grow old and die. Living in the bonds of enslavement, this had always come about quickly. Around 1808, the importation of African slaves was stopped. Within a certain number of years, those slaves would get old. Without replacements, the institution would die with them. The plan failed. There is no way to explain why it failed without making a controversial statement. It failed *because white Southern slave owners treated their slaves better than any slave owners had ever treated slaves in the annals of humankind*!

The United States was a capitalist country, run by prosperous merchants, businessmen, and entrepreneurs. Slaves were investments for them. They were treated poorly by the English, Spanish, and Portuguese shippers who transported them to the States because they had little incentive to treat them well. Some black revisionists have attempted to declare that so many slaves were thrown overboard during the ocean crossing that the migration habits of sharks were changed forever. That is a lie. But they were treated poorly.

Once sold into slavery, however, most were treated humanely. The stories have been told and retold, and part of the political agenda of African Americans is to paint the worst possible picture. It was not a rosy scenario, but they were treated better than slaves had ever been treated.

They were fed, clothed, and housed. They usually had one day a week off. They were given medical care and allowed to worship God. But the key, and this is why the plan "failed," is that they were allowed to marry and have children. Their children were more often than not born healthy and raised healthy. These children became healthy adults who were allowed to marry and have more healthy children.

Because of this, slavery did not die out by the late 1820s. All those healthy children made for a more thriving slave institution. Some families were split up. Some slaves did die of disease. Slavery was a hard life. Slaves also became free on a regular basis. Sometimes they escaped, were let free by their masters, bought their freedom, or had it come about in some other manner.

Like the war with Mexico and the Indian Wars, slavery involved an activity that saw the U.S. government make its share of mistakes and at times act in an immoral manner. It also represents the United States acting in a more moral manner than most other countries on the face of the earth *would* have acted.

Unlike the war with Mexico and the Indian Wars, slavery was not "inevitable." These two conflicts involved policies that were in this nation's national interest. In looking back at slavery, there is only one answer to the question "What should we have done?" That answer is to have ended slavery.

During the Constitutional Convention of 1787, the Northern states should have insisted that the South end the practice as a price of admission to the Union. Very likely, some (not all) of the former Southern colonies would have refused. Two separate nations would have existed. It is possible that, over time, the common American purpose and legacy of defeating the British would have compelled a Southern desire to be part of the United States. In a spirit of compromise, they may have acquiesced to the demand of abolition, or at least made strides toward it.

However, there is great irony in this speculation. If this course had been followed, and the South did not "come back" or make the desired compromises, slavery might have existed for many years longer than it did. Without the issue coming to a head and tearing the Union asunder, the Civil War most likely would never have been fought. Abraham Lincoln would not have become president. The Emancipation Proclamation would not have been enacted, and slavery might have gone on until . . . World War I.

This is how the devil works—through end runs, false "necessities," and moral equivocations that allow otherwise good men to justify their expedient means, leading to insatiable ends. In the meantime, the reality is reality. In war, people die. In Communism, excellence cannot thrive. In slavery, people are chained and imprisoned. To many white men and women of the seventeenth, eighteenth, and nineteenth centuries, the black Africans who made up the slave population were less than human. They were not civilized. The advancements of history had "proven" the manifest superiority of some races over others. This was seen as justification for their actions.

The "Americanization" of masters and slaves among the English colonists occurred rather quickly, especially in the South. The environment was radically different there from that in Great Britain and New England. The people felt American. There was little speculation or "carpetbagging," whereby English investors sought to make fast money on planting ventures and then return to England. Absentee ownership was common in the Caribbean but rare in the American South. Masters were active in running plantations. African Americanization also took place among the slave population. When the Revolution began, about 20 percent of American slaves were African-born (although the concentration of Africans remained higher in South Carolina and Georgia).

After the outlawing of new slave imports in 1808, the proportion of African-born slaves became tiny, and a native-born slave population emerged. African-born slaves (imported primarily for their ability to perform physical labor) included few children. Men outnumbered women by about two to one. American-born slaves were equally divided between males and females.

Slaves in the United States experienced "natural population growth." In Brazil, Jamaica, Saint-Domingue, and Cuba, slave mortality rates exceeded birthrates. The growth of the slave population depended on the importation of new slaves from Africa. When that importation ended, the slave population declined. Deaths among slaves exceeded births in the American colonies at first.

In the eighteenth century birthrates rose, mortality rates fell, and the slave population became self-reproducing. The result of this was that after outlawing slave imports in 1808, slaves tripled from 1.2 million to almost 4 million in 1860. By the beginning of the Civil War, slaves thought of themselves as Americans, not Africans.

Masters looked on their slaves (and themselves) differently as time and generations passed, to the detriment of the slaves. The masters who bought the slaves often saw them as important investments. They did not necessarily have great compassion for their humanity. They did wish to protect them as they would protect horses, cattle, and other property. The slaves born in Africa were more likely to be defiant, even proud, some skilled in the art of war or hunting. Many second-generation masters, unlike their parents, grew up with slaves and came to regard them as inferior members of their extended families. The slaves in turn fell in line with this view of themselves. The masters thought of themselves as "kindly patriarchs" who ruled firmly but fairly, looking after the slaves' needs. But such slave owners employed foremen with no familial attachment to the slaves. They relied heavily on the lash (and other forms of punishment) for discipline. The kind of man who gravitated into this kind of work was simply more likely to have a brutal streak than the kind of man who became an engineer or a newspaper reporter. The result was that slaves did not see their owners as kindly guardians.

Nevertheless, extreme physical abuse became less common for two reasons. One was that such abuse was not economically beneficial. The other was it became more apparent that to treat their slaves inhumanely was immoral.

The last third of the eighteenth century saw widespread questioning of slavery by white Americans. The American Revolution created a more egalitarian way of thinking. Many of the Founding Fathers, including

George Washington and Thomas Jefferson, while slaveholders, were troubled by the practice. They initiated a series of acts meant to create a climate they thought would lead to slavery's gradual abolition.

In all states north of Delaware, slavery was abolished. A few states did away with it immediately. Pennsylvania passed gradual emancipation acts in 1780, where all children born to slaves in the future would be freed at age twenty-eight. In 1787 the Northwest Ordinance barred slavery from the Northwest Territory (which included much of what is now the upper Midwest). A compromise reached at the Constitutional Convention allowed Congress to outlaw the importation of slaves in 1808. A number of states passed acts freeing slaves by individuals. As a result, in the upper South huge numbers of slaves were freed. Tens of thousands of slaves escaped from their masters during the war. The free black population surged.

The war appeared to have set the tone for a relatively quick abolition, but in the aftermath of fighting, as men made their way back to their farms and worked to build them back up to prosperity, the antislavery movement failed to make headway in Georgia and South Carolina. Planters imported tens of thousands of Africans before the 1808 cutoff. In the upper South, Revolution-inspired egalitarianism was replaced by a defiant desire to maintain unique regional characteristics. This is a great American tragedy.

Because the slave population self-reproduced, the end of importation did not undermine slavery, as many of the Founding Fathers expected. The ultimate result of the first antislavery movement was to make slavery a sectional, albeit thriving, institution. During the antebellum (pre–Civil War) years, slavery was fueled by the world demand for cotton. Slavery spread quickly into the Southwest. Alabama, Mississippi, and Louisiana formed the heart of the "cotton kingdom." Between 1790 and 1860, about one million slaves (almost twice the number of Africans shipped to the United States during the whole period of the transatlantic slave trade) moved west, partly due to a new domestic trade from seaboard states to Southwest planters.

Abolition of slavery in the North had begun in the Revolutionary era and was complete by the 1830s, dividing the country into the "slave" South and the "free" North. This defined the South. To defend slavery was to be "pro-Southern." Opposition to slavery was "anti-Southern." While most Southern whites did not own slaves (the proportion of white families that owned slaves declined from 35 percent to 26 percent between 1830 and

1860), virtually all whites in the South supported the institution. The issue was the single brushstroke that the rest of world used to paint their pictures of the South. By the middle of the nineteenth century, slavery remained only in Brazil, Cuba, Puerto Rico, and the Southern United States. "Backward" and "repressive" were catchphrases of foreign association with the South. Many people correlated it with serf-holding Russia.

The aristocratic nature of the South also became a major disadvantage. In the North, egalitarianism created a system where most people could read. Opportunity was available to a wide range of people. The average person could aspire to move beyond his or her "class." Class, in fact, was becoming an outdated concept.

But the South was still a place where a small number of rich people had access to education, and people knew their "place" in society. This class structure had an effect on attitudes regarding slavery. Poor whites had somebody below them. The "dumbing down" of large segments of their society would prove a huge problem in fighting the war and becoming a mainstream part of the country.

Northern states abolished slavery and then saw the growth of an articulate abolitionist movement. Southern whites found themselves applying their intellectual capital to an issue seen by more and more people as not only immoral but also requiring a certain amount of ignorance, for lack of a better word, to defend. As Southerners rallied around slavery, they became more and more despicable in the eyes of others. Some defenders tried to say it was a "practical necessity." Others went so far as to call it a "positive good." They pointed to the Biblical "curse of Ham" to explain the origins of black bondage, portraying slavery as part of God's plan for civilizing a primitive, heathen people.

In this respect, the Southerners tried to entrench their philosophy. Today, in light of greater knowledge, such arguments seem stupid. As mentioned earlier, slavery was a thriving practice that had permeated virtually the entire world for time immemorial. The Greeks said it was natural. Even the Bible provides some language that can be interpreted as tacit "approval" of some kind of activity that demands servants adhere to the wishes of their masters, just as wives were instructed to obey husbands and children to respect parents. There was a great deal of "evidence" supposedly supporting the Southern argument.

During the 1840s and 1850s the South was harmonious, orderly, and religious. The North was tumultuous, heretical, and mercenary, torn by radicalism, reform, individualism, class conflict, and abolitionism.

Southern slaves allegedly were treated better than Northern wage laborers, who endured free-labor capitalism "wage slavery" that was cruel, exploitative, and selfish. The degraded condition of supposedly free British paupers and Irish peasants was pointed out. Free-labor spokesmen argued that slavery kept the South backward, poor, inefficient, and degraded. Slavery advocates said that only slavery could save the South (and the world) from the evils of modernity.

Beginning in the mid-1840s, and especially after the war with Mexico, slavery became the central American political issue. New Western territories were exclusively free, but Southern spokesmen wanted to expand slavery there. The federal government was "meddling," a grave affront to Southern honor. In 1860 the election of Abraham Lincoln as president on a free-soil platform set off a crisis. Seven states in the Deep South seceded from the United States and formed the Confederate States of America. The United States and the rebel Confederates went to war in April of 1861, leading to the additional secession of four states in the upper South. Four other slave states—Maryland, Delaware, Kentucky, and Missouri—remained in the Union, as did the new state of West Virginia (which split off from Virginia.)

Just as Osama bin Laden's decision to crash planes into the World Trade Center on 9/11 resulted eventually in *exactly the opposite of what he hoped to happen*, Southern politicians supporting secession in order to preserve slavery found that their action *led instead to slavery's death*. Over time, Northern war aims shifted from preserving the Union to abolishing slavery and *reconstructing* the Union. Two shifts began to take place. Southern blacks, seeing weakened authority at home, began to refuse to behave like slaves. Northern whites accepted the Radical Republican position that the war should result in abolition.

Slavery ended for hundreds of thousands of Southern blacks long before the war ended. The Union moved further into the South, freeing slaves along the way while others fled from their owners, seeking refuge within Union lines. Federal officials experimented with free and semi-free labor. Northern missionaries established schools to help turn slaves into citizens. The freed slaves showed enthusiasm for education, and Northern whites who saw this backed President Lincoln's "new birth of freedom."

The Emancipation Proclamation was issued on January 1, 1863. Although it applied only to areas under rebel control and did not end slavery in the United States, it was the turning point that marked the beginning of the end. The Proclamation now made the War Between the States a war for freedom. A federal victory would mean the death of slavery. As slavery crumbled in much of the South, more than 188,000 African Americans, both Southern and Northern, joined Union forces and fought, in a number of cases bravely and in important battles. The 13th Amendment to the Constitution, passed by Congress in January 1863 and ratified by the states in December of 1865, completed the process, outlawing slavery everywhere in the United States.

Despite this great achievement, the future for former slaves remained murky. Freed slaves wanted economic security, social autonomy, and civil rights. Former slave owners were burning with animosity. Northerners argued over Reconstruction. The result was a national commitment to turn former slaves into citizens, anchored by the 14th and 15th Amendments to the Constitution and the Reconstruction Acts of 1867 and 1868. Together, these measures provided basic civil rights to former slaves, enfranchised black males, and imposed a largely self-administered democratization process on the former Confederate states, under federal supervision.

Emancipation brought personal freedom that came with no longer being someone else's property, along with the attendant hardships. But full equality was a myth. Reconstruction was in many ways a failure. African Americans lived in poverty, were exploited, and were subject to violence at the hands of whites determined to reimpose black subordination. A variety of state laws instituted rigid racial segregation in virtually all areas of life. In violation of the 14th and 15th Amendments, white resistance effectively disenfranchised black voters. The struggle had only just begun.

Had slavery not existed, there never would have been a war, but the issue was not articulated in such a way at the beginning as to be understood by all. The issue was peripheral to the Civil War at the beginning of the conflict. It was the central tenet of the war at the end. In 1861, great care was given to not alienating the border states and avoiding Northern dissent. In the early part of the war, one reasonable goal of Abe Lincoln's was to achieve peace in return for saving the Union, while allowing slavery to continue.

In his inaugural address, Lincoln stated, "The maintenance inviolate of the rights of the states, and especially the right of each state to order and control its own domestic institutions according to its own judgment exclusively, is essential to the balance of power on which the perfection and endurance of our political fabric depend."

In July 1861, a resolution introduced by Senator Andrew Johnson of Tennessee was adopted in the Senate by an almost unanimous vote, declaring that "the war was not prosecuted for the purpose of over-throwing or interfering with the rights and established institutions of the states, but to defend and maintain the supremacy of the Constitution and all laws made in pursuance thereof, and to preserve the Union with all the dignity, equality and rights of the several states unimpaired, and that as soon as those objects were accomplished the war ought to cease."

Christian abolitionists saw perfidy in Lincoln's stance. He had debated Stephen Douglas, using fervent and sometimes religious phraseology that created the image of a modern-day Moses, opening the floodgates of freedom and turning the prairies of America into a new Red Sea.

Other Voices: Winston Groom

Winston Groom is the author of Forrest Gump *and is also a University of Alabama football historian.*

I never heard about Bryant saying, "This here's what a football player looks like." I wrote a history of their football program, and I heard so much B.S., so many little anecdotes, and when I went to try to pin it down, it generally turns out it never happened, and that just pisses you off. If you want to do it right, you've got to find out where you heard that, and where did he get it. I never heard any such thing as that.

I've got plenty of friends there, and off the top of my head, it would be insane and totally out of character for Bryant to get another player, bring him into the locker room, and just humiliate his team. Somebody said it, but I have no knowledge of it. I had graduated by then.

Johnny Musso and Scott Hunter were there. Between these two, if somebody had done that and said that, I'd think they'd have been aware of it.

Having studied it, it would have been the most improbable event imaginable to have a coach go into another coach's locker room to drag a player before a dejected team. Bryant may have said something like this back in Tuscaloosa before Sunday, or at Monday practice, maybe in film. If he said it to [Johnny] Musso he learned something, because he went on to become an All-American.

Other Voices: Dwight Chapin

Dwight Chapin was assigned to both the USC and UCLA sports beats for the Los Angeles Times *in the early 1970s. Although he was in Oregon covering UCLA on September 12, 1970, he did know John McKay very well. He is the coauthor, with Jeff Prugh, of* The Wizard of Westwood.

I heard Bear Bryant speak a lot, and I can't recall ever understanding *any-thing* he was saying. He was an all-time mumbler. So who knows about that famous quote? I'm strongly guessing he never brought Cunningham into the locker room and said what he is supposed to have said. I didn't know or have any dealings with him at all, in fact, except for a very few contacts during my years with the *L.A. Times*.

I think somebody at Alabama *knew* they needed black players to win, and that Bryant-Cunningham incident was invented to speed the process. Just a guess, but an educated one.

Tommy Prothro, a Southerner who coached UCLA when McKay was at USC, told me once that he fought, not always successfully, against the racist views that were a part of his upbringing and heritage all of his life. Prothro, by the way, was not only a helluva coach but also a helluva guy. Far and away my favorite of all the coaches I worked with in my L.A. days.

As for McKay, whom I knew much better than Bryant, I always respected him greatly as a coach. I well remember that when I covered the Trojans daily on the beat for the *Times* in the late '60s, if he saw me coming on the practice field and didn't want to talk to me, he'd drive off on his cart and go up on his coaching "tower." I felt his trademark wit was often programmed, too. The jokes that played so well to audiences of boosters and such were ones he used over and over. He could be a very funny guy, especially when he was in one of those marathon "talk" sessions over drinks at Julie's restaurant with writers such as John Hall (and me), but I found him to be moody, too. No question, however, that he was one of the top coaches of his time (probably all time) and a heckuva recruiter, too. The talent he had in those years was awesome. A lot of it rarely if ever saw the field (such as Mike Holmgren) because the Trojans were so deep.

CHAPTER Four

Christian Idealism and Influential Contrarians

What is truth?
—*Pontius Pilate*

Richard Nixon embodied conservatism, and it is no surprise that during his presidency he developed a strong professional and personal friendship with the great Christian evangelist Billy Graham. Hollywood had already started to skewer Christianity. The 1950s Burt Lancaster film *Elmer Gantry* supposedly "exposed" the "charlatanism" of Christian revivalists. There was nothing charlatan about Graham, and it was not a coincidence that he was from the South, deriving his greatest popularity from that region. It is also not a coincidence that Nixon was from California—born, more specifically, in Orange County.

The partnership of Nixon and Graham was a partnership of geographic regions and the shared politics of those regions. Nixon and Orange County represented a Christian alternative to Hollywood. The Christianity that powered Orange County was the source of both Nixon's inner strength and political support. It was the nexus of his relationship with Graham. It was what made men such as Nixon, Ronald Reagan, and Barry Goldwater palatable to the American South. It was the middle ground that softened hearts, and after all the hitting, shouting, fighting, and consternation, it was what drove change—desegregation—in Dixie.

Therefore, in order to understand this dynamic, one must understand Christianity.

Jesus Christ is the man responsible for the end of the Roman Empire, nearly five hundred years after His death. In so doing, He replaced warring minds with a message of peace. He was probably born in 6 BC. It is easier to attribute His birth to six years prior to His birth date than it is to change all the landmark dates of human history. Historians have determined that mistakes were made in determining the Christian calendar in relation to His life. December 25, for instance, is probably not His birthday, but rather the day we have decided to celebrate it.

All that is known about Jesus of Nazareth appears in the first four books of the New Testament. Matthew, Mark, Luke, and John wrote them years after his death. All tell different stories. Jesus Christ was a contrarian, a revolutionary.

When the Founding Fathers (almost all of whom were Christian) wrote the Constitution and instituted the U.S. political system, they were concerned with what the Greek "Greats" had been concerned with: minority rights. They spoke of the "tyranny of the majority."

Greek democracy consisted of a series of votes over all decisions. All major questions were settled by a large vote of the eligible citizen population. The Americans saw the bulkiness of this process but wanted something different from the English Parliament. They chose representative democracy, which is called a republic. This vested decisions in the hands of elected public officials who would cast votes on behalf of their respective constituencies—districts or states.

Had a Greek-style vote been held throughout the history of the Jim Crow South, from the end of the Civil War, through Reconstruction, and in the ensuing one hundred years, that vote would have consistently denied civil rights and most other rights for blacks. Blacks were held from the vote through any number of nefarious means—poll taxes, tests, literacy demands, whatever could be used to keep them down.

Even if blacks had the vote, they were still in the minority. However, the American system would have given them power. Political districts would inevitably place large numbers of black voters in certain geographical locations, resulting in the election of black congressmen and other representatives.

However, any statewide vote would always outnumber them. Any regional vote—the whole South, for instance—would also outnumber them. But federal law superseded state laws. It was federal law, whether Supreme Court decisions, laws passed by the House and Senate then signed by the president, or laws mandated by White House order, that caused "problems" in the 1950s and 1960s. Southerners argued, with some justification, that their "states' rights" were being trampled on.

This would be a pure democratic republic in action. Conversely, in the 1960s, had state-by-state elections been held regarding questions of segregation; "colored-only" schools, drinking fountains, lunch counters, and rest rooms; integration of football teams; and all the other peculiarities of life at that time, Southern states would have democratically upheld the Jim Crow "laws" already in place. Certainly, Southern senators and congressmen (all Democrats) had officially voted against the actual Civil Rights Act and its attendant laws (called by LBJ the Great Society), which emanated from the 1964 to 1965 political period and were still being enacted, argued about, or rejected in 1970.

Herein lies the heart of the American political question and its tenuous dance with morality, which can be a code word for religion. It infuses the modern issue of abortion, to name the most obvious example. The "tyranny of the majority" is the worst-case scenario of democracy. Adolf Hitler, for instance, had once been democratically elected to lead Germany, and by the time the Nazis had successfully "campaigned" on their "issues," a majority of Germans would have ratified these into law if given that chance.

So when is democracy good, and when is it immoral? Just because a majority wants something does not make it the right thing to do. John F. Kennedy's Pulitzer Prize–winning *Profiles in Courage* detailed how American political figures went against the grain of public opinion, often at great expense, to vote according to their respective consciences. Would the living Jesus Christ win a vote on questions regarding his status as Messiah?

Racism and segregation are immoral. These are "self-evident truths" that emanate from "natural law," yet the great "self-evident laws" that make this country great did not do away with slavery. Was segregation moral in the South because a majority of people there said it was, then became immoral only when a majority said it?

Is gay marriage immoral because the majority deems it to be, or because the Old Testament says it is? Was abortion immoral in the 1950s because a majority said it was? Is it suddenly not immoral because a modern majority would support a pro-choice agenda?

These eternal questions go to the concept of moral relativism, a term used today to describe why terrorists murder innocent people. But all politics is local, and individuals argue all politics. The genius of freedom is in allowing for reasonable discourse among all, including those who disagree, are in the minority, or are called "contrarians." Socrates was put to death by his state for being such a man, but history accords much respect and credence to our contrarians. Winston Churchill was once a contrarian.

In the 1960s, Martin Luther King Jr. was a contrarian. So was Bobby Kennedy and Richmond Flowers Sr. If it were not for contrarians, change would rarely occur. Understanding the more influential contrarians of history is important in understanding how change is effectuated, whether it be in 1970s Alabama or under any other circumstances.

In 1969–1970, another contrarian was planning a revolution in Birmingham, Alabama, but in the quietest way possible. His name was Paul "Bear" Bryant.

Other Voices: Rod Martin

After starring for both John McKay and John Robinson at Southern California, Rod Martin went on to a great career with the Oakland Raiders. He starred in the 1981 Super Bowl, leading Oakland to victory over Philadelphia. He now works at USC.

I got to meet John McKay through Willie Brown. I went to L.A. City College, where I was an All-American and the Defensive Player of the Year. Vince Evans was our quarterback, and he was the Offensive Player of the Year. We tied in the Potato Bowl. Evans went with me to USC, and like me he later played for the Raiders.

So, I was highly recruited and wanted to stay on the West Coast. San Diego State, UCLA, and USC went after me. Brown came by to recruit me quite a few times, but I'd told Dick Vermeil I'd go to UCLA. I loved Bruin basketball, so I was leaning there. Through basketball, Vermeil, who was in his first year taking over, had me nearly committed to UCLA.

That is, until McKay came to the house where I lived in L.A. He was on his way out of town, and Coach Brown set it up. He was humble and nice to my mom, and he had the gift of gab that could hypnotize me. He was honest and down to earth. He told me what USC had to offer. What stuck in my mind and changed my decision, I don't know if he knew about my basketball, but he said, "If you're a great basketball player, you should go to UCLA, but you *are* a great football player, so then you should go where the great players are, and that's USC."

Vermeil tried to change my mind. Vermeil gets emotional, and the man starts crying in mom's living room. I had to ask my mom to ask Vermeil to please leave.

At USC I was in awe about all the talent, but I loved my decision. I came in with another linebacker, David Lewis, and the position was opening up. When I came in, I got hurt against Arkansas. I bruised my knee and didn't get well fast enough. This is the 1974 national title year. Once I got healthy, I determined the USC way, the way they played. It was an honor to even be red-shirted, because I was working the guys, making 'em better. Guys on the scout squad could start on any team. That's a testament to their recruiters. It was such a great family atmosphere; guys stuck together. This came from McKay and Marv Goux. He was in charge of the scout squad and kept us fired up.

Despite red-shirting, I felt like I was an intricate part of that national championship run. McKay would ride around on a golf cart, beeping his horn. When you heard that *beep* you knew it was McKay, and you'd perk right up. Every now and then McKay and his assistants would get together, and the coaches would relay this message to the players. McKay stayed away and let his assistants do the coaching.

The Manfred Moore story about Coach not rescinding his scholarship when he got his girlfriend pregnant, that's the human side of McKay. I'm originally from West Virginia, too. People there are honest, blunt, and to the point. Truthful, that was Coach McKay. If he wanted you, you knew it. If you weren't good enough, he'd tell you. He didn't try to feed you a story, and he earned your respect.

I remember talking about that 1970 game growing up. I wasn't into football, I was mostly into basketball, but we all knew about Sam Cunningham and what he did. He had a great game, but I emphasize not to take away from the great success of Martin Luther King. The civil rights leaders opened Bear's eyes—he wants to win, he has to bring in the best talent, and he needed blacks. Bryant stood up and was a man about it. He loved Alabama football and didn't care who didn't like it. Was he in a position to do that two or three years before? I don't think it was the right time to do it yet.

Don't forget that Booker Brown was on the line opening holes for Sam. There were a lot of great black athletes on that team, and it opened a lot of people's eyes.

Other Voices: John Robinson

Make no mistake about it, John Robinson is a legendary USC football coach, deserving of mention in the same league with Howard Jones, John McKay, and Pete Carroll. A product of Serra High School in Northern California, he grew up best friends with John Madden, who became the Oakland Raider coach and a TV football superstar. After college, Robinson took to a coaching career, landing a position on McKay's staff at USC during the greatest period in Southern California history (prior to the Carroll era). In 1975, he "prepped" for the head coaching job at Southern California by working under Madden at Oakland. After McKay departed for Tampa Bay, Robinson took over, and there have been very few transitions that carried forward so smoothly at any level, in any sport, pro or college. His 1976 team was 11–1, defeating Michigan in the Rose Bowl. His 1978 team marched into Birmingham and whipped Bryant's Crimson Tide, 24–14, en route to a national championship. The 1979 team was supposed to be the greatest in college football history. Despite a single tie that cost Troy a repeat national championship, they are remembered as possibly the most talented squad ever assembled. While McKay is known as a coach with genius for the running attack, Robinson coached two Heisman Trophy winners, Charles White (1979) and Marcus Allen (1981), and with the Los Angeles Rams called the shots when Eric Dickerson broke O. J. Simpson's single-season rushing record in 1984. After leaving the Rams, Robinson had another stint at Southern California (1993–1997). His 1995 team beat Northwestern in a memorable high-scoring Rose Bowl. He eventually took over at the University of Nevada–Las Vegas. Robinson was media friendly and made football fun for his players, even when there were two seconds left on the clock and a yard and a half separated Troy from the promised land or bust. He is retired and lives in the Phoenix area.

What I remember before that 1970 game was that McKay and Bryant were good friends. Their friendship was important in understanding this whole dynamic. They talked about that, integration. This whole thing was planned out, I assure you.

Sam Cunningham was a catalyst, a great guy and a great athlete, but those two men, by the nature of their relationship, bridged the gap and saw some of that change before it happened.

USC had enjoyed success in 1962 with a national-title team. In 1970, 1971, and then in '72 they had the greatest team of all time. Sam was a fullback on that team. Those USC teams had a great impact in a lot of ways. I was an assistant on their staff at that time.

Now, if you think about the effect of the West Coast on society and how it plays out in sports, I think we're kind of wacky anyway. A lot of civil rights things were happening, and California was part of that whole scene.

Up at the University of Oregon, we were like a radical triple-A ball club. They sent you up there for "training." There was a lot of unrest, new ground being opened in those areas. People in other parts of the country were reluctant, but a lot exploded on the West Coast, not just in civil rights like in the South, but in the everyday expansion of things. In terms of athletics, it seems that so many talented African American kids got a chance to play in high school in the L.A. area, and you're not gonna succeed unless you had recruited those players.

Over a twenty-year period from 1962 to 1982, USC was probably as strong in football as any college program ever was. Our location was advantageous. We're right in the middle of the inner city, so many kids grew up wanting to play at USC. If they were basketball players, they wanted to go to UCLA. With all that was going on, it was having a major effect, and nationally USC had always benefited from the fact that African Americans felt welcome there.

There's no question that USC got it right. A lot of black kids looked at UCLA as being in the rich part of town, so we had this strange mixture of all things that linked us together. Maybe Miami was like that, during that stretch when they were so good, you saw Miami and USC similarly did not have great facilities, but each had great weather, and athletes felt at home at these schools, and discipline was not a hallmark.

There's a coalition of people in the stands at a USC game that a politician would dream of. I'd drive through South Central L.A., and people would wave at you if you were from USC.

One other thing is that African American athletes became very socially adept at USC. Maybe this was because of the Hollywood connection, or because the school's located in a major city. There's always media around, and McKay was brilliant—he exposed his players to the media, to alumni groups, and so they became very comfortable and polished. Listen to Cunningham, Mike Garrett, Lynn Swann, Marcus Allen; they are savvy with the press, are well spoken, and represent the school beautifully. Not all athletes, black or white, do this role well.

It's not just football players or black athletes. Look at John Naber, Pat Haden, Tom Seaver. Famous people go there. O.J. obviously flipped, but before that, before he had his collapse, he was a star in Hollywood and sportscasting.

It's a major metropolitan area with two, three, four newspapers and a lot of TV coverage. It's different if you go to, say, Athens, Georgia, and the local guy is asking a player a question, and down there it's, "Yes, sir; no, sir; proud to be here, sir," those kinds of questions.

USC and UCLA athletes were exposed to so much more and were from a town with two pro football teams, two baseball teams, two basketball teams, and a broader social world. It's very interesting and ironic that in the 1980s and early '90s it kind of turned things the other way with the riots, and this made it—L.A.—a negative place. USC basketball and football took a dip. It was not as attractive as it had been, but in recent years the city, the state, and USC have made a comeback.

It was fun to be there. A lot of those athletes were great friends of mine. The 1979 team, the only negative was that Anthony Munoz got hurt in the first game and played just the last game. Marcus was a sophomore, we had a great secondary, and we were loaded from freshmen to seniors. The 1972 team was a veteran team; both were really good teams. I was assistant, Marv Goux and myself. We were both guys who were there with McKay. It's sad that Marv passed on. That '72 year was magical, especially after I'd been at Oregon.

I was at USC for a number of years under McKay, then Madden had me for one year in order to broaden my range for head coaching, as USC had me in mind to replace McKay. That happened. Sometimes the hardest thing is to be promoted from assistant to head coach, so my one year at Oakland kind of helped me transition. If you go away, they think you're better. To be successful, I advise a coach to take on different jobs under different coaches and develop a range of experience.

That's what Pete Carroll's done, and now he's bringing all this back at USC.

CHAPTER Five

"I Have a Dream"

Nonviolence is not sterile passivity, but a powerful moral force
which makes for social transformation.
—*Martin Luther King Jr., 1946*

History is a funny thing. Major events often occur within a short span of time. Such was the conversion of the emperor Constantine, which changed Christianity forever. As history tells us, in the blink of an eye, Constantine saw a vision of the cross, and the Roman Empire was now a Christian one.

But the religion had grown all throughout the empire for almost five hundred years prior to Constantine's epiphany. The writing of the New Testament, the works of Augustine, and the political power of Pope Leo all served to make the Christian Church a powerful social force. Just as the fall of the Berlin Wall was not an isolated incident but the result of years of struggle, so was the world "ready" for Christianity when Constantine declared that he was a Christian. Thus was the empire under His command.

It is important to understand this, as it applies to the 1970 USC-Alabama game. That game was not merely a singular event that changed the South. Like Constantine's vision and the fall of the Berlin Wall, this game came after years of struggle, resulting in a tipping point not unlike the Roman emperor's vision or the German people's bold attack on the wall.

* * *

The attempt here is not just to gain some understanding of the human animal. The purpose is to apply what we have learned to a study of the unique American character and how that character was embodied in a game of football played in 1970. In the United States, we have made better and more moral decisions for the public good than any previous power. Still, we have not achieved a perfectly harmonious society. Immoral decisions prefaced the morality that followed that game. Practicality played a large role in the subsequent events. It was not all harmony and serene thoughts.

First and foremost, as interviews with the participants, the observers, and others involved with the 1970 USC-Alabama game can attest, the picture is never as clear as it would be made to seem. The South for years had been caricatured as "ignorant" by the liberal media and Northeastern "do-gooders." Yet five years before the game, the streets of "enlightened" Los Angeles had burst into flames over perceived racist treatment by cops in the LAPD. The Trojan football team that traveled to Birmingham may have been painted as harmonious. However, years after the fact, their mediocre records in 1970 and 1971, despite a roster full of superstars, are explained by racial tensions. Their perfect 1972 team is said to have been brought together not by new forms of communication but rather by the fellowship of Bible study.

In the years following the game, while the South was desegregating, whites in that most judgmental of Northern cities, Boston, were rioting in the streets to protest a court order sending their children to school with blacks. In 1973, a black criminal gang that became known as "the Zebra Killers" started randomly killing whites as retribution for racism, not in the South but in the city of "the Summer of Love," San Francisco. Groups such as the Weathermen and the SLA rose up in an effort to give liberalism an army, like the IRA in Ireland. In 1995, the myth of white-black harmony was exploded when a black former USC football star, O. J. Simpson, was put on trial for the murder of his white wife and her white friend. This time, all the old "rules" were reversed when an all-black jury, despite seemingly overwhelming evidence of his guilt, acquitted him.

Nobody would make the argument that racism was vanquished from Dixie by the game or in subsequent years. However, the moderating elements of payment for its guilty past, possibly even in the form of "political correctness," have created a paradigm shift. Whites and blacks now have an understanding in the South that may be absent from other parts of America. There is a sense of camaraderie in their interactions that comes from shared experiences, common language, and rural common sense—the kind all too often missing in big Northern cities.

Just as the depictions of Bull Connor, police dogs, and water hoses do not tell the whole story, white or black, in the 1960s South, neither would it be fair to characterize all the subsequent progress as the benevolent result of Christian healing. Rather, the unique values of America seem to have come into play here. This includes, of course, the redemptive powers of religion, mixed with the genius of our political system and a successful capitalistic marketplace. Through these factors, everybody has been able to share together in a "rising tide that lifts all boats," giving them some sense of ownership—an investment in the great "experiment," as the Founding Fathers called it.

* * *

Rudyard Kipling wrote the poem "White Man's Burden" to "justify" America's military incursions into Cuba and the Philippines. A few years later, Mark Twain remarked, "What about the brown man's burden?" The history of interaction between white people and nonwhite people is a history of conflict. The most recent history concerns colonization and expansion of the British Empire and what must now be called the American Empire.

The British occupied much of Africa, the Middle East, the Far East, and points in between. The Americans first engaged in wars with Mexicans and Indians, then set forth on the de facto colonization of Cuba, the Philippines, China, Hawaii, and points in between. Most of the white European countries, however, have long histories of interaction with the "native lands." The Roman Empire. The Spanish Conquest. The Crusades. For a couple thousand years, armed whites have ventured into the lands of the nonwhites and done some serious damage. At this point, a very large portion of the nonwhite world hates the whites because of it.

The relationship of whites to nonwhites is often characterized as being one in which the nonwhites are disproportionately hurt, enslaved, exploited, and destroyed by the whites. There is no question that in adding up the "score," whites have done far more damage to nonwhites than vice versa.

The question, which is not asked without controversy, is whether the nonwhites are better or worse off for having dealt with the whites. Any blanket "excuse" for white exploitation, prejudice, and violence is easily dismissed as immorality. On the other hand, we live in a world shaped by

Western civilization, or by "dead white males" as some like to say, with a little bit of derision.

The great principles of Western civilization have been left to roll around in messy confluence with the great evils of Western civilization. Either way, the world has been shaped, for the most part, *by* Western civilization. Western civilization is not the only civilization. The ancient world includes the antiquities of the Middle East and the philosophies of the Far East and Near East. Europe has given us its fair share of major stinkers. The French Revolution led to a century of revolution, eventually resulting in the Nazis and the Communists. Nevertheless, the contributions of Western civilization far outweigh the evils.

The age-old question again is asked. Are nonwhites better off, or worse off, on the whole, for having been forced to coexist with the white world? Are the descendants of slaves better or worse off for their ancestors having been brought to America? These questions have an inherent controversy attached to them because they force one to address whether there was justification in what happened. Of course, there is no sense of moral relativism that can ever be used to give credence to slavery or any other evil. But just as American involvement with brutal dictators who opposed Communism must be viewed under the larger picture, so too must the convoluted, complicated relationship of whites and nonwhites.

Today, Liberia is a country in West Africa that is rife with genocidal violence. Freed American slaves, under the dictates of President James Monroe, founded this country. The capital of Liberia, Monrovia, is named after him. Are the descendants of these slaves, who barely survive the day-to-day struggle against AIDS, war, anarchy, disease, and evil, better off than descendants of slaves living in, say, Detroit, Michigan?

The black-white relationship is more complicated in the United States than in other nations. Great Britain, for instance, is so old that one simply accepts their past misdeeds. There is too much history to try to "explain" it. But America was founded on enormous principles of goodwill and love for our fellow man. The contrast with treatment toward blacks is something that we do try to come to grips with. The beauty of America is that we do not sweep our problems and secrets under the rug.

Furthermore, there is no denying that a great majority of the world's best modern inventions—electricity, penicillin, air travel, roads, railroads, modern hospital medicine, the printing press, books, films, radio, TV, just to name a very, very few off the top of the head—are products of "white people." Are nonwhites better or worse off for having access to these modernities?

The converse argument is that white people (namely Christopher Columbus) brought diseases to nonwhites, but the premise that but for Columbus and his "ilk," no diseases ever would have made their way into these paradises is specious. People *are* better off learning how to read, learning how to drive cars, and getting treated for sexually transmitted diseases. In a perfect world, the utopians would have had Westerners provide all these "services" free of charge, without taking any self-interest in anything beyond pure benevolence. This is to deny human nature, black, white, brown, or otherwise.

In actuality, there were many whites who did indeed practice this kind of benevolence. They were called Christian missionaries. If we sent more of them today, while fewer rock stars raise money that ends up in the coffers of African despots, Africa would be better off. By a long shot.

Certainly many "modern inventions" have been made to do evil work. Brilliant white scientists and engineers are responsible for the weapons of mass destruction that result in the kinds of military holocausts that make up the twentieth century. Of course, the Chinese, who are decidedly *not* white, invented gunpowder. The argument, made with some merit, also goes that nuclear weapons saved the United States and the USSR from fighting World War III. Military technology has allowed America to free most of the world.

Still, expediency and the devil are never far away from our justifications.

What is certainly true is that whites do not hold any monopoly on morality. This may have been the false premise that brought down the British Empire, the concept of *superiority* as opposed to *partnership*. The two most evil political ideologies of all time, Nazism and Communism, are the products of modern white European minds. Any notion that the white man was morally superior to his fellow man was wiped out by these horrors.

However, it is a lie to argue that nonwhites are morally superior to whites. Terrorism, which is not an Arab Muslim invention (but is being perfected in those circles) is nowhere close to Nazism or Communism. Yet. However, it is evidence of the premise that nonwhites are capable of enormous immorality on a grand scale. The bottom line is that, at least up to this point in time, to borrow a Darwinian term, in the evolution of man, white people have been in control of things. Therefore, since they have been in charge, they have done the most damage. The fact that they have also done the most good is part of the duality of the human dilemma.

While the Greeks did hold the Olympics in ancient times, for upwards of two thousand years after they stopped doing that, man was too busy fighting, dying, dealing with disease, warring, and surviving to get involved much in sports. Then, along came America. We had the weather. We had the wide-open spaces. We had hardy folks who were physical and liked a challenge. Sports came naturally to us.

Throughout all the years in which whites and nonwhites dealt with each other as enemies, the glue needed to bring people together, to form a common purpose, was missing. As sports became an integral part of American society, few really could guess that sports would turn out to be the glue, or the cement mixer, as Jeff Prugh called it, that did just that. Out of sports emanated all the ideals of Martin Luther King's "dream."

Who knew?

The death of Abe Lincoln is particularly tragic because, had he lived, blacks might have been allowed real freedom instead of being sentenced to another hundred years of de facto slavery. Many blacks in the South more than likely lived worse after the Civil War than they had when they were property. The administrations of Andrew Johnson and Ulysses S. Grant were rife with corruption and ineptitude. Reconstruction, which had started with such high hopes, ended in the 1870s as an abysmal failure. People in the South were more resentful than ever. The easy scapegoats for their hatred were the poor blacks living within their midst. It was a recipe for disaster.

Maybe, had Lincoln presided over the first four years of Reconstruction, he would have demonstrated enough leadership to enact real peace. Maybe he would have failed, and his legacy would have suffered because of it. Either way, what did come out of it was something called "Jim Crow."

The term originated in a song performed by Daddy Rice, a white minstrel-show entertainer in the 1830s. Rice covered his face with charcoal to resemble a black man and then sang and danced a routine in caricature of a silly black person. He called the character Jim Crow. By the 1850s, this Jim Crow character was a popular depiction of black inferiority.

There is no clear-cut explanation as to why this term was eventually applied to laws used to keep black people segregated. What is clear is that the laws were in place and used to subordinate blacks to the dictates of whites. Segregation took a clear turn immediately after the Civil War. Both whites and blacks instituted it. "Carpetbagging" whites came to the South, "mixing" with Northern blacks. The populace quickly scorned this practice. Southern whites had no desire to share their lives with blacks. Blacks were not comfortable making any attempt to mix with them.

The former slaves established their own churches and schools. "Black Codes" enacted to legally impose discrimination were short-lived, but the federal government declared these "laws" illegal. The passage of the 14th and 15th Amendments, along with the Civil Right Act of 1866 and various Enforcement Acts of the early 1870s, curtailed the ability of Southern whites to formally deprive blacks of their civil rights.

For a period of time, African Americans made progress in building their own institutions, passing civil rights laws. They elected officials to public office. Secret organizations such as the Ku Klux Klan were created as a backlash. The result was brutalization and terror. Federal attempts to stop it were weak, in part because they feared starting a "second Civil War."

In 1877, Republican president Rutherford B. Hayes ended Reconstruction, essentially abandoning Southern blacks. This was *not* the Republican Party's finest hour. In the 1880s, mob lynchings, a brutal prison system, and chain gangs were imposed upon the black population. The Supreme Court sanctioned segregation by upholding the "separate but equal" clause of state laws in *Plessy v. Ferguson* (1896). It was the second time the Supreme Court had gotten it wrong. The Dred Scott case prior to the Civil War sanctioned the view of slaves as legal property in certain states. The federal government failed to enact antilynching laws.

By the twentieth century, blacks and private Northern white groups started black colleges. Whites in the South had refused to build black public high schools until the twentieth century. Private education became the only avenue for blacks. Their literacy nearly doubled from 1880 to 1930, rising from less than 45 percent to 77 percent. By 1910, segregated black institutions enabled a small middle class of prosperous black participants who lived "behind the veil," in the words of black intellectual W. E. B. Du Bois. Southern blacks adopted appeasement tactics called "dissembling," or a psychological ploy that manifested itself as shuffling, feigning irresponsibility, and "turning the other cheek." African Americans endured words such as *boy, girl, uncle, auntie,* and *n—r.*

African Americans resisted by mocking whites in songs, jokes, and stories, called "putting on the man," or playing Sambo (a black minstrel caricature of the era) to manipulate white masters and alleviate suffering. The result was mixed. Whites were too smart to be fooled by the mockery, which simply inflamed their anger more. But the worst part was that in playing, or actually being, the stereotype, blacks found that whites came to expect this docility. In later years, when the civil rights movement picked up steam, the contrast between the Sambo caricature and serious petition became a culture shock for whites that they could not handle.

Literature and film of the period immortalized characters such as Uncle Tom, Uncle Remus, Jim Crow, and "Old Black Joe." D. W. Griffith's *The Birth of a Nation* (1915) depicted elected black Reconstruction congressmen as ape-characters eating bananas on the House floor. Black film actors were cast as lazy, submissive, and docile.

Amid the disturbing realities of life under Jim Crow were acts of resistance. Four thousand African Americans were said to be lynched, mutilated, or burned alive from 1882 to 1968, mostly for challenging or breaking Jim Crow laws.

Owning a prosperous grocery store could make blacks stand out, therefore incurring white wrath. Prosperous blacks took to living in unpainted houses, maintaining "run down" and unpainted businesses, and avoiding new carriages and automobiles so as to stay unnoticed. Black newspaper editors, church leaders, and civil rights advocates were especially vulnerable.

By 1905, the debate on how to deal with Jim Crow was between the followers of Booker T. Washington and W. E. B. Du Bois. Washington was born in slavery. He advocated segregation, farming, and community support, choosing to "lay low" in order to avoid violent confrontation that he knew blacks would not win. He helped form the Tuskegee Institute and discovered that there was a great deal of white goodwill and philanthropy. He chose not to antagonize his white sympathizers, realizing that his cause would never be won unless he had the backing of enough whites. He preached training in the arts of agriculture and teaching. Economic security, Washington said, had to be achieved before any other freedoms were possible.

Du Bois was a Harvard-educated, New England–born intellectual who said Washington was an appeaser. Du Bois insisted that Constitutional rights of the citizenry come first and that a talented elite of black Americans would lead the rest, making the fundamental decisions for the masses.

Du Bois and William Monroe Trotter founded the Niagara Movement, advocating activism over gradualism. The Niagara Movement eventually became the National Association for the Advancement of Colored People (NAACP), an interracial organization that emerged in 1909. In the 1920s, the NAACP filed numerous lawsuits and lobbied Congress to pass federal antilynching laws. The nationwide laws never came to fruition, but the media exposure reduced the practice.

The philosophical divide between Washington and Du Bois also led to a disturbing trend in which "light-skinned" blacks were favored by their own community over "African" blacks. Most of the black intellectuals had a great deal of white blood in them. They affected white hairstyles, called "conking." This was the practice of "straightening" the natural kinky hair of Africans into the longer styles of Caucasians.

In the 1930s, the NAACP under Walter White and Charles Hamilton Houston challenged segregation and disenfranchisement in the United States Supreme Court. This was the genesis for the *Brown v. Board of Education* Supreme Court ruling of 1954. It was a landmark case that reversed the Court's support for the "separate but equal" doctrine, opening the floodgates for the civil rights movement.

Organizations such as the National Urban League, the National Negro Congress, and the Communist Party all were prominent in the civil rights movement. Communists, seeing racial inequality as a niche with which to gain a toehold in American society, defended the Scottsboro Boys in the 1930s and formed an offshoot called the League of Struggle for Negro Rights. The Scottsboro case involved the trumped-up convictions of nine black youths falsely accused of assaulting two white women. Rural African Americans joined the socialist Southern Tenant Farmers' Union.

Blacks riding trains were required to sit in the "Jim Crow car," even if they had bought first-class train tickets. Laws banning interracial marriages were passed, although people who dared such a thing would likely meet with violence long before they faced a court of law. The situation in the South became more than just backlash. It had started as revenge for losing the Civil War and hatred for all things having to do with the Union. By the late 1880s, however, a disturbing religious character seeped into the South's racism. The concept of "white superiority" became more prevalent. Many felt it was a "sacred duty" of sorts to "save" the white race from the blacks. Mixing the races threatened the very survival of the "superior" white race, according to this logic.

Southern states passed suffrage laws and poll taxes. Though many blacks of Georgia and South Carolina voted in 1880, almost none could vote by 1888. Ballots were stolen, misdirected, or simply not counted. Mississippi disenfranchised black males through literacy tests, poll taxes, and "white primaries." Actual laws replaced fraud and force. By 1910, the entire former Confederacy had adopted these laws. During slavery, blacks and whites frequently commingled, but now social contact became virtually nonexistent. The result was total lack of empathy or understanding on both sides for the other. For instance, the practice of white nurses volunteering to deliver children or tending to the sick in black populations was outlawed.

* * *

In the North and in some Southern cities with nightlife, such as New Orleans, new musical forms of ragtime, jazz, and blues were a reaction to repression. Jazz, which adapted African- and plantation-based rhythms to European harmony, was a huge success with white audiences. It did as much to bring races together as any other social factor. Sports became the next great avenue for black success. In the West, black athletes played side by side with white teammates. All-star exhibitions were played between the Negro and Major Leagues, with the black teams faring at least on an equal footing, if not better.

In 1936, Jesse Owens put on his great Olympic display, defying Adolf Hitler and the Nazis who hosted the games. After World War II, more changes were in the offing. Jackie Robinson crossed baseball's color barrier. Robinson's success on the field and greatness as a man were of vital importance in the struggle.

In the 1960s, Jews, who had experienced their fair share of prejudice, formed an alliance with black civil rights organizations. This had mixed results. In the South, antipathy toward Jews had sometimes approached, in some cases perhaps exceeded, derision toward blacks. Various Christian "cults" after World War I formulated their own Biblical interpretations perceiving Jews and Catholics as "Christ killers" now in league with each other in an unholy Satanic alliance. Jews and Catholics were seen as "Northern" hybrids of a corrupt Yankee regime. Furthermore, the Joseph McCarthy era revealed a disproportionate number of Jews and Northeasterners to be Soviet spies and Communists. The linkage between Jews and baseball, strengthened by Robinson and his Brooklyn connections, had not taken hold in the South, thus blocking hoped-for assimilation.

Black protest literature reached full expression in the Harlem Renaissance of the 1920s. "New Negro" poetry and literature emphasized self-respect and defiance. World Wars I and II cut off European immigration, creating a labor shortage and opportunity for blacks in the North. Cities such as Detroit and Cleveland had huge increases in the black populations because of the factories. On the West Coast, Sausalito, Oakland, and Los Angeles saw migrations of blacks to work in shipyards. They took advantage of less severe attitudes. The North was not the "promised land."

Whites resisted the blacks, and race riots erupted in East St. Louis, Houston, Chicago, Tulsa, and many other places.

The NAACP and the National Urban League worked toward integration, but the Universal Negro Improvement Association and African Communities League took a different approach. Led by Marcus Garvey, it advocated self-help and black autonomy, which became the "back to Africa" movement. The movement did not materialize because many blacks came to realize that despite racism, America still offered the best opportunity in the world. U.S. laws, the courts and political system, the free press, economic opportunities, and a wide range of social factors combined to lead folks to understand that within the framework of America lay their best hopes.

Many blacks served as soldiers in the two world wars of the first half of the century. This experience had a twofold effect. On the one hand, they were repulsed by further racism in the armed forces, reinforcing their desires to get out of the South upon discharge. On the other, they were exposed to American values and saw the need to defend democracy, and in comparing the United States with her enemies, namely Germany and Japan, the realization that the United States was the greatest country in the world strengthened resolve to achieve social goals. At the end of the day, America was too great for social injustice to overcome it. We live in a world in which people of every color, nationality, and religion *come* here. Almost nobody ever *leaves* here.

African American leader A. Philip Randolph had threatened in 1941 to lead fifty thousand blacks in a nonviolent march on Washington, D.C., to protest segregation in the military. President Franklin Roosevelt had already gained popularity with blacks by creating "relief" during the Depression. Blacks were astounded to find that they could receive checks from the federal government for not working. Many found panacea in the Democratic Party as a result. Eleanor Roosevelt was a passionate advocate for civil rights. African American voter registration rose from 150,000 in 1940 to more than a million by 1952.

* * *

On December 1, 1955, forty-two-year-old Rosa Parks stepped onto a city bus in Montgomery, Alabama, after spending a long day working as a seamstress. She took an empty seat in the "colored" section, but the "white" section in the front filled up. The white driver then told Parks to relinquish her seat. She said no. Rosa was arrested and put in jail. The act inspired the Montgomery bus boycott, pointing out a truth about race relations: whites were happy to take blacks' money but "reserved the right to refuse service" to blacks if the circumstances did not suit them. The Montgomery bus company made a significant portion of its income from black riders. The blacks realized that economic protest was a powerful tool. It was a successful nonviolent protest, receiving national publicity, ending with a Supreme Court declaration that bus segregation was unconstitutional.

A new activism, now known as the civil rights movement, was also called the "Second Reconstruction" because it completed congressional action embodied in the 14th and 15th Amendments, passed in the decade after the Civil War. This movement also coincided with the fall of the British Empire. It drew inspiration from the decolonization of nonwhite nations throughout the world. Dr. Martin Luther King Jr. decided to pattern the movement on the nonviolent tactics espoused by Mahatma Gandhi.

With the passage of the Civil Rights Act of 1964 and the Voting Rights Act of 1965, legal segregation and the disenfranchisement of African Americans came to an end. The improvements made in society since then have been so drastic that few modern college students even know what "Jim Crow" means, associating it with a vague notion that it once had something to do with segregation, which to young people today is simply ancient history. Unfortunately, the enormous changes have left many young blacks ignorant of the sacrifices made by their elders.

In the 1950s, the federal government began to "get behind" the civil rights of blacks, and federal laws superseded state laws. It was federal law, such as the Supreme Court's *Brown v. Board of Education* decision, plus President Dwight Eisenhower's version of the Civil Rights Act (vetoed by Democrats, later revived by Lyndon Johnson), that caused "problems" in the 1950s and 1960s. These decisions and federal mandates were at the core of Ike's move to send National Guard troops to Little Rock, as well as John Kennedy's threatened use of the same when dealing with Governor Ross Barnett during the James Meredith crisis at the University of Mississippi.

The states' rights issue, personified by Governors George Wallace of Alabama and Barnett, derived its strongest power from the notion that the majority of citizens in these and like-minded states wanted to live a certain way and did not wish to have their desires usurped.

In the 1960s, Martin Luther King Jr. was a contrarian. If it were not for contrarians, change would rarely occur. In the midst of tumultuous times, Dr. King led the March on Washington and in 1963 gave his wonderful "I have a dream" speech. When Dr. King elevated the civil rights movement past its other incarnations—"light-skinned intellectuals" versus "African appeasers," Communist manipulation, Black Muslim "nationalists," and militant radicals—two factors became apparent. First, Dr. King's movement was laced with Christian phraseology. Second, black athletes, who by the 1960s were heroic figures to millions of young white kids, tended to come from conservative, family-oriented environments and were usually rock-solid Christians. It would be these very qualities that would make Wilbur Jackson the right man to break Alabama's color barrier.

Other Voices: Clarence Davis

African American Clarence Davis had the daunting task of replacing the great Heisman Trophy tailback O. J. Simpson at USC in 1969. Clarence made All-American in his first season, and after being drafted by the Oakland Raiders, he caught Kenny Stabler's desperate last-second toss into the end zone, despite having a "sea of hands" of the Miami Dolphins draped around him, to win a key 1974 AFC playoff game. He is a legend at both USC and within the Raider Nation.

I was born in Birmingham, Alabama, but my parents divorced. I moved to the Bronx, New York, with my mother, but then she moved out to Los Angeles when I was about thirteen. I had two sisters, Beverly and Marie. My mother basically moved around because she had a job waiting for her, and we were just with her.

After I got out to California, I saw that life in L.A. was different from life in New York. It was just different, but I think people were friendlier in L.A.

At Washington High, I was a shot-putter on the track team and a pulling guard on the football team. I was not a running back in high school, so nobody recruited me. After graduating in 1967, I went to East L.A. Junior College, and it was there that I became a running back. I was there two years and was recruited by Kansas and Arizona, and I took a trip to Washington; but I chose USC, and I was there for two years. O. J. Simpson tried to recruit me. I'd broken his junior college records, but I was not really familiar with USC's great tradition or their record of having great running backs.

I never thought about the pressure of replacing O.J. One guy asked me if I should be "Lemonade" instead of "the Juice." I just said, "I'm here to play ball, not to try to replace a legend."

On racism in the South. I still had family back in Birmingham when we played there. I really did not see all that much of the troubles down there. My father had a car, and I rode the bus; but you know, I did not see that.

I think [USC assistant coach] Willie Brown was from Alabama. When we played Alabama and walked on the field, all we heard was, "Bear meat." I looked at the guys and just kept going. We were there for the game. I was one of those players who take it seriously.

On USC's black players bringing guns to Alabama. I remember Tody Smith. I called him Toto. I was not aware he brought a gun. I wasn't worried; I was just concentrating, not knowing about all this stuff about Tody and the gun. This is the first time I heard anything; I was unaware of this meeting.

On the role of Christianity in the game. My uncle back then was Uncle Claude. He was married and had two daughters. I was close to them. My mother and my grandmother went back from L.A. to see that game, and Claude was very happy that I had a good game. Claude was a minister. As for the role of Christianity in that game, I'm not sure; I think it had a lot to do with it. Folks in the South did have a lot on their minds.

My grandmother took me to church, and I still go to church to this day. I'm definitely a believing Christian. As for redemption, and how redemption is part of this football game and how the South changed, I'm not sure. I more or less look at it and ask what others think, but I can't answer that. I can't speak about the way others looked at religion; I just put my faith in God's hands. . . .

I'm thankful, I'm blessed with whatever God gives me. I'm not a prejudiced person. I guess that's because of my religion. I played pro ball, high school ball. I played with white players such as Fred Biletnikoff and Bobby Chandler. I played with Ken Stabler. When I played with him he was telling me about 'Bama, but we never talked about racism. He never talked about Bryant.

On the controversy surrounding the Bryant quote. I'm not familiar with Bryant's "this here's a football player" story. I was blocking for Cunningham. I was on my face most of the time, blocking for Sam. I'd look up, and Sam would be running over two people. Sam and I were good friends. Sam had a good game. He was a young player. I looked at him as another talented player.

Other Voices: Dr. Culpepper Clark

Dr. Culpepper Clark is the dean of the communications school at the University of Alabama. He was in Chapel Hill, North Carolina, finishing up his PhD in 1970. He arrived in Tuscaloosa the year 'Bama beat Southern California, 17–10, in Los Angeles. Dr. Clark is the author of a book on desegregation at his university, titled The Schoolhouse Door: Segregation's Last Stand at the University of Alabama.

I was in Chapel Hill, North Carolina, getting my PhD in history from the University of North Carolina in 1970, but I was on the verge of getting an offer from the University of Alabama to teach there. I arrived when we won in L.A. I'm a deep "blue state" guy in the middle of a "red state," which goes with the territory, I guess.

When it comes to the subject of football, anyone would say that if you take popular culture and inject social change into it, then it is easier to effectuate that change. Charlie Scott played basketball at North Carolina before 1970. Obviously, when Wilbur Jackson and John Mitchell arrived on the scene, it began to have some effect at Alabama. Change that had already taken place in other sports came late to the table.

On faith and racism. In trying to assess the theory of Fareed Zakaria (author of *The Future of Freedom*), which is that Western civilization advanced through the triple forces of Christianity, democracy, and capitalism, I think this is more of an eighteenth-century concept than a modern-day notion. That said, many have made compelling cases for progressive evolution using this kind of concept. It is not lacking merit, but it is more complex. Nonetheless, clearly, football in the Deep South is often said to be a religion. Clearly this is the Bible Belt, a conservative place of evangelical tendencies. That expression of Christianity and football has cohabitated in the South comfortably, for whatever reason. I guess I can't shed more light on this aspect of the game than that.

No one in the nineteenth century would ask about racial tensions or about racial separation and Christianity. People believed in a Victorian hierarchy, in which cultures were more or less stratified, and African Americans simply did not hold the same standing as whites.

These questions begin to get answered in the 1920s, 1930s, 1940s, and 1950s, when, dare I say, a paradigm of cultural relativism became a more dominant theme. The history we see perceives cultures not as better or worse but as different, so a mental change regarding the place of blacks in the social order took place because of it. Religion plays a powerful role in this, but primarily this is through liberal denominations, mostly Methodists more so than others, such as Baptists.

The civil rights movement played to heavily Christian themes, looking at the brotherhood of man and treating others as you would treat yourself, and found fertile soil in the white community; but it was not really part of religion tied to football. Some football fans might have made this connection, but more football fans were conservative, with entrenched religious tendencies that were slower to come to desegregation.

The media played a major role in the civil rights movement. Martin Luther King did not succeed in Georgia because he was 150 miles from Atlanta, but he succeeded in Birmingham because it was a media center and there were TV cameras there. He needed a national audience, and the country was not yet aware of its own racial passions. It was "good" to have the South to whip on; it isolated Birmingham, and that allowed legislation that had been passed to be enacted. That allowed us to cure our defects without people in the North having to look at their own defects. I'm glad it happened that way. Had King taken Malcolm X's strategy and called all whites "devils," he would not have gotten anywhere. King's strategy worked: to isolate evil and get it spotlighted.

Now, regarding religion, it could be said that it was a "miracle" that between the murder of Emmett Till in 1955 and King in 1968, only forty people lost their lives in the movement. The blood was up in the South; there could have been many more people killed. It was a time of white-hot temper, yet the movement pulled it out. King might give credence to the concept that a benevolent God guided this movement and that the hand of God kept the death count to such a low total instead of the bloodbath it could have been. I won't do that, but I do think King got it right in emphasizing the concept of "keeping the eyes on the prize."

The Vietnam War came to overwhelm the social movement we call the civil rights movement. It fed off the same passions but sucked the life out of what the movement sought to accomplish. The movement ended with legislation in 1964–1965. *Time* magazine focused on the war beginning in 1966 and sublimated the movement after that.

Seeing blacks and whites dying together on TV I don't think had much influence; but it could have. The moral is one that seems not to have really had an effect on hearts and minds on the race question.

On the legacy of the game. In that 1970 game, I doubt at all that the immediate reaction being played out before the fans in the stands had nearly as much effect as the lore that developed out of it over time. I don't know the truth about the lore, but it is awfully important, whether true or not, when we consider a retrospective of that game, but not something anybody reacted to at the time. People in the stands had seen plenty of teams with blacks on them. It was not novel. Nobody would've sat around and said, "Isn't it interesting that there are a lot of black athletes on the USC team?"

A lot of the feeling at that time was that the team had been slipping. This was a culmination of a four-year degeneration of the team, and there was a lot of feeling that Bear had seen better days, he was drinking too much, or whatever it is people say when they think something is going downhill.

There are statements that may be more lore about Bear than truth, saying, "I never will be beaten again because I don't have black players." Winston Groom's book has that line. The University of Alabama desegregated athletic teams around the same time as all of the Deep South. Teams in the border states started, then the middle states, then the Deep South. Other states were making progress, so it's not remarkable in terms of Alabama leading or not leading. We *were* actively recruiting them and saw the wave of the future. Where this game stands out is the nature of the game and its timing. It came on the heels of events that led up to it. Then the game was played, and it was a blowout. It was not close. Had it been more competitive, it would not have had the effect it did. Because it was a blowout, it became a seminal moment of change that people remember and, as I say, embrace as folklore.

On Bryant's contested statement. Now, did Bryant bring Cunningham in to the locker room and say, "This here's what a football player looks like"? I don't know. Someone may have discovered that Bryant said it. People believe it. It sounds right; it was right to say it; it's still compelling.

Bryant may not have said it, but he would have. He must have said something like that, somewhere, that became iconic.

On racism in the South. Jackie Robinson was born in my hometown in [Cairo] Georgia and grew up in Pasadena, California. His description of racial patterns in Pasadena was just about as gripping as in Georgia, but the difference was that it was *legal* in the South, not legal in California. Robinson could resist in California.

Based on what has happened, the political demographics in the South, Wallace got four runs at the presidency off of his schoolhouse stand, and he pulled out Wallace Democrats who were mad at the

Kennedys. These Wallace Democrats became Reagan Democrats, and that began the process of transformation of the South into being solidly Republican. The region doesn't have enough black votes to overcome white votes, with profound political consequence.

When LBJ passed the Civil Rights Act, he turned to Bill Moyers or somebody and said, "We just handed the future of America to the Republican Party." He was right.

CHAPTER Six

Our National Pastimes

I've always said that sports are the concrete mix of society.

—Former Los Angeles Times sportswriter Jeff Prugh

Accprding to legend, baseball started in a pasture in Cooperstown, New York, in 1839. U.S. Army officer Abner Doubleday (later a Civil War hero), whose specialties were surveying, mapping, and planning construction sites, apparently laid out a baseball diamond. The national pastime was born. Later, the Doubleday story was refuted. Baseball came to America in bits and pieces, mostly emanating from the English sports of rounders and cricket, but the Hall of Fame was erected in Cooperstown anyway.

Union soldiers played baseball during the war. The first professional team was the Cincinnati Red Stockings, who went undefeated in 1869. The National League was formed in 1876, the American League in 1901.

Prior to World War I, professional baseball players were looked down upon by the upper classes. They were uneducated, and they chewed tobacco, drank heavily, consorted with gamblers, and were not to be trusted with women. Christy Mathewson of the New York Giants was the first "role model." An All-American from Bucknell, Matty was handsome, intelligent, and upright. He was one of the greatest pitchers in history, winning 373 games for John McGraw's Giants, including three shutouts in the 1905 World Series against Connie Mack's Philadelphia A's. Mathewson was a tragic figure who joined the Army when World War I broke out, was exposed to mustard gas, and died from its effects a few years later.

The American League joined the National League, known as the "senior circuit," in 1901. In 1903 the first World Series was played between the Boston Pilgrims (later Red Sox) and the Pittsburgh Pirates. Boston surprised the baseball world by winning. In 1904 McGraw refused to play his Giants against Mack's A's because the A.L. was a "busher league."

It was only forty years after the Civil War when Ty Cobb entered the major leagues with Detroit in 1906. Cobb was the product of a wealthy Georgia family. His father was a state senator. The father had gone on a business trip, but he suspected Cobb's mother was having an affair. He snuck in through the bedroom window to catch her in the act, and he was shot dead. The story was that she thought he was a burglar, but it was theorized that she was with another man, who murdered him and then covered it up with the burglar story. Cobb was devastated by the event. His psychological makeup was forever shaped not just by his idolized father's violent death but also by the knowledge or suspicion that his mother had cheated on his father, then killed him.

Cobb was met by enmity from the Northerners on the Tigers. He was described as "still fighting the Civil War," coming up from the South with a "chip on his shoulder." He was a violent racist, as was another star player of the late nineteenth century, Cap Anson. Cobb was a remarkable player, though. He hit .367 lifetime, with more than four thousand hits, revolutionizing the game. His violent temper, racism, and murderous rages, however, forever stained his legacy. Cobb may have been an intellectual genius. He became a manipulator of the stock market on a par with Joseph P. Kennedy, making millions when the country was in the Depression. He never found happiness or peace, dying alone and unloved.

After the turn of the century, sports and race became a sticky subject. Jack Johnson, a huge, gifted black boxer whose skills were decades ahead of the rest in the "sweet science," ascended to the heavyweight championship of the world. He antagonized the white establishment by consorting with white women, spending money lavishly, living in style, taunting his fallen white opponents, and lording over the white fans who hurled every epithet at him—all with a huge white-toothed smile outlined by the blackest possible face. Predictably, the white establishment brought him down. He was indicted, using the Mann Act, a little-known federal law meant to criminalize the transport of women across state lines for the purpose of immoral behavior. The act was meant to curb prostitution but was worded broadly enough to "justify" its enforcement on Johnson, who in fact did travel with a coterie of women, some of whom were known prostitutes.

Johnson hit the sporting scene some thirty-five years after the Civil War, a relatively short period of time. Reconstruction had officially ended in 1877, replaced by Jim Crow laws. Hopes for improvement in black life in the South had not materialized. However, it can be argued that Johnson set his people back even more. During Johnson's boxing career, lynchings and other crimes against blacks rose throughout America. Worse, Johnson created extra antagonism in the North and, discouragingly, in the *West.* Johnson lived part of the time in California. He trained and fought in the state, as well as other Western states. His controversial actions, and the response from non-Southerners, fueled Southern arguments against blacks.

Boxing was the way out for many Jews, often toughened by having to defend themselves against Irish and Italian kids in Eastern cities. Eventually, sports became a form of assimilation for Jewish Americans, especially in heavily Jewish enclaves such as Brooklyn.

In 1912, an American Indian named Jim Thorpe won both the pentathlon and decathlon at the Stockholm Olympics. King Gustav of Sweden told him he was the greatest athlete in the world.

"Thanks, King," said Thorpe.

At that same Olympics, a young Army officer, George Patton, failed to medal in the modern pentathlon, which was a different event involving the firing of guns.

When America entered World War I, many baseball players served in the Army. The game was expected to revitalize morale after the war ended in 1918. Instead, it was embroiled in the worst controversy in its history.

Charles Comiskey was the tightfisted owner of the world champion Chicago White Sox. He cheated his players out of bonuses and paid them the minimum, even though the White Sox had a number of star performers. Eight White Sox players were approached by gamblers associated with a million-dollar bookie named Arnold Rothstein. They agreed to "throw" the 1919 World Series against the underdog Cincinnati Reds. After losing the Series, the "fix" was discovered. The players were charged. In 1920, they were all acquitted and expected to go back to their team, which was at the time in first place again. But the new commissioner of baseball, Kennesaw Mountain Landis, banned them from the game for life on the grounds that baseball could not afford a whiff of scandal. One of the banned players was "Shoeless Joe" Jackson, an ignorant South Carolina farmboy who was said to be too dim to have understood the concept of "throwing" the Series. Jackson got his nickname because as a boy he supposedly played without shoes, but the legend of his lack of intelligence was exaggerated.

Jackson knew about the gamblers but did not report them. He played hard, obviously not trying to lose. His ban from the game is steeped in tragedy and legend. Today many lobby that he should be posthumously admitted to the Hall of Fame.

The game was really saved by Babe Ruth, who was traded by the Red Sox to the Yankees prior to the 1920 season. Ruth grew up in a Baltimore bar, where his father was the saloonkeeper. He was an incorrigible youth, sent to an orphanage, where he learned to play baseball. He was the best left-handed pitcher in the game with the Red Sox, whom he led to two world championships. Boston owner Harry Frazee, in order to finance a Broadway play called *No, No Nanette*, sold Ruth along with several stars to the Yankees, who in their previous history had been an average team. Ruth transformed them into the greatest juggernaut in sports history. The Red Sox did not win a World Series again until 2004. Beantowners attributed this fact to "the Curse of Babe Ruth."

(The real "Red Sox curse" actually had nothing to do with Ruth. In the late 1940s, a Boston scout submitted a report on Willie Mays, then an Alabama teenager. The report specified the kind of awesome skills Mays possessed. Boston passed on him because he was black. To the extent that such a thing as a "curse" exists, it is much more attributable to this than to the selling of Ruth!)

Baseball, seeing the excitement created by Ruth's home-run hitting, "juiced" the ball prior to 1920 and outlawed spitballs. During the Roaring Twenties, Ruth was bigger than life. Yankee Stadium, "the House That Ruth Built," was erected. Ruth set career and single-season home-run records. To this day he is arguably considered the greatest baseball player and athlete of all time. This subjective title is tempered by his drinking, his overweight physique, the fact that he did not compete against black players, and the sleek athleticism of later stars such as Mays and Barry Bonds. But Ruth still holds the "title" for two reasons. For one, his status as a star pitcher before becoming a slugger on the greatest teams in baseball cannot be matched. While others have broken his records, nobody ever stood as far above their contemporary competition as Ruth did. He revolutionized his sport more thoroughly than any athlete.

Blacks were not allowed to play Major League Baseball, but on the West Coast they played on integrated high school and college teams. Baseball's Negro Leagues produced some star performers, namely Satchel Paige, Josh Gibson, and James "Cool Papa" Bell, who was said to be so fast he could "turn the switch off and be in bed before the lights went out."

Over the years, baseball has attempted to create various "all-time all-star teams" and award "greatest player" titles to various players. As Negro League lore became more and more known, it has become commonly understood that some of the Negro League stars were better than their white Major League counterparts. All-time all-star teams that once included catchers such as Bill Dickey, Mickey Cochrane, and Johnny Bench now replace these players with the likes of Gibson, a home-run slugger who, if he had played in the big leagues, would have challenged Ruth's home-run records. It is a worthy argument that all-time pitching staffs, including the likes of Walter "Big Train" Johnson of the Washington Senators, could substitute Paige. Satchel gave us homilies such as "Never eat fried foods, it stirs up the blood," and "Never look behind you, somebody might be gainin' on you."

The Negro League players barnstormed in the winter, occasionally playing Major League all-star teams even up (or better). In the 1930s they traveled to Latin America. Tin-pot dictators, eager to distract the masses from their repressive regimes, created baseball teams to entertain the people. The reason baseball is so popular in Latin America is because of the Negro League stars who brought the game there.

Sports and politics became intertwined. William Howard Taft became the first president to throw out the first ball on opening day of the baseball season. In 1912, the Boston Red Sox were led by a dashing young superpitcher named Smoky Joe Wood, who won more than thirty games. Wood bested Mathewson in game seven of the World Series. The Mayor of Boston attached himself to the Red Sox, to his great political benefit. His nickname was "Honey Fitz." He was John Kennedy's grandfather on his mother's side.

The Olympics were a forum for politics and social change. In 1924, the Summer Games were held in Paris, signaling peace in Europe after World War I. In 1932, Los Angeles "introduced" itself to the world as the city of the future by hosting the Summer Olympics. Sports and politics further mixed when the 1936 Summer Olympics were held in Berlin. The Germans used the world stage to display the facade of clean streets, a crimeless society, and the myth of Aryan physical supremacy. Adolf Hitler's display was almost successful, as German athletes performed remarkably. The image was broken up when African American track star Jesse Owens of Ohio State dominated a series of events.

In 1948, London demonstrated renewed peace in Europe by hosting the Summer Games. In 1960, the U.S. hockey team, made up of college players, defeated the Soviets, a team of world-class professionals, at the Winter Olympics in Squaw Valley, California. That same year, UCLA decathlon star Rafer Johnson defeated his Bruin teammate, C. K. Yang, along with a Soviet decathlete, Vasily Kuznetsov, in a thrilling competition at the Summer Games in Rome. The event was rife with political symbolism: a black Californian and his college teammate from the embattled anti-Communist island of Taiwan, forced to compete for Red China, along with a "Soviet automaton" who insisted, in what seems wistful in retrospect, that "sport and politics are separate" from each other.

In 1964, Tokyo used the Summer Games to show that they were a trustworthy country again. Germany attempted to do the same in 1972. The Black September wing of the PLO put a crimp in those plans, when Yasser Arafat's murderers killed Israeli athletes in cold blood. Jimmy Carter pulled the United States out of the 1980 Soviet Olympics after the Russians invaded Afghanistan. The USSR retaliated by not sending a delegation to the Summer Olympics in L.A. in 1984. In the 1980 Winter Games held at Lake Placid, New York, the Americans, again consisting of untested collegians, defeated the Soviets, considered the best team in the world (professionals, all of NHL caliber), in what was dubbed the "miracle on ice." In 2008, Beijing, China will no doubt try to put a happy face on their withering Communism when they host the Summer Games.

German-U.S. sports rivalry preceded World War II in boxing when Max Schmeling defeated African American Joe Louis. Many white Americans rooted for the German over Louis. When they fought a rematch, the Germans had begun aggressive military moves in preparation for invasion of Eastern Europe. Americans now backed Louis, a major turning point in race relations. When he knocked Schmeling to the canvas, Louis became a national hero and a god to his people.

Baseball star Lefty O'Doul led barnstorming teams to Japan in the 1930s, where the fans took to the game, receiving him as a star. Crowds yelled "Banzai" while watching O'Doul and his mates display their considerable skills. After World War II, O'Doul returned to U.S.-occupied Japan, where the citizenry was depressed by the experience of defeat in the war. His baseball exhibitions were a major part of reviving morale in Japan. General Douglas MacArthur said O'Doul had done more for Japan than any diplomat or policy. The country picked itself up and became a member of the family of nations again. Brooklyn Dodger owner Walter

O'Malley and others took teams to Tokyo to play exhibitions. The game became as popular in Japan as it is in America.

When World War II broke out, many Major League stars joined the armed forces. The most prominent of these was Ted Williams, a southern Californian who joined the Red Sox, hit .406 in 1941, and was considered the equal of Ruth as a hitter. Williams joined the Marines, becoming a fighter plot. After the war, he returned to baseball, twice winning the Triple Crown and MVP honors. When the Korean War broke out, he went back to the Marines, where he was John Glenn's wingman. Williams was a conservative Republican who made his opinions known, causing enmity among the liberal Kennedyites in the Boston media. His heroics speak for themselves.

After Pearl Harbor, the Rose Bowl was moved to North Carolina. Major League Baseball officials debated shutting the game down. President Roosevelt urged them to keep playing for the sake of American morale. Joe DiMaggio was a superstar center fielder for the Yankees. Like Williams, he was a California native. He became an enormous hero to Italian Americans, who were perceived as being either mobsters or Mussolini Fascists. DiMaggio's hero status was protected by the New York media, but unlike the hero Williams he was closer to the Italian stereotype than his fans would have wanted to know. DiMaggio regularly hung out with New York Mafiosi.

Williams and DiMaggio represented an enormous influx of talented athletes from California. Theories even made their way around that the warm weather and the oranges somehow created bigger, faster athletes. There may be some validity to it. Indeed, a higher proportion of physically able humans populated California than any other part of the country. Originally, only the strongest and most fit braved the cross-country trip, so their offspring tended to be more physically impressive. The weather created a population of people who played sports and performed outdoor activities on a year-round basis. Hollywood brought a new generation of impressive physical specimens to the state. Over time, attractive, athletic men and women married, producing athletic children. Sports became a way of life on the West Coast.

Over the years, no other state has produced more athletes than California. California also was a more tolerant place than the rest of the country. In the late 1930s, a black athlete named Jackie Robinson rose to prominence there. Robinson prepped at Muir High School in Pasadena, where he starred in baseball, basketball, football, and track and was L.A.

city tennis champion. He moved on to UCLA, a state school that in its short history was dominated by its prestigious crosstown rival, USC.

USC and UCLA became important cogs in the wheels of social progress. It was at these two rival Los Angeles colleges (along with Columbia) that some of the first real opportunities for blacks in team sports occurred. USC's first All-American football player, Brice Taylor in 1925, was black. A three-sport black UCLA athlete of the 1920s, Ralph Bunche, eventually won the Nobel Peace Prize for his work mediating the war in the Mideast that erupted after the formation of Israel. Prior to the 1970s, black and white athletes were playing with and against each other for almost fifty years at USC and UCLA.

Robinson and another black star, Kenny Washington, put UCLA on the map, tying the Trojans in football and, for the first time, establishing parity. Robinson ran track and played baseball, too. When the war broke out, he became an officer. In an incident at a Georgia Army base that foreshadowed the Rosa Parks affair, Robinson refused to give up his seat on a bus. He was court-martialed. He stood up for himself and was acquitted. After the war, he played professionally in the Negro Leagues until he was chosen by Dodger president Branch Rickey—a devout Christian—to break the color barrier.

Other Negro Leaguers such as Paige and Josh Gibson were passed up because Rickey was looking for just the right kind of player and person to handle the rigorous challenge ahead. Robinson possessed all the criteria. He was a superior player but also a college man and an Army officer. He was handsome, articulate, and dignified, with a lovely wife and young family. Brooklyn, a true melting pot, was the perfect place for the "experiment" to take place. Robinson was told that he had to be "man enough not to fight back" against his combative instincts.

His first few years in the league were grueling and excruciating, but he continued to triumph. Fans booed, called him a "n--r," and threw black cats on the field. Other teams razzed him, threw at him, and spiked him. Robinson refrained from punching his foes, but he used other methods—thrown elbows, upturned spikes, and bunts down the first base line resulting in body blows to offending pitchers.

When an entire stadium turned on him, Dodger shortstop Pee Wee Reese, who hailed from Louisville, Kentucky, went to Robinson and put his arm around him. It was a beautiful gesture. Robinson was a great player who became the first black in the Hall of Fame. His integrity and leadership qualities on the famed *Boys of Summer* teams, embodied by Roger

Kahn's book, allowed blacks to integrate into baseball and other sports. Had the Robinson experiment "failed," it could have pushed integration back for years.

Robinson was a Connecticut Republican who backed Richard Nixon, although he withdrew his support when Nixon failed to intervene to get Martin Luther King Jr. out of jail in 1960. His son had problems coping with the pressure of being an icon's child, and Jackie himself succumbed to a heart attack in 1972, long before his time.

Following Robinson, black and Hispanic players not only were allowed to play but also became dominant among the hierarchy of stars. The last vestige of sports integration would be college football.

Baseball expanded to the West Coast in 1958 when the Dodgers and Giants took their ancient rivalry to Los Angeles and San Francisco, respectively. Basketball became highly popular in the 1960s, developing into an urban art form dominated by black athletes such as Bill Russell, Wilt Chamberlain, and Oscar Robertson. Amazingly, in the twenty-first century, the new superstars of basketball are no longer American blacks. The end of the Cold War revealed a treasure trove of basketball wunderkinds from Croatia, Lithuania, Serbia, and other Eastern European nations. If anybody doubted this phenomenon, the mediocre performance of America's all-black 2004 Olympic basketball team against this international competition erased the last vestige of invincibility. For years, it had been considered a given that blacks are the finest athletes, bar none. The Olympic basketball defeat, while not discrediting the notion, did weaken it.

Television changed the face of sports, and cable television even more so. College basketball's Final Four became one of the most wildly popular institutions in the world. There is so much money in professional sports now that the athletes are the new economic titans of a gilded age. Gambling in Las Vegas and on the Internet has added a startling dimension to sports popularity. Even college baseball, once a lazy weekend activity for true fans, features its popular College World Series showcased on ESPN.

The Super Bowl is now a worldwide event. American sports have captivated every corner of the globe. In many ways, the charisma of American athletes, teams, and personas—colors, logo, symbols—has cemented the United States as the most influential of all nations.

American superstars such as Barry Bonds, Michael Jordan, Magic Johnson, Tom Brady, Larry Bird, Carson Palmer, and Joe Montana are household names *everywhere*. It is not uncommon to go into a bar in

Germany and hear Germans argue the relative merits of the Packers versus the Cowboys. Sports have integrated society; made millionaires out of peasants; created rivalries, city pride, and identity; and transformed the landscape of entertainment.

Other Voices: Scott Hunter

Scott Hunter was the senior quarterback and leader of the Alabama team in 1970. A high school star from Mobile, Alabama, he was part of the "new breed" of college students from the South, and his views reflect the new thinking that was happening on campuses throughout the country. In the early 1970s, Hunter found himself next to his idol, Alabama-bred Bart Starr, who was finishing up his career with the Green Bay Packers. Hunter helped guide Green Bay to a return to play-off contention, inspiring a memorable Sports Illustrated *cover announcing, "The Pack Is Back."*

On the controversy surrounding Bryant's statement. Let's start with your question, did it or did it not happen? In 1970, did Coach Bryant bring Sam Cunningham in, prop him up on a stool in front of us, and declare, "This here's what a football player looks like"?

It absolutely did not happen. I can unequivocally state that it did not happen!

It's one of those great tales that takes on a life of its own; it's almost too good to not be true. The story, it started going around, how or where it started I don't know. I'm sorry it didn't happen. I don't know who first said it. I started hearing it a few years after the game, players talking, maybe a writer here and there.

As for the Jerry Claiborne quote, that Cunningham did more [for civil rights] than Martin Luther King, Bryant said it. But Jerry and [Bryant] were good friends, so they both probably said it.

On racism and integration. Alabama was one of the last bastions of segregation. In that sense, although the SEC [Southeastern Conference] was integrated by Lester McClain, still schools were not really integrated. I think it took a catalyst to do that. Coaches around the league saw clips, and it was obvious to all concerned and fans of all SEC schools that it was time for full integration of football teams. After that game, there were no arguments.

I had been to Vietnam on an NCAA trip with Mel Gray, the wide receiver, and some other black players. Mel was black, and I threw him a pass on the beach at Na Trang. I overthrew him, but with his speed he caught up to it. I thought, *Man, I wish I could throw to a guy like that in a game.* In my mind I'd crossed the line, but there was nothing I could do. It just took one person and one game like that, and after that everything changed.

I never really sit down and pore through the changes of that time; I just knew that so many things were going on on campus, so much change. There was a new world out there, and I knew we were never gonna go back to the way it was. After the summer of 1970 in Vietnam, I knew nothing was gonna be like it had been.

For me, playing in Green Bay, there was no problem whatsoever with black players. I never had a problem. In fact, many blacks were from the South, and we spoke the same language. When I played under Bryant, class was something he spoke about all the time. He was friends with McKay. They went to that eleven-game schedule, and that got it going. I was extremely pleased to play Southern Cal. I was a USC fan. I always made a point to watch the USC-UCLA game, and I always rooted for the Trojans, O.J. over Gary Beban. I liked their offense; it was wide-open football. I liked West Coast football. I was a passing quarterback, and I almost thought about going to Cal. . . .

Martin Luther King's legacy helped usher in an orderly integration of football, which caused harmony, not disharmony. Fans might have attitudes and prejudices, but when they saw white and black players patting each other on the butt, whooping, and hollering, the attitude they had before ended, and this caused the harmony King dreamed of. The cause of this harmony between races was football. . . .

My being a young man then, up until King's speech at the steps of the Lincoln Memorial, where he said he hoped we would be judging a person by the "content of their character," why this was what Bryant is saying. So if I pay attention to Bryant, I have to do the same thing, to respect what King said. So do I disregard King but pay attention to Bryant? No.

On Bryant's intention for the game. McKay and Bryant may have been thinking that if an integrated team won the game, it could influence the minds of our fans. Maybe not, I can't really plot it out that well regarding Wilbur Jackson and John Mitchell, but USC's black players impressed 'Bama fans.

It was time for change. Regarding the question of why Coach Bryant would schedule a game against a team that could beat him, it was different then. Today, coaches are looking for wins with bowl games, so teams don't do that anymore. But I loved 'Bama-USC; it was a great series, a great recruiting tool. I think the schools should play two games against each other every ten years.

From a political standpoint, it was a watershed event in the Deep South. There's prestige in football; even Auburn fans put prestige in 'Bama football. For an integrated team to beat us as soundly as they did, it opened eyes. At that point, all bets were off, and we could recruit blacks without anybody saying a thing about it.

'Bama football fans want to win games, number one. But capitalism, the freedom of democracy, and Christian morals—don't get me wrong, Christians do and should want to win, there's nothing wrong with it. The general blanket attitude of every person's attitude was, "We need players who can run and tackle these guys on Southern Cal." Everywhere in between, that middle ground, is where there's some moral consideration. So some of it is winning, and this ties in with the program—making money. And some of it's the promise of America—democracy. But it's all centered on doing the right things.

Our fans had watched USC play so well. They hated to lose, but it set the tone for the rest of the 1970s in Alabama and on into the 1980s for all Southern football.

Other Voices: Sam Dickerson

Sam Dickerson is a USC legend, but don't mention his name in Westwood. In 1969, after a controversial pass interference call went against the Bruins, he caught a long pass in the very back corner of the end zone from Jimmy Jones to give the Trojans a 14–12 victory over UCLA. The game characterized USC's Cardiac Kids reputation. An athletic six-foot-two, 194-pound split end, Dickerson did not attain the records of other USC receivers because John McKay preferred "Student Body Right" to a wide-open aerial attack. In the 1970 game at Birmingham, he spent most of the time upfield, blocking for Sam Cunningham. Dickerson was drafted by the 49ers in 1971, and today he works for the city of Modesto, California.

On his background. I was born in Texas but grew up in Stockton, California, where I attended Franklin High. I was an end and defensive back at Franklin. John McKay recruited athletes, then found a position for us. I ended up being a receiver. He brought Bobby Chandler in and didn't know where to play him. He was a quarterback and a defensive back when they brought him in, and he ended up being a star wide receiver in the Rose Bowl and the NFL.

On camaraderie at USC. Jimmy Jones and I were all right off the field. The majority of time we spent off the field was playing basketball during the off-season. As I say, McKay recruited the best athletes. Most of the football players had played basketball—a lot of 'em were good basketball players. Everybody was a two-sport or three-sport player in high school. Just about everybody was a multisport guy, so we stayed in shape by playing basketball. This keeps us together; there's camaraderie, and you create a winning attitude breaking a sweat.

On black quarterbacks. As for Jones being a "breakthrough" black quarterback, I know Willie Wood was a quarterback, but maybe Jones was the first "modern" quarterback who was a drop-back passer, but if flushed out of the pocket he could run and show all-around athleticism.

As for Jones's leadership style, the coaches had Jones wrapped up, so everything that came through him was from the coaches. He had confidence, and he possessed leadership ability. He had displayed leadership in high school and brought it on to USC, so if you mix that with all the others, who were winners the majority of their lives, it was cohesive, and we all executed what we were supposed to do.

Jimmy did have on-field charisma, and you could see his leadership in basketball, the way he ran the offense. Jones kept his composure and had all the confidence in the world, and that carried over.

On being black at USC. Once you got to the weekend, you partied together. I had family in L.A., so I'd spend weekends with them. I joined a fraternity through my cousin, Richard, when I was a freshman. I was one of the few black athletes in a fraternity, Kappa Alpha Psi, which was the black fraternity.

I remember Sam Cunningham, who was a sophomore, two years younger than me. We were all friends. Dee Dee was Sam's girl. There were not as many black athletes. There were fewer when I left as a senior, but over time that was increasing. The fraternity was an escape. We spent all our time during the week together with football.

On the game. Regarding that game in Birmingham, they, the other black athletes, had something to worry about, but I didn't understand it. It wasn't that way in California; you grow up and hear about segregation, but you don't live it. After I grew up and became friends with people who lived in the South, I came to learn more. I learned that if I'd stayed in Texas, where I was born, I would have known that situation.

On the "black players' meeting." Tody Smith died, maybe of a heart attack, probably about five or six years ago. I don't know too much about that L.A. meeting, about the "brothers watching each others' backs." I had been on trips with Jimmy Jones, to Nebraska, and they had a reputation; let me say it like this, if people were scared I didn't know about it. We had to cross tracks to go to junior high, but it wasn't something that was all that different. In Stockton there were people of all races and nationalities, even in elementary school. After school, everybody'd go by the store, then walk home.

On the times. In the 1960s, we knew guys in high school who'd gone to 'Nam. One guy ran track at Edison. He was killed in Vietnam. I'd seen the Alabama race riots on the news. It was hard for me to believe that was going on in another part of the country. It was hard to visualize myself in that position.

In 1970, I never had a problem in Mobile for the Senior Bowl. I never knew there was something to fear. I'm not saying that in the fourth grade I didn't know about something; we got bused, but I didn't know about the South, racism. I came from a melting pot. I never understood why we got bused. Maybe it was for us to become more integrated. It was not like walking home, and your parents feel good about it.

If I'd stayed in Texas, I would have been bused to the school my mom went to. I go to my mom's reunions and find out all the things that would have happened had I stayed in Texas.

On religion. I try to go to church once a month. When I was a kid I went every Sunday. After I got to L.A. on my own, I spent less time. Now I start to go more, on an irregular basis. I joined a men's choir that sings every fourth Sunday.

As for the question of how much of a role Christianity played in the South's changing, I look first to Reverend King. He had a great impact on the civil rights movement. At that time, you know, there were the Black Panthers, who wanted to fight fire with fire. Others saw the dividing line; now what King saw was "no violence." He died while I was in college. I was running track; I was at a freshman track meet. I came home and heard the news, that Reverend King had been shot. It hit the news media and brought a lot of attention to what was going on, by someone who thinks he has supreme ways, his race. It brought attention to people starting to search their souls. Looking back, why did some people feel we had the right to bring slaves over here? The attitude of the nation changed. Not everybody changed; some people are racist and always will be, but each generation it changes more and more. It never goes away, but it just weakens.

On the Alabama experience. As for the meeting in that room, I don't remember if it happened. I may have been there, but if so did I say, "What do you think is gonna happen?" It doesn't stick out in my mind. I didn't think anybody would come and blow us up. I don't know, a lot of stuff may have happened, but I had no clue. The strangest thing was when we got on the bus to travel to the stadium, and on the way to the bus a rope was set up between spectators and us, a path to walk, and people on the other side were talking, "There's the Bear meat."

I don't recall anything like cheers coming from outside the stadium. I never thought about it. If it happened, then I assumed the cheers were coming from our fans in the stands. A lot of this was my naïveté to all that went on at the time. I had not realized that USC with blacks handily beating an all-white Alabama at home would have such an impact.

On Bryant's locker-room appearance. I don't remember Bryant coming in to our locker room. I would do my best and try not to miss the bus. We'd have our prayer, now go back and party. I never heard about "this here's a football player" until I saw a video.

I spent some time in Mobile last year and was watching Alabama and Mississippi State in a bar on main street, and they were saying Sylvester Croom should have been the coach at 'Bama.

I played with Scott Hunter at Green Bay. He just said, "Hey, you guys came down here and cleaned our clocks." We talked about how that game went, and we kicked their butts. We weren't really expecting a blowout 'cause we'd had a lot of comebacks in '69.

CHAPTER Seven

The Religion of Football

Football lends itself perfectly to evangelical tendencies.
—*University of Alabama professor Dr. Culpepper Clark*

Early football was greatly influenced by the game of rugby, which had been introduced by McGill University, a visiting Canadian college. In the late nineteenth century it became popularized under the "American rules" at East Coast colleges such as Rutgers, Harvard, Yale, and Princeton. The game was so violent that deaths piled up. The government had to enforce rules to make it safer.

But after World War I, football became a very popular sport. Originally, it had been relegated to the Ivy League crowd, but eventually it became all the rage across the country. Doughboys who started college in their twenties took to the game in order to get their aggressions out. The first great postwar team was the University of California Golden Bears, known as the Wonder Team.

The University of Notre Dame, a tiny Catholic school in South Bend, Indiana, put its name on the map in 1913 when their end, Knute Rockne, devised a new play called the forward pass, which was used to defeat mighty Army.

While large stadiums were being built around the country, Notre Dame Stadium would not be completed until 1930. In the 1920s, Notre Dame began to travel the nation, taking on a barnstorming quality. Now the head coach, Knute Rockne made a smart marketing decision, which was to play games in large cosmopolitan cities in the East, the West, and the Midwest—places where Irish, Italian, and Polish Catholics lived and would love to see "their" team up close. Fans flocked to their games, taking to the team as their own. They became known as Subway Alumni. The Irish traveled to New York, where the Four Horsemen of Notre Dame defeated Army at the Polo Grounds under what fabled sportswriter Grantland Rice called "a blue, gray October sky." They went to California and beat Stanford in Pasadena's Rose Bowl in 1925. In 1926 they beat the University of Southern California Trojans at the Los Angeles Memorial Coliseum. These games drew enormous crowds.

Southern California and Notre Dame decided to make it a yearly rivalry. In 1927 and 1929, USC traveled to Chicago, where they lost thrillers to Notre Dame in front of crowds that reached 120,000 at Soldier Field.

In the Midwest, University of Illinois running back Harold "Red" Grange thrilled capacity crowds with his exploits. His nickname was the Galloping Ghost. He was signed to play professionally in the new National Football League, and he drew capacity crowds to games at Soldier Field, thus ensuring the success of the NFL. It was Grange who gave the young National Football League just the push it needed.

College football in the 1920s grew into big business and a cultural phenomenon. Eastern football gave way to the West, but national arguments sprang up. Who was the best? Who deserved to win the national championship? Who was the best individual player?

In 1935, the Heisman Trophy was awarded to the "best player in college football." In 1936, the Associated Press began a poll to determine "who's number one?" Tremendous regional pride and excitement were attached to these honors, to natural rivalries, geographic and otherwise. Bowl games pitted champions from one part of America against the best team from other regions.

Catholics, particularly the Irish, who at one time were a highly discriminated-against minority, can attribute their assimilation in large part to Notre Dame's success. The unglamorous Midwest, with its harsh winters and farm landscapes, found pride in the success of the Michigan Wolverines, the Ohio State Buckeyes, the Illinois Fighting Illini. The city of Los Angeles grew into greatness in unison with its two great football teams, USC and UCLA.

In the South, Georgia Tech was the dominant power through the World War I years. Texas, Auburn, and Oklahoma claimed national championships through the many and varied "systems" used, often years later, to determine such things. But the South was looked down upon socially and athletically.

In the 1920s, a religious revival turned ugly when the Ku Klux Klan changed its focus to "white supremacy." Hatred among Protestants, Catholics, and Jews emanated from this, even manifesting itself in the way Notre Dame was treated (one of the reasons Rockne chose to play in large cities instead of rural settings). But the University of Alabama put themselves and their region "on the map" when they beat Washington in the 1926 Rose Bowl; tied Stanford in the 1927 Rose Bowl; and earned national championships in 1925, 1926, 1930, and 1934.

The last vestiges of Civil War animosity were swept away by world wars and college football. Soldiers from the South and the North mixed in the military during World War I and II. It was in these kinds of environments where they would engage in friendly debate over who was better: Alabama or Penn State? Tennessee or Pittsburgh?

* * *

The American South has always been a passionate place, a place where, as University of Alabama communications dean Dr. Culpepper Clark says, "the blood runs hot." It is a region of the country that has taken to football with a particular fervor over and above the rest of the nation. The South is the Bible Belt, a land of Christian believers and churchgoing folk, black and white.

"Football," says Dr. Clark, "lends itself perfectly to evangelical tendencies."

"Football is religion in the South, right there with huntin' and fishin'," says Mississippi State football coach Sylvester Croom, the same Tuscaloosa Sylvester Croom who thought Joe Namath looked like "a cool jazz singer."

The country mind-set of the rural South has always looked for manly challenges. Its denizens have met those challenges in war and in the hunt. Tales of Confederate battles have long inspired the Southern psyche: Pickett's charge at Gettysburg, Stonewall Jackson in the middle of the fray, Lee's army on the march.

Nothing outside battle has more perfectly fit that psyche than football, a game of field generalship, real estate captured, charges stemmed by courageous stands, and forms of "espionage" such as the red dog blitz or the called audible.

The casual observer of high school football in the South may be struck by the realization that herein lies the reason America wins its wars. There is no place in the world that quite matches military pageantry like the big prep contest, with its marching bands, John Philip Sousa music, young gladiators pumped to the extreme edge of "Testosterone City," and pretty cheering girls waiting to show their appreciation once they return from battle.

Perhaps the reason for all of this was the Civil War, which created in Dixie the ultimate form of inferiority complex. The menfolk had "failed" to protect their homes, their women, their children—their very way of life.

Botched Reconstruction created isolation. With few checks and balances from the North, which had distanced itself from its old enemy, and with the hopes of the nation turned to the shining future that lay out West, the Old South was alienated. Poor blacks were caught in the maelstrom of one hundred years of recrimination.

With nobody seemingly paying much attention, Southerners—white *and black*—took to football as their pastime. It became a rallying point for communities, a social event, something to take their minds off grinding poverty, racism, and that inferiority gnawing at the soul of a proud region that once produced Presidents, Constitution drafters, and great statesmen.

Football was the focus of family get-togethers, politics, business meetings, and religious gatherings. Everything was centered around it. In the off-season, it was the main point of discussion.

The Florida-Georgia game became known as "the world's largest outdoor cocktail party." The Alabama-Auburn game turned into a blood feud of Hatfield-McCoy intensity. Football in Texas had emotional overtones on par with the Battle of the Alamo.

But what football really did, more than anything else, was give Southerners something to be proud of. The Civil War and their racial crimes ground into their collective conscience that unmistakable sense of inferiority. Football was that one thing they did as well as anybody. Nobody embodied it better than the Alabama Crimson Tide, and *nobody* exemplified the excellence they loved better than Paul "Bear" Bryant.

When Alabama burst on the American grid scene with their consecutive national titles in 1925 and 1926, just the sound of the phrase had a ring that seemed to echo with the sort of pride that once rang out of the mouths of soldiers at Bull Run and Shiloh.

National championship.

In the 1930s, when 'Bama again stood tall, with All-American end Don Hutson leading them to the pinnacle, Bear Bryant lined up on the other side of the field. When Hutson went on to star for the Green Bay Packers, the entire state of Alabama "starred" for the Packers.

After World War II, the South and Alabama football experienced down times. Jackie Robinson's breaking of the color barrier brought to light the obvious discrimination still happening in the South. Blacks playing in the minor leagues throughout the region, or in spring training settings in Florida and Georgia, told tales of racial woe that increasingly found their way into Northern newspapers.

California for years sent teams such as St. Mary's and Santa Clara to southern New Year's Day bowl games. In 1951, the University of San Francisco found themselves disinvited from the Orange Bowl because they had black players.

President Harry Truman desegregated the Army, but black soldiers, some of whom were World War II or Korean vets, were shamefully discriminated against in Southern hotels and restaurants. The *Brown v. Board of Education* decision infuriated Southerners because it represented the hated concept of Northerners (read: the federal government) coming to their land and telling them how to live. Television invaded their sheltered world, creating the colossus of public opinion marshaled against them, as in *us versus them*.

Enter Bear Bryant.

In 1961, Bryant's Crimson Tide won the first of his four legitimate national championships (the 1964 and 1973 "national championships" are asterisked by bowl losses), and its effect cannot be fully understood outside the region. Notre Dame collected its national championships like a scholar collects straight As. Southern Cal cheered their titles and moved on. Ohio State and Michigan asked in frustration why they could not do it more often.

But at the University of Alabama, a state and a region saw this as a validation, a mandate for their way of life. It was something they did better than anybody. It was excellence personified; the gruff, mumbling ol' Bear, with his whisky slur and his houndstooth hat—by gum, he was every bit as good as Bud Wilkinson, Woody Hayes, or Red Sanders. Nobody was better. The Tide was robbed of the 1966 number one ranking when the "Catholic vote" awarded once-tied Notre Dame with a tainted title over unbeaten, untied Alabama. 'Bama's segregated status was a factor with voters that stuck in their craw, too, but the classy Bear refused to complain about the slight.

Bryant was up there with any coach in the history of college football, whether that coach be Knute Rockne, Amos Alonzo Stagg, Frank Leahy, Bud Wilkinson, Woody Hayes, John McKay, Tom Osborne, Bobby Bowden, or Joe Paterno. His record proves it: he retired the all-time winningest coach in history.

The effect of this kind of American excellence emanating from and representing Alabama cannot be compared to many other things in this country when it comes to the issue of pride. Bryant indeed did "walk on water" in Coke ads. As George Wallace acutely understood, by the mid-1960s had Bryant run for governor, he would have won.

"Auburn people would have voted for him just to get him to quit coaching," said Crimson Tide quarterback Scott Hunter.

In Bryant and 'Bama there stood, in the mid- to late 1960s, a conundrum. On the one hand, he reached the pinnacle of his profession and led his program to that pinnacle using all white football players. This had the disturbing effect of reinforcing the racist concept, not unlike Hitler's vision of the Aryan superman, of a physically and mentally superior white athlete, possibly indigenous only to the ruggedly individualistic world of the American South.

The flip side of that very conundrum was unseen. It existed in the mind of the sly fox they called Bear. It consisted in the fact that the coach knew the concept of the superior white football player was a myth that would soon explode; and when it did, he needed to have some answers.

Bear Bryant was planning to come up with those very answers. The result would be a seminal moment of change in American history.

Other Voices: Dave Brown

Dave Brown was a lineman at USC on the 1970 team. Like Manfred Moore and Charle' Young, he was and remains a very spiritual man who led in a quiet way, despite not being a superstar athlete. He was good enough to play in the now-defunct World Football League and has dedicated his life to teaching and coaching. He currently teaches history and coaches football at San Clemente (California) High School.

I became a Christian when I was seventeen years old. One night, sitting in my room, I gave my life to Jesus Christ. I always thought I was philosophical and anti-God; but I realized—I knew—I needed to make a change in my life. I went to USC in 1968 as a freshman. It wasn't easy; I was not a big star. In high school, we're all big stars; but at USC, I was just one of the guys, not penciled in as a starter. Not starting, many times I felt like giving it up, but my mom used to advise me that nobody in my family had ever graduated from college, so I hung in there to honor my mom, and I'm glad I did.

That Alabama game was my first game—not as a team leader, but God was good to me. . . . I was wide-eyed, a rookie getting off the plane. I'd never, ever even been to the South; this was the first time I ever traveled. But I was up on current events. I knew about the civil rights movement and Martin Luther King. They greeted us with the Million-Dollar Band, and I'd never seen anything like that in my life. People were surrounding us, and it was a real big deal that Southern Cal had come to play Alabama. My eyes were wide, and I was thinking, *This is amazing.* I just didn't realize that people felt that highly of football in the South. In southern California, it's different.

Bill Holland, an African American from Los Angeles High School and a super guy, he was hanging with me most of this time. I remember distinctly seeing this one place; it looked like an old factory or warehouse, with dilapidated buildings. I looked out there, and I said, "That's amazing." All these black high school students were doing band drills in the yard. This school looks horrible, and Holland just says, "This is the way it is here."

Segregation du jour, that's the way it was. Integration was not really happening yet. As the bus rolled down the road, I saw the marked difference in socioeconomics of each neighborhood, and all the while I'm thinking, *This is amazing.* It was shocking.

Later, standing in the hotel with Bill, he takes me to a wing of the lobby, and this little kid comes by asking for autographs. We've all got USC blazers on; this is the Holiday Inn, Birmingham. This little kid mixed into the group. He's maybe five or six, and he turns to his mother and says, "Gee, Mommy, they sure have a lot of n--rs on that team."

I turned to Bill, and I asked him, "Hey, how are you holding up?"

He says, "Yeah, you know, I face that in L.A. That's typical."

That opened my eyes. I come from a white community in L.A., and I'd not realized that before. I'm twenty years old, and this is my education.

We played well against an all-white team, and they were not what we expected. They had no team speed, and it was not a very good game, to be honest with you.

On his faith. Regarding my Christian influence on that [1970] team, I wasn't a leader at that point. People knew it about me, and I tried to act

like it. Guys were older and did not hold those values, so I was not mainstream; but God was faithful to me because by 1972 we had a really good
core of men on that team, guys with good values, a lot of Christians. Sam
Cunningham was a Christian. We Christians started fellowships when we
were seniors. We said, "We're going to give our season to the Lord," to
honor Him with our team.

I didn't know how good we'd be. My sophomore and junior years we'd
not played well. My senior year we played at Arkansas and were not supposed to win that game. We were tied at the half. We won that game, 31–10,
and they were number one or close to it going in.

On the 1971 Notre Dame game. In 1971 we were 2–4 and racially divided
over the Jimmy Jones–Mike Rae quarterback controversy. Notre Dame was
6–0. The week we were to travel to South Bend, I went over to Coach
McKay, who was often unapproachable. Sometimes we feared him. I said
to him that we always pray before games, so I asked if he would let us pray
after the game. So that night we prayed and were thankful. The team took
off and went 12–0 the next year; it was the most fantastic team ever. I
coached twenty-six years in high school and junior college, and I've never
seen a team like that. I've never seen such camaraderie and unity.

On Fellowship of Christian Athletes. That year was from God. Others
would just say it was a great team, but as a coach I know you've gotta have
more than just great talent—you need to overachieve; and that's what
God's granted you. That team had it.

I got involved in Athletes in Action and the Fellowship of Christian
Athletes. I lifted weights with a guy who was with Athletes in Action in the
late '60s, so I invited him to come to our team. That was the Notre Dame
week in '71. McKay said he wouldn't mind if the guy puts on a demonstration, as long as it's voluntary. We had a good time up there; a lot of
guys prayed and accepted Christ that day—a lot of guys, maybe 80 percent.
We went and beat Notre Dame by a big score in South Bend, and that team
never lost again in '71 or '72.

On his teammates. John Papadakis was a real fiery guy, a good athlete in
high school and at USC. He was charismatic; he was a guy we looked to on
the team. He was always doing something off the wall, always trying to get
people to play better. He was a leader defensively on the team. I came in as
a freshman, and he was a better athlete than I was; he never had to red-
shirt. He was a good guy to have. I can't remember all the things he said
quite right, but he always had a Greek saying; he was always "acting
Greek." We would discuss Christ. He didn't get involved that much, but he

was a Christian and we would have discussions about God. I think he was Greek Orthodox. I wouldn't characterize him as a person who got really involved in that fellowship, which kind of took off after he was gone.

Sam Cunningham is a super guy, a really humble, very friendly man, sensitive to others. He was really team oriented. He could have gone to another program with great statistics instead of being a blocking fullback, not carrying much more than seven, eight times a game. In another program he'd have carried twenty times a game, but he just wanted to win. He started coming to AIA and FCA. He's very moral. I rarely heard him swear.

On integration. Thirty-five years later, their football game down there [in Alabama] was supposedly integrated. They had a few blacks in school, but from what I understand, some of those students that had entered the school years before didn't stay too long. Segregation legally ended, but it lasted much longer. We even see patterns of it to this day. Today we see a black community, a Latino community, a white community, sometimes blacks even self-segregating, which is sad. We just have to keep making it better every generation.

I never thought that much about it, to be honest with you. At USC we had whites, blacks, a few Jews, Latinos; I never thought about it. Here we played an all-white team, which was strange in college. I was thinking as I looked at Alabama, *How do these guys think they can compete like that? This game's gonna pass 'em by.* The next year they had an outside linebacker named John Mitchell who was black and a defensive end who was black; and they won that game. They realized integrating was their way out.

On USC's progress. As far as our program's getting back to where we had been, our tipping point was the Notre Dame game in 1971. We started our fellowship around that time, and we got serious. We were a big underdog back there, and we beat 'em 28–14. We never lost to them at USC after that.

I thanked God that I listened to my mom and had opportunity. I played in the World League in 1974–1975 before it went defunct. I tried to play in the NFL, but I was a six-foot off center. So I got my teaching credentials, started education at twenty-eight, and pretty much always was involved in coaching. God's called me to do it.

Other Voices: Manfred Moore

African American Manfred Moore was a great Trojan on the football field and remains one to this day off the field. Soft-spoken and erudite, he articulates in the manner of a college professor. Moore choked up when recalling the profound influ-

ence John McKay had in keeping him steered on the right path. Moore, who has remained active in the USC Alumni Club, is a very spiritual man.

On his teammates and coaches. Wilbur Jackson was my teammate. He was a great guy. He was a running back, and I was a fullback. He started; he was quiet but tough, and he could run the ball fast. In 1976, the league added Tampa Bay, and John McKay picked me up.

We lost every single game, so somebody asked McKay, "How do you feel about your team's execution?"

"I think that's a good idea," he replied.

Sam Cunningham was a guy with integrity—a big brute of a guy, yet soft-spoken, very aware of people's opinions and situations. He knew people had different issues. He's wise.

One thing was that Rod McNeill, Edesel Garrison, Charle' Young, Sam Cunningham, and I got together, and we called ourselves the Big Five. It wasn't about ego, but we hung together; we supported each other. I knew alumni groups, and I'd introduce those guys to the groups for speaking in the off-season, and we'd get perks, clothes or whatever. We took care of each other.

Marv Goux was a brute, a tough guy; but if he respected you, he'd talk to you like a human being. If not, he'd let you know you needed to get tougher to do your job. He was all about business on the field all the time with his players. He was a short guy, and linemen are big guys; but he'd grab you by the jersey, point at what direction to go, and man, if you did what he said you got good results.

John Papadakis, he was upper class. I was a red-shirt. You didn't want to go up against him, to block him. I was on the "goon squad"; you had to be heads-up always, and he'd get around the defensive end and chase you down, hard. He was intimidating on and off the field.

On John McKay. John McKay affected my life in a profound manner. When I was a freshman, I got married to a Caucasian lady. She was my high school sweetheart, a cheerleader. We had a son. McKay had recruited me with a scholarship, but now we had to come face to face with issues that in those days were not so cut and dried. He could have rescinded the scholarship, cut me off; and he could have had a legitimate excuse that my getting married and having a son would distract me from school and football. Instead, John McKay said, "He [Moore's son] doesn't make any difference." McKay helped with married student housing; he was a man of his word, yes sir. I love my son. I took him to classes; I took him to practice.

McKay saw I had a son. He could have said, "Don't bring a kid around here . . . don't bring him to class." Instead, John McKay, at the end of practice, told my little son Jason to come over and line up at halfback. He handed him the ball for him to "run" for a "touchdown." He was only four years old. John showed that love and affection, so now with tears in my eyes, if I can show him love and affection by telling you this story, then that's what I'm gonna do.

The next year we lost to the Ohio State Buckeyes [in the 1974 Rose Bowl]. Coach McKay was disappointed and must have had a lot on his mind; but when the press spoke to him, this is what he told them: "If it's the last thing I do, I'll make certain Manfred Moore gets drafted into pro football."

Maybe sometimes he didn't relate well to people, but he was honorable and bright. He called me Manny; they all started calling me Manny. My experience with him—he gave me a scholarship and got me into pro football. Under him I was voted most inspirational and most improved. This is directly attributed to Coach McKay's influence.

But wait, there's more. At Tampa Bay, we're 0–14. The worst team in the league. He needed to make roster space and had to trade me. He could have traded me anywhere in the league. Where does he send me? He sent me to the Oakland Raiders, the year we won the Super Bowl in 1976. My hometown [he was originally from Richmond]—the best team in the world. I won an L.A. city championship at San Fernando High, a national championship at USC in 1972, and a world championship at Oakland in 1976. McKay affected my life with an impact I'll feel forever. *That's* some of the things McKay affected.

So, remembering John McKay . . . it was just another reminder that God puts people on your path that help you achieve your goal and purpose in this life. They may not have talked or behaved like angels (on or off the field), but they were a blessing on the way to fulfilling your purpose in this life—to know God and to make Him known!

CHAPTER Eight

California Dreamin' Meets the American Dream

Quite simply, without any nonsense, you take out the
old monster of injustice, which has been accustomed for
centuries to being bowed and scraped and curtsied to, and
you sentence it to death.
—*Boris Pasternak,* Doctor Zhivago

California was the land of opportunity for gold miners, railroad barons, water engineers, migrant farmers, and suburbanized soldiers returning from the wars. In the East, neighborhoods were divided—Irish Catholic, Jewish, Italian, WASP, and black. In the West, neighborhoods were not marked by racial and religious bloc identity. Blacks came to these warm lands, many to work the shipyards during World War II. They were met by prejudice, but less so than in any other place in America. They were able to attend the same schools and play on the same teams as whites.

Los Angeles was a sleepy pueblo surrounded by the sea, desert vistas, canyons, mountains, and valleys where oranges and other "exotic" fruits and vegetables grew in wild abundance. The Spaniards dominated the political and social influence of southern California. Father Junipero Serra, who traversed the state founding Catholic missions, led them. Catholicism was the dominant religious ethic. The citizenry was mostly Hispanic. The Mexicans who lived in the area and owned much of the land considered themselves Americans, for the most part. Over time, however, white Americans populated the area. As the whites moved in, emboldened in part by the U.S. victory over Mexico in the 1847 war, more and more Spanish and Mexican land barons moved out, sometimes by force. A seething resentment on the part of the Hispanic community began. It still lives, to some extent, to this day.

The "big city" in California was not Los Angeles. It was San Francisco. Next came Sacramento, which was the hub connecting the Trans-Continental Railroad to San Francisco in the west and the Sierra Nevada in the east. Historians have often asked why the railroad was built over the Sierras. The safer, easier route was to the south, then across the deserts that could have bypassed both the Rockies and Sierras, through Arizona and on into southern California to L.A. Connecting rail lines to San Diego in the south and San Francisco (and Sacramento) in the north would have been easier to construct over the Tejon Mountains, or along the Pacific Coast, than the treacherous Rocky and Sierra passes that were constructed.

The answer to the question as to why the "Southern route" was not chosen is simple: Abe Lincoln and the Civil War. Lincoln was a huge supporter of the railroads, who in turn supported his candidacy with money and favors. When the slavery question threatened the War Between the States, it was decided that the lines would not be built through Confederate states. Slaves likely would have been conscripted to perform the labor, which eventually was handled, in large part, by Chinese immigrants.

When the line finally was built, and the war did end, people in the Midwest and the South came to California. Before the Trans-Continental Railroad, San Francisco was the "civilized" city that was populated by people from the East Coast. They favored the Union. The City—the moniker given by San Franciscans to describe their . . . city—was populated by Europeans, many from England, and Asians. The first settlers came via covered wagon, but this was a perilous journey. They were motivated by gold, discovered in the Sierra foothills in the late 1840s. Later "sophisticates" preferred ships, which made their way via the Cape of Good Hope or from Asia.

With the creation of the railroad, men and women from America's heartland came to California. Four hundred miles separate San Francisco from L.A., but those four hundred miles represent (and today is no different) a psychological divide between north and south, or to use political terms, the North and the Southland. Southerners did not "cotton" to the East Coast Yankees who made up San Francisco's power structure. They tended to find their way to L.A. Midwesterners, up to their ankles in frozen winters, chose the year-round sunny climes of the Southland over the oft-foggy Bay Area. San Francisco's "elites" tended more toward ribald Barbary Coast hedonism and less toward traditional Christianity. The new Los Angelenos were more conservative and churchgoing.

Over time, many changes would occur. Los Angeles and environs became more populated, its vast expanses and weather providing an enormous attraction. The population expansion become possible when, in 1904, L.A.'s "city fathers," led by chief engineer William Mulholland, cut a controversial deal with the Owens River Valley in the southern Sierras. An aqueduct was created to divert precious water to L.A. Many more canals, aqueducts, and dams were built over the years to quench the seemingly insatiable thirst of a continually growing populace.

World War I and World War II showed L.A. off to servicemen passing through for training or on their way to and from the fight. The Rose Bowl became a huge spectacle, drawing more and more Midwesterners to L.A. until Long Beach became known, as *L.A. Times* sports columnist Jim Murray termed it, "Iowa West." But the original mind-set, in which San Francisco and the north were viewed as liberal, while Los Angeles and the south were seen as more politically conservative and Christian, has never truly gone away.

California's great colleges found themselves to be part of this changing world by virtue of their popularity on the gridiron, but they quickly developed sterling academic reputations above and beyond football success. USC provided educational opportunities for L.A.'s first black professionals in the field of architecture, law, medicine, and the arts as early as the turn of the century. In a 1935 event that actor Denzel Washington is planning to bring to the big screen, USC's national champion debating team gave an opportunity to a debating team from a traditional black college that had been denied the chance to compete in the official contest. It was a spirited, fair debate, the polar opposite of affirmative action. Both sides acquitted themselves like gentlemen and scholars. The Trojan debaters gave it their best. The black debaters won!

After World War II, southern California became a bastion of the Republican Party, particularly in Orange County, just south of L.A. and north of San Diego. Richard Nixon and Ronald Reagan were the most prominent to rise from this new dynamic, described by some as the

"Goldwater West" of "rugged individualism" after 1964 GOP presidential candidate Barry Goldwater of Arizona.

California was a state of unrest in the late 1960s, its campuses embroiled in protest over the Vietnam War. Out of the civil rights movement grew the antiwar, free speech, women's rights, and gay liberation movements. Liberalism mixed with radicalism at the "open-minded" California schools, Berkeley and Stanford. USC, a conservative institution, remained peaceful. Yet the image of an idyllic racial climate in California was marred by some uglier realities.

The political differences between the regions have been reflected in their colleges. In the north lies the state's major public school, the University of California, Berkeley, located just across the San Francisco Bay from the City. UC Berkeley became a hotbed of radicalism and Communism prior to and during World War II, when its prominent leftist scientist, Robert Oppenheimer, promoted subversion in the sciences as it related to the sharing of atomic secrets with the Soviet Union after the Manhattan Project. From 1964 to 1971, UC Berkeley was the de facto staging grounds of American Communism. During the Vietnam War, the North Vietnamese derived their greatest aid and comfort from actions taken on the campus!

Stanford University, a private school located in Palo Alto, just south of San Francisco, took on a more and more liberal political persona beginning in the 1960s. It has never been as radical as UC Berkeley, but its wild and crazy halftime marching band reflects the eclectic "march to the beat of a different drummer" attitude that permeates its conscience. Strangely, Stanford students at football games often ridicule USC as the "University of Spoiled Children," when in fact Stanford students come from wealth and affluence that at least matches USC's.

On one occasion, sportscaster Chris Schenkel observed incredulously, "The Stanford band's doing . . . a tribute to . . . *Chairman Mao!*" Indeed, down on the field the Stanford band was hailing Chinese dictator Mao Tse-Tung. This was during the Cultural Revolution (1966–1976). The man they were honoring was, at that precise moment, in the middle of a purge resulting in the murder of an estimated 35 to 55 million human beings!

On another occasion Stanford's student body hurled racial epithets at USC's football players that, in their minds, were okay to say because they were the ones saying them. This is elitism at its worst. USC football coach John McKay disliked Stanford's liberal elitism, which he regarded as academic snobbery. In the late 1960s, he brought his Trojans, filled with powerful black athletes, to Palo Alto for a game on "the Farm."

"As the team emerged from the locker room," McKay recalled in what was one of the last interviews he granted before his passing in 2001, "my team was peppered with the most vile, disgusting racial epithets that I've ever heard in thirty years of college and professional coaching." The man who once said "a billion Chinese couldn't care less" whether his team beat Notre Dame certainly cared about the bigotry coming from the allegedly enlightened Stanford liberals.

"I felt that the liberalism at Stanford was an example of academic hypocrisy," McKay said. "These were people who put down those who didn't share their ideals, who told everybody else how to live. But now I was hearing the exact opposite of what that school supposedly preached. They ridiculed us as a 'football school,' said we were spoiled rich kids, but we were giving more and greater opportunities to blacks at that time than they were or anybody else, for that matter. The whole thing made my blood boil, and that's why I later told the press I wanted to beat Stanford by 2,000 points."

In the Southland, there is UCLA, a state school that has grown into a world-renowned institution of learning and research while building itself one of the most powerful athletic departments in America. It has accomplished this while avoiding the pratfalls of major campus radicalism. In L.A., it may be seen as the school of "the people," attracting a more egalitarian student body than USC's perceived "rich kids." UCLA is the preferred choice of a majority of L.A.'s large Jewish community. To the limited extent that such distinctions can be made in an area as diverse as Los Angeles, the San Fernando Valley and the Westside might be called "Bruin country."

UCLA has produced its fair share of leftists. Antiwar actor Tim Robbins is a UCLA man. Angela Davis, the black Communist who supplied the guns used to kill a white California judge in 1970, has been given, instead of a lifetime prison sentence, lifetime tenure and a political platform at UCLA. But overall the school has never allowed itself to be a hotbed of Che Guevara anti-Americanism.

Then, of course, there is the University of Southern California, also colloquially known as USC, SC, Southern California to many outside the region, Southern Cal (despite official admonitions from the sports information office *not* to call it that anymore), and—to UCLA, Stanford, and Cal students—the University of Spoiled Children. Tony enclaves such as San Marino and Newport Beach might be thought of as "Trojan country."

USC has always remained a conservative institution. Richard Nixon's wife, Patricia, was a USC graduate. Nixon's presidential administration (1969–1974) was filled with USC (along with UCLA and Stanford) graduates. Appointments secretary Dwight Chapin (not the *L.A. Times* sportswriter) was a USC man. Donald Segretti, the first target of Bob Woodward and Carl Bernstein when they began to investigate Watergate, was a member of the so-called USC Mafia, a term used in the film *All the President's Men*.

In 1983, Watergate "plumber" G. Gordon Liddy was received as a hero at USC's Bovard Auditorium when he came to promote his best-selling autobiography, *Will*. In 1984, Democratic presidential candidate Walter Mondale chastised students chanting, "Reagan country."

"You oughtta be ashamed of yourselves," said Mondale, who like most liberals was fawned over at 99 percent of America's other institutions of higher learning. "This is the school that produced Dwight Chapin and Donald Segretti."

In 2004, controversial filmmaker Michael Moore showed *Fahrenheit 9/11* at USC. According to reports from students, when Moore began to advocate against President George W. Bush and the Iraq War, he was "booed off the stage." Moore reportedly "left in a huff." Like Mondale, he assumed every college walked in lockstep with left-wing orthodoxy. Dismayed at USC's independence, he "shouted at the students as he left." After that he took to wearing a UCLA hat.

Other Voices: Coach Willie Brown

After starring for John McKay and playing in the NFL, Brown was tapped as USC's first black assistant coach. He was on the staff of the 1970 team. Today he works in the university's athletic department.

I was born in Tuscaloosa, Alabama. My family moved to Long Beach, California, when I was eighteen months old. I graduated from Long Beach Poly High School, played for Coach McKay from 1960 to 1963, and graduated in 1964. The Los Angeles Rams made me their first-round draft pick. So did the Chargers of the American Football League, as this was prior to the merger. I signed with the Rams and played with them for three years, then with the Philadelphia Eagles for three years.

On tension before the game. McKay and Bryant set up the 1970 Alabama game, and it did volumes for race relations. Prior to the game, though, there were a lot of concerns on the part of our black players, going in to the South. Politically, there was a lot going on. Racially, there were incidents happening all throughout the country.

I talked to Charlie [Weaver] the other day. I heard that [he and Tody Smith] had guns, and I'm not surprised if they did. A lot was riding on it. We received hate letters sent to McKay and some of the players, so going back to the Deep South, our guys were not used to that, and now they were exposed to that situation. I heard about that gun story, but I didn't see it. But I'm not surprised.

On attitudes in the South. Bear Bryant and McKay were close friends and all. Bear offered me a job to go back to Tuscaloosa. I would have been one of the first black coaches, but I didn't want to go back to the South. My father had grown up there. My father recalls going to 'Bama games and sitting in the section for blacks, high in the stands. He went to Spelman College. The University of Alabama would give 'em hand-me-down equipment. You know, though, as much prejudice as there was, the black community, they thought the Crimson Tide was their team. When we played in that '70 game, I had relatives pulling for me but who still wanted 'Bama to win!

I remember black people outside the stands, cheering for USC, plus people in the stadium, blacks jumping up and down cheering. They recognized the bus and cheered us after the game. They surrounded the bus, there were blacks everywhere, and they were very happy. They were rooting for us; they'd come down and were cheering for us. Our black players just took it all in and did it with wonder. As I sat in the bus, I did recall they held candles and Bibles. People were crying; it was very emotional. This was *not* a regular game. It was just monumental. The players, who normally would be rowdy after a win, they were quiet. They'd played well, and the players knew something important was going down!

Sam Cunningham was someone who played a big part in it, to what Paul Bryant was trying to do. It was him and McKay, trying to set up something. He did come in our locker room and all. I think Sam did meet some of their players, maybe not on a stool but individual players, plus the press was all around Sam.

It served a wonderful purpose, a wonderful purpose. Man, I really believe sports transforms a lot of things. It just helped relationships; it pushed it along.

Other Voices: Keith Dunnavant

Writer Keith Dunnavant wrote Coach: The Life of Paul "Bear" Bryant *and at the time of our interview was working on a book (*The Missing Ring*) about the 1966 Alabama team that was deprived of a third straight national championship when the Catholic and anti-Wallace votes awarded the title to once-tied Notre Dame.*

I was a teenage sportswriter, covering preps and the SEC when I was in high school. I went to Alabama on a scholarship arranged by Paul "Bear" Bryant. I wrote for a national sports daily and was a football writer before I wrote books. I wrote about Bryant because I understood him, and no one had written a definitive biography on him. One aspect that always interested me was the whole civil rights movement in the context of football. Just between us, the 1966 team was the last lily-white team.

On the controversy surrounding Bear Bryant's statement. I don't know whether Bryant ever brought Cunningham into that locker room and said, "This here's what a football player looks like." I honestly don't know. I tried to get to the bottom of it when I wrote his book, to see if it was true, apocryphal, or partially true. The bottom line about that game, which is lost on a lot of people, is that I agree with the *premise* of the quote, in terms of race relations. What is not accurate is that it prompted Bryant to begin recruiting blacks. Wilbur Jackson was in the stands that night, a freshman on full scholarship. 'Bama had recruited several black athletes up to that time.

That said, you can't underestimate the importance of that game. Clarence Davis was from Birmingham. Somebody said the other day that Clarence should be in the Alabama Sports Hall of Fame because that game showed the times were changing, and 'Bama could either go with it or not. Bryant was never a racist, but a realist who wanted to win. He was saying to the fans, "The days of segregation are over." People cared about winning even if they didn't believe in integration.

Jerry Claiborne wasn't there in 1970, regarding his supposedly saying, "Sam Cunningham did more for civil rights in three hours than Martin Luther King did in twenty years." That statement was not meant as an insult; it was a compliment for Sam Cunningham, Jimmy Jones, and Clarence Davis. Not to interject myself into this, but I was born in 1964; I grew up in a small town—Athens, Alabama. I have five older brothers; they all went to segregated schools. I went to school starting in 1971, and I was in integrated schools all the way. I was a big 'Bama football fan. When I was a little boy and we were choosing teams, I was just as likely to want to be

[African American players] Wilbur Jackson or Calvin Culliver or Ozzie Newsome. The integration of Alabama had a profound impact on me.

It helped create a more color-blind society. This game is part of a number of mileposts, and the first of them was this game. In 1956, Pitt played in the Sugar Bowl, and they had a black player [fullback Bobby Grier] who was quite good. They played Georgia Tech. Because of that game, the state legislature passed a law mandating segregation [a "social segregation law" applying to sporting events], enforcing the law so that the Sugar Bowl could not have a Northern team.

Now, my brothers were not racists, but the difference is I had black heroes. In my book, the importance of Wilbur [Jackson] at Alabama is that he was a revolutionary figure; he could tell races to share their heroes, which is more important than lunch counters or water coolers.

On Bryant's motivation to schedule the game. The question of the facts is romanticizing the idea that Alabama scheduled that game in order to grease the skids for the recruitment of the black athletes that followed. Knowing Bryant as well as I do, he would never make a game with somebody he thought would [defeat him]. He'd never put his team in opposition to a team like that just to make a point. But that said, he *was* astute, and he knew how much better USC was than his team at that time.

Here is a possibility: Bryant may have wanted to bring in a strong, integrated USC team coached by his friend, John McKay. He may have been thinking that it would be a close, competitive game. Certainly a game between Southern Cal and Alabama holds out that possibility much more than a blowout in most given years. Win or lose, he may have thought that the sight of an integrated, classy USC team would leave a positive impression on the fans, thus creating a more hospitable greeting for Jackson the following season.

On the other hand, if he truly felt it would be a blowout, it is hard to imagine he planned such a thing. For instance, if in 2005, Alabama, struggling under Mike Shula, suddenly had a schedule opening, would he invite Pete Carroll's two-time defending national champions to come to Alabama and probably lay a beating on the Tide? I think not. They'd schedule Alabama-Birmingham or Louisiana-Monroe.

At some point, though, Bryant didn't think like that. In his life, he had been offered big money to go pro. He was offered $1.7 million to take over the Dolphins prior to 1970. He was making about $25,000, not including leveraged side deals that upped his yearly income to around maybe $100,000. He was offered a ton by Miami, who took Don Shula when Bear turned it down. This means he was in it for the long term, so perhaps his thinking regarding this game was strategic, to take a step back in order to take two forward. If so, his record in the 1970s shows he was a genius if this was his plan.

John McKay said in my book that they were visiting Bryant and his wife, at a condo on the Alabama coast owned by Bear, in the off-season after 1970. One alumnus came by, and at some point Bryant excused himself to walk on the beach. During that time this alumnus told McKay, "I think the old man's lost it." That guy had no idea, McKay said, but coming off 6–5 and 6–4–1, this is the spring of '71, with all this stuff going on, people thought Bear was over the hill. . . .

Bryant stated that the athletic director, which was him, would decide when the coach needed to go. Bryant was at his lowest point as a coach prior to that 1971 game, which launched the greatest decade in college football history.

Honestly, no, I feel Bryant would not have scheduled a game just to get beat. He was too much of a competitor. Yet he was enough of a realist regarding his team and culture that I think it's fair to say Bryant would want an integrated team to play a competitive game versus him.

He had gone up against the great Nebraska teams of 1965 and '66, who had great black players. The Penn State game in 1959 was a big deal. Bryant relished that and understood it would help integrate. He spoke to his teams and told his players to treat 'em like anybody else: "Knock 'em [down], then help 'em up."

On politics and religion. Regarding politics, I'm one of the guys produced by this new thinking that I grew up with. The Southern strategy made a big difference. The perception now by some on the Left is that the Southern strategy was a way to speak in code of racism, and this was transferred to Reagan; but I don't buy that. What you have to remember is that race baiters were all Democrats. Governor Wallace was a Democrat; Lester Maddox was a Democrat. The South did not leave the Democratic Party, the Democratic Party left the South.

Now, Christianity. Religion had a tremendous influence. It is easy to look back on the segregated South from the vantage point of the twenty-first century and paint all of it with the same brush, but it's not that simple. All of it is in shades of gray. There were plenty of evil people, people who used the night riders and the KKK and killed; they were just evil. Then you have people such as [Governor] Wallace, who were not racist per se but were smart enough to use race for political advantage.

Then there was a group of people who had problems with things going on but remained silent. Most Alabama Christians believe in redemption, which led to change and to doing the right thing. In the late 1960s and early '70s, so many people had been raised believing segregation was just the way things were, not necessarily right—not to treat blacks badly, but that things would always be that way.

This doesn't justify it. Racism was never wiped out, but slowly, realities of peoples' lives changed. This is the Christian faith that permeated the South. It's cliché to say football is a religion, but there's some truth in the sense that football in that era was perhaps the ultimate extension of the American Dream. Bryant's teams were the connective tissue of American values. Ronald Reagan and Bear Bryant are the two heroes of my life. I've been in the media since I was fourteen, and except for people in sports, I know four who are right of center. The connective tissue, in terms of football in the South and what it means in that era—I'm writing about the '66 team—in that era there was a real "us versus them" feeling for people in Alabama, transmitted through the football team.

Alabamians always had a chip on their shoulders, an inferiority complex, created by Wallace. Bryant was the antidote to that. Not only was he very good at what he did, but he was the kind of guy they wanted to represent them.

The Reagan-Bryant connection was about strength, old-time values, hard work, perseverance, self-reliance. I love Bear because primarily I knew that it didn't matter how much talent you had; if you had enough heart you could play for Bryant, or do whatever you put your mind to.

Bryant was not just a football coach but also a personification of the idea of America. Not wealthy but beloved. I believe the respect Bryant had for McKay made 'Bama fans understand the other side of the issue. People look at that game and say, "If it's okay for Coach Bryant, then it's okay for the rest of us." Now that was powerfully revolutionary yet subtle. . . .

I think football is so important, and at Alabama it was the leveler, the opportunity to compete on a level playing field with the rest of the country. Between those white lines, it doesn't matter who your daddy is; it matters how much do you want to win, are you willing to work hard? It is a metaphor for putting forth effort, achieving great things, and taking personal responsibility.

CHAPTER **Nine**

The Tradition of Troy

It's a good day to be a Trojan.
—*USC football coach Pete Carroll*

As the nineteenth century became the twentieth, sports and the railroad line connected USC with both Cal and Stanford. Natural rivalries developed on the gridiron. Aside from those teams, USC also played other local colleges, such as Pomona and even Los Angeles High School. During wartime, they played tough games against the various Marine, Army, and Navy outposts that have always dotted the southern California landscape.

But football helped redefine the West. Many of the players were doughboys who had served in the military and now were in college. They were bigger, stronger, and more mature. In Berkeley, Coach Andy Smith's Wonder Teams of the early 1920s were one of the greatest dynasties of all time. Smith was the first coach to actively recruit, plucking blue-chippers from southern California through the efforts of an assistant, Nibs Price, who had coached high school ball down there.

USC was a power, but coach Elmer "Gloomy Gus" Henderson was unable to beat Cal. In a move that would foretell many firings of many coaches over many years, Henderson was dismissed. USC went after Knute Rockne, but he remained loyal to Notre Dame. Rockne recommended Iowa's Howard Jones, who was hired and became an instant success beginning in 1926.

By the 1920s, Southern California, California, and Stanford were national football powers. In 1923, USC defeated Penn State in the first Rose Bowl game played in the brand-new Pasadena stadium. In 1925, guard Brice Taylor became USC's first All-American. He was not only black but also handicapped, having been born without one of his hands. He was partly of Cherokee Indian descent.

In 1928, USC won the first of their (to date through 2006) eleven national championships. After losing to Notre Dame the first two years, they managed to beat the Irish. In 1931 they went back to South Bend, Indiana, for a "battle of titans." Notre Dame seemed unbeatable at home. The game was played in cold weather, on November 21. The Irish led 14–0 entering the fourth quarter. USC rallied to win it on Johnny Baker's field goal, 16–14. The game established USC as the dominant power in the college game following the death of Rockne in a plane crash earlier that year.

USC's train ride back to Los Angeles was met with crowds reminiscent of a political campaign. All of L.A., it appeared, came out to welcome them upon their return. USC won the national championship that season and again in 1932, when they defeated Notre Dame (13–0 at the Los Angeles Memorial Coliseum) and Pittsburgh (35–0 in the Rose Bowl) to finish 10–0.

In 1938 and 1939, USC defeated Southern teams entering the Rose Bowl game against them unbeaten, untied, and unscored on. On January 1, 1939, backup end Antelope Al Krueger caught four passes, the last for the winning touchdown, from fourth-string quarterback Doyle Nave in a 7–3 win over undefeated Duke. In 1939, USC won the national championship, Howard Jones's last, by beating Tennessee 14–0 in Pasadena.

USC, spurred by the great rivalries formed by yearly games with UCLA and Notre Dame, had by the 1950s maintained their status as a national football power but not a national *champion*. A paradigm shift in college football supremacy had shifted back to the Midwest, not only to four-time national champion (in the 1940s) Notre Dame but also to Big 10 juggernaut Michigan. When the Rose Bowl became a game contractually matching the Big 10 with the Pacific Coast Conference, West Coast teams appeared soft in a string of losses to their "three yards and a cloud of dust" rivals. Frank Leahy's Irish dominated the rivalry, but in the 1950s, as a population shift to California began to take shape, Notre Dame and Michigan fell on down times while USC prospered with the likes of All-Americans Frank Gifford and Jon Arnett. However, two new powers emerged in the

Big 10 and the PCC. Ohio State under Woody Hayes and UCLA under Red Sanders climbed to the pinnacle of the college game, with the Buckeyes capturing two national championships and the Bruins one.

Crowds in the 1950s routinely were over 100,000 for the UCLA and Notre Dame games. In later years, when theater-style seats were installed, the capacity was reduced to its current 92,000. The teams shared the Coliseum until 1982, when UCLA moved to the Rose Bowl. Recruiting scandals and NCAA sanctions hurt USC and other Pacific Coast teams in the 1950s, despite the efforts of successful USC head coach Jess Hill.

While John McKay is credited with creating the greatest opportunity for black athletes, Hill certainly should be given his due, too. After Brice Taylor, UCLA had done better, but Hill was determined to rectify the situation. Running back C. R. Roberts is not as well known as some of USC's legends, but he should be.

"We played in Austin, Texas, in 1956, and things went smoothly," Hill told Ken Rappoport in *The Trojans: A Story of Southern California Football*. "No racial problems at all."

Others remember it differently, but in studying race and the South, the discerning historian quickly discovers that the "white experience" and the "black experience" are as different as . . . black and white. In fact, Hill did deal with a major brouhaha, but "we beat Texas really badly, something like 44–20, and Roberts had gone crazy that day—ran for 257 yards. After the game, Roberts was sitting in a restaurant with some of our people, and this guy who had been at the game walks up to the counter and says, 'I don't know too much about this thing, segregation, integration, and that. But whatever it is, I've been watching that Roberts guy—and I believe in HIM.'"

Indeed, C.R. made an impression on September 22, 1956, the opening game of the season. History records a groundbreaking football game between USC and Alabama, played at Legion Field in Birmingham fifteen years later. The ebb and flow of history revolves around circumstance, opportunity, and timing. Roberts was spectacular in an environment that was inhospitable in the extreme. His performance was important, but not groundbreaking on a national level. The time was not right. Still, honoring his efforts is truly worthwhile because the freedom of others down the road came about because of events such as the one Roberts made happen.

Roberts said that he faced great prejudice at USC, but he felt a duty to his race to go there, deal with it, and forge a path for others.

"I felt that somebody had to go and it might as well be me," Roberts said. "I wanted to contribute something."

Art Spander grew up in Los Angeles and attended UCLA, where he worked in the sports information department. Later, he worked for the *Santa Monica Evening Outlook* before moving to the *San Francisco Examiner*, where he worked for decades.

"Not to take a knock at USC, but the Trojans were late at integrating until C. R. Roberts," said Spander. "UCLA remained competitive in basketball and football because they brought in lots of blacks. Rafer Johnson and guys like that. They got the best black athletes in southern California."

Spander, being a Bruin, may be excused for taking "a shot" at USC. The school had provided opportunities for black athletes and black students for half a century prior to C. R. Roberts. But Spander was right in that it was UCLA who provided the *most* opportunity up until this time. This was the pillar of their rapid rise in all sports.

Roberts gained 1,309 yards in his career, averaging 6.5 per carry, but it was a struggle. As a freshman, he found himself on the second string, and he strongly suspected that race was at issue. He received anonymous letters urging him to quit school. He claimed that in practice his blockers "laid down for me" and tipped the defense off as to the play, causing him to get gang-tackled. But by late 1955 his talents had shone through. He got significant playing time in the UCLA and Notre Dame games.

By the time USC traveled to Texas in Roberts's junior year, he had earned the admiration of his teammates. Now it was time to reach out to the rest of the world.

"This was one of those rare times when an integrated team came down to Austin, and I was supposed to stay somewhere else than where the team stayed," Roberts said. "But the team said they'd prefer to have me with them, and the team wouldn't go unless I stayed in the same hotel. It was quite a problem then, because the whole team got hate mail after all—all from California. The guys didn't get excited, though.

"Black people from Texas came in and took me out. That took the edge off everything. It was one of the most wonderful road trips I ever had."

Hill's assertion that there had not been any racial problems may have been viewed through the prism of rose-tinted glasses. The fact is, there were problems, and his response to it was heroic. When Roberts was barred from the team hotel, at great expense and logistical trouble, Hill moved the entire team to other lodgings. This no doubt took away from the team's concentration and the staff's preparation, but rather than leave the Trojans befuddled, it seemed to coalesce them as a group.

Roberts played only twelve minutes, all in the first half. In that time—and this is not a typographical error—he gained *251 yards*! The joke was that he set a record for yards gained but did not get enough playing time to earn a varsity letter.

"Most of my runs were like for 60, 50 and 47 yards," Roberts said. "Hill took me out early because he thought there might be trouble. Actually I was glad to get out. The other players said a few bad things. I expected it."

When Hill reached 250 yards, he said Texas actually started saying "nice things" to the stocky-legged running back from San Diego County. According to reports, the Longhorns were convinced by Roberts's performance; they offered congratulatory handshakes, saying he was a "good man" and "a better man than me."

The fans continued to catcall Roberts to the end. The response of the fan in the diner who, according to Hill, had said, "I don't know too much about this thing, segregation, integration, . . . and I believe in *him* [Roberts]," may have been an isolated incident, but not one reflective of a whole state.

Marv Goux was a teammate of Roberts's in 1955. He was not at the game in Austin, but he had the unique perspective of being C.R.'s teammate and Cunningham's coach at Birmingham. Goux would be an assistant under John McKay and John Robinson until 1982.

"C.R. was a competitor," Goux said in one of the last interviews he granted, in 2000, prior to his untimely passing in 2002. "A man like that, when he earns something, he's gonna take what's his without asking. That was our philosophy at USC. We played clean, we played hard, we played to win.

"The fact is, C. R. played a better game against Texas than Sam did against Alabama, but Sam's game is the one we remember, because the time was not right in the 1950s. Later, with Vietnam and the protests, Martin Luther King and the civil rights movement, Sam was the right man in the right place at the right time. But C. R. Roberts was an extraordinary player, man, and Trojan!"

The USC-Texas game is an important benchmark in the integration of college football, but the last hurdle would not fully be overcome until well after it had happened in baseball, basketball, pro football, boxing, track, and tennis.

However, there were other landmark events. Years earlier, Michigan had agreed to sit out a star black player whom Georgia Tech objected to if

Tech sat out one of their own players. Michigan star Gerald Ford, later the president of the United States, hit a Tech player who uttered the epithet "n--r" so hard the man had to be carried off the field.

The 1955 Navy-Mississippi Sugar Bowl and the 1956 Pitt-Georgia Tech Sugar Bowl also were significant. The former was the first major game in the South where there was not segregated seating because Navy had distributed its tickets without racial consideration, and the bowl honored that. The latter was the first major game in the South with an African American (Pitt's Bobby Grier) starting for one of the teams. After that game, Louisiana passed a law not allowing integrated play, but the "genie was out of the bottle." The Supreme Court struck down that law later on.

The role of the Sugar Bowl was huge in both drawing attention to segregation and (reluctantly at first) helping to eliminate it. The Sugar Bowl, being the premier college game in the South at the time, had a national significance that other games did not. Until the Pitt game, teams from the North who played in the game would either not bring their black players or agree not to suit them up. In the years after World War II, St. Mary's and the University of San Francisco had dealt with problems trying to play in Southern bowl games.

Other great black stars made major marks on the game. Syracuse built themselves into a huge powerhouse with Jim Brown. Brown is probably the greatest running back in NFL history. He was just as good at Syracuse but did not win the Heisman Trophy, mostly because he was black. Later, black running back Ernie Davis would win the coveted Heisman for Syracuse in 1961. He was the first black recipient of the trophy.

C. R. Roberts would have other great games, but none as spectacular or as important as the Texas game. Prejudice did not end that day in Austin. He continued to find it, sometimes in unlikely places, such as when a Washington player bit him in a pileup.

Interestingly, Roberts "chose" USC, not vice versa. A top-notch student at Carlsbad High School, he was hoping to go to West Point, which was making a major push to integrate its school after the war years. But Roberts wanted to make the point that a black player could succeed not just at an egalitarian public school, UCLA, but also at a private one, USC. He was weak in math, but the school offered him a tutor, and he made it through.

Roberts missed his last year because of the recruiting scandal, playing for the Toronto Argonauts in Canada. He returned to finish his business studies at USC, then signed with the New York Giants. He was not Frank

Gifford's teammate very long, though. He was traded to Pittsburgh, but he left because he claimed Pittsburgh's racial climate was "intolerable."

Roberts landed on his feet with the San Francisco 49ers, where he teamed with Y. A. Tittle, R. C. Owens, and J. D. Smith in the great all-initial backfield that earned fame in the years prior to Vince Lombardi's Packer dynasty. He played alongside Stanford's John Brodie, but after settling their Trojan-Indian differences it worked out well.

C.R. (R stands for "nothing," but C stands for Cornelius) played briefly again in Canada, then returned to teach at Lawndale High School, near the Los Angeles Airport.

"I'd do it all over again," he said. "It was a tough row to hoe, but it was worth it."

Roberts's game at Texas was a shining moment in USC's civil rights legacy, but for a period of years, UCLA did provide more opportunity for black athletes than did USC. As a result they won the 1954 national title and were every bit the Trojans' equal on the football field, at least until the scandals hurt both programs.

Then came John McKay. Nobody opened more doors for black athletes than McKay. A new golden era not only of USC football but also of the USC-Notre Dame rivalry began in the 1960s. The legendary Coach McKay's Trojans won the 1962 national championship in an undefeated manner. This began a twenty-season run that is arguably the most dominant in college history. McKay captured more national championships in 1967, 1972, and 1974. His replacement, John Robinson, won one in 1978. Between 1965 and 1981, USC tailbacks won four Heisman Trophies, establishing the school as "Tailback U."

McKay's and Robinson's success were nearly matched during the "era of Ara"—the ten-year run of Notre Dame coach Ara Parseghian—and in subsequent years in which Joe Montana led the Dan Devine–coached Irish to the 1977 number one ranking.

In 1964, McKay's Trojans trailed off toward season's end, while Parseghian's Irish rolled through their schedule unbeaten. Their final game was versus USC at the Coliseum. In those days, Notre Dame eschewed bowl games, so winning the season finale meant their first national title since 1949. Led by Heisman quarterback John Huarte, Notre Dame led 17–0 at the half, but USC quarterback Craig Fertig brought Troy back in the second half. Fertig hit Rod Sherman over the middle with little time left to spoil Ara's first season.

Running back Mike Garrett, now USC's athletic director, won the Heisman Trophy in 1965, and O. J. Simpson matched that in 1968. In 1979, Charles White won his, and Marcus Allen won one in 1981.

The 1972 Trojans (12–0) were for years considered to be the greatest single-season team of all time. Two years later, USC finished number one again after scoring fifty-five straight points in seventeen minutes to beat Notre Dame and coming from behind versus Ohio State in the Rose Bowl, 18–17. In 1978, the Trojans won again under John Robinson.

After a down period, Pete Carroll (hired in 2000) declared, "It's a good day to be a Trojan!" In 2002, quarterback Carson Palmer won the Heisman Trophy. USC won two consecutive national championships in 2003 and 2004, establishing itself as the greatest collegiate tradition ever. The 2005 team threatened to replace the 1972 Trojans as the "greatest of all time" until losing to Texas in the Rose Bowl. Quarterback Matt Leinart won the 2004 Heisman Trophy. Teammate Reggie Bush won the award in 2005. In 2006, Bush was the second pick in the NFL Draft. Leinart went number ten in the first round.

On top of all this, USC counts the most baseball national championships (twelve), the most Major Leaguers, the most Hall of Famers, the most All-Stars, and various dominant players. Despite USC's not being known for basketball, a disproportionate number of Trojans from the 1940s and 1950s are considered hoops pioneers. The "triangle offense" was invented at USC. Such stalwarts as Bill Sharman, Alex Hannum, and Tex Winter played under coach Sam Barry. Hannum and Sharman were inducted into the Basketball Hall of Fame in Springfield, Massachusetts.

USC also boasts (along with UCLA) the most Olympians and the most Olympic champions, and if the university had been a country in 1976, it would have been a medals leader at the Montreal Summer Games. The USC track team has won an insane twenty-six NCAA titles (plus two indoor titles), the school has earned nine swimming and diving national championships; sixteen men's tennis and seven women's tennis titles; six men's volleyball and six women's volleyball titles; and various other national titles in men's and women's gymnastics, water polo, basketball, and golf.

* * *

Outside of USC and Notre Dame, the other great powers of college football are Oklahoma and Alabama. These teams already had incredible traditions in 1969, a time in which the country and college football were changing or about to change. Oklahoma, despite its location in the hard-scrabble Southwest town of Norman, courageously integrated its program under legendary coach Bud Wilkinson in the 1950s.

Alabama and the South—certainly the Deep South—were still all white. In Texas, coach Darrell Royal was able to hang on to his all-white policy, winning national championships in 1963 and 1969. His Longhorns defeated another all-white team, Arkansas, in 1969's so-called game of the century. By 1971, Texas integrated with running back Roosevelt Leaks.

By the 1930s, Alabama was a power, led by All-American receiver Don Hutson. In 1961, coach Bear Bryant erased doubts by winning the national championship. His 1964 team, featuring the great Joe Namath, was voted number one after the regular season, but the Tide lost to Texas in the Orange Bowl. Arkansas (with future Cowboys coach and owner Jimmy Johnson and Jerry Jones) is popularly thought to be the legitimate 1964 national champ.

In 1965 Bryant won an undisputed title. In 1966 Ken Stabler took his team to an Orange Bowl victory. They were denied the national championship by voters, very possibly as an unofficial "sanction" against their segregated roster (although Texas, with President Nixon's "blessing," won the vote over unbeaten, integrated Penn State three years later).

Still, with multiple national championships in the 1960s, Bryant was a bona fide legend in Alabama and throughout Dixie. But the game *was* changing.

Other Voices: Tom Kelly

The first time many people heard the story about Paul "Bear" Bryant holding Sam "Bam" Cunningham up before his team and declaring, "Gentlemen, this here's what a football player looks like," was when Tom Kelly stated it in the 1987 Trojan Video Gold, *which accompanied his book detailing the first hundred years of USC football. Tom has for years covered USC football on radio and television.*

John McKay was the greatest quotemeister of all time. By contrast, UCLA's Tommy Prothro gave one memorable quote. He said something about "the only guy who could have caught him is the one who made the catch." That was a direct rip-off of Gene Mauch, who said of Willie Mays, "The only guy who could have caught it hit it."

McKay and USC integrated the South with this game. I was there, in the press box, but not in the Alabama locker room. This was not the first time that USC integrated the South. C. R. Roberts and the Trojans went down to Texas in 1956. C.R. told me that first of all, there was another member of the team who was passing as white. When they came to the hotel, the guy at the hotel said to Jess Hill of C.R., "Is he with you?" and Jess said if he can't stay we're not staying. Word got out, and the room was full of ministers, cab drivers—the whole black community showed up afraid that somebody was going to get killed. They protected C.R.

As for 1970, I fully understand the story about McKay and Cunningham and Bryant, and about how it could have happened in the hallway instead of the Alabama locker room. Yes, that place was crowded, and it could have been there. Legion Field is in the "darkest" part of town; you have to drive through a terrible neighborhood to get there, not unlike the Coliseum. But I never knew much about race problems. All I knew is we had a hellacious football team.

That team was loaded with talent, but Stanford beat us two years in a row. I don't care about Don Bunce or Jim Plunkett. I've often thought but nobody said it, these were freshmen or sophomores who'd make up the 1972 national champions, but I've often thought they had racial problems of their own. They were too good not to win. Stanford was good, but we had no business losing. I respect Rod McNeill, and if he and a few others say the 1970 and '71 teams had some racial problems, well as I say, I never said it but it confirms suspicions I've had for years. I do think there was tension over the fact that Jimmy Jones was a black quarterback, while Mike Rae, who was spectacular, sat behind him.

I think the bottom line is we might have had better talent than 'Bama. In all the games they played, Bear beat him here and we beat 'em down there. Bryant could sure coach.

Just to think, on a team with racial problems, Marv Goux intimidated people and would call linebackers "spider monkeys," and eight of ten of 'em were black, but he could care less what a man's skin color was, not to mention if somebody took umbrage with Goux he'd probably sock 'em.

If you wanna read a good book, read Jim Perry's *McKay: A Coach's Story*. I really don't know what to say about the game that season. McNeill said there was a race problem; maybe it was just the fact they were that good and got overconfident. It might have been animosity toward Jones and Mike Rae. . . .

I'd have to go back a long way, but Brice Taylor was an All-American in 1925, and Willie Wood played quarterback for McKay. It was never "Who wants a black quarterback?" Maybe McKay felt he was forced to play Jones.

I just don't know, I was too close to it. Rae was highly recruited and later played behind Stabler in Oakland. He played extremely well in 1972, but I thought the 1979 team, talentwise, was the greatest ever in college football. I say to Paul McDonald, your all-time biggest problem was who to hand off to, Heisman winner Charlie White or Heisman winner Marcus Allen? Anthony Munoz is blocking. Ronnie Lott's on defense. Holy cow!

The all-time greatest college football programs are Notre Dame, Ohio State, Oklahoma, Texas, Alabama, Florida State, and USC, not in that order. Over any given ten-year period, each one could have the number one spot by themselves. Florida State went from a girl's school to a national power. Oklahoma always has a big reputation. Notre Dame's hit hard times, but the average fan thinks they're sensational. Ohio State is always a worthy opponent, and USC starting with McKay, God rest his soul, brought the West Coast up to the top. Until McKay, the Big 10 thought the Rose Bowl was a time to meet pretty girls, go to the beach, then kick a–s. Nobody's a better coach than McKay. John Robinson's players got along better, but McKay must have learned his lessons because from 1972 to 1974, nobody's ever been better.

Until he and his good old friend Bob Flour had their last misunderstanding, he was 7–0 going to 7–5 in 1975. He quit at Cal. Chuck Muncie's on that team, too. Before the end of the half, USC didn't score from the two. They rolled over and died and ended up in the Bluebonnet Bowl or someplace against Texas A&M. Marv Goux took over and refused to let 'em go down with six losses in row.

There are guys for the times in business, politics, and sports. He was a man for his times for USC, as was the man who hired him, Norm Topping.

I love the John Wayne story "flipping off" the Texas fans with his Longhorn "finger." Half those Texans didn't know he had gone to USC.

Other Voices: Mike Walden

Mike Walden is one of those guys who, when you hear him, you immediately recall. He has the perfect sportscaster's voice—deep and melodramatic. Mike was USC's radio man, describing the game from Birmingham to Southern California football fans on the evening of September 12, 1970. Prior to that, he had worked with Ray Scott on Green Bay Packers broadcasts during the Vince Lombardi–Bart Starr era that was the 1960s, thus immortalizing his style in endless NFL highlight tapes. Aside from USC football, he also announced for crosstown rival UCLA, making him the only local announcer to broadcast for both schools.

Well, that game opened the floodgates to get blacks recruited in Southern schools. I did that game; it was the first game of the 1970 season from Legion Field, and there were about eighty thousand people in the stands to watch Bear Bryant's Crimson Tide versus John McKay's USC Trojans.

Now Corky McKay was good friends with Mary Harmon Bryant, and of course Bryant and McKay were very close, so the extent to which this game involved some kind of plan as it relates to integration seems very plausible to my way of thinking.

I was not unfamiliar with the South, as I'd been in the Air Force in Montgomery when Bart Starr was coming up, and of course with the Packers I'd known Starr and was most familiar with Alabama through him.

On the famous quotes from that game. Now, you're telling me that the Bryant quote, "This here's what a football player looks like," which is something I have always heard and never questioned, is something that some people in that Alabama locker room are now saying never happened. Unfortunately, I cannot verify it one way or the other. As soon as the game was over, I had to dash to the airport for an Atlanta–St. Louis Cardinals football game, and then a flight to New York, as I was doing a New York Mets baseball game. What I do remember was Beano Cook was on the same plane with me. I also remember a story where Bryant supposedly said, "I've gotta get me some a those *Puerto Ricans.*"

Now Sam Cunningham was from Santa Barbara, but Clarence Davis was from Birmingham. As for who might have said that Bryant quote, about Sam being what a "football player looks like," it could have been a writer. Mal Florence used to tell people that, at Rotary Clubs and gatherings, you know. I think Tom Kelly was there, too. I was the radio announcer from 1966 to 1972. John McKay convinced me the 1972 team was the best in the history of college football, but I now feel the 2004 USC team under Pete Carroll is the greatest team I've ever seen.

Jerry Claiborne said, "Sam did more for civil rights in one game than civil rights leaders over the last twenty years or so."

On USC's performance. Johnny Musso was called "the Italian Stallion." I recall Musso did not have a great game that day. Charlie Weaver put the clamps on him. Another factor was that the USC quarterback, Jimmy Jones, was black.

I don't recall hearing black fans outside the stadium, but I had a headset on. Maybe I heard a chant, but the crowd was quiet, I do recall that. I was on the third floor of the press box. They were feeling like, "We're gonna show 'em. They can't come down to our house." Well, USC sure *did* show 'em.

Now, John McKay is overlooked. Everybody talks about Tailback U. and all that, but he was a damn good defensive coach with great assistants. Joe Gibbs was on that staff.

On the Southern football culture. Now, the publicity guy from Alabama, Charlie Thornton, who was well known, used to do a show with Bryant on Sunday. Maybe it was on that show that Bryant said Cunningham "looked like a football player."

I recall that it was the first game of the season, and everybody was anticipating great things from 'Bama. I really don't think they knew all that much about USC. They knew about McKay, of course. When the Trojans just came out of the gate the way they did, it turned the crowd way down. I felt the crowd; they were almost all in their seats fifteen minutes prior to the game, not like an L.A. crowd, which is late arriving—guys trying to meet girls, a big social whirl at the Coliseum, you know how that is. But they take it seriously down there.

We did not realize it at the time, but we could look back and realize it was a big tipping point. It just wasn't a big thing at that time, about Alabama having no blacks. As the season ended, then on reflection, I realized the game was special, and maybe it focused on the fact that, yes, there were problems down South and they needed to be addressed.

Now, I know that John McKay said he wanted to beat Stanford by two thousand points, but I don't know that story about Stanford students yelling racial epithets. I don't know about that. I do know he had a "thing" going with Jack Christiansen. After the 1972 game, I think, McKay said, "I never want to get in a pissing contest with a skunk."

But regarding the Southern people, well football is so big there; they realized they can't get it done with white players only. Now, I don't make it out to be a big moral thing with them. In my view, I would just say it was football. They wanted to win, and they realized if they wanted to be at that level, "we can't let 'em [blacks] go." At Illinois, Ray Elliott had J. C. Caroline and Mickey Bates, and Caroline was from the South, and that made a big difference. He was from South Carolina and played for the Bears. Bates played for somebody, too. I can't recall.

On his USC experience. Chick Hearn was doing USC football, but he was also the announcer on Channel Four and then the Lakers. The athletic director was Jess Hill, and he said if Hearn is going to be the USC announcer, he has to make a choice, and he chose the Lakers. Then Tom

Kelly came on the scene. I was in Wisconsin doing Milwaukee Braves games. Tom goes to Channel Eleven, and then they bring me in

Tom Kelly is from Peoria, and I'm from Springfield, Illinois. I did USC football on radio from 1966 to 1972, then went back to something later called OnTV. I recall Pat Haden lived in the McKay household, and somebody asked if McKay was worried that another school might get Haden and McKay's son, J. K. McKay replied that one guy slept in the upstairs bedroom, and he [McKay] slept with the other guy's mother.

That comment was typical of McKay. He and the L.A. media were a marriage made in Heaven. McKay and the media had a more enjoyable relationship than what we see today, which is departmentalized—you gotta go to this guy for this contact. My method of operating was to make it a point at noon on Thursday to talk to all the assistants. I got great staff stories in themselves this way. I'd do this between 3:30 and 5:30 on Thursday; this was forty hours before the game.

On USC's personalities. Marv Goux could be so dynamic. He could get players to run through a brick wall, especially before the Notre Dame game. He was a fierce competitor. When he was at USC, about 1954–1955, he played center and linebacker at 180 pounds.

Sam Cunningham was so powerful a runner, with a big smile, a great grin, but I'd not see him every day. I'd see him on Thursdays, but his performance was just like he was, a powerful guy.

John Papadakis—pronounced PAP-A-DAKE-ISS—his mother was a screenwriter. He runs a restaurant in San Pedro. I used to sit next to his mother once in a while on game days. John was an outstanding linebacker who made key plays. I would go to his restaurant in later years. Great place, and he'd put on a show with the plates and with his parents. We just would go down there for dinner after games.

Nick Pappas was another Greek fellow. There always was a big Greek community at USC. Pappas was friends with John Wayne.

My first game in 1966 was on the road versus Texas. There'd be a press gathering in Austin, what they called "smokers" down there, where everybody got together. Well, Wayne was down there making *War Wagon* in nearby Mexico, and he shows up with Bruce Cabot.

"I'm gonna have some whiskey," Wayne says to the bartender, who pours it, and Wayne just looks at it, shoves it back, and says, "*I said WHISKEY!*"

Texas had a quarterback they called Super Bill Bradley who was supposed to be outstanding, but USC just controlled the ball and won, 10–6.

Afterward, Goux came in and said wasn't it great, "We didn't get anybody 'chipped off.'" Well, Wayne and Cabot were somewhere, and someone got in an argument the next morning, and their makeup artist was dead of a heart attack. It was confusing. I don't know for sure what all happened. Wayne and all of 'em were out drinking all night and came in at seven in the morning; maybe it was too much for this guy, but this makeup artist died.

Well, Cabot said, "*We* got somebody 'chipped off,'" after Goux said, "We didn't get anybody 'chipped off.'"

On black players at USC. Jimmy Jones was a leader. He was well liked and had a good arm. Jones had a good receiver named Sam Dickerson; he made some great catches in the old Coliseum to help USC win a lot of games, particularly the end of the 1969 UCLA game. Jones was intelligent. I understand he's a Christian minister now, but I don't know really what a kid does regarding his religious values. My radio interviews were only for three minutes.

Jones was not the first black quarterback. Minnesota had a guy named Sandy Stephens who was black, playing for Murray Warmouth, maybe in 1962. There was Jimmy Raye at Michigan State.

My final thoughts are that expectations and hopes were high after that game, then USC hit a slump through the midpart of the season, so it was not quite the great year we all thought it would be. They think 2005 is gonna be a big year; USC is favored to try to win it [the national championship] for the second time in four years, but to repeat is easier said than done.

I remember the Green Bay Packers hired Phil Bengston. He was an outstanding assistant, but not a great head coach. This is like Norm Chow. Everybody wants all the credit, but only some coaches are cut out to be head coaches.

John McKay was a "Jekyll and Hyde" kind of personality, but I always respected him after the 1966 Notre Dame game. He lost 51–0. Notre Dame had an All-American center, I think named George Goedecke. He played only one or two games that year; he'd been injured but had earned All-American the previous year. On the last play of the game, Notre Dame sent him in and McKay told players not to block him, to see to it he didn't reinjure himself. After the game, and remember this was the first year of the Cultural Revolution, McKay told the writers that "a billion Chinese don't give a damn whether we won this game or not" to put it into perspective.

Still, USC played hard in the Rose Bowl. Unlike Ara Parseghian, who had laid down and gone for a tie, when USC scored at the end to make it 14–13 in favor of Purdue, he chose to go for two instead of a tie. USC failed, but I respected him for it.

I started doing UCLA basketball after 1972. I wanted J. D. Morgan's blessing, so I insisted we get ahold of him vacationing in Hawaii, and he just said, "Mike, I've always respected your work, and you'll be just fine."

CHAPTER Ten

The Generals

In a few years, you're all gonna be black.
—*Bear Bryant speaking to his team,* Unconquered

Paul "Bear" Bryant looked like a hound dog, his visage accentuated by the fact he wore a houndstooth hat. He had big floppy jowls, sleepy eyes, and craggy, sunburned skin; and his ears made him look like a taxi going down the street with the doors open, which probably was the reason for the houndstooth hat.

Bear was friends with Oakland A's owner Charles O. Finley. One of the A's minor league affiliates was in Birmingham. The club's general manager was Bryant's son, Paul Jr. In 1966, Bryant attended a game there as a guest of Finley's. The A's top minor league prospect was Reggie Jackson, who had also been a football star at Arizona State, playing for the legendary disciplinarian Frank Kush. At the conclusion of the game, Finley took Bryant into the Birmingham locker room, introducing him to Reggie. Jackson was quite a sight: bare chested, with huge biceps, a bulging chest, and full lats.

"You're just the kinda n--r we could use at Alabama," Jackson says Bryant told him.

"I didn't let it upset me," Reggie later recalled. "I took it as a compliment, which is how he meant it; it was how men of that generation and region talked."

Extensive interviews with Bryant's colleagues and intimates, in Alabama and throughout the United States, lend dispute to Jackson's claim. Nobody, black or white, could recall Bryant using the word *n—r* at any time. Perhaps he used the familiar Southern moniker *nigra* or *Negro*. Maybe Jackson's memory of the event is faulty.

In a movie about Richmond Flowers Jr., titled *Unconquered*, Bryant (who helped young Richmond get a scholarship to the University of Alabama Law School) is depicted as predicting the future.

"In a few years," he told his players, "you're all gonna be black."

John McKay was an iconoclastic, cigar-chomping, conservative Republican West Virginia Irish Catholic. He was a good ol' boy at heart and by Southern upbringing. He did not particularly like to hunt and fish, but he liked to sip whiskey. He could be persuaded to go duck huntin' if he had a flask to bring along.

McKay had made his way out West, to the University of Oregon, where he played football for the Ducks. His athletic talent was good but limited. He was also a tail gunner in World War II.

His coaching talent was not limited. After his playing days and military service ended, McKay landed a position on the Ducks staff. It took very little time for his star to rise and for his name to be bandied about as a potential head coach.

The standards at USC were almost impossible to meet, thanks to Howard Jones and his four national championships from 1928 to 1939. In 1959, Don Clark, a very creditable coach who had taken over from Jess Hill in the wake of a recruiting scandal that knocked the whole Pacific Coast Conference off-kilter, led the Trojans to victories in their first eight games.

After going 1–9 in 1957 and 4–5–1 in 1958, things looked to be back to normal at Troy. The last two games were against traditional rivals UCLA and Notre Dame. The Trojans demonstrated zero offense against the Bruins at the Coliseum, falling 10–3 before 85,917. The next week they traveled to freezing South Bend and fell again, 16–6, to Notre Dame.

In three years, Clark lost three straight to the Irish and twice (with a tie) to UCLA. Southern California had not won at Notre Dame for twenty years. On top of this, USC found itself on probation again, and not just the football program. USC's baseball team, which in 1959 was 23–4–1 and thought to be the best collegiate team of all time, was denied a chance to play in the College World Series due to football transgressions. Enough was enough.

The selection of McKay resulted in a great big rhetorical *thud* in Los Angeles, though.

"John *who*?"

He was a young man, with a crew cut and piercing eyes, usually in a white dress shirt with a thin tie on game day. At practice he wore a letter jacket and a USC baseball cap. He cracked jokes, but without the backing of a record they fell flat. In 1960 and 1961, he fell flat, too, going 4–6 and 4–5–1, including combined losses to Notre Dame of *47–0!* He beat UCLA the first year but in 1961 fell to the Bruins, 10–7.

Clark had been gone in three years. USC has never been a school that messes around. In the modern era, McKay would have been given the heave-ho like Paul Hackett, who from 1998 to 2000 enjoyed considerably more success than McKay from 1960 to 1961.

"I need speed," McKay told his staff.

Speed? Read: black athletes.

UCLA had all the best black stars. Jackie Robinson, Kenny Washington, Rafer Johnson, just to name a few. USC had a decent record, with players such as C. R. Roberts, future Packer Willie Wood, and future baseball star Don Buford. However, UCLA had passed USC because they had the best black football players, and now their basketball coach, John Wooden, was on the verge of building a dynasty using the same strategy.

UCLA under Red Sanders, a Southerner who liked to pull a cork and chase skirts until he died in flagrante delicto in a Sunset Strip cathouse, had gone after the black stars who dotted the Los Angeles prep landscape. They won the 1954 national championship, and in that decade UCLA beat their crosstown rival by scores like 13–0 and 34–0, in front of enormous crowds that topped a hundred thousand at the Coliseum. They had all the city bragging rights, and it was downright embarrassing.

So when John McKay said he wanted *speed*, his recruiting staff knew exactly what that meant. It took a couple of years, but by 1962 the Trojans had speed. Willie Brown from Long Beach Poly High School and Mike Garrett from Roosevelt High in L.A. were two examples of black blue-chippers who, a few years earlier, would have chosen to be Bruins.

In that 1962 season, Southern California exorcised twenty-three years of demons. They beat UCLA 14–3 and Notre Dame 25–0. They beat Wisconsin 42–37 in a wild Rose Bowl, when Brown intercepted Ron VanderKelen's last-second pass into the end zone. They were the national champions again.

In 1963, Bear Bryant and John McKay attended a coaches' clinic. It was one of those high school get-togethers in which top collegiate coaches would be headlined at a camp full of prep hopefuls, whose parents either paid for their attendance or, if they were good enough, who were sponsored by their high schools. Today, these camps are big business, advertised in sports magazines all over the nation. In 1963, it was still a pretty cozy affair. For coaches such as Bryant and McKay, it was a chance to relax, get in some recruiting, play golf, and drink.

These became regular events for both coaches. Sometimes Bryant would bring his elegant Southern wife, Mary Harmon, and McKay his spunky spouse, Corky. Sometimes they did not. In the twilight of the evening, they would relax in the glow of cocktails, tell tall tales, and make knowing laughter. A friendship was born.

Bryant loved California and made it to the Golden State whenever he could. When his teams won more national championships, his recruiting base expanded. No longer did he pick his team from a wild-eyed, play-above-their-heads group of Alabama country boys. With success came the notoriety of prima donna high school stars from Florida, the Midwest, and California, a nice problem to have, maybe, but one that caused more than a few bumps in the road.

McKay also enjoyed off-season trips to the South. He had his pick of black prep stars in Bryant's neck of the woods. They were going to schools such as USC and Michigan State because schools such as Alabama and Georgia were off-limits. McKay would drop in on the Bear, and they would head down to a lodge Bryant kept on the 'Bama coast—"the Redneck Riviera" they liked to call it. They would sit in duck blinds sippin' whiskey and talkin' football, women, and life. They would take a few shots at the ducks. They were better at drinkin' and coachin' than at huntin', but they had camaraderie.

McKay never rubbed it in, the fact that he could get the Jimmy Joneses, the Tody Smiths, the Clarence Davises, while Bear's idea of ethnic recruiting was restricted to guys nicknamed the Italian Stallion (Johnny Musso) or Greek fellas from Ohio (Christ Vagotis). Vagotis was so exotic that when he was introduced by a booster at the team banquet, the drunkard stated, "Well, hell, this fella *Fag*-otis, why we don' know what he is, but at least he ain' no *Negro!*"

This was what Bear Bryant was up against when it came to changing the world. McKay was sympathetic to his plight. The two would talk about how someday things would be different, and when that happened it would be better for everybody.

"We'll come out there to the Coliseum," Bryant told McKay, referring to a future with blacks wearing the Crimson Tide, "and it'll be like a *high-speed train*." McKay did not see black or white, only Cardinal and Gold. In 1965, his star black running back, Mike Garrett, won the Heisman Trophy. Three years later, O. J. Simpson won it, too. USC won national championships in 1962 and 1967. McKay's offensive schemes were not intricate. The press took to calling his pounding running attack Student Body Right. When asked why he handed the ball to O.J. so often, McKay quipped, "Why not? The ball ain't heavy, and he's not in a union."

In 1969, USC went undefeated with black quarterback Jimmy Jones and black running back Clarence Davis, who hailed from Birmingham, Alabama. Texas still won the national championship. They would be the last all-white team to finish number one, but something was in the air.

* * *

In the 1960s, Bob Troppmann was an innovator. A native of San Francisco, he had grown up in the glory days of the city's high school sports, days when the likes of Joe and Dom DiMaggio, Frank Crosetti, Joe Cronin, Jerry Coleman, and Tony Lazzeri competed on the windswept fields of old Big Rec Park.

Troppmann starred at Lowell High School, then entered the Marines, where he served during World War II. He entered the teaching profession and became a football coach at a brand-new high school in the growing suburbs of Marin County. In the 1960s, Redwood High under Bob Troppmann was a Bay Area gridiron power.

In the mid-to-latter part of that decade, Troppmann came up with a great idea. He saw the growing popularity of the coaching clinics like the one where Bryant and McKay had met, and he started one of his own. It was called the Diamond B Football Camp, and it was an immediate success because he was able to attract top college coaches, among them Bear Bryant and John McKay.

Bryant admired Troppmann, who had a first-class football mind and could have taken it to the next level but chose instead to remain an unsung high school hero. Bryant was quoted as saying, "When I need advice on developing the short passing game, I consult Coach Troppmann's diagrams." It was a little hokey, but it was nice advertising for the Diamond B camp.

McKay would show up with Marv Goux. It was like a fantasy camp for kids, with Goux barking orders in drill sergeant fashion at the kids from the liberal, rich Marin homes.

"Your a–s is mine for the next week. . . ."

"If you don't like it, go cry to your mamas."

One kid who *loved it* was Troppmann's star quarterback and safety, a bright-eyed kid with a natural mind for football named Pete Carroll.

At the end of the Diamond B camp, a banquet was arranged. Bryant, McKay, the camp staff, and other dignitaries drank, laughed, and made speeches. High school coaches from far and wide would show up.

"Send your A students to Cal and Stanford," Bryant told the assembled coaches. "They'll get a fine education. Send your B students to Southern Cal and UCLA. Hell, I'd send my own kin there. Send your C students to one a your fine state schools or junior colleges. They'll find themselves. But y'all send your whiskey-drinkin', skirt-chasin' D students to 'Bama, and ol' Bear'll turn 'em into *football players!*"

The crowd would roar in laughter, appreciating the unspoken reference to two very famous whiskey-drinkin', skirt-chasin' D students named Joe Namath and Ken Stabler.

Sharing a nightcap with McKay after the banquet, Bear contemplated what he had said to the coaches. Sitting next to them, like a guy in those photos of Churchill, FDR, and Stalin at Yalta with a barstool view of history, was a quiet Bob Troppmann.

"Ya know somethin', ol' buddy," Bear said. "About sendin' some a your kids to play for the Bear? We been sendin' our share to play for y'all."

McKay understood his meaning. Bear was talking about black players, but this was a subject that was dealt with in code.

"I think the time's a-comin'," continued Bear, "when that practice is gonna cease."

McKay just tinkled his glass to the other man's.

"From your mouth to God's ears," said John McKay. He turned to Troppmann, who did not realize that he was hearing Bear Bryant talk about things in a way he never talked about in front of his staff. There was the Alabama Bear and the other Bear, the vacation Bear, the California Bear. "Whaddaya think of that, Coach?"

"I would have no objection," replied Coach T.

Other Voices: J. K. McKay

The elder son of Trojan football coach John McKay, the younger John always wore the moniker J.K. to separate him from his father. A star on the 1974 Trojan national championship team, young McKay played in the NFL for Tampa Bay. Known as a laid-back guy who enjoyed partying at Southern California (while his roommate Pat

Haden burned the midnight oil in the other room), McKay eventually went to law
school before forging a successful career as an L.A. attorney and real estate execu-
tive. He has been active in the city's efforts to bring a pro football franchise back in
the years since the Raiders and Rams left town.

When you're talking about the effect of that 1970 game at Birmingham, I
think the caveat I might add, and there's no better fan than I was of Bear
Bryant, but he was frustrated and not sure how to integrate the University
of Alabama. He was a man of great principle, but he was first a football
coach, so you can't underestimate the importance of winning. He was
highly competitive, so winning games was part and parcel of the same goal.
It's a perfect example of a practical goal allowing for an idealistic goal to
flourish.

How it all started, I think they were at a golf tournament out in the
desert. My dad didn't talk after the fact about scheduling it before the
game. I remember him telling us that he and Bear had decided to play. Bear
had asked, and my dad said yes. My take on it then was that it would help
Bear get his program back where it was before.

After the game, my dad told a million times how Bear brought Sam
in to his locker room, introducing him as "what a football player looks
like."

Bryant asked my dad if he could "borrow" Sam, but I'm not sure if it
came in the locker room or when they shook hands on the field. My
impression was he came in the locker room. The story that Bryant's statement occurred in the hallway between the lockers and was in front of
alumni and old-timers, with the door open so Sam could see the Alabama
players undressing, as you tell it, makes sense to me. At banquet after banquet, I know my dad repeated the story. I don't think Bear would say it in
a confrontational way to make a point. In Sam's mind, that hallway may
have seemed like a crowded locker room. Also, 1970 is just two years
removed from 1968, so he probably had a little trepidation.

I've heard the gun stories from John Papadakis. He told me that story,
and it makes some sense. My political take of that 1970 game, you'd
almost have to ask that to the Alabama people, but it meant different
things to different people. The impact on the schools in the South was
tremendous, but not from the immediate USC perspective. Coming out of
difficult times in our country, the game was profound. Those USC teams
were struggling, and I think even USC struggled with race relations. USC
had more white players and fewer black players those years. They had more

than the other schools, but in 1970 and '71, my dad's worst years, you have to ask those guys, but I think there was suspicion. There were problems. When I got there it was in the past if it ever existed at all, and beginning in 1972 our team really came together. Overall, an event like that 1970 game helped achieve that, but it was a rocky road.

You can't go so far as to say the game had a direct cause and effect, but politically it was emblematic of that change, and of the nature of the game that happened since then, but it's part of that story, the transformation of the South, of acceptance of different political points of view.

The interesting larger story, as it relates to my dad, is he's emblematic in the part played by conservatism in the changing of the South. He was a conservative Republican who was totally race neutral. He received death threats in the old days when he started Jimmy Jones, which was not popular even in southern California back then. He was race neutral in all regards. He did not advocate affirmative action, but in his case he believed and lived up to the principle that the job goes to the best man for the job.

His quote about wanting to beat Stanford by not one thousand but *two thousand* points, he said it because he was getting abused by the Stanford rooters. I've heard him tell that story. He talked about the things that were said. He was criticized for having too many blacks, as if Stanford was providing more help to blacks by not having so many. But he provided more opportunity by having more blacks than not just Stanford but also other programs, some of which were more liberal than he was but were not doing as much for minorities.

Other Voices: Sylvester Croom

Sylvester Croom grew up in segregated Tuscaloosa, Alabama. He played for Bear Bryant with the Crimson Tide from 1971 to 1974, played briefly for the New Orleans Saints, and then went back to Alabama as a graduate assistant for one and a half years. Bryant hired him full time in 1977. He was a member of the staff until Bryant's 1982 retirement, and he stayed on under Ray Perkins through 1986. Croom moved to the NFL, at Tampa Bay (1987–1990), Indianapolis (1991), and San Diego, where he coached running backs before taking over as Bobby Ross's offensive coordinator in Detroit through 2000, then at Green Bay through 2003. In 2004, Croom took over as the head football coach at Mississippi State University, making him the first African American head football coach in the history of the Southeastern Conference.

Through football and coaching, I've seen America. That's the great part about it. I adjust to every new city, but I really give credit to my wife, Jeri, because she has to adjust with me. Change doesn't bother me normally. Now I embrace it.

I have friends in every place I've been. I loved San Diego, I loved the organization in Green Bay, I loved Tampa, even Indianapolis, which is my favorite city in pro ball. I've played or coached in all the major cities and seen all kinds of cities when we play abroad. We've played in Japan, in Germany. Football has taken me all over the world. When it comes to education, there's no substitute for travel, and I still have places I want to see.

On integration at 'Bama. The idea of a black player in that program at Alabama was not possible; even when Tennessee got a black player, it was not a possibility to me. Yes, Alabama had a few black students; they had a couple of token walk-ons. But when they signed Wendell Hudson to play basketball, then you thought, *It's a possibility.* Then they signed Wilbur Jackson, and after this game we're talking about, *Why, anything could happen, you see.*

As a player, you're not sure if you're good enough. The high schools in my area weren't integrated until the ninth grade. John Stallworth's brother was the first black in my community with any degree of success at a dominant white institution. The whole time I played football, at the same time there's no notion as to where it would lead. You can't see that far; there was no pattern set.

Black athletes up until then went to play up north or out west. Michigan State or Southern Cal got most of 'em. I remember the great Michigan State team with Jimmy Raye, who was from Carolina. Willie Brown was coaching on that USC team. His family was from Tuscaloosa. No black athlete was ever offered a scholarship by Alabama.

In 1970, Wilbur entered the school and there's this game with USC, so suddenly things are caving in now. I graduated [from high school] in 1971, and I guess I was good enough, because here comes Bear Bryant calling.

Now, Craig Fertig says there were five [black] players in the stands from Alabama whom USC was recruiting. John Mitchell ended up at Alabama. I don't know the others. John was the only one who came in the next year, and he gave 'em two good years as a defensive end. I wasn't one of 'em; Southern California never recruited me.

All I know is, John was at Eastern Arizona J.C. But the thing was that, traditionally, Alabama didn't recruit junior college players. I can't name five the whole time I was there.

On Bryant's motivation for setting up the game. I firmly believe the account that Bryant was greasing the skids for Wilbur. He planned everything. He never played a [regular season game against a] team with blacks before then, so why would he schedule the very first game to be in Birmingham? I can't believe it was an accident.

Here's the thing. Bryant was going to do what gave him the best chance to win at the national level. He was far more farsighted than most would be, and I've always believed this: had the climate been right, he would have integrated his team earlier. Look, when I was in junior high, we went places where fans were throwing stuff at us, calling us "n--rs." Bryant was smart enough not to put his team in that situation. He didn't want to have to worry about his team in the hotel. A team eats together as a team, sleeps as a team; you needed an environment that would not treat anybody differently. He was waiting for the right political climate. As long as the times would not allow it, Bryant would not push it ahead of its time.

On the black fans at the game. I was in Tuscaloosa, not Birmingham, so I can't comment on the story about black fans outside the stadium, but Clarence Davis had family there. Family is important in the black community. It's our fallback position, so anytime there's a game, that compounded the situation regarding minority players in the South. In Alabama, at a game, you look for your family.

On progress. As for the change that 1970 brought on, well, it's like Bryant would say about a football game: "Never quit. You never know how it's gonna happen, but it's how it's gonna finish that matters."

The 1970s were a culmination of a hundred years of work. It seems short when it happened, because it took so long [to get there]. Jerry Claiborne's comment about Sam Cunningham doing more in a few hours than Dr. King had done, that signifies as much the great reality of what football is in this part of the country. It was a time of turmoil, not an easy time, the 1960s and '70s, but I wouldn't give it up for anything, for having lived that time. There was so much change, when you talk about from 1954 on up to the 1970s, and it just accelerated in the '60s, what with assassinations, civil rights, Vietnam, women's rights—so much was happening. Yes, it was difficult but exciting. It was always something new, change. The civil rights movement was a big part because for the first time you could openly talk about the problems about race.

On religion's influence on the game. Now, you ask about the moral equation . . . the "trinity" of democracy, Christianity, and capitalism—why I've got to say, I think you're on to something there, yes, you are!

Football was king in the South, with huntin' and fishin' right after that. No question, that was the catalyst; but again, other things had been playing in the South as the schools were integrating. Yes, there was a moral standpoint, from Christian vows to democracy. That was the thing: when will the nation's principles be a reality in this part of the country? You gotta understand, during this time, athletes and students at integrated schools were handpicked. Athletics was so critical as far as making integration move forward. You had to make sure the black students would do nothing that would impede acceptance.

So this goes to the question of hearts and minds. Regarding this game, it was played and the outcome has happened, so white folks now are saying, "In order to compete, we need to integrate schools at all levels." Now, acceptance really happens. This is what's so important. . . . When blacks entered colleges, *myths* were broken—myths that we could not compete academically or athletically, that our morals were less—all that was shattered. A lot of white students, I know this, this was the first time they were exposed to blacks at every level, and you could tell from the questions they asked.

This made a huge difference. It's still huge to have black heroes; that's the significance of my hiring at Mississippi State. This goes to what you were telling me about Keith Dunnavant, who grew up in the 1970s and his heroes were Ozzie Newsome or Wilbur Jackson. Still, the problem exists today. Here it is, thirty years later, and we're still talking about a lot of the same things.

On Bear Bryant. Coach Bryant treated me well for the eleven years I was there. If you are racist, racist at the core, and you're around for eleven years, it'll show up. Nobody's that good an actor.

He never did or said anything in which he did not have all of his players' interests at heart. We'd have a staff meeting, and the whole hour in the meeting, we'd be talking about a kid—as a person, what life would be like for him when he got out, maybe even talk about a player who's graduated, does he need help? Bryant was concerned about *all* his players. Forget the games he won; the games were a by-product of his genuine concern for all players, black and white. He had personal feelings for all of them. Now it's too much about business, all about how many games we win, the money you make, not the players' welfare; you even see it in high schools plus college. Bryant wanted you to graduate if it took seven years. He always said, anybody who went there, there was absolutely no reason not to graduate.

Bryant understands and was smart enough to stay out of politics. One year he endorsed the governor's race, maybe it was Richmond Flowers Sr., and oh what a mistake that was. Bryant understood why Flowers's son needed to go to Tennessee; there was no way that kid could survive at Alabama. What his family went through, they are unsung heroes of the civil rights movement. I would not have wanted to go through that.

You see, leadership is service. It's sacrifice. If you want to lead, you have to serve. Now people think a leader is in charge or in power, but a leader is like the life of Christ. There was no greater leader or server.

The Bear was a complex individual. A lot of people will never totally understand all that he did; they see a country guy, but he was as "crazy as a fox." No question, everything he said and did had a motive to it. Bryant understood his team better than anybody. He was not gonna put himself in a situation not to win—he wanted that game—but I believe in my heart that he saw the bigger picture, and that some way, somehow, he saw that a loss to an integrated USC team at Legion Field would hurt, but over time it would pay off with wins. You can't argue with the next ten years of success he enjoyed!

CHAPTER **Eleven**

The University of Spoiled Children

The USC-UCLA game is a gathering place for the beautiful people.
Everybody's tanned and rich.

—*A comic on Fox Sports'* The Sports List, *hosted by Summer Sanders*

USC linebacker John Papadakis starred at Rolling Hills High School, located on the beautiful, affluent Palos Verdes Estates. However, he was originally from the blue-collar town of San Pedro, which gave him a unique perspective on his rich classmates. He did not move to Palos Verdes until he got to high school. His background was a mixed blessing. On the one hand, Palos Verdes Estates was a place of tolerance, but life there separated him from his less-well-off college teammates, particularly the inner-city and rural Southern African Americans. On the other hand, he was a product of his childhood upbringing and Greek heritage, in which he learned about the nobility, morality, and striving for justice inherent in Greek philosophy. John had become a devotee of Ayn Rand, herself a Platonic admirer who wrote about an objectivist approach to the world designed to replace want with the kind of economic opportunity that would provide "a rising tide that lifts all boats."

When John arrived at USC, his naturally outgoing nature, combined with his swarthy good looks, made him stand out from the other white players, who more resembled the blond surfer persona made popular by California beach bands of the era. He made quick friends with his black

144

teammates, attended their parties, and dated their women. He became one of the central personalities who took a group of young men who might have been divided and instead brought them together. Through Papadakis, they became a family. John McKay was their father.

Sam Cunningham had gone to high school in the idyllic, affluent community of Santa Barbara. He knew prejudice, but it would be fair to say he probably was subject to less of it in a place like Santa Barbara than almost anyplace else in America. One of the nation's greatest high school players, he had little idea that he would be a central figure in the civil rights struggle. In 1970, he was still a "scrub." In those days, freshmen could not play on the varsity, so he was a rookie sophomore.

Sam's African American family had moved to Santa Barbara a few years prior, from another laid-back California beach town, Ventura. Sam was the best athlete at the oldest high school in the state, starring in football and track for the Dons. In southern California prep sports circles, his name was known far and wide.

Santa Barbara was the mythical launch site of the *S.S. Minnow* in the popular 1960s sitcom *Gilligan's Island*. Life there was not unlike living on the set of a later popular show, *Baywatch*. It was about sun, sand, and fun. People there liked to party, and the girls who populated the beaches, the high school, Santa Barbara City College, and the UC-Santa Barbara campus were the tanned beauties of the Beach Boys' classic "California Girls."

Older blacks of that generation knew full well what kinds of obstacles lay beyond the friendly confines of a place like Santa Barbara. One of the most common refrains from African Americans advising their young sons was how to deal with white girls *don't!* By 1970, that kind of talk went over like a lead balloon with the new generation. In Santa Barbara, if you wanted to talk to girls, white girls were the great majority. There was a small black population and a more sizable Hispanic community, but overwhelmingly people—and pretty girls—were white. Most of the guys found ways to excuse themselves from conversations with the old folks.

Sam Cunningham could go where he wanted to go, when and with whom he pleased. As a sports star, he enjoyed some celebrity, although not the kind of pagan idolatry reserved for high school heroes in the South. Sam was young and naïve. He knew about the civil rights movement, but it had never truly hit home with him in this place. His biggest decision coming out of high school was which scholarship he would accept. USC had the best football and track program in the United States, so taking a ride to play for the Trojans was not difficult.

In 1969, Cunningham had toiled for the USC freshman team. Going into his sophomore year, he was looking to start. He had impressed his coaches and was the leading candidate for the fullback job, but USC had so many talented players that a single slipup could mean a significant loss of playing time. Cunningham's main competition for the job came from two white players: John Papadakis and Charlie Evans. After losing out to Cunningham, the Greek junior-to-be accepted his fate, concentrating on a new position: linebacker. Evans would not go down so easily. If he were to lose his job to Cunningham, he would take it hard.

Julie's is closed now, but it was an institution for years. Julie's was a popular watering hole across from the L.A. Memorial Coliseum. It was McKay's hangout. The assistant coaches liked to knock back cocktails with the head coach there. Julie's was a patio-style restaurant with a swimming pool in the back. On occasion, USC coaches would take a dare, such as "If my team makes the NCAA tournament, I'll jump in the pool at Julie's," as basketball coach Stan Morrison did in the late 1970s. McKay never needed to engage in such shenanigans. His teams won as they were expected to. McKay did not need extra publicity.

It was at Julie's where McKay, lubricated by drink, loosened up. McKay often carpooled, with assistants who lived nearby, from Covina. Covina is about thirty minutes east of the campus on the 10 Freeway. McKay had two sons in the Catholic school in nearby La Puente, at Bishop Amat Memorial High School. His older son, J. K., was a heralded wide receiver. Richie, the younger, was not as physically gifted but possessed uncommon intellectual skills. McKay had two daughters, Michele and Terri. Both had to deal with the realities of being a girl in a man's world of football and Catholicism.

While J.K. was enrolled, the Bishop Amat Lancers, who were one of California's top prep football powers, were quarterbacked by a handsome, blond young man named Pat Haden. Haden was entering his senior year of high school. He would complete his Bishop Amat career as the leading passer in state history (a record broken in 1987 by Craig Fertig's nephew, Todd Marinovich of San Juan Capistrano).

Haden, also a brilliant student, was J.K.'s best friend. The two of them were a potent pass-receiver combination. But Haden's father was about to be transferred by his company to Walnut Creek, creating a dilemma for the family. Should he uproot his son and transfer him to a new school in the San Francisco Bay Area for his senior year?

Coach McKay came up with the solution. The McKay household would soon have another resident. He invited Pat to live in their home during his last year. How convenient! Pat would play out his All-American senior season, throwing touchdown passes to J.K. In the meantime, a stream of college recruiters would be forced to sit in Coach McKay's living room, touting their programs. McKay would just sit off to the side, smoking a cigar with a cat-ate-the-canary look on his face.

When asked whether he was worried that either J.K. or Haden would be "lost" to another school, McKay quipped, "No. I sleep with the mother of one of 'em, and the other sleeps in the upstairs bedroom." In the end, McKay's influence, and the chance to play together at USC, won out. Haden and J.K. would lead USC to two Rose Bowl victories and a national championship in 1974.

At USC, J.K. would be known as a partier, often trying to draw Pat into the living room for some relaxation. Haden preferred to study. J.K.'s younger brother, Richie, never attained great football success on the field. But he earned his bachelor's degree from Princeton and a JD from Stetson's College of Law before becoming one of professional football's most successful general managers, now with the Atlanta Falcons.

McKay's daughter Michele was matriculating at USC during this period. She had the reputation of being rebellious toward her conservative Irish Catholic father. To McKay's dismay, she enjoyed the company of some of the black football players. Rumor has it that one player, Ty Hudson, had his star career curtailed because he got too close to Miss McKay. McKay's word was law in the football program. To his assistants, when he spoke, whether in his office, on the practice field, at the Coliseum—or at Julie's—it was like hearing from the Burning Bush.

The L.A. Coliseum is in a neighborhood across the street from the USC campus, just south of the Rose Garden and museums. It always was a neighborhood to avoid. Only the "old school" ventured there. Students had no desire to cross that street except for football games, when they had the numbers in their favor. This was long considered the reason USC's basketball team drew poorly at the Sports Arena, where games were usually played at night in the winter. The small crowds created a self-fulfilling prophecy. Suburban fans couldn't get past the notion that they were in dangerous territory. A new basketball arena, however, changed much of that. The Galen Center opened at the beginning of the 2006–2007 season across from Felix Chevrolet at Jefferson and Figueroa. It not only upgraded the program and increased attendance, it also created some viable nightlife in the form of restaurants and bars.

The combination of the Galen Center, the recent resurgence of USC's football fortunes, and the building of the Staples Center in downtown Los Angeles has created a two-mile corridor of neighborhood renewal in and around the USC campus. However, for years before that the campus was said by detractors to be in "the ghetto."

The school is located in one of L.A.'s oldest neighborhoods. When USC was founded, the area was one of the finest in the city. But by 1970, it *was* a ghetto known as South Central, located adjacent to the infamous Watts projects. Only five years had passed since Watts had erupted in the flames of riot.

Students at USC quickly deciphered the lines of the "social zone": Figueroa Street to the east, Jefferson to the south, Hoover to the west, and West Adams to the north. Unlike UCLA, located in glitzy Westwood and bordered by even glitzier Bel Air, Beverly Hills, and lovely Santa Monica with its adjacent beach communities, USC was like Baghdad's Green Zone—an oasis of wealth and privilege surrounded by hardcore urbanism.

"They've had two riots in L.A. over the years," recalled McKay in 2000, "but the campus was never touched, because the local people know how important the school is to the community."

This is true. USC is the biggest employer in the area and among the biggest in the entire city. It has always maintained friendly relations with the largely black and Hispanic neighborhoods surrounding it. In recent years, USC has endeared itself to the community through outreach programs that include revitalizing neighborhoods, building projects that encourage professors to live in the area, offering school sponsorships, opening day-care centers, and awarding scholarships to outstanding academic students from nearby high schools.

Fraternity life at USC was and remains a hallmark of campus society. A typical question asked of Trojans is, "Are you in a house?" or "Are you in a sorority?" To answer no is seen as a sign of second-class status. Frat Row, located just a few blocks from campus, is the center of social life at USC. Unlike UCLA, USC's nearby bars tended to be seedy, even dangerous—especially for women. To venture to the nightspots of the South Bay, Westwood, or Santa Monica for the drunk driver meant a treacherous return through Cop Land. The result is that the students stay close to the campus for their fun, their drinking, and their romantic flirtations.

A comic once remarked that a USC-UCLA game is "a gathering place for the beautiful people. Everybody's tanned and rich." USC students tend to be the richer of the two, but regarding the physical appeal of their students, both schools are world class. The tuition at USC, a private university, is and always has been among the highest in the country, and along with it, a sense of arrogance has pervaded. It is derided as the University of Spoiled Children. Class envy has always been a part of USC's rivalries with other schools, whose student bodies like to wave credit cards in the air at the USC faithful as the band plays "Conquest."

USC is the preferred school of the children of famous Hollywood celebrities. It is not uncommon to see stretch limos tooling around the streets surrounding the campus, occupied by gorgeous girls in black gowns and handsome young gods in tuxedos. It is all fair imitation of Oscar attendees arriving at the Shrine Auditorium, across the street from the school, in the years in which the Academy Awards were held there.

Frat Row has the look of classical Greek architecture with its well-manicured lawns and columned pillars. Every semester, it is the site of a party tradition known as "rush." Throughout the year, while individual fraternities hold their share of invitation-only parties, there are usually open-keg blasts available to all. Fraternity traditions are inspired by the ancient Greeks, but by 1970 "Greek life" on campuses such as USC's meant little more than sex, debauchery, and drunkenness, all in the name of future business networking.

Not everybody at USC, however, is in a fraternity or sorority. Despite its emphasis on white wealth, USC has always attracted a large nonwhite population. It is geographically located in the middle of the Los Angeles metropolis, the gateway to the Pacific Rim. International students from the Middle East, Africa, Asia, and everyplace else call themselves Trojans. These tend to be serious students who eschew fraternity life.

The other group that is less likely to join a house is USC's athlete population. Football, baseball, basketball, track, and other athletes—male and now increasingly female—are often drawn to their own kind. The athletes are usually on scholarship and do not come from wealth. They often chew tobacco, hail from blue-collar towns, and are less refined. USC athletes tend to think of their teams as their fraternities. Their friendships forged on the playing fields are often more lasting and real than those found in frat associations.

Life at USC has always been a mixture of both, however. It is a small-scale version of the relationship between entertainers or politicians and athletes. The frat boys attend the games, cheer for the Trojans, and thump their chests with pride at the success of their teams. They like to socialize with the athletes, who bring a sense of machismo to the environment. The athletes enjoy the payoff, which comes in the form of pretty girls, free booze, and social contacts that can open doors down the road.

In the late 1960s and 1970s, USC, like much of America, was somewhat two-faced when it came to race relations. An African American athlete had to navigate a perilous road. Basketball superstar Lew Alcindor (now Kareem Abdul-Jabbar) of UCLA put it this way:

"In New York, where I was from, you knew who hated you," he stated in a *Sports Illustrated* piece. "The Italians and the Irish didn't want you in their neighborhoods. In California, I was welcomed with open arms by white people, but after a while I realized that these same cats who were giving me the Pepsodent Beach Boy smile were calling me a n--r behind my back."

Alcindor's UCLA experience mirrored the USC experience for many of the "brothers," a term popularized in the 1960s by Malcolm X, whose Black Muslim religion made reference to fellow Muslims as brothers and sisters. A black athlete had to walk a fine line. White women were often attracted to black men for a variety of reasons. Blacks are the best athletes in the world, a fact that may be argued but is almost impossible to refute. One of the reasons they are great athletes is that they tend to be faster, stronger, more agile, and physically larger in every way. Women have been known to get "jungle fever," a disparaging phrase describing their desire to experience the mysteries of the black male. Other white girls, racked by liberal guilt or a desire to be inclusive, give extra attention to blacks to see to it that they do not feel left out.

Mix all these sociological criteria with alcohol, drugs, rock music, and young away-from-home adults in the midst of full hormonal rage, and the results are predictable. At USC, most of the black athletes were smart enough to steer clear of obvious trouble, but trouble could find them—and often did.

Enter four black men (Charle' Young, Charlie Weaver, Ty Hudson, and Tody Smith) and one white girl . . . John McKay's daughter, Michele. Specifically, enter them into the SAE fraternity at USC.

Young: All-everything tight end from Fresno. Extremely smart, highly Christian, future Hall of Famer. A crusader. First name spelled C-H-A-R-L-E, with an ' for style.

Weaver: Militant black, big Afro, the kind of unimpressive student that could get into USC and play football, and cause Cal and Stanford to cry foul about it. Raised in the slums of Richmond. Crazy. Also an All-American defensive end.

Hudson: Handsome, smart aleck, loved the ladies, particularly white girls. Great, fast star of the defensive secondary.

Smith: Six foot five, 247 pounds, black. Hometown: Beaumont, Texas. Older brother: Bubba Smith of the Baltimore Colts. Disposition: Crazy.

Tody's older bro had starred at Michigan State. He was one of those great black athletes from the South who could not play college football there unless he went to Grambling or one of the traditional black colleges. Bubba was big time and wanted everybody to know it. Duffy Daugherty brought him in, and he had played in the 1966 "game of the century," a 10–10 tie at East Lansing with Notre Dame. Now, he was All-Pro at Baltimore.

Tody followed him to Michigan State, got into some kind of dispute with Daugherty, then packed his bags and headed for the bright lights of L.A. and the USC Trojans. He was a great player, a defensive tackle who would later play for the Dallas Cowboys.

All four of these black football stars were physically imposing. Threatenin'.

Miss McKay: A "hippie chick," a product of the Age of Aquarius. In the spring of 1970 she was a poster child for it. The beads, the headbands, the flowing shirt, the peace symbol painted on her face.

She had grown up in a football house. Brothers J.K. and Richie were Friday-night heroes. Blue-chipper Pat Haden was brought in to bunk with Richie so he could play his senior year at Bishop Amat. A frequent house-guest was John Sciarra, who would lead UCLA to a Rose Bowl victory in 1976. Then there was the old man, who was *sooo* Catholic and *sooo* Republican; he was set in his ways, a drinker, a cigar smoker, old school. Oh man was he old school, which of course was not the term kids used in those days. McKay was *square*.

So here is Miss McKay, away at college, only she's not "away." She's still near her father, and he's got more spies at University Park than the Central Intelligence Agency. On this night, despite the warnings of Charle' Young, she had openly accompanied Ty Hudson to the SAE house.

I smell trouble, Young thought to himself. He could *discern* such a thing.

"Try not to drink too much, baby," he told McKay's daughter.

"Lighten up, Charle'," she said.

Lord have mercy, thought Charle'.

He cased the joint. Frat boys drinking beer. The usual scene. Sorority sisters. White girls. Hot chicks.

"I'm gonna get me into a mess a trouble, baby," Tody Smith told Young. A "mess of trouble" meant that he was gonna get knee deep into some of these sorority sisters. Miss McKay was not the only white girl whose "liberal guilt" led her to these black men. There were plenty of others on this night, and one of them was making goo-goo eyes at Tody Smith.

It was hormone time on Friday night.

"Hi, baby, what's shakin'?"

"Hi, I'm Sarah."

"I'm Tody."

And I'm watchin' your back, said Charle' Young to himself, just a few feet away. Now, pan just a few more feet away, and observe White Frat Boy One, White Frat Boy Two, and White Frat Boy Three, drinking beers. White Frat Boys Four through Fifteen are all within hailing distance. The conversation is predictable:

"You see those brothers? They act like they own the place."

"They're cool."

"It ain't cool that that great big brother's hittin' on my girlfriend."

"She's not your girlfriend anymore."

"Are you with me or not?"

"Aw, s--t. . . ."

A few beers, some dance moves, a few more beers, a slow dance . . .

The whole of the story is a well-worn one. Tody and the white girl. Tody's hand on her butt. A smile, a kiss, a flirtation turns a little more serious, and the next thing the defensive end of the Southern Cal Trojans knows, Frat Boys One through Fifteen are on him, to make an apropos analogy, like "white on (black) rice."

Tody Smith was an enormous, incredibly strong man, but he could not overcome fifteen drunken fraternity brothers. Luckily for him, Charles "Tree" Young "had his back," saw the whole thing coming—Ray Charles could see it comin'—and managed to get into it quickly. So, too, did Hudson and Weaver.

Crazy Weaver, as most people described him. Young knew that his "job," aside from babysitting McKay's kid and watching Smith's back, was to keep *Weaver* from doing something nuts. It was a melee, but of course most of the frat boys really did not want to mix punches with these football players. Young was an acrobat, pulling guys off Weaver and Smith.

Lord, give me strength, thought Young to himself.

There was some luck involved, but Young managed to extricate Tody from the fray, along with crazy Charlie Weaver.

"Let's get the heck out of here," said Charle' Young.

Images of the LAPD, the South Central Jail, and the face of Marv Goux at four in the morning bailing them out suddenly appeared like an epiphany before their eyes. In the amount of time that it took to call an audible, they were out the door and gone from the scene.

And these are our classmates, thought Charle'.

Young just looked at his teammates.

"His will be done," he said under his breath.

Other Voices: Rod McNeill

Rod was an African American running back at USC from 1969 to 1973, and he played in the NFL with the Saints and Buccaneers. He has worked for the better part of two decades in the technology industry, most lately with AT&T in Orange County, California.

On the tension before the game. We had safety concerns. I never heard any indication of any weapons whatsoever, but I was from North Carolina before we'd moved out West. I'd experienced segregation. When we lived there, my father and older brothers participated in marches, stuff like that. They spent an overnight in jail, did the sit-ins, and all the people in my neighborhood were black. I was never in contact with white people until we moved to California when I was thirteen. Suddenly I'm in a neighborhood that's completely white, so it was from one section to another.

I had no trepidation, but I knew it would be volatile in Alabama. But it was business as usual, as far as the guys were talking. Getting off the plane, we had police escorts everywhere we went. What was overwhelmingly powerful was the anticipation, the feel to it, at the airport, the hotel. The majority of the hotel support staff was black, and you could sense the hope in their eyes. It was like we were down there and they wanted us to help 'em out—that in some way what we did in that game, that through our performance on the field, we could change their lives. I didn't play that night, but I had a chance to have a bird's-eye view from on the sidelines. It was very unique. Sam had an incredible game. Manfred and I were with Sam; we'd come together as freshmen, and we just had a feeling we'd be good. That became the 1972 national champs.

In 1969, we played the California North-South Shrine Game at the Coliseum. There was a huge crowd; all the high school players wanted to play that game. The majority of us met at that game and found ourselves at USC. The whole experience at USC was like a movie from start to finish; it was like "win one for the Gipper." It was bigger than life.

At 'Bama, as I say, we had police escorts. We were talented, but we had our struggles internally. As a team, there were racial things going on with us. Marv Goux dealt with it. We were all football players representing USC. We were supposed to do that the best possible way, never embarrass yourself, your university, or your family. He preached it over and over for all of us. I never saw Marv disrespect anybody except freshmen.

On his teammates. John Papadakis was a middle linebacker. I was a running back, and running backs and linebackers have a unique relationship, trying to make names on each other. I had a few head-to-head plays to see who's the better player. He was the kind of guy you want to have on your team. As I watched USC, I saw guys with names like Rossovich, Vella, European kinds of names. It evoked that image, and Papadakis had the same ring to it.

He was a gung ho player, he was. I never really saw John get in the middle between blacks and whites. Sometimes there's automatic segregation that guys impose on themselves—white with white, black with black—but John was one of those guys who never let those barriers keep him from mingling or hanging with anybody he wanted. I tried to be the same. With my background, it was natural for me to want to have good race relations.

On Bryant's statement. I'd have to go to the horse's mouth to find out about whether Bryant ever said Sam's "what a football player looks like." Sam himself told me it never happened. More to the point is was it demonstrated on the field—nothing should minimize what he did. We adequately demonstrated it on the field. As far as whether it happened, Sam said it didn't. But the stories demonstrate the reality of what that game meant. The whole of USC football is larger than life; it's mythologized. Some stories are so good, people have them etched in their memories. My personal view is it would be unfortunate if it did come down that way because it would smack of a slave auction.

On the 1972 team. We had so much talent in 1972. Charle' Young was at tight end. We had Lynn Swann, J. K. McKay, Edesel Garrison. The whole thing about USC is that it's an opportunity to realize your fantasy in life. It's a chance to win the Heisman and the national title; it's all in your reach. I did get hurt and missed some playing time, but I wouldn't trade the USC experience for anything. . . .

McKay was an icon. You like to put him in with the big names, in the same category with Frank Sinatra, Bob Hope, Dean Martin, the Rat Pack. He had a huge persona, a quick wit with that white hair and big cigar.

On football now. Thirty-five years later, the game itself is evolving. Today it's commercialized; it has lost some of the pristine aspects that existed when I was in college. The remarkable thing about Pete Carroll is he brings back the traditional values, a way of dealing with athletes, setting high standards, and expecting guys to live up to them. That speaks to why he's so successful there now. The game is a microcosm of life: struggles, ups and downs. It's a ready example that if you stick to it and persist, through teamwork you can overcome all. That's why sports are so great.

Other Voices: Pat Haden

Pat Haden set California high school passing records as a quarterback at Bishop Amat High School in La Puente. He led Southern California to a national championship in 1974, earned a Rhodes Scholarship, and studied politics at Oxford College in England. He quarterbacked the Los Angeles Rams to the 1976 NFC championship game and earned a law degree from Loyola. He has practiced law in Los Angeles for many years and has also been a national college football television analyst.

Well, you know the story. I was the quarterback at Bishop Amat High. My best friend was the wide receiver, John K. McKay—son of coach John McKay—whom we knew as J. K. My dad was transferred for his job to Walnut Creek in the San Francisco Bay Area, but I wanted to stay at Bishop Amat and play my senior year. The dilemma was solved when Coach McKay offered to let me live in his house that year. I roomed with Rich McKay, now the general manager of the Atlanta Falcons. So, I was living with Coach McKay's family in the fall of 1970, when that game between USC and Alabama was played.

Regarding this game, I do not recall much about Coach McKay speaking to me with great significance about it. I've read about it, and thirty-five years later it seems more important than it did then. It was not on TV. Perhaps he saw Alabama was predominantly or entirely white, but their ethnicity was not apparent from my vantage point. I didn't hear much about it then, but since then it's grown in importance. I didn't know much about it at the time; the social context of it was not discussed particularly.

It may have been the big thing that people say it was, but I have mixed emotions about it. I consider whether the revisionist history is that Bear Bryant had on his mind that he would bring an integrated team with African Americans down to play, just to integrate his program. I could be wrong, but that's not my perception. I just think he had a drink in the off-season with McKay, and they decided to play that game.

McKay never talked about the scheduling of that game, but I was a high school senior playing my games, and he never spent much time at the house, and he didn't speak much to Johnny, Rich, or me, so I didn't notice the significance of the event at the time. Over time, I can appreciate it more, but I also think some revisionist historians have tried to make it more than what it was.

Craig Fertig would have a better feel for it than I do. It's one of those moments in time in athletics—a game happened, and afterward, it had social context—but maybe we're now attributing events that were not here or there. Different people are saying different things about whether Sam Cunningham was in that locker room. Hollywood will put it out that way.

The larger politics of it has made it much larger than the real context, so I'm just not positive what kind of effect it really had, especially with the story being that it was the incident that integrated SEC football. I don't know, maybe it sped the process up, maybe it did. I don't know the minds and hearts of people down there in the early 1970s. I was alive and vibrant at that time; one would think it happened fifty years before my time. It's shocking that as late as 1970 blacks still were denied opportunities. I'm skeptical about putting too much social context on that game.

As for its effect on social change at that time, not being from the South, I don't know, but I lay it on top of the social unrest that was predominantly led by Dr. Martin Luther King Jr. It was mostly African Americans being sent to the Vietnam War, so you mix that together, and it creates interesting sidebars.

Yes, I grew up in a Catholic environment, but I don't quite understand the question of whether fundamental Christian beliefs in the South effectuated this change, or whether it was just a cynical, dollars-and-cents decision to bring in blacks in order to win games. I'm just not sure. I'm thinking that Martin Luther King was the "tipping point." It was his leadership. I see this game more for its integrating of athletic teams than the overall civil rights movement. Jerry Claiborne may have said Sam Cunningham did more for civil rights than King, but coaches saying that, they don't always have the broadest cultural context.

CHAPTER Twelve

Dirt Poor versus
Wealth and Privilege

The poor wish to be rich. The rich wish to be happy.

—*Ann Landers*

University of Alabama football coach Paul "Bear" Bryant grew up dirt poor in a place where "poor" meant living off the land of humble Moro Bottom, Arkansas. He was sympatheic to poor people, a trait shared by some "poor whites" in the South. It might be said that the difference between "poor whites" and "white trash" was that poor whites empathized with others because they shared their plight, while "white trash" blamed others for their plight. The most virulent racism in the South had never come from the slave-owning classes or the aristocracy. Instead it emanated from the foremen who derived their wages and bonuses from slave toil and then pinned their economic downturn on the blacks, whom they saw as taking their jobs, their land, and their opportunities.

Bryant's football mentality worked against any instinctive racism. As a man whose entire life was football and competition, he understood fully the nature of achievement. He had seen enough athletes succeed or fail to know that the two factors that played the decisive role were physical ability and mental desire.

Racism, an evil disease that makes good people believe lies about other people, inculcated the logical reasoning ability of otherwise-intelligent men and women. These people had grown up with separate drinking fountains, restrooms, schools, and churches, sheltering them from blacks. Whites certainly had no desire to share lockers, showers, sweat, and blood with blacks.

For centuries, including the better part of the previous hundred years, blacks believed these lies too. But society had changed. It had changed because of two world wars, books, mass communications, human nature, sports, and American politics. But most of all, it had changed because of Christianity. No longer did the blacks believe in their own "inherent" inferiority. Their brand of Christianity—self-affirming, loud, and proud—had begun to develop a pride in themselves. They were itching to prove themselves. They knew that on the "other side of the tracks" on Sundays, white folks were worshiping the same Christ they were, and sooner or later the twain shall meet.

No one denied that blacks possessed physical ability. That was part of the racists' creed, in a way. Gambling guru Jimmy "the Greek" Snyder got into trouble talking about this very thing when he stated that in slave times the owners would mate "the big black with the big woman." The theory was that this mating would produce big children, who were better suited by virtue of strength and size to labor in the fields. Snyder's sociological view was that this process repeated itself over time, eventually producing what might be termed a "super race" of athletic blacks who now made up the best athletes in the National Football League, as well as other sports.

While physical ability is the most important factor in athletics, many physically great athletes fail because they do not possess the intangibles, such as *heart*, partly defined as the desire to succeed despite hardships and obstacles. In contrast, other athletes possess less-impressive physical attributes but succeed because of their heart.

Still other athletes are not overly gifted but have a "niche" quality that allows them to succeed in particular circumstances. A quarterback like Joe Montana might fall into this category. Montana did not have the best size, speed, or throwing arm, but he had football intelligence, on-field courage, and the ability to lead men in stressful situations. He found his "niche" in throwing a variety of soft-screen passes and tight-end reads, drawing defenses in and then hitting fast wide receivers who could make up for his lack of long-ball throwing strength. He played at just the right time and place for coach Bill Walsh, who devised the West Coast offense that perfectly suited Montana and his San Francisco teammates. To this day, the "physical versus intangible" argument still carries with it some inherent racism.

Somewhere, coaches were brainwashing themselves into believing that while blacks could be great pro players, that was a mercenary game. Or college blacks could compete with whites up North, out West, or in the East, but not in Dixie. Southern football was still, despite evidence piling up to the contrary, a more "manly" game than that played in other regions. Old notions of class and aristocracy were archaically being applied to Southern football.

Bryant, while not a believer in these lies, still embodied part of the myth that Southern whites were clinging to in 1970. He had tried to integrate Kentucky when he coached there in the 1950s, and he often spent Friday nights watching all-black high school games. But Bear also installed a drill called "the Cage." It was supposed to determine the strongest-willed *and* most able-bodied players.

These drills were based on discipline, loyalty, and character. Players squared off two at a time in the Cage and literally fought to the finish in hand-to-hand combat. The Cage set linemen against each other in an actual cage in which being knocked off balance or forced to rise up resulted in knocking their heads against a steel bar. Many white coaches thought blacks would wilt in the cage—and in the fourth quarter.

Bryant, the Cage, and the accoutrements of 'Bama football circa 1970 were all suited for each other. Assistant coach Clem Gryska thought the program had been bogged down by "prima donnas" from outside the state after winning national championships. By 1970, Bryant was rebuilding by going back to basics: tough country boys from in state.

The average Alabama football player of this era was markedly different from the average USC football player of the era. It was a complete role reversal. Alabama's white boys were mostly poor.

"Those kids couldn't afford to buy a thing," said *Forrest Gump* author Winston Groom, a 'Bama graduate who also wrote a pictorial history of Crimson Tide football. "They were dirt poor," just as Bryant had once been.

Bryant was not above breaking some rules in order to effectuate the "survival" of his program, as individuals and as a unit. Alumni and boosters routinely lined the pockets of Tide football players—if $10 or $20 to a kid who really needed and appreciated it was really "lining their pockets."

Then there were USC's players. John Papadakis grew up on the Palos Verdes Peninsula. Sam Cunningham was from a place Hollywood used as the setting for an island paradise. Many Trojans prepped at expensive Catholic schools such as Sherman Oaks Notre Dame and La Puente Bishop Amat. Lineman Dave Brown grew up in the comfortable surroundings of Eagle Rock. Many of USC's white players, such as receiver Bob Chandler, effectuated the blond surfer mannerisms associated with SoCal nostalgia.

The black Trojans, while not an affluent group, probably came from higher family incomes than Alabama's whites! The 'Bama kids lived in the sheltered world of Tuscaloosa, where they were feted by fawning alumni, worshipful students, and sympathetic press. However, this did not lend itself to a sense of worldliness. They were protected from many social realities outside the confines of their little college town.

The Trojan players, on the other hand, dealt regularly with a sophisticated media. They were expected to be able to handle themselves in interviews with newspaper, radio, and TV interviewers, often with national affiliations. More was expected of them than the kind of "yes sir, no sir" answers an Alabama player could get away with when speaking to a reporter from the local TV station.

In a city like L.A., with the varied press outlets charged with covering USC football, it was impossible for McKay to "protect" his players from the press, even if he had been of a mind to (which he was not).

There was a "religion gap," too. Both whites and blacks prayed to the Lord Jesus Christ, but their respective visions of Christianity, at least as it related to their own lives, were still very different. Whites tended to thank the Lord for the blessings bestowed upon them. In America, they had found the promised land of opportunity. Blacks tended to pray for the strength to persevere in a land in which those blessings seemed tantalizingly close and yet so far.

Christianity, as it related to the 1970 Alabama and USC football players, was evolving. Alabama's kids were born and raised in the Bible Belt. They accepted the tenets of the New Testament with unwavering acceptance. USC's players, most of whom were from California, were on the front lines of an American "cultural revolution" in which the new sacraments were sex, drugs, and rock 'n' roll.

Many of the "sophisticated" Trojans looked down on Christianity, calling its adherents "pussies" who lacked the toughness to be great football stars. In a story that would develop over the next two years, they would find themselves only when they found Christ. But the 1970 team was still divided by race and religion. Some thought that, since they were now living in the Age of Aquarius, they could come together through harmony and understanding. Instead, they were torn apart and would stay that way until Dave Brown helped lead them out of the deep valley they were mired in.

Finally, the wealth and privilege of USC's student body, its fraternity associations, its Hollywood connections, its beautiful "daddy's girls"—all of this created an osmosis of polish that could not help but rub off on their athletes, further differentiating them from their Alabama counterparts.

* * *

The NCAA announced that they were adding an eleventh game to the fall football schedule early in 1970. After hearing about the extra game, Bryant gathered his "brain trust" in his second-floor office, the same one where he watched Wallace make his infamous "stand at the schoolhouse door" seven years earlier.

Bryant's brain trust included his coaches. There was Jerry Claiborne, his loyal number two man, who was said to be his heir apparent when the day ever came. Mal "Bud" Moore was a hard-liner but smart, and someday he would take over as the school's athletic director.

The young guys included Jack Rutledge and Clem Gryska. Rutledge was a seeker, a man who lived in the violent world of football but actively sought the best in each person's humanity. He had played at Alabama as a married man, a rare thing under Bryant. He was the kind of fellow who countered his own impulses, the rough, hard edges of football—the swearing, the cussing, the womanizing, and his own part in this lifestyle—by meditation with the Lord Jesus Christ. He would need the strength of the Lord in fighting off a series of cancer surgeries.

Gryska lived and breathed 'Bama football. He revered Bryant and would not think to call him Paul or Bear but rather Coach or Sir. He was just happy to be there.

Bryant's coaches were a different breed of cat from John McKay's. The West Coast assistant was a mercenary (with exceptions such as Marv Goux). Staff members such as Wayne Fontes and Joe Gibbs had not played at USC. Their goals were to coach at different places, maybe even get some experience on offense and some on defense, some college and some pro, and parlay ten years or so of this into a head coaching position somewhere.

Bryant's guys generally had played at 'Bama, either for Bryant or the previous man, J. B. Whitworth. Being on Bear's staff represented their lifelong goals. Many stayed their whole careers in the same place. Retirement from coaching meant an administrative job with the university, and retirement from *that* meant part-time work at the Paul W. Bryant Museum.

Maybe they were Bear's brain trust, but regarding the issue of this added game, they were merely his audience when he announced that the Tide had an extra contest to prepare for and that it would be the Southern Cal Trojans on September 12 at Legion Field.

"Coach Bryant, now hold on," said Moore. "Let's think this thing through."

"That's what I always do, Bud," said Bryant.

"Coach," said Moore, "Southern Cal's undefeated, they're fast, they're . . ."

Nobody had to say it. They had *blacks*. Lots of *fast blacks*. One could hear Aunt Bea wailing about it right now.

"Andy, Andy, there's blacks at Legion Field."

"It's the best thing for the program, Coach," Bryant said to Moore, but it was directed at the assembled staff. "It'll be a big game for our fans, like a bowl game in September."

"They got Davis," said Claiborne.

Davis was Clarence Davis, an All-American tailback in 1969. Davis was black. He had also been born in Birmingham. He had left with his mother at a young age when she decided that opportunity did not beckon in Alabama. They had lived in the Bronx, New York, until he was thirteen and then moved to Los Angeles. In L.A., Clarence had blossomed into a fine football player. After one year at East L.A. Junior College, he had, like another juco transfer, O. J. Simpson, accepted a ride to USC. Despite the pressure of replacing "Juice"—writers tried to call him "Lemonade" but it did not stick—Davis had starred for the 10-0-1 1969 Trojans.

"The papers'll have a field day," said Claiborne.

Indeed, Davis had become a poster child for a growing chorus in the media to integrate the football program. It was not just the black media, and there *was* such a thing. They covered the black high school stars and the black colleges. The "white" papers wondered about Davis, too. He was one who most certainly had gotten away.

"It'll help with Wilbur," stated Bear.

Wilbur Jackson. Ah, the elephant in the corner. A running back/wide receiver from Ozark, Alabama. One of the best high school football players in America. His dad was a railroadman. Big family. *Conservative*, very Christian.

"Yes sir, no ma'am" all the way.

Black.

With a full-ride scholarship to the University of Alabama, slated to enter with the freshman class in the fall, where he would be expected to star on the frosh team. In 1971, barring disaster, he would be on the field of play, competing at full throttle for the Crimson Tide.

Bear Bryant never made mention of race, at least not in the context of what this game with USC would mean, but greasing the skids for Wilbur Jackson was Project 1-A, and he had his way of doing things.

Bryant's mind was made up. He was also already recruiting Mobile's John Mitchell, a black star whom John McKay thought he had wrapped up for his Trojans. Moore, Rutledge, and everybody else around Bryant were in the dark about his true intentions regarding this game and its effect on the all-important "second game" of recruiting.

Craig Fertig was not yet thirty years old in the spring of 1970. Fertig's father, Henry Fertig, was the police chief of Monterey Park, California. He was a colorful character known as Chief. In 1966, USC opened the season at Texas. John "Duke" Wayne, a one-time Trojan football player in the Howard Jones era, rode around the field on a golf cart before the game. Chief Fertig poured whiskey into his paper cup the whole time. When Duke flashed the Texas fans the "hook 'em horns" sign, they cheered wildly.

"Hey, Duke's a Longhorn fan."

What they did not hear was Wayne, the whole time he was flashing that sign, saying to Chief, "F--k the 'horns."

As a star quarterback, Craig engineered that miraculous victory, coming from 17–0 down at the half to defeat Notre Dame in 1964, thus denying Ara Parseghian his first national championship. In so doing, he earned his eternal place in the glory halls of Troy.

Now, however, he was a lowly assistant coach. He had made it past the graduate assistant stage, but not by a whole lot. He was assigned bed-check duty. When McKay had his fill of whiskey at Julie's, a nearby watering hole, Fertig (whose unofficial duties included keeping up with the old man) was tasked with driving him home to Covina. On this smoggy winter day, Fertig again found himself playing taxi driver.

"He says, 'Come on Craiger, let's go,'" recalled Fertig in *The History of USC Football* DVD. "Well I get in the car, I'm born and raised in L.A., you tell me where you wanna go and I'll get you there, but he doesn't say anything."

Out the door they went, to the parking lot, where McKay handed Fertig the keys to his car, a big old gas-guzzling cardinal Toronado. McKay told Fertig to drive but gave little in the way of direction other than the next immediate left or right.

"Yes, sir," said Fertig after each instruction.

As they edged out onto the freeway, Fertig refrained from his need to inquire.

"And I never speak unless I'm spoken to," continued Fertig. "So I turn here, turn there. . . ."

"The whole thing had the feel of a Godd--n spy novel," McKay recalled in 2000. Fertig silently was putting the pieces together. He knew Bear Bryant was Alabama's athletic director. He knew the NCAA had just added an eleventh game. He knew that Bryant and McKay were friends. He knew Bryant was in Palm Desert for the Bob Hope Desert Classic. . . .

Traffic coming off the Hoover entrance, clearing up around San Vicente, boxing them in again around the interchange with the San Diego Freeway, clear to Washington, then airport traffic the rest of the way. Fertig figures out that they are going to the airport, but he knows nothing more than that.

Are they flying somewhere? He has not packed a thing, not even a toothbrush.

"And finally we get to the airport, so I said, 'Short term or long term?' and he says, 'Short,' and I says, 'Aah, short flight,'" recalled Fertig.

Los Angeles International Airport, their home away from home. How many times had they flown in and out of this place, for games and recruiting? But a top-secret meeting?

"And I never forget, at 10 o'clock in the morning, we go to the Horizon Room of Western Airlines," recalled Fertig.

"Scotch on the rocks," said McKay.

"Vodka," said Fertig. "With O.J. Just like Simpson."

A round of drinks delivered by the waitress.

"And he says, 'I'll have a cocktail here,' and he's still not talkin' to me, and he looks at his watch and he says, 'We'll have another one here,'" said Fertig.

McKay glanced at his watch.

"And he says, 'He'll be here in about five minutes,'" said Fertig. "I don't know who 'He' is."

Four minutes later, "'He' walks in with his houndstooth hat on," said Fertig.

Fertig's recollection in a 2005 interview was even more classic.

"One drink, then two," Fertig said thirty-five years after the fact, "then three, then four, and then *in walks Paul 'Bear' Bryant.* Like Mount Rushmore with legs."

Sunburned from days on the Palm Desert golf course, Bryant extended his hand. Fertig had never met him before and was like a child.

"'Hi, Paul,'" Fertig recalled McKay saying.

"Hi, John."

"What do you wanna see me about, Paul?"

"Well, John—we'll have one more round here."

The waitress senses something too. She hovers over the men.

"Martini," mumbled the Bear.

Another round, small talk. Nice weather. Love California. *How's Corky? How's Mary Harmon?* Then . . .

"What's this all about, Paul?"

"John, I'd like to offer a package that would bring in between $150,000 and $250,000 for the Trojans if they would come to Birmingham to fill up the open date of September 12," stated Bryant.

"'We'll have another one'—and McKay tugs at his cigar and says: 'Okay, I'll tell you what I'll do, Paul, I'll give you $250,000 if you come out the following year and play us in the Coliseum,'" said Fertig.

No hesitation. McKay knew what to expect.

Fertig just stared.

"They shook hands, and that's what started that football game," said Fertig.

"Coach McKay was thinking how much bigger the L.A. Coliseum was than Legion Field," said Fertig. "He thought an attraction like Alabama could sell thousands of tickets more than anyone else we could have scheduled. They had a drink, shook hands, and got up to leave."

Fertig was "sitting in on a historical moment," he continued. "Coach McKay and Coach Bryant both understood what had just happened, but I didn't catch on right away. They had just agreed to play the first integrated college football game in Alabama."

Then the realization came to young Craig Fertig.

Bear's integratin' his program, he thought to himself. *Jesus, Mary and Joseph.*

Sure, everybody knew about Wilbur Jackson, but in the spring of 1970, whether Jackson would really play was still an open question. A couple of years earlier, Bryant had brought in three black walk-ons to practice with the team. He was known to keep a recruiting list in his top drawer that carried the names of the top black players in the South. When challenged in a court case, he told the black lawyer bringing litigation that he would offer scholarships to blacks, but none of the state's best black players wanted to play at the University of Alabama. In December 1969, however, Bryant had signed Jackson.

Bryant once said he wanted to be the "Branch Rickey of football." In a 1965 *Look* magazine article he stated, "Negro players in the Southeastern Conference are coming." But radio host Paul Finebaum said Bryant could have done more sooner.

"He had more power than any football coach in the South, maybe the country, and any public declaration from him would have helped enormously," Finebaum recalled.

Perhaps Bryant could have done more sooner. Perhaps not. Either way, on that winter day at the L.A. airport, Bryant was indeed "doing more." It would be the ultimate "public declaration."

But the Trojans, with all those black guys with their Afros, at Legion Field? Holy cow.

Details were worked out, pleasantries exchanged, more drinks consumed to toast the occasion, and finally Fertig had to get the old man home.

"Coach," Fertig asked McKay in the car, "why'd Coach Bryant choose us for this thing?"

"Young Craig Fertig," McKay announced, "the 'prowling Bear' has chosen the Trojans to help 'change the complexion' of college football."

Fertig laughed. Great double entendre. Pure John McKay. The artificial turf in Birmingham, thought Fertig, would not be the only challenge for his team.

McKay announced the eleventh game, which would be the season opener for both teams, during spring practice. He told the Trojans that USC had won twenty-nine games in three years, been awarded a Heisman Trophy and a national title (two Heismans and two national titles since 1962), gone undefeated, and made four straight Rose Bowl appearances—but the game in Birmingham would be the most important they had yet played. He did not directly make reference to the issue of race, but he made it clear that he understood the social significance of the contest. It would also be his first head-to-head matchup with his friend Bear. McKay also made it clear that he had the highest respect for Bear. This says a lot about Bryant. McKay was a legend with a reputation for being "totally race neutral" as his son, J. K. McKay, said. If Bryant were a racist, it is not likely a man like McKay, whose success was so dependent on black football players, would have respected and liked him so much. It is also not likely that a "racist" Bryant would embrace a progressivist like McKay.

News of the opening game, featuring an integrated USC team against the all-white Crimson Tide, caused quite a stir in the black communities. In black churches, parishioners prayed for the Trojans. In white churches, believers prayed, too.

Other Voices: Coach Clem Gryska

For twenty-four years, beginning in 1960, University of Alabama graduate and former football player Clem Gryska was an assistant coach under Paul "Bear" Bryant in Tuscaloosa. He is considered a "keeper of the flame," the source for material on the late, great coach. Coach Gryska works in the Paul W. Bryant Museum in Tuscaloosa as managing director.

I was an assistant coach under Coach Bryant for twenty-four years, and I can say that we were really friends, although our relationship was always a private one. I started at first with Coach Bryant in 1960, on the kicking team. [After college] I was the recruiting coordinator, and I had the freshman team until 1976.

As I recall, the decision to schedule that game with Southern Cal came about because Coach Bryant and John McKay had met after a bowl game, after an NCAA meeting. The NCAA held meetings in different parts of the country. Don Hutson and Bryant would go out to Palm Springs and play golf. At some point Coach Bryant and Coach McKay had a meeting, maybe after golf or at one of those NCAA meetings, and they struck up a conversation about playing each other. The NCAA had recently allowed for an eleventh game, so the schedule had an added week.

Coach Bryant chose USC, probably over a couple of drinks, out of friendship with McKay. It was not about contracts or TV. I think it was Coach Bryant's personality that they just said, "Let's play." Anything other than that would be a change of character. I don't think the fact that Coach McKay had an integrated team had any effect.

I don't really feel that Bryant wanted that game against Southern Cal for racial reasons. I think he just knew that USC had been in Rose Bowls, they won Heismans, so I think he felt USC was a great program and would be a real draw. He never really talked all that much about that 1970 game. Bryant never really reminisced about the game other than we took a physical beating.

On the controversy surrounding Bear Bryant's statement. As for the statement that Coach Bryant had said, "This here's what a football player looks like," to my knowledge, Sam Cunningham was not in our dressing room. I was usually the first one in, and I would have seen it. I first heard this story a long time ago, maybe ten or fifteen years ago. It's not true. I have no idea where it comes from. In the last ten years, Sam was in Mobile and stated there that he didn't remember it.

On recruiting black players at Alabama. Sam was not the first black football player to play in Alabama. We had signed a freshman who was black; we already had an African American who was a really good basketball player, Wendell Hudson. They say that Sam was the best football player they had, but Clarence Davis was their best back, an All-American.

The whole question comes down to why we had not recruited blacks before this. You have to understand that we were a state institution, and George Wallace was still the governor. Coach Bryant knew he could not buck Wallace because of the controversy it would create. You know, he had tried to recruit blacks when he was at Kentucky, but they wouldn't let him.

There is a story that Alabama fans were not happy about the Tide playing an integrated Penn State team in the 1959 Liberty Bowl, but as far as I can remember, they were tickled pink that we went to a bowl game. There was no controversy about that Penn State game.

The story about how we got John Mitchell is that we played Oklahoma in the Bluebonnet Bowl. We had the pregame meal, then a squad meeting, and after that Coach McKay called Paul that night to wish him good luck. During that conversation, Coach McKay let it slip that he was after Mitchell. Well, Coach had an assistant drive straight to Mobile to check him out. Mitchell was home for the Christmas holidays. Frankly, I didn't think Coach McKay was really that interested in Mitchell, but according to Coach Bryant, if McKay wants him, he'd better be a good one, so Bryant wanted him at that point.

I think Coach was very reserved. Coach Bryant was financially cognizant of all the things going on around him and wanted to do something for the university. The Sugar Bowl wanted him, so Coach Bryant called Joe Paterno and invited Penn State to the Sugar Bowl.

On the 1966 season. Now, in 1966, it's said we had the national championship taken from us for political reasons. For the record, we had Kenny Stabler at quarterback, and we were going for a third straight national championship. We were undefeated and untied, and we won the Sugar Bowl. In the meantime, Notre Dame had tied Michigan State in "the game of the century." In those days, Notre Dame didn't go to bowl games, so they finished the year undefeated with a tie, yet the voters denied us the number one vote.

Coach Bryant never said much about that '66 team, other than he thought it was one of the best teams he ever had. He never entered into discussion of whether it was a racial thing. Coach knew if he said the wrong thing, it would hurt the program, so he let it slide. The writer John Underwood said Coach admits that the '66 team was one of his best teams.

On Coach Bryant's recruiting. Coach Bryant did not have the philosophy of recruiting only the best players. As I say, Wallace was the governor, and so it was problematic to recruit black athletes because of that. Coach Bryant wanted to bring in black players, only he wanted them to possess certain ingredients of character. He wanted athletes who worked hard, not blue-chippers who might have a prima donna attitude, white or black. This was the situation that affected both what kind of black players he wanted and why the team had gone down for a couple of years after the 1966 season.

First, Coach Bryant knew that a black player in the program would have to compete, to be of a certain type who could deal with the pressure. That was Wilbur Jackson. Wilbur was a country boy from Ozark, Alabama. Pat Dye, who later coached at Auburn, recruited him. Jackson's family was real conservative. He was a kid who could run like the wind and do anything he was asked. He was no prima donna. That had been the problem.

After winning three national titles, almost a fourth, everybody wanted to come to play for Coach Bryant, and we got us some very highly rated kids; but they were, as I said, prima donnas. Coach Bryant would rather have a kid who was not as talented but had a bigger heart. . . . Wilbur Jackson fit that model.

Kenny Stabler had been a guy who gave us a few problems. He did something and Coach suspended him, made him third string, and that turned his head around. It worked on a few others, but not all of them.

Bryant loved Stabler because he was a street fighter who'd do anything to win. When the ball was teed up and it was time to play, he was very competitive, and Coach could see that in him. But when we brought in some of the so-called best players, they saw themselves as stars who did not conform to Coach Bryant's way of playing. Coach admitted this was the reason the team went down.

In order to get back to where we were, we had gotten greedy. We went to Cincinnati, Miami, and California for recruits, but those brought prima donnas in, and they did not like his tough approach.

When Joe Namath came in, it took just three or four practices on the freshman team to see he was a Cadillac, not a Ford. But he never acted like a star. Coach coached him, talked with him after practice, and won Joe over.

On Bryant's nickname. They say Coach Bryant didn't like the nickname Bear. He had a million friends, and only four or five called him Bear. His friends called him Paul; others called him Coach. People felt they did not want to get that intimate with him or hurt his feelings.

Other Voices: Coach Craig Fertig

There are few Trojans who better represent USC, over a longer period of time, than Craig Fertig. Craig was a member of USC's 1962 national championship team and earned his spurs when he led the Trojans from a 17–0 halftime deficit to a 20–17 victory over Notre Dame, knocking the Irish out of a sure 1964 national championship (and giving it to Alabama in the polls, to Arkansas in the old "systems"). Craig was an assistant coach in 1970 and later became the head coach at Oregon State before embarking on a long career as a TV football analyst. Throughout all these years, Craig has been a spokesman for the school and a regular with the media and at events of all kind.

I probably shouldn't say it, but the 1970 USC-Alabama game changed the complexion of college football, and it occurred because of two guys, Bear Bryant and John McKay.

According to Coach Bryant himself, it happened because of his relationship with Coach McKay. In the South in those days, you couldn't come out and say, "I'm gonna do this" and "I'm gonna do that." It had to happen quietly. One day at 10:00 a.m. I get in McKay's car—I'll never forget it; it was a cardinal Toronado—and we turned left then turned right into the L.A. Airport. I finally ask Coach, "Short or long term?" He says, "Short."

We go to the Western Airlines Horizon Room. "Vodka on the rocks, make that three. He'll be here in a minute. Bring us another." Then, here comes Paul "Bear" Bryant, *like Mount Rushmore with legs.*

"Paul, how are you? What's this all about?"

"I want you to open the season in Birmingham next year for $150,000."

Coach twirls his cigar.

"If I come down for $150,000, next year I'll guarantee $250,000 if you come out to USC."

Those two guys created something with a handshake, no contract. Bear was out here for the Bob Hope Desert Classic. Me, I'm sitting in on history.

We had five black kids from Alabama we invited to that game for recruiting purposes, and they all ended up at 'Bama. I forget their names except for John Mitchell; they all ended up at Alabama. We hadn't realized what we were doing. We were creating the nucleus for the Alabama juggernauts of the decade of the 1970s!

I think Coach Bryant was way ahead of his time. I know McKay was. They were two great brains. Now, I think there was the Bryant I saw, the Bryant McKay hung out with, and then there was the Bryant that *they*— people at Alabama—saw. He talked differently out here than in Alabama. I think this explains why, when you talk to his players and assistants, you get different interpretations of these events.

Now, the night before the game, it's his birthday. It's a big day for Bear. They pass that over to us, so it's a big time for Coach McKay, who left the team to go to Bear's birthday. They played golf and drank together, two college coaches who typify what it's all about.

I'll never forget this as long as I live. . . . It's just me and Marv Goux walking next to Coach McKay after that game. We walk over, and *Bryant's smiling.*

"John, I want to thank y'all."

I think, *What is that? He's almost euphoric after losing 42–21?*

I think they had it planned. I'd bet on it. Sophomore Sam "Bam" Cunningham, why, we just turned him loose. I didn't know what he was going to do, but he could run and we blocked. They just stayed in the same defense, so Mike Rae asked over the phone, "When do we get to throw?"

Well, Sam Dickerson was double covered, which takes two of their eleven. Genius I am, I just told 'em to keep giving it to Sam; the ball ain't heavy, and he's not in a union. Sam just ran over everybody.

Before the game, I saw one of the greatest things I've ever seen in my life in coaching. I'm checking the phones, I'm calling the plays, and here comes this plaid hat, and now here's this rising clapping as he walks on the field, kisses a baby on the cheek just like a politician, then walks over and leans on the goalpost. Now the other guys on the Crimson Tide, wearing sport coats, come out. Bryant motions where he's at, and they walk toward him.

So now the game's over, and they're shocked. Bear's a competitor, and he's just been beaten pretty good in his hometown, and he's *smiling.* This intrigues me 'cause we just defeated them in their opener, and they're good. He says, "John, thank you," and they shook hands. I run off the field with Coach. I didn't know it at the time, but none of the 'Bama guys saw this.

Now, we're in our locker room. We're jumping up and down—it's a big thing; it's no black and white thing. We were scared to death playing these guys, and we've just defeated them.

Bryant comes to the door. Old Bear mumbles, "John, may I borrow that Sam Cunningham boy for a moment?"

I'm the backfield coach, so McKay says to me, "Craig, make sure we get him back." I stood outside their locker room. I know Sam went in that locker room. I don't know what happened in there.

Now, I didn't exactly see it, but Sam said, "He put me on a bench." Sam's wearing just his hip pads—I guarantee that's all he had on—and Bryant says, "Boys, listen up. Here's what a football player's supposed to look like." Sam repeated those words when I brought him back. McKay didn't ask what the dialogue was.

Now, I never told this story until lately. I talk about it when I speak at different things; this is what this country is built on. I know Tom Kelly repeated it too. . . .

Now I know Scott Hunter says it didn't happen, and I don't know. All I know is he's saying it didn't happen, and I know Sam ain't a liar. Sam on a bench? I'm standing next to the door—hey, I don't know. But that's what Sam told me.

When you get beaten in the opening game, maybe you might not pay attention. Bryant wanted to make a point, which was, "Let's change the South." Football, if you want to get down to everything that happened, is so important to those people. We at USC never looked at it like this; that's the way it was. Blacks were going north to Michigan, Michigan State, Ohio State. None stayed in Alabama.

So no, I wasn't repeating this story ["This here's what a football player looks like"] in the early '70s. It wasn't a big thing. They were the best, and we beat them. Sam probably told friends.

McKay would say, "Sometime you'll be on the other side of the field and know how it feels." He and Bryant had a special relationship. Those two, I mean to tell you, they were friends. I've never seen two coaches so close together; they're what college coaches are all about: mutual respect!

I was with Bryant in Tampa a month before he died, to recruit a player. Coach McKay, Bill Battle, and me. Bryant comes in to help, and he goes to dinner and McKay gets tired. Battle's gotta see this kid. McKay says to me, "Make sure Coach Bryant gets home," so it's back to the Bay Club. We hear music through the lobby, and Bear says to me, "Craig, I think we should have one more."

That was Coach Bryant's philosophy of life: to have one more of whatever it was life offered, you know? That's what I loved about that man. He died one month later.

I'm not sure who first said, "Sam did more than Martin Luther King for civil rights," but I've heard it many times. I think it brought it down to anybody's perspective. USC-Alabama, at Legion Field, made people open their eyes and say, "Maybe we should be doing this, integrating."

I've been to banquets with Sam, and this never really comes up, USC versus Alabama. From our part of it, we just beat 'em, and that was it. Our players tell you that.

On Southern racism. The only thing I can think of about the black-white issue is that Willie Brown is a black guy, so he dealt with some of those issues and may have perspective I don't have. I did do bed checks of the rooms, and I come to Clarence Davis and Lou Harris. They're lying in their beds, and I see something flicker, and Lou laughs. Clarence tells him to be quiet, and Lou just says, "Aw, Clarence, show Coach."

Willie Brown and I saw that Clarence had a six-inch Cub Scout knife.

"Coach," he says, "I was born in Birmingham." I never knew about racial deals.

Now, you're telling me some of the black players brought guns, which is news to me. Charlie Weaver might do anything; he was crazy. I don't believe that part. They didn't need guns. If somebody came after one of our guys, we'd all be there for him.

I can't comment on the gun story, from what I saw. McKay had gone to Bear's party; we brought 'em home, checked rooms. Maybe it happened, the guys got together. A football coach won't know everything. He'll let the seniors run the team, if you're good. Maybe they got together. If McKay or Goux had to come get you out of jail, though, you might as well go to Sing Sing or Leavenworth. They all respected McKay; I can see why Sam would be afraid of him. If he gets on to you, you've had it. . . .

CHAPTER **Thirteen**

Something to Believe In

Be careful to leave your sons well instructed rather than rich, for the
hopes of the instructed are better than the wealth of the ignorant.

—*Epictetus*

After the assassinations of Malcolm X in 1965 and Dr. King in 1968,
along with the murder of John Kennedy in 1963 and Bobby
Kennedy five years later, the civil rights movement had taken a radical turn. It was no longer a Christian, Gandhi-inspired, nonviolent peace
movement. Instead, the black militancy was symbolized by the Oakland,
California–based Black Panthers, who in turn spawned radical movements
such as the Weathermen and the Symbionese Liberation Army.

In the 1960s, the civil rights movement divided the country. The
South was "officially" desegregated by the Great Society legislation
President Johnson had initiated in 1964–1965, but it was still just a facade.
People in the rest of the nation looked on in disgust. Folks looked at
California, and they saw something new and fresh. Here was the promised
land, where—at least in theory—white and black brothers and sisters
walked hand in hand. They went to school together, socialized together,
worked together.

No place demonstrated this brave new world better than the football
program at Southern California, where coach John McKay was a modern-
day Moses of progressivism. His Trojans were classy champions, a well-
oiled machine. The "madman" Marv Goux kept them fired up through a
combination of fear and bravado, his speeches in the "dungeon" taking on

175

the quality of his hero, Patton, exhorting the troops to "use their living guts to grease the treads of our tanks."

Football at USC was indeed color blind. Fans saw black and white brothers blocking for each other, hitting each other with precision passes, patting each other on the backs. Off the field, an open social whirl of parties, pretty girls of all ethnicities, and Los Angeles diversity beckoned like sirens hailing Ulysses to the shore.

Coach McKay smugly observed his social unit, confident that he had gotten it right, but to some extent, by 1970, the image of the happy Trojan family was also a facade. The Vietnam War was raging. The University of California, Berkeley, campus was awash with protest. Furthermore, the civil rights movement had taken a turn—for the worse.

After the King and Kennedy assassinations, riots had embroiled America's cities. The movement was now militant, perhaps even violent. King's Gandhi-style nonviolent passivity was replaced by Black Muslims, Stokely Carmichael ("Violence is as American as apple pie"), and the Panthers, who were riding around town with shotguns, which they claimed was their constitutional right. Black kids were sporting Afros. They had *attitude*. To a lot of white folks, it was a little scary.

USC was idyllic, conservative, patriotic. There was no obvious sign of discontent as the Trojan ship sailed toward what promised to be another undefeated season. Tom Kelly, one of their play-by-play announcers, who spent a lot of time at practices, started to see something, though. He was a young man then, perceptive and hip, a handsome Irishman with a voice as smooth as caramel. He started noticing that black quarterback Jimmy Jones had his "people," and they were black.

White quarterback Mike Rae, the hotshot sophomore who wanted Jones's job (and had plenty of backing in the press) had his group. They were all white.

Black players tended to take their "complaints" to black assistant Willie Brown. White players congregated around the white assistants, Dave Levy or perhaps Joe Gibbs.

Kelly was a drinking buddy of Coach McKay's. He did not ask the tough questions and probably did not want the tough answers. All he really had was this little voice telling him that something might not be quite right at Troy.

USC offensive lineman Allan Graf starred at San Fernando High School. San Fernando is a "valley town" that had been annexed by the City of Los

Angeles as part of the great water, land, and aqueduct deal William Mulholland pulled off in 1904. According to the 1974 classic, *Chinatown*, the whole thing was a nefarious land grab, typical of capitalistic greed, Manifest Destiny, and a little incest just for good measure. Hollywood's version of America.

San Fernando High in the 1960s was a divided campus. On the one side were the Mexican kids, some from old valley families, some whose parents had just crossed the border to pick grapes with Cesar Chavez. On the other side were the blacks, who were taking jobs at the huge Budweiser beer facility in Van Nuys and whose children were demonstrating extraordinary athletic ability on the valley's sun-drenched fields of play.

Then there were the white kids. They were finding themselves, year by year, to be the minority. There were fewer and fewer jobs for them at the Budweiser factory as the blacks "moved in." By the late 1960s, this was a source of tension. Allan Graf was not from San Fernando proper. He was from Sylmar, a small community north of San Fernando. Located right on top of a major earthquake fault line, Sylmar was still a part of the Old West. It was a town of pickup trucks and gun racks, of feed stores, farms, and ranches. Coyotes stalked the foothills, raiding chicken coops, killing domestic cats. Oranges and other fruits and vegetables grew in the fields. The town was still white. The kids grew up wearing cowboy hats and s--tkicker boots. They hunted and fished. The completion of Interstate 5 and the 405 Freeway would make Sylmar a half-hour drive without traffic from downtown Los Angeles, but despite its proximity the town more resembled rural Alabama than suburban California.

Allan Graf was Sylmar all the way. A six-foot-two, 243-pound "big ugly," as Keith Jackson would put it, he wore the s--tkicker boots and spoke with a slight Bakersfield drawl. At San Fernando he had starred in football, had mingled with the blacks and Latinos who were his teammates, but retreated afterward to Sylmar. He was good enough to receive a football scholarship from John McKay to play at Southern California. In the fall of 1969 he found himself part of what college football historians say may have been the most talented incoming freshman class ever. McKay had always recruited a lot of black athletes. He had incurred his share of criticism for it, from opponents and alumni alike. But this class was "darker" than usual. It would prove to be unique, in ways that nobody could yet see. Enter into this mix of race, football, 1960s social experimentation, and charged-up competition Sylmar's own Allan Graf.

At six foot four, Charles Young was tall. They called him Tree. He was unique, too. The first indication that Charles "Tree" Young skipped to the beat of a different drummer was that he did not go by the familiar name of Charlie.

"No, it's spelled C-H-A-R-L-E'."

Charle'? Sounded like a French fashion designer. This guy plays football?

Yes, Charle' Young played football. Charle' Young grew up in an all-black environment in Fresno, California. This gave him perspective. Out of this perspective, as life would move on, Charle' Young came to understand that in order to make sense of life one must develop *discernment*. The ability to read between the lines. He was a thinking man.

The black experience in Fresno was an entirely different one from that of Los Angeles. The first thing Charle' discerned was that there were not a lot of blacks in Fresno, but they all lived in the same neighborhood. On the other side of the tracks. It was a little like a camp. It was a free country, and they were free to live where they wanted to live, and that was in this little camp.

But the wide-open spaces of the San Joaquin Valley gave these people a perspective that was much different from that of black folks living in their "camps" in the Watts section of L.A. or in the little Crenshaw Boulevard valley between the Santa Monica Freeway and the hills with the road that ran up to the oil rigs centering the odd urban-rural landscape of the city that isn't.

The famous Johnson brothers had come from nearby Kingston. Jimmy had been an All-American at UCLA and was now an All-Pro with the 49ers. Big brother Rafer was an international legend, having won the 1960 Olympic decathlon in Rome. Lord, that had been more than a sporting event. It was a Cold War battle royal. When Rafer won, it was a victory for America, for democracy, and for black Americans. Since he was one of theirs, it was a source of pride for people like Charle' Young. It was because of heroes like Rafer Johnson that Charle' felt all possibilities were now open to him. It was the wide-open spaces of the California valley that gave his fellow blacks a sense of rural independence, if you will, that many urban blacks did not have.

Charles "Tree" Young was one of those high school football superstars who turn it on and make jaws drop. He could do it all. He could catch, run, hit, and carry the water bucket, too. He was *fast*, with nimble fingers and soft hands. The ball just settled into his palms like a baby in a cradle. He ran by people, over people. The recruiters came around like ants seeking sugar. Oh, how quickly a black kid from Fresno becomes popular with white folks when he can play football!

The Edison High senior was feted like a supermodel on a photo shoot. One of the suitors was an unusual-looking man, a short, *very* powerfully built fellow with *black* hair and *black* bushy eyebrows. His face looked like the United Nations—a little bit of every ethnicity. He penetrated Charle' with his stare, his sheer *will*. This guy was a football coach, but maybe that was just a cover for some secret Cold War mission. He had to be Delta, CIA. He was a cross between G. Gordon Liddy, Zorba the Greek, and George Patton.

"Son," this man said to Charle', "do you want to be the best?"

"Yes, I do," said Charle'.

"Well, then, there's just one place where you will be challenged to be the best," the dark-haired man told him. "You can go to one of these other horses--t schools where they pretend to be something they're not, but there is only one place where you will be called on to reach inside yourself and pull out all the stops. I will be honest with you right now, and I will never stop being honest with you. I will take you to dinner and buy you the biggest steak on the menu. I'll come to your house, and I will be polite to your folks, because they deserve respect. We'll talk about education, religion, social values, and I'll convince them that to be a Trojan is the noblest purpose you can pursue.

"But when you get to the University of Southern California, I will push you to the limit, and you will hate me for it. But four years from now, when you are a first-round draft pick with a national championship ring on your finger, you will walk into life fully prepared for *anything*—any kind of bulls--t anybody tries to throw your way, and it will be because you accepted the challenge I am putting on you right now."

I'm scared to death of this madman, Charle' Young thought to himself. *He looks like he's gonna break my sternum. I better sign with him or he just might.*

Marv Goux got his man, just as he had gotten O. J. Simpson and Ron Yary and Marlin McKeever—all Trojan legends; winners of the Heisman, the Outland Trophy; consensus All-Americans.

At USC, Charle' looked around him and thought to himself, *Where are the blacks?* The nonsports blacks were *light skinned.* "More acceptable to the consumer," he called it.

Man, this is the University of Southern *California.*

In the fall of 1969, Allan Graf and Charle' Young competed on the USC Trojans' freshman football team. In those days, the NCAA barred freshmen from playing on the varsity. Their teammates included hotshot black running backs Sam Cunningham from Santa Barbara and Rod McNeill from Baldwin Park and a hotshot white quarterback from Lakewood named Mike Rae. The only thing that any of these people really had in common was that they were hotshots.

They were joined by a white center named Dave Brown from Eagle Rock High, near Glendale. Brown was no hotshot. He had to pinch himself just to make sure he was here, at the University of Southern California, competing with what looked to be the *Parade* High School All-American team.

Over the next four years, some of these players would ascend to great heights of glory and fame, and with that ascension the USC Trojans would ride the crest of college football's wave. Brown would never be a "name" player, a star, a cover boy, but among this collection of superstars, he would become very possibly the most important player on the squad.

In the summer of 1970, USC's players were given various odd jobs to make some extra money before reporting for late-summer camp. Handsome, blond wide receiver Bob Chandler lucked out with lifeguard duty, but most of the others toiled in more blue-collar surroundings.

Sylmar's Allan Graf and Fresno's Charle' Young found themselves thrown together at a construction site in Beverly Hills. They both lived near the USC campus. Allan had a car. He would swing by every morning to pick up his teammate.

Graf would smile, and Charle' would smile back. Graf wore his hair in a crew cut. Young was sprouting a baby Afro. They looked like a racial "odd couple." They would hit the Santa Monica Freeway for the five-mile ride to the Robertson exit. Allan would have country music on the radio. Charle' would not say anything, but if he had his druthers he would change it to the Motown station. Small talk ensued. They were friendly, not friends.

Maybe it was because Graf was a burly lineman and Young was an elegant, smooth receiver, but their backgrounds were different. Graf had played with some flashy San Fernando blacks—the school was known for that, with Anthony Davis and Charles White—and he really preferred the low-key approach. Score and hand the ball to the referee, don't spike it into the stands. Do it like O.J., act as if you had done it before.

Young had spent little time with white folks, but he knew Allan Graf. Country guys with Bakersfield drawls, people who grew up in L.A. County but sounded more like Abilene, Texas. Rodeo guys. Hank Williams guys. Oh, heck, he was gonna give Graf the benefit of the doubt before he would think him a racist, but these two were gonna be teammates for three more years, and at some point they were either going to come together or split apart.

Graf looked at Charle', and the first thing he thought was, *What's with this spelling? Charle'?*

He did not ask him about it. It would come out. But what is it with these black people? They always want to give each other some funky name. Something un-American. *Charle'!*

So the two football hotshots drove in fits and starts of silence and small talk through the moneyed streets of Beverly Hills. Both young men looked at the world outside their windows, and it might as well have been Mars to their way of upbringing. Beautiful women in miniskirts, poodles on leashes, fancy cars, a café society just a fifteen-minute drive from the mean streets that surrounded USC. Young looked at all this white wealth and just sighed, thinking to himself that this world was what Graf could aspire to but he could not.

Graf looked at it, and he saw a world every bit as different from his Sylmar as it was from Young's Fresno. They would find the site, park, and go to work. A big USC alum owned the construction company. Not much was expected of them. Hammer some nails. Pick up some bricks. Haul a wheelbarrow. But it gets hot in L.A. in the summer. Sweat soaked Graf's shirt. Young glistened.

About 3:00 or 3:30 it was quittin' time. A little early but a good day's work. Back to the car. Hot as all get-out, the windows rolled up all day in the baking sun. Graf maneuvers the car into the sticky Beverly Hills traffic. A nightmare at this time of day. Stopped. Absolutely stuck.

There's that country music. Some complaints about the construction foreman. A yahoo. The car inches along. A red light, a green, red again. Still stuck on the same block. Slowly but surely Graf gets his green Pontiac down the street, but it's even more backed up than usual.

There, up ahead. Something's . . . happening here. What it is ain't . . .

"Ah, s—t, it's a protest," Graf blurts out.

There, in front of a large public building, was a genuine anti-Vietnam War protest.

"Well I'll be . . . darned," said Young. A highly religious young man, he resisted the other terminology.

The Beverly Hills Police were there. Some of them had their clubs out.

There were long-hairs with signs:

OUT OF VIETNAM

DUMP NIXON

GIVE PEACE A CHANCE!

"Those cops don't need to have their clubs out," said Young.

"What, and let these a--es s--t all over the flag?" said Graf.

A couple of hippies were wrapped in Old Glory. It offended his sensibilities.

"They've got an opinion," said Young.

Graf stared at the demonstration as they inched along. It was Steven Stills and Buffalo Springfield's "For What It's Worth" come to life before their eyes. Graf stopped, looked around.

What was that sound?

"Those people are just noisemakers," Graf said.

Young pondered this. Some silence ensued. Both men, realizing that further analysis of the protest might lead to a place neither was comfortable going, maintained their calm.

Slowly, the green Pontiac worked its way through the traffic, eventually inching onto the Santa Monica Freeway for some more rush-hour traffic back to the USC campus. Finally, Young could stand it no more.

"Hey, man," he said. "What about Martin Luther King in Selma and Montgomery? Were they just 'noisemakers?'"

Graf knew he was being put on the spot. Truth be told, he was not a fan of Martin Luther King. He was not prejudiced, but he did not like the way black folks were always putting white people on the spot. Nothing whites said ever was "right."

"You know what, Charle'," he replied, "I just think there's a better way to demonstrate, a better way to make change."

"Don't you have a social conscience?" asked Young.

"Take Birmingham," said Graf, as if he had not heard Young's question. "In September."

"Yeah, what about it?" asked Young.

"We're goin' back there," said Graf, "whites, blacks. They're all white. Man, *that's* wrong. We have a chance to make a difference, and it won't be through a protest march. It'll be by playing together and demonstrating excellence. Truth. Yeah, truth. No b--t, just the truth."

"What'll be the truth?" asked Charle', imagining Pontius Pilate asking Jesus that very question.

"That's up to us," said Graf. "I know I can't get into these people bad-mouthin' America, but goin' back to Alabama and beatin' those people in front of their Confederate flags . . . *that's* somethin' I can believe in."

Birmingham. Allan Graf had said it. In the 1960s, that loaded word meant more things to more people than just about any other symbol of the decade. Graf saw the Trojans' upcoming trip to Birmingham as an opportunity. Charle' Young and his black teammates were a little more wary about that "opportunity." A lot could go wrong in Birmingham, both on and off the field.

But Charle' Young smiled as he gazed out the window, observing the smog-shrouded neighborhoods to his right, south of Jefferson. The big ol' country boy from Sylmar, Allan Graf, had the ability to *discern*. To Charle' Young's way of thinking, if somebody had that, he or she was ahead of the curve. Charle' also thought about Alabama football coach Paul "Bear" Bryant. This game was his idea. It was a risk for Bear. A big risk. The Trojans were loaded and had the guns to go back there and *embarrass* his team. It occurred to Young that Bear Bryant knew that, and that the coach also had the ability of *discernment*.

Charle' Young looked at Allan Graf and knew he had just made a life-long friend.

Other Voices: Charles "Tree" Young

The term legend *gets thrown around a lot, but at USC many players are worthy of the title. Thus was Charles Young, a sophomore in 1970 and a unanimous 1972 All-American on the "greatest ever" national champions. Inducted into the National Football Foundation's College Hall of Fame in 2004, Young starred for the 1981 world champion San Francisco 49ers. He also played in the 1980 Super Bowl for the Los Angeles Rams.*

Let me start from my point of view, the naïve windows of my life. When I came to USC, it was called an ultraconservative school along the lines of a John Birch Society type of thing. The school attracted people from all sections of the country who came there in the early 1970s. You must understand, two or three years earlier, there were race riots all over the country.

In Birmingham, Alabama, they had a bombing of a church. They had Bull Connor, George Wallace, and "segregation now, segregation forever."

In painting a picture as best I can on a window of that time, on a canvas of time, going back to take a look at it, well, this requires consideration.

Ours was one of the greatest classes ever. There was Sam Cunningham, Rod McNeill, Manfred Moore, Mike Rae, Dave Brown, Pete Adams. It was a group of guys from different backgrounds who were outstanding individuals able to transcend the situations. Into this comes Sam Cunningham, a man who had the ability to communicate with everyone.

Sam's ability to communicate with blacks, whites, Hispanics on our team was invaluable. He was more than a guy who had ability. McNeill grew up in an all-white environment. I grew up in an all-black one in Fresno. Because my high school coach was Greek, I perceive this about them: they think they're that much more civilized.

My high school coach would talk about Greek history and how he was an educator; he mapped out everything, in being an educator, through the superiority of the Greeks. Now John Papadakis is Greek. John had a flair of arrogance.

So all these people are together, and Sam Cunningham is from Santa Barbara, and he knew everybody from growing up—white, black, Hispanic. He brought that team together.

On recruiting blacks at USC. You can put two people in a room, and unless there's understanding, the attitudes that come in the room with them will prevail. When I came to USC—O. J. Simpson and Al Cowlings recruited me— I looked around and asked, "Where are all the blacks?" They had light-skinned blacks, which were more appealing to the consumer, but not too many dark blacks; call them a different shade of black. As we came in, McKay made a statement that he was bringing in different kinds of blacks who were hungry to play, and he was determined to make a difference.

On USC's record. We were all assembled at USC. We were undefeated my freshman year, and we all thought we'd go four years without losing. We figured we'd break Oklahoma's forty-seven-game winning streak. It's not unlike what USC is looking at now, thinking they're unbeatable. That's when you're vulnerable.

Let me put this biblically: "Pride goes before the fall." The history of antiquity, from the standpoint of any great team or nation, falls from within, not from without. They fall from within.

This is how we failed. We were great individuals, but we didn't come together as a unit until we set aside our personal differences. You mention [offensive lineman] Allan Graf; on each team, there are seven guys who are leaders, and those seven have at least three who follow or associate with them. If those seven don't come together, those twenty-eight don't come together. Then the sixty-two don't come together. That was our problem: we were a divided team.

On his teammates. We came together only on the field; that's where Sam came in. Sam was much more than a football player or an ambassador. He was more than "Bam." He was a diplomat extraordinaire. I learned a great deal from Sam. There was a group of us called the Big Five. They came together, all of the extreme talent, and brought it to the University of Southern California. All these different backgrounds.

An example: During that time, if the police stopped me, I'd question the cops and they'd always give me a ticket. So Sam gets stopped by an officer. He gave this officer only graciousness seasoned with wisdom. When it was through, this officer let him go. The lesson: you catch more flies with honey than with vinegar.

I went to Sam's hometown and saw how he got along with people in Santa Barbara. There were all these families, and everybody loved Sam; they basically adopted him. I saw this one gentleman who was a mentor to Sam. Sam transcends all those cultures.

At USC, he implemented all those things, because we had blacks who didn't want anything to do with whites and whites who wanted nothing to do with blacks. Dave Brown, Sam, Pete Adams, Mike Rae, and a bunch of other guys got together off that team. Dave Brown did it, he started [the local chapter of] Fellowship of Christian Athletes, and that brought us together. There are at least five ministers from that team. I hear Jimmy Jones is a minister too. Did you know that he beat out Mike Holmgren for the starting quarterback job in 1969?

Jones was playing with Mike Rae on the bench. The mentality at the quarterback position was that it's a leadership position. All of our education and history, from that standpoint, was that blacks could not lead. So people were looking for any type of reason to get Jones out of that position. He went through hell. To be a black quarterback at USC in 1970, with the mentality of the 1970s, oh man, here he is all the way from the other side of the country, and he has to endure all of these trials and tribulations, all of these setups. You can imagine how many people tried to set him up or provoke him to lose his position.

I believe the best [quarterbacks] have confidence and a touch of arrogance. Jimmy and [Mike] Rae had that. The white guys would console Mike and say he should be playing. The blacks would go with Jimmy. Some blacks raised in a white environment didn't know what to think. All that season was peppered with all that. Jimmy and Mike, then Sam and Charlie Evans at the running back position, as you found out. Evans still holds some of that after thirty-five years. Then there were other positions: Marv Montgomery, a black lineman; tight end Gerry Mullins; and me.

Edesel Garrison was a world-class sprinter and an outstanding receiver, but he played the same position as J. K., and there was tension there. A lot of animosity in regard to all of that, from the standpoint of the coach's son, and he would get a lot of opportunity that another person would not get. A lot of these were crafted in back rooms, but observant persons would see that and question it in their minds or in their actions, in their performance.

On culture at the time. So that's the background, which explains what was transpiring in the early 1970s. There's resistance to all this kind of thing, and it was right here in Los Angeles, California. What was unfolding in Birmingham was a paradigm shift of cultural philosophy on the battlefield, but it was about culture. I was young and naïve, and didn't know anything about it. We were guinea pigs, and these were testing grounds for that battle. We were put in harm's way.

Jimmy Jones took the brunt of it. He was put into an environment of racial hostility, a hotbed of bigotry against blacks who were not allowed on that field. Yet we came down and began to play. The philosophy, in my opinion, was we have a group of whites who believe in white supremacy, thinking they can win with an all-white team against a team that has blacks, with a black quarterback and a black running back, plus the defense was half black.

I think we had six on offense, six or seven on defense. It's an eerie feeling. It's hard for me to say, going back thirty-five years, but I can recall the bus ride from the airport to the hotel, vaguely. On the bus I was always a person; when I went into a town, I didn't go out. I was there strictly for business, to do what I had to do. I stayed in my room and rested for the contest.

But on the bus—people who grew up in the South had different perspectives. Fresno tends to be conservative, but I'm an athlete so I'm not treated like other blacks. I was tolerated, like I was gray, because I had economic value. But driving in that bus, I'm looking at blacks in shanty homes; we call them "shotgun" homes. It's like looking back in time. Tody Smith had a briefcase, and in it, I don't know if it was a .38 or what, but it was a gun. I asked, "Why do you carry a gun?" He said he grew up in the South and said, "Anything can happen down here."

There was an agreement between Bear and McKay. Bear gave his word we'd have protection. Bear was the man down there, and in most cases they'd listen to him. He could get things done.

The KKK was still prevalent. A lot of those guys were part of that; if Bryant had been in 'Bama all that time it's reasonable to think he had an association with that. They'd had every prominent person involved in that organization. But he was trying to get something done. He used McKay. They used each other.

There was no security in the stands. Most of the time, when assassinations are orchestrated, the thing is, the security is usually *involved* in it. If you truly look at history, when presidents are assassinated, people in the cabinet or in the government had something to do with it. Even John Wilkes Booth had government coconspirators. Caesar was killed by people in his own party. The whole time I saw Hank Aaron chasing Babe Ruth's record in Atlanta in the early '70s, this was probably on his mind.

On his memory of the game. I enjoyed that game from the standpoint that they always told blacks we could not do it, that we were not good enough, we were inadequate, inferior. That was the ultimate lie, but we were conditioned that way—trained, educated, or "lack of educated" that way. Now when we get on the field of competition, on a football field or battlefield, it's about survival, and there's no way racism can survive in a foxhole. That's what I like about sports. What I learned about that game, that's why the '72 team paid off, through our trials and tribulations.

What happened in 1970 was the foundation of that '72 team, which some have called the greatest team ever. "Great" means overcoming great obstacles. Without the obstacles we had to overcome, we never would have had that greatness, which was the foundation of that team being laid.

On the role of religion in the game. My overall philosophy is that God rules in the affairs of man. Even in the time of John Papadakis's Greek history, the Romans, the Babylonians, the Egyptians—God rules the affairs of men. Look at this country; our founders came to this country, which was started by King George of England and the King of Spain, Magellan's voyage. During that time they needed workers to work on things. We came over as indentured servants, some of us as slaves. There were opportunities to bring more slaves; and in order to justify it, they had to dehumanize us. A lot of people came over for religious freedom; others to make money; some were outlaws. Kings would send undesirables out here to populate the new land and bring back a fortune. It was a business deal, and because of this they enslaved us. But during that process, some people believed it was wrong. They became abolitionists. Most of them were God-fearing people, and they set out to change all of this.

Going back now to its effect on this game, which we're talking about. The question is, so, is there a divine order in which God intervenes? Yes. If you're asking am I religious, do I believe in God? Yes. I do understand that God rules in the affairs of man. No matter how strong or brilliant you are, or how much money there is in your bank, you are *nothing* without God!

This contest was not a football game. It was staged as a football game in order so that change could be made. It was a paradigm shift, not a revolution. Bear was a part of that; he instigated that. I'm not foolish enough to believe that all whites hated blacks or all blacks hated all whites. It was a *system*. Bryant was in this system. What did I say about empires? Change comes from within. If the devil created the system, then God infiltrated Bear Bryant into that system to do His good work! God used Bear Bryant, whether he was a willing participant or knew what was going on, it does not matter. God used Sam; he got his chance and did what Sam's going to do.

On Bryant's statement. Legend has it that Bryant came to Coach McKay and graciously asked for Sam. I'm sure his approach was seasoned with wisdom. McKay agreed, and Bear took Sam in the locker room. I'm not privy to that, and as legend has it, Bryant has all his players and lets them know, "This is what a football player looks like." What he was telling them, in his own words, is not that "You're not football players because you don't look like this," but "We'll be getting some of these football players."

Sam was uniquely designed to do that. He has a strength and the power of a rhinoceros, but the wisdom and knowledge of that guy Rafiki in *The Lion King*. Power, grace, and wisdom. That's only half of Sam's mental strength.

John Papadakis indicated that the Greeks admired physical beauty, and Sam was an Adonis. That is true, Sam had those qualities, but his real strength was his ability to think, understand, discern. Without discernment and understanding, the physical part never really develops.

In the history of time, God always raises a person, an individual whose work needs to be done. Now we're back to Birmingham, where all that philosophy was being unfolded on the playing field of time. Understanding culture at that time, the way education was being disseminated—all of that to be disproved was a shock to people in that stadium, listening on the airwaves, or watching on TV [the game actually was not televised]. On the other side, it was a source of great jubilation for the lowly janitor or maid or guy selling programs, this team from out West coming out with huge, fast African American vessels of God.

When it came to civil rights, this was not an area for great achievement. It did not begin because the regular rights of citizens, passed in the 1800s but appealed in courts of law, created a flawed system. We never wanted a handout. Maybe that's why a football game symbolizes our achievement in this area. We didn't go to Legion Field asking for a handout. We went down and exhibited the gifts that God gave us.

Other Voices: Coach Dave Levy

Dave Levy played at UCLA but was an assistant on John McKay's staff at Southern California every year McKay was at USC (1960–1975). Many felt Levy should have been his successor, but the job went to the more "telegenic" John Robinson.

I really can't say I have a definitive answer from McKay's perspective, but it seems to me one day he said we'd scheduled a game with Bear. He was associated with Bryant, beginning early in 1963 at a football clinic. I knew Bryant before that. I met him at a clinic at North Dakota State, the kind where we have three practices, then a guy volunteers to play in a game, and the fourth practice is a game. In some states, not all, these were like events where "our" all-stars played an out-of-state all-star team. A combination clinic/game kind of thing.

On the Bryant-McKay relationship. In 1963 we all got acquainted socially and had a good time, so they became social friends and they'd see each other at clinics. As best I know, they just were talking one day and the coach announced it.

What I remember was Bryant coming in to our locker room. He spoke to our team. Now maybe I'm in the coach's dressing room, but after he congratulated us and so on, he asked Coach for permission to take Sam Cunningham. I know it happened, because I know I just looked at it and said, "I'll be damned." Add to that the euphoria of winning the game, but after that you just are concentrating on getting dressed and getting out of there.

I do remember a mostly black crowd around our team bus, but I didn't personally think it so unusual. Our black players had relatives and friends in the area, and obviously they'd not be congregated around the Alabama bus, so it's not really surprising that they'd be in the parking lot, but I don't recall people holding Bibles.

I got dressed and got on the bus. The big thing before the game in the papers was that "blacks are going down to Alabama" and so on, but I don't remember being concerned. There were conversations about what hotel we'd be in and their security, but Bear would make sure there were no riots, so I had no concerns.

On society in the 1960s and 1970s. That said, I don't doubt the gun story. Maybe somebody said it or we got somebody with guns or something, but not everybody was "packing heat."

The players remember more than I do the little details of that game. From the sideline it was very exciting when we got ahead. I thought in preparing for that game that they'd be better than they were. The South had a mystique then. You'd not play them as often, when you have plenty of TV games like today.

I don't ever recall any incident in which any of our players came to us and said, "I got beat out 'cause I'm black." It wasn't perfect harmony; winning brings morale, but we were winning pretty good. I just don't recall any major or even minor incidents.

Society in 1965, as campuses went, USC was in the top one percentile of least problems. It's a private, small university. I think we had less than ten thousand undergrads. Over time, guys would grow their hair, they'd wear those medallions. Campus dress was changing. In 1960 we still had a dress code. The dean would see a student in a tank top and send him back to the dorm to get a shirt. It was nothing like Berkeley.

USC was a conservative campus. The only story I can think of concerned Marv Goux. Some students arranged for a speaker named Brother Lenny, a peripatetic type of guy, a beatnik I suppose, to speak at a sociology class. The class got canceled; I don't know if the professor heard about this guy and didn't want him in the class. So he goes to Tommy Trojan. Well, there's some kind of construction going on in the area, so there's a mound of dirt. Brother Lenny got up to the top of this mound and gathered a crowd, a few hundred maybe. He goes on for about fifteen minutes. Marv and I were in McKay's office looking out at this.

Goux said, "Look at that son of a b--h." He was a real patriot; his father had died in the Battle of the Bulge. McKay says, "Let's forget that, I'll see you after lunch." So that was the last I thought about it until John McKay called me in and said that, apparently, Marv went up and pushed his way through the crowd to Lenny and said, "Why don't you get your a-s out of here." Some are cheering Marv, and others are calling him a Fascist.

The school president told McKay, "You gotta call Marv in."

"Now Marv, you know me, and I feel like you do, but you've got two choices: apologize or refuse." Marv says, "Let me think about it."

The next day he says, "I can't apologize." McKay told the president, I can't swear on it, but I think it was Dr. Norman Topping, and he just said, "Good."

That whole week, this whole thing is getting into the papers, first the *Daily Trojan* and then the *L.A. Times*, with people writing in, some supporting him, some not, all various opinions.

In the last thirty-five years, I recall in my career two specific conversations with athletes about race. One was at Long Beach Poly. I remember talking to Willie Brown, who came to USC, and another halfback at Poly. I said, you gotta use these athletics to get yourself out and make something of yourselves. We talked prejudice, and what they told me caught me by surprise, but as I talked they agreed to some degree that what I was telling them was true.

The next was Mike Garrett. I was the backfield coach. He's an intelligent guy, very intense. He was trying to get an apartment in Pasadena, which at that time I think had no blacks [even though it was the hometown of Jackie Robinson]. We talked about prejudice, me saying to him if we can't allow people to change, nothing's going to change, that each generation's raised with certain social mores, but if they're wrong they have to be able to change. It was not an argument, just a good discussion.

We have to allow people to change. I saw alumni attitudes change. You could see it when you got exposure to different kinds of personalities; as you saw people's performance, it helped [redefine] mores.

Speaking of Mike Garrett, I think he roomed with baseball player Tom Seaver. They had long intellectual discussions. Actor Tom Selleck played sports at USC at this time, too.

John McKay was a leader. To some extent you have to have great athletes to win, but athletics in general are the fairest parts of society. Not always, but mostly. He sought black athletes, not looking to be a social leader, but he thought it was fair and knew they were great. He hired Willie Brown as his first black coach. He liked to get a guy we've had, so he says, "How 'bout Willie Brown?" I think he said, "I'll do these things before we're forced to." But he never, ever said or asked, how many black guys are we starting?

He was attuned to anything coming out of Stanford. He loved to beat Stanford by two thousand points; it was just a thing he had for them because he thought they were hypocrites. That was just one way he found to get ready for Stanford. McKay could get that game face on in a hurry now, especially if the Stanford hecklers were calling him John. Stanford was the perfect venue for these hecklers as we were making the gauntlet into the stadium.

Tom Kelly with the great Sam "Bam" Cunningham. Kelly's caramel-rich voice has described the greatness that is Trojan football for more than forty years. Courtesy of Tom Kelly.

Tom Kelly with Trojan legends John Robinson, John McKay, and Marv Goux. Courtesy of Tom Kelly.

Jeff Prugh, who wrote the game story of the famed 1970 Alabama contest, is seen interviewing Greg Slough in 1970. Courtesy of Jeff Prugh.

Jeff Prugh covered USC and UCLA sports, then later covered politics in the postsegregation South of the late 1970s. Courtesy of Jeff Prugh.

Wendell Hudson was the first black varsity athlete at Alabama when he joined the basketball team in 1969. Courtesy of Paul W. Bryant Museum.

John Hannah, Alabama's All-American lineman, was a sophomore in 1970. He was a teammate of Sam "Bam" Cunningham's in New England for a decade before entering the Pro Football Hall of Fame. Courtesy of Paul W. Bryant Museum.

Coach Paul "Bear" Bryant (right), wearing his trademark houndstooth hat. Courtesy of Paul W. Bryant Museum.

Brice Taylor was USC's first All-American in 1925. He was of African American and Cherokee descent, born without use of his left hand. USC led the way in the area of opportunity for black athletes long before the rest of the country integrated. (Courtesy of the Amateur Athletic Foundation of Los Angeles.)

John McKay (center, holding cigar) won four national championships between 1962 and 1974. (Courtesy of the Amateur Athletic Foundation of Los Angeles.)

Dave Brown and Cliff Culbreath.

Craig Fertig (left) was a coach on John McKay's staff in 1970. Mike Garrett (right) was the second black Heisman Trophy winner and is USC's athletic director today.

John McKay and his staff in the early 1970s.

Sam Dickerson as a Trojan.

USC coaches
Marv Goux (left) and
Dave Levy.

CHAPTER **Fourteen**

Packin' Heat: The New Breed

The blacks on our team had a swagger.
—*John Papadakis*

I n the film *American History X*, the white racist played by Edward
Norton, despite being from L.A., is a Celtics fan. His black fellow
prison inmate, naturally, prefers the Lakers. The reason is the Celtics,
led by Larry Bird, personified the "blue-collar" stereotype; code for smart,
hardworking white athletes who through "heart" can defeat the black players, even if the blacks are better athletes. The Lakers represented "flash,"
"Hollywood," "Showtime," as represented by Magic Johnson.

There have been many hardworking black athletes, such as former
49ers superstar Jerry Rice or the Bears' Walter Payton, whose workout reg-
imens are legendary. There are numerous black stars who are considered
"money players" in the clutch. Basketball great Michael Jordan is an obvious example. Oakland A's pitcher Dave Stewart, playing a position like a
football quarterback that some might not normally associate with blacks,
was a particularly fierce competitor in postseason play, dominating his
more-heralded white rival, Boston's Roger Clemens.

In 1970, Bob Gibson of the St. Louis Cardinals was one of baseball's
greatest pitchers. A proud black man who had played basketball at
Creighton University, Gibson demonstrated the full measure of both pure
athleticism and desire. His manager, Johnny Keane, kept him in the game
for nine innings, despite Gibby's fatigue, to win game seven of the 1964
World Series because "I had a commitment to his heart."

Gibson's performances in the 1964, 1967, and 1968 World Series are, to this day, probably the greatest exhibition of clutch postseason pitching in baseball history. Despite examples such as Gibson, Jim Brown, Gale Sayers, O. J. Simpson, Bill Russell, Oscar Robertson, Willie Mays, Hank Aaron, and others too numerous to list, some white coaches still hung on to the belief that blacks lacked the heart, brains, and spirit to compete.

* * *

Trojan quarterback Jimmy Jones led USC to an undefeated season as a sophomore in 1969. He was a rarity in that era, a black quarterback. In 1966, Michigan State had finished number two in the nation led by a black quarterback, Jimmy Raye. Despite the success of both Raye and Jones, it would be years before a black quarterback would be widely accepted. The common perception was that blacks could be option quarterbacks, running quarterbacks, multitalented athletes, but the traditional quarterbacks—drop-back-in-the-pocket passers who were smart leaders—were still white. There was Johnny Unitas of the Colts, Bart Starr of the Packers, Joe Namath of the Jets, and Len Dawson of the Chiefs, just to name a few. But the black athletes playing for John McKay were a "new breed."

A junior in 1970, Jones was the leader of the USC Trojans. In his three-year career, he would set a number of records. In the late summer of 1970, with the game at Birmingham coming up, he sensed urgency on the club. Preseason camp was rougher than the previous year. There were more fights, more arguments, more acrimony. He was noticing a disturbing trend, the same thing Tom Kelly was noticing: it was too often black on white, white on black, whites crying to Coach Levy, blacks to Coach Brown—"It's all right, Jimmy, don't worry about it, just make the plays, forget about it, man"—but he could not forget about it. He called an emergency meeting in his apartment. Just blacks, just upperclassmen.

The younger blacks were unaware of it. Other players included remnants of the Wild Bunch defensive front of 1969, "crazy" Tody Smith and Charlie Weaver, and running back Lou Harris. A few others. Not everybody knew about it. Sam Dickerson and Clarence Davis have no recollection of it. Sophomores such as Sam Cunningham and Charle' Young were not invited.

"We gotta come together," Jones announced. "We gotta come together for Birmingham."

Platitudes were exchanged, the usual playerspeak about teamwork and self-sacrifice, but what was at hand was more extraordinary than that.

About thirty minutes, maybe an hour went by. In the August heat of an off-campus apartment with no air conditioning, tempers started to flare, accusations were made, voices were raised.

Then defensive lineman Tody Smith created a whole new dynamic. He told his teammates he was planning to bring a gun.

"I don't know about you suckers," he announced, "but I'm packin' heat to Birmingham."

Packin' heat? *A gun?*

"Are you out of your mind?" shouted Jones. He sensed that now he was being faced with the biggest challenge of his young life. The future minister from Harrisburg, Pennsylvania, tried to find a way to dissuade Tody Smith from bringing a gun to Alabama.

The whole idea was not nearly as crazy as it might sound today. The Panthers were making gun ownership in the black community a popular thing. But just a couple of weeks earlier, at the Marin County Civic Center, a black criminal named George Jackson had blown the brains out of a white judge named Harold Haley. A black Communist agitator, Angela Davis, had through Jackson's younger brother helped smuggle the weapon into his jail. Jackson had produced a shotgun and held captive Haley and the prosecuting attorney, Gary Thomas.

A photographer covering the highly politicized trial captured a photo of Jackson holding the shotgun to the head of the bespectacled Haley, an elderly man who looked like everybody's granddad. It would appear in *Life* magazine and earn the Pulitzer Prize. A few minutes later, Judge Haley lay dead, and Thomas was paralyzed for life with a bullet in his side. The event would lead to the installation of metal detectors at courthouses, and a few years later, in response to terrorist hijackings, at airports. But Tody Smith would be perfectly free to pack heat in his briefcase on the plane. Jimmy Jones knew that if a bunch of threatenin' Afro brothers from South Central L.A.—which is how they would have been depicted—were caught in or on their way to white Birmingham with weapons, "all hell" would break loose.

"Tody," said Jones, "I'm askin' you, brother, *do not* bring a gun. These crackers are just waitin' for us to screw up just like that."

"Man," replied Smith, "I'm from the *South*, and I know that down there, anything can happen."

"Hey," piped in Charlie Weaver, an All-American defensive end from Richmond, California, "I'm bringin' a gun, too."

It went back and forth like that for another hour. Finally, an impasse. Jones composed himself.

"All right, here's the plan," the quarterback announced. "From the time we get on the plane until the time we leave Birmingham, all the brothers are gonna stick together. We're gonna watch each other every second. Stay close to that hotel, and always have a brother by your side. Don't venture from that hotel. Stay clear of white women. Just stay in the hotel, there's nothin' but trouble outside the hotel. This ain't Seattle or Berkeley."

Nervous laughter. Jones just looked at his teammates.

"Are we all agreed on this?"

His teammates nodded agreement.

"Yeah, Cap."

"Right on!"

This was going to be one heck of a road trip.

"The blacks on our team had a swagger," John Papadakis told Neal McCready of the *Mobile Press-Register* in 2003. "They knew they were playing in a place where they were highly accepted and promoted, based on their athleticism. Our best players had been black players, at least some of our best players. In any case, they had a swagger and they were loose and they weren't short on words.

"Well, I could tell once we announced that Alabama game, and especially in the fall practices when we gathered, the blacks grew tighter and tighter. You know, like you tighten a drum. They were growing tighter and tighter and tighter and extremely fearful about going down South."

* * *

On the field of athletic strife, honor and loyalty are far more than hoary phraseology. They are the underpinnings of success, the connective tissue of trust that is indispensable to winning in sports. Any baseball double-play combination, any football passer-receiver tandem, any dynamic basketball guard-center duo can exemplify Plato's perception of people "seeing each other in ourselves." Each of these embodies not just the physical attributes of the act but also the spiritual trust and investment that teammates build over hours, days, months, years of practice, repetition, and dedication.

It is in the earthly ideal that Plato's vision begins to take real shape, just as a football team takes shape. Coaches call this "buying into" their team concept. If this doesn't occur, a team is nothing more than individuals, no matter how many all-stars are on the roster. In their conversations that summer, USC's players saw the upcoming game in Alabama as the chance to effectuate real American change. They were led by coach John McKay, a visionary who saw an opportunity waiting at Legion Field, an opportunity that would be anything but utopian. He and his team saw a new world; to them, this would be the *real world*.

The young Trojans, influenced by the symbolism displayed for television news, were looking for something, like Socrates, that was beyond the external world. They had not yet found it. They did not know it yet, but young philosophers searching for the meaning of life dotted their roster. Like Allan Graf and Charle' Young, they were all looking for something to believe in!

Held at the swanky Long Beach Yacht Club, USC's football banquet promised another big season. Sam Cunningham was not thinking about the papers or racial issues. He had put himself in a position to earn the starting fullback job from Charlie Evans. Cunningham, at six foot three and 230 pounds, had competed in the decathlon, considered to be the ultimate test of athletic ability, while still a prep in Santa Barbara. Photographs of the young Cunningham reveal an Adonis with a perfect body like a Greek statue. He was the epitome of what blacks at the time were saying: "Black is beautiful."

When Coach McKay talked to the audience about how the team would be traveling to Birmingham to play a great Bear Bryant-coached Crimson Tide team, he knew that the anticipation would be at a fever pitch, just as it had been when the Trojans (with alum John "Duke" Wayne in tow) opened the 1966 season at Texas. The implications of the game were obvious. Much had changed between 1966 and 1970. The game promised to be a civil war.

Other Voices: Jim Perry

Jim Perry was the longtime sports information director at the University of Southern California. In 1974, he coauthored McKay: A Coach's Story, *the autobiography of John McKay.*

On changes between 1970 and 1978. I was a sportswriter covering UCLA. I moved over to the USC beat, and my first game in that capacity was the 1971 game at the L.A. Coliseum with Alabama. I remember they had a player named John Mitchell and at least two other black players. Whether it could have happened earlier . . . in the early '60s it just wasn't feasible.

I was in Birmingham in '78. USC won twice there, and they won twice in L.A. USC won 24–14 in that 1978 game. I advanced that game and had no feeling of black-white problems. It was just another game in that regard, although it determined a shared national championship. It was a huge game, but not seen as anything remarkable off the field.

On Bear's statement. The story that says Bear Bryant did not have Sam Cunningham on a stool in front of his players, but rather in the crowded hallway between the visiting and home lockers at Legion Field, and that he said, "This here's what a football player looks like," more for the benefit of old-line alumni and administration, makes a lot of sense. He already had black players, but he had a bigger problem with the administration, the fans, and to some extent the media.

On Coach McKay. I cowrote *McKay: A Coach's Story*. McKay wanted it to be called *1st and 25*. It was 1974 when the book came out. McKay scheduled that game with Bear. He made little reference to this game in the immediate years after it, but looking back thirty-five years, having worked on the book with him in 1973, I can see now that three years later it had not reached mythical status yet. That was a 6–4–1 season, not a great year. The focus of the book was on the Notre Dame games, coaching rivalries, how he learned to "let players play," and recruiting.

McKay was close to Bryant; he called him Paul. They liked to drink together, they talked a lot, and their wives were close. Bear's wife's name was Mary Harmon. He did address how tough it was to coach against friends, such as Duffy Daugherty and Darrell Royal. He said after the game he was never comfortable about shaking hands with the other coach. Security wasn't great in those days. Somebody could be hit or stabbed. If he lost he didn't feel like seeing the other coach, and if he won he didn't feel like gloating. In '71 he lost to Alabama.

McKay was a unique personality. USC had very few black athletes before McKay. There was C. R. Roberts, Don Buford, Brice Taylor, and not many others. But it didn't take McKay long to recruit blacks, and he had a lot of them. Jimmy Jones became our first black starting quarterback in 1969 as a sophomore.

More blacks than whites started. McKay was conservative in some ways politically, but his football line was "win the damn game."

"Shut up and play."

"Do your job."

McKay's ambition from the beginning was to win, but to win successfully. If the best players were black, that was not an issue. He didn't talk about USC's black-white relations. They were pretty good in tumultuous times. He'd just play the best player in the game no matter who he was.

McKay was Catholic, but I'm not sure he was real religious. Others might know his religious convictions, whether he was churchgoing, better than I.

McKay's favorite movies were old John Wayne movies, but he was also highly influenced by the film *Patton*, starring George C. Scott. He used to lecture me. One time, I'm at UCLA, and he's asking, "Why are you writing that s--t about UCLA?" and he said, "You should see *Patton*." I'm twenty-eight and antiwar; I think I snorted something.

"I know how you feel," said McKay, "but you should see it. It's revealing." When his assistants saw that movie, they felt that McKay *was* Patton—an absolute dictator who cared about his men but was tougher than hell. You knew who was the boss. That was McKay. *McKay* felt he was Patton.

Craig Fertig was like a second son to McKay. Dave Levy was more cynical. Levy respected him but had not played for him and had a differing view. McKay was very demanding, decisive. Coaches are afraid to make the call on the goal line, but he made those decisions. He'd not walk away. He was stubborn in his beliefs and knew how to coach the running game. You know the old line about why O. J. Simpson was carrying the ball so much: "It's not heavy, and he doesn't belong to a union." McKay was very bright, and he respected people who were tough; if you came back at him he respected that. You could change his mind. He was in charge, he was old-fashioned, but on occasion his mind could be changed. He and Bryant were alike in that way.

Bryant was a "tough guy" coach who was in power and coached from a tower. McKay sat in a golf cart. If something upset him, he would get out of that golf cart in the middle of his players. He didn't like coaching from a tower; he wanted to be in touch with his players. He had an incredible sense of humor. He could be a very funny person, but sometimes he was a terror. But when trying to be funny, his one-liners were incredible. He'd be complaining about something, and I'd show up. I'm the only person there, so he's not doing it for the benefit of an audience, and he'd say such funny things. The 1975 team was struggling, and McKay said, "Our offense couldn't move the ball against a strong wind."

Other times he'd say, "I hate the first game of the season. I'd rather open with the second game." In pro football you can get the kinks worked out in the exhibitions, but in college you have nine months, then you open the season for real. In 1974 we won only half the national title because we lost to Arkansas in the first game.

McKay could be one of the funniest guys I've ever heard. He'd visit seven or eight booster clubs with large crowds, and he'd entertain people, taking things from the previous year and putting his spin on it. McKay could have been a stand-up comic.

He had a dry wit, was laconic and moody. When you approached him in the office you never quite knew what mood you'd get, so he had the edge on people that way. Part of it was his short temper, but that was a little misleading. At other times he had great patience, depending on his mood. He could give you an icy stare that was chilling, but if he wanted to be charming, he was the most charming of men.

When I worked on his book he was good on a tape recorder, and I'd get his surly flavor. I told my wife how tough he could be, so the first time she met him he charmed her socks off. She said he "wasn't at all like you said."

When I finished taping for the book, he needed to do more, but we had run out of time. He said, "I'm coaching an all-star game"—the NFL won't allow these games anymore because of injuries, but thirty years ago they had these games, the College All-Star Game and one in Texas he coached in 1973, the Coaches All-American Game, and he says, "Why don't you come down. I'll have a lot of time."

I went down. That's where I got to know John Robinson. We went drinking with him, Ben Martin of Air Force, and Duffy Daugherty. If you do a book in their voice, it gets in your head, and you understand their temperament. I had to ask something of my wife, and I went up to my wife, Cathy, and I barked out some order. We'd been married two months. Corky McKay said to Cathy, "You don't have to put up with that." I had started to sound like McKay!

On rivals. The two games that made the biggest impression on McKay were the 51–0 1966 loss to Notre Dame and a 20–16 loss to UCLA and Gary Beban in 1965. The Notre Dame loss was the worst in USC history. In that UCLA game, Beban threw two touchdown passes late. In those days, if you don't win the Pac 8 [the AAWU in 1965] you don't go to a bowl. USC dominated but had too many mistakes and blew a ten-point lead in the fourth quarter. Tommy Prothro had beaten McKay when he had been at Oregon in 1960, and McKay didn't like Prothro. It was the most galling loss ever, that and the 1966 loss. People said Prothro outcoached him.

Fertig said McKay watched that '66 Notre Dame and '65 UCLA games several times a week. McKay said, "Not a day goes by in which I don't think about 51–0. For a year not a night went by in which I would go to bed and not think about it. It still stuck in my throat."

In 1967 USC, who had not won in South Bend since 1939—we're number one but a twelve-point underdog because of that history, and because Ara Parseghian was a damn good coach—well, USC won, 24–7. It was a huge win. I always thought the most impressive thing he ever did, not the four national titles, the unbeaten teams, Tailback U., and the Heismans; nothing was more impressive than turning that series around. In the early years McKay won only twice. He lost five of seven. Parseghian was a fabulous coach, I think a little underrated, and in '66 had humiliated him, and McKay's team went to the Rose Bowl after losing to Parseghian.

Pete Carroll turned the whole USC program around, as McKay did, but the Notre Dame teams McKay was beating were the best in the country every year. McKay was facing a guy who could coach, with good athletes, who knew what to do with 'em. Ron Yary said he was amazed at how big the Notre Dame guys were. Alan Page and Carl Eller, I think. They were big, strong, and well coached.

"We were all psyched up and gained just one yard," Yary said.

In a span of games from 1966 to 1974, every game had an impact on the national title. Every year. It was a string of games like none ever, before or since. Not all games were on TV in those days, but this game was always on nationally. The ratings were fabulous. USC and Notre Dame represented the pinnacle of the college football world.

Other Voices: Jeff Prugh

Jeff Prugh is uniquely qualified to address the 1970 USC-Alabama football game and the social aftermath of that event. He coauthored (with Dwight Chapin) The Wizard of Westwood, *a book about John Wooden and UCLA basketball that focused on the social questions revolving around college students in L.A. He also wrote* The Herschel Walker Story, *which deals at length with the civil rights aspect of sports in the South.*

Prugh was the L.A. Times *beat writer for Trojan football, writing the game story that appeared under Jim Murray's column, "Hatred Shut Out as Alabama Finally Joins the Union," on September 13, 1970.*

I covered USC for the *L.A. Times* in 1969 and '70, then went back to USC for the 1972 season. Jim Murray and I went to Birmingham to cover this game—me first, Jim second, on Wednesday. The next day, we drove to

Tuscaloosa, and Jim good-humoredly described our appointment with Bryant as "elephant disease." We went in at 10:00 a.m., and his office looked like that of the president of General Motors—mahogany paneling, Oriental trappings—with Bryant sitting at his desk in a dress shirt and tie, and the shirt looked like he had slept in it. As he talked, he spat into a large ashtray. Whether it was snuff or not, I don't know.

It was very clear in talking to Bryant that he understood the social implications of this game. He volunteered that he was bemoaning the fact that USC had Clarence Davis at tailback, that he was born in Birmingham, and he was one who got away. Davis was the symbolism that Bryant was trying to convey. If Davis had stayed in Alabama all those years, he'd've been at [the University of] Alabama.

On the significance of the game. The 1970 USC-Alabama game is a story that few people saw as significant at the time. Murray did, but neither of us really knew how significant it would be over the future years. It was easier for Jim, but both he and I sensed, without saying it, that Bryant was "crazy like a fox." To play this game at Legion Field, as you know, with the history of racism in the South still very fresh and very much alive at that time. The only sport that had integrated in the SEC was basketball, and that was very limited.

I believe Perry Wallace at Vanderbilt broke the basketball color barrier; I think it was 1967. There may have been a handful of black basketball players in 1970, but don't hold me to that. I don't believe there were any on Pete Maravich's team at Louisiana State.

A little anecdote is, I reported this on the Monday follow-up, I was at the Holiday Inn in Birmingham, and men were sitting around the table, obviously football fans. I overhead both men say, "I bet Bear wishes he had some of them nigra boys on their team." That was the new sentiment, the postmortem, and it was revolutionary. It was obvious that things were going to change from that day forward, but I could not anticipate the pace and speed of change. Later, I went to Atlanta to become our bureau chief there.

On progress in the South. I thought, regarding that game, that it was a great experience for me. It was enriching covering a lot of the aftershock of the civil rights era, stumbling on stories both mainstream and otherwise. For me personally, the 1970 game crystallized the thinking that there was much more to write about than just sports. With regard to this game, in many ways it did for the collegiate sports landscape in the Southeast what Carrier did with air conditioning. Carrier is the father of air conditioning. This seems simple, but the rise of the modern South is not just about civil rights but can be traced to the economic development in the region that came about once the buildings could be cooled in the summer via air conditioning.

I never quite looked at it from this standpoint, but I see it from sports and commerce. As you know, the foundations of the civil rights movement are its black churches. I see sports and entertainment as the cement mixers of our world. Those are two areas that tend to break down ethnic social barriers, and it went a long way toward silencing George Wallace.

One thing, as a sidelight, is that after I had moved to the South for two to three years, I did break a story about how Wallace's stand, basically the day he stood in the door to keep blacks from enrolling, how it was rigged up so it helped both sides! I went down there to lecture in 2001 about Wallace and other civil rights stories. They were good to me at the University of Alabama, and I said the kind of things that if I had said them in 1970, I would not have been received kindly. It brings to full circle the South, which I had left in 1990.

It shows the amount of change that did follow. I talked about this game; this was in 2001, but many of the students had no context about it.

On why Bear chose USC. I'm not sure whether Alabamians really felt that USC was a school that stood out in terms of being the "right" team to make such an impression. A lot of people from the South confuse USC with UCLA and don't know that USC is a private school. The fact that USC is an affluent school, with a large, well-to-do alumni base that is conservative and strong in Orange County, I'm not sure this registered in Alabama football fans' minds as the game was played. I can see that Bryant chose McKay out of friendship, more so than choosing somebody else, based upon being less bitterly divisive than a school from the Yankee North.

On racism. In 1976, I wrote a story for the *Times* that was never published. It was about Gerald Ford versus Georgia Tech at Ann Arbor, Michigan, in 1934. A lot of racial angst existed in advance of that game because Michigan had a black end named Willis Ward, who later became a judge in Michigan. In a nutshell, what happened was Georgia Tech refused to play the game if Ward suited up, so all kinds of fury ensued. Finally, Michigan caved and said they'd sit Ward if Tech decided not to play its starting end. Ward heard the game on the radio at a frat house.

In '76, Willis stood up for Ford against [Jimmy] Carter and told a story that there was some allegation that a Tech player shouted across the line about Michigan not having their "n--r." On the next play, Ford and a teammate blocked that man so hard he had to be carried off the field. Ward said he heard that and came back to practice; and there Ford came up and told him, "We got one for you, Willie." Michigan won that game.

On the tension at the game. I almost got in a fight with a guy in the press box at this USC-Alabama game in the first quarter. This guy's pounding on the table, yelling whenever Johnny Musso got the ball. He yelled so loud that I couldn't hear what the PA announcer was saying, how many yards Musso had and so on.

So I asked him to please try to keep it down so I could concentrate on my work, and he says, "You're from the West Coast, ain't ya, rootin' for Southern Cal?" He kept yelling, so I asked Charlie Thornton, the Alabama SID, to take care of it; and Thornton had a couple of guys come and remove him. He says to me, "I'll see you after the game." And I just said, "I'll be around."

Afterward, I ran into this guy and he apologized. "Your team was so good and our team was so bad, I just lost control," he said. That setting in Birmingham was like few I've ever seen.

CHAPTER Fifteen

Pregame Jitters

I wish we had guys who ran that fast.
—*Alabama quarterback Scott Hunter, speaking of black players with whom he visited Vietnam*

Crimson Tide quarterback Scott Hunter wanted to watch USC game film. He was from the Deep South and understood the long-term implications of the game. Bart Starr had come from the University of Alabama, as had Namath and Kenny Stabler. Starr and Namath had become famous on integrated pro teams, as would Stabler. Hunter was a big deal in his state and would later play for the integrated Green Bay Packers. So, following in the tradition of Starr, Namath, and Stabler, Hunter understood that he had the responsibility of upholding tradition. In Alabama, playing quarterback was a great honor.

By virtue of his position, young Hunter was finding himself to be a big man on campus in a way that only Southerners treat their football heroes. There is a disconnect from reality that comes with that role, sometimes at a heavy price. Hunter could walk the streets of Tuscaloosa and call his own shots so long as he was the starting quarterback for the Tide—and so long as the Tide won. Southern belles at the University of Alabama are beautiful, with mellifluous voices so tempting they drive men wild. These girls found Scott Hunter to be the apple of their eyes.

But Hunter, being a Southern boy of a certain breeding, was a gentleman, respectful of his elders, who in his neck of the woods prefer their young to address them with "yes, sir" or "no, ma'am." This kind of politeness is also expected of an Alabama quarterback. Hunter would be required to lead by example.

Hunter had played sandlot ball with blacks, which was not entirely unusual. Young athletes, full of fire and competitive edge, like to test themselves. Occasionally, white kids would cross the tracks to run races or play football games against black kids. A scene from the 1988 film *Everybody's All-American* depicts Dennis Quaid doing just that. Hunter had also played in high school all-star games with blacks. He knew they were fast and talented.

However, when Hunter looked at tape of USC's January 1, 1970, Rose Bowl victory over Michigan, 10–3, he came away feeling that USC was not as fast as he thought they would be. This was an odd observation, considering they gave up only three points to a team that a little over a month earlier had beaten the number one ranked Ohio State Buckeyes, 24–12, a defending national championship team that some thought was the greatest of all time.

But Hunter was clearly still concerned about the game. When Alabama's star running back Johnny Musso, a burly Italian American, asked Hunter to assess USC, Hunter told Musso about the "black dudes" he played with touring military bases. "I wish we had guys who ran that fast," he said.

Hunter's counterpart, Jimmy Jones, was under pressure. His fellow black teammates understood it well.

"Jones went through hell," recalled tight end Charle' Young.

Separate camps—blacks for Jones, whites for backup Mike Rae—had formed, with certain "moderate" elements who "didn't know what to think," according to Young.

Rae would, in fact, lead USC's 1972 national championship team—a club still considered by some to be one of the greatest in college history. Rae would go on to become a fixture as Ken Stabler's backup on the championship Oakland Raiders teams. But in the spring of 1970, Jones was unsure of what to worry about most: Rae, racism, or both.

USC's African American players were nervous, and not just about Birmingham.

McKay and Bryant had established a friendship over the years, based on their mutual love of football, whiskey, and duck hunting. They were better at coaching football and drinking whiskey than they were at duck hunting, but the serenity of the hunt provided them a chance to talk freely, sometimes with the encouragement of the alcohol.

They were equals, probably the two best college coaches in the country. Woody Hayes of Ohio State had his supporters. Bo Schembechler had just started to revive Michigan after a moribund period. Penn State's Joe Paterno had his team at the top, and of course Darrell Royal of Texas and Frank Broyles of Arkansas were heroes in the Southwest Conference. But Bryant and McKay were legends already, with truly national reputations. Their personalities—homespun, charismatic, a twinkle in their eyes—had won over the sports media. Thus, a friendship based on mutual respect emerged.

Coach Bryant presided over his practices sitting in a high tower where he communicated via megaphone, sounding like a Southern version of John Huston playing God in the 1966 classic *The Bible*. Down below, the "big uglies," as John Madden calls them, men such as future All-Pro John Hannah (who would be a teammate of Sam Cunningham's with the Patriots), battled it out in the Cage. These battles were won through brute force. He liked guys like Hannah, who could drive a bull out of the Cage.

But the game was not entirely won in the trenches. All the size and strength in the world would be of no value if Bear's big men could not catch up with USC's black men.

Bryant knew all of this to be true. He knew that USC would come in with fresh legs in their season opener, not racked by the kinds of injuries that slow a team down the stretch. He knew that McKay was an innovator who had changed football and was continuing to do so. The USC coach instituted the I formation, revolutionized the quarterback from a "triple threat" to a field engineer, and had opened the game up with play action, much like Kansas City's Hank Stram had done in the AFL.

Bryant still represented the old stuff: "the Cage mentality." Whether or not he would change with the times would determine his place in history. That meant not just opening up his offensive schemes but also opening up a closed society. He knew his team could lose to an integrated squad in front of seventy thousand fans in their home stadium. He knew that if this happened, it would occur to a lot of people that not merely the formations and plays would have to change.

Maybe, just maybe, he was counting on it.

As practice heated up in Los Angeles prior to the trip, small rifts continued to make their presence known. Too often, it would take on a black-white dynamic. White players spoke to the white assistant coach, Joe Gibbs. Black players such as Clarence Davis sought out the black assistant coach, Willie Brown. Davis was feeling some real trepidation about going back to Birmingham. Brown was sensitive to the concerns of any African American during those trying times. McKay had hired Brown, a Trojan legend and NFL veteran, largely to relate to his black players. He especially needed his help on this trip. The challenge for McKay and his staff was to take this nervous energy, these "pregame jitters," and use them to get the team geared up for Alabama. Their differences would have to become their strengths against an "enemy" as easily identifiable as the all-white Crimson Tide.

Offensive lineman Dave Brown, a white member of the Christian group Athletes in Action, invited his teammates to come to their next meeting. Many of the players thought Christianity was a joke. In 1970 Brown, still an underclassman with no clout, was in the minority. His team was divided. Brown knew that the racial fissures could be turned into an emotional yet superficial source of bonding in Birmingham, and that left unmanaged, over time these fissures would crack. He knew that for the team to rise to their full potential, both on and off the field, they would have to truly come together. He knew only one source capable of making that happen!

Local leaders tried to apply pressure on Bryant not to schedule the integrated Trojans, but Bryant had powers he did not have in 1959. He understood that a new day had dawned. Bryant was now emboldened by his successes over the years. He made it clear to any detractors or noisemakers that the game was on.

Other Voices: Coach Christ Vagotis

Christ Vagotis played under Coach Bryant and was an assistant on his staff. He was the main recruiter responsible for bringing in Wilbur Jackson as the first African American scholarship football player at Alabama. He became an assistant under Howard Schnellenberger in Miami and is currently on Schnellenberger's staff at Florida Atlantic.

I played for Coach Bryant from 1963 to 1966, was a grad assistant from 1967 to 1969, almost into 1970, then I graduated in the spring of '70 with my master's degree. I recruited Wilbur Jackson as a graduate assistant for Coach Bryant. I also recruited John Mitchell. I was at Alabama in 1963 when the state legislature was debating all that stuff that was going down with Governor Wallace. I've been with Coach Schnellenberger since he took over.

On integration. Integration actually was thought about in the legislature. They held everything back there in Alabama, as far as letting Coach Bryant do what he wanted to do, but after that 1970 game he went to Montgomery and told them he could no longer compete without having black athletes. Legally, integration had started, but hearts and minds had not changed yet. That's what had to happen, so he needed to go. You've got to remember, this is Alabama, and all of this stuff happens at a slower pace. I'm from Canton, Ohio, so I had to adjust my way of thinking and living, to develop a whole different perspective.

When Coach Bryant went to the legislature, he wanted to get rid of opposition, to create political unity that would open doors, to let us compete in the athletic arena with the rest of these people. You can't win with a singular group of players. I was from the North and I'm of Greek descent, and for this reason I was chosen to recruit blacks. It was not said, but it made sense to me. I think it was sort of like breaking the ice. Alabamians didn't used to think of me even as an American because I was Greek and from Ohio. I wasn't considered a full-fledged American.

We went to a banquet. I was a freshman, and one of the Alabama alumni said, "We got this guy named *Fagotis*"—he couldn't pronounce my name correctly—"and we know he's not a Negro. We don't know what he is, but at least we know he's not a *Negro*."

On Southern culture. This seemed ironic to me, since if you look at Southern history, aristocracy, and architecture, you'll find many of their public buildings and plantation mansions are built with columned pillars reminiscent of the Greek Parthenon. The Founding Fathers and Southern aristocracy studied Plato and Greek philosophy; they had a great impact on our early documents and throughout Southern education.

On 'Bama's black players. Anyway, Wilbur Jackson may not have been the "black Ray Perkins," but he was a "black Johnny Musso." He was a clean-cut kid; he spoke articulately and was obviously going to be a good student. He couldn't fail at it; that would make us all look bad. I'm sure there was suspicion on his part. He had to be a pioneer and a pathfinder at that time, so things were told to him: "You can't make mistakes." At the same time, we assured him, "We can't fail with you [on our team]; we're picking you." He had all the assurance in the world that he was the right guy. We wanted it to be as natural as it possibly could be. We gave him the option of staying with someone or having his own room. We just wanted to make it as easy as possible. On the other hand, we didn't want to set up something just for him because he was a minority. That wouldn't sit right with him; it wouldn't be natural.

We didn't want to lose Wilbur Jackson to somebody else. His parents, to us they were nice, but I'm sure they had a lot of questions and animosity. Letting their son go or not was a big decision. A lot of Northern schools were after him, but you also have to remember, Grambling or Florida A&M wanted him too.

There was a lot of anticipation about Wilbur and questions about whether this was the right thing, from a school standpoint as well as from the black community. Fans of Grambling and other black schools were upset. The traditional black schools, now we're cutting into their recruiting, so they were very upset. They were telling him, "You're gonna be treated like dirt by a bunch of crackers. Do you really wanna take your family through this?" and dragging his folks into it.

On the modern game. But these arguments were internal and not something I had to contend with. It was in the newspapers, white and black both. Looking back, thirty-five or forty years ago, in order to win national championships, you had to have the right amount of everything. Now it's minority players: If you have too many whites, it's not gonna be right; but too many minorities are not right either. You can't have too many Hispanics; that's not right. You gotta have just the right mix. We have different cultures among minorities now. Within black athletes, you have suburban blacks, inner-city blacks, country blacks. When they come together now, that's where the strife is. It's not white-black anymore, but different cultures within minorities.

We were learning from each other in the '60s. Now that we know each other better, we're competing, when in the past we were learning from each other. The competition now is not just on the field but also for cars, girls, things outside of the field, materialistic things. And with that pot of gold when you leave, if you go to the NFL, it's too much money, too fast.

On Bryant's insight. It was innocent in the 1960s, which made it happen. The insight of Coach Bryant to see that game and take that step—he was an innovator in football; now he was an innovator who could walk in [to the issue of civil rights] very gently. Bear Bryant is a major figure in civil rights because once Alabama did it, it was like one of those forest fires they get when the land is dry out in California. *Boom!* And that fire just spread.

Other Voices: Wilbur Jackson

Wilbur Jackson was the first recruited African American incoming freshman scholarship football player at the University of Alabama. He was a freshman in 1970 and starred for the Crimson Tide in the early 1970s. He started out as a homesick, lonely kid from Ozark, Alabama, and ended up being voted captain of the team his senior year before embarking on a successful career with the San Francisco 49ers.

I played for the 49ers for six years. There was a big cultural difference between San Francisco and Alabama, but the football difference was really night and day. In Alabama, it's part of life. In California, it's just laid back. Near San Francisco they have a "Big Game" between Stanford and Cal, but that's no comparison with Alabama-LSU or Alabama-Auburn.

When I was recruited, my first contact was in my junior year in high school, by Pat Dye. There were two other seniors in Ozark being recruited, so Dye came down in the spring. He'd seen tapes of mine in spring training; my high school coach showed him. He and I talked to a counselor. I didn't put a lot of stock in it at that time, but Dye was there again the next year. They started to recruit me heavier as the year went on. My father had put my sisters through school on a railroadman's salary, so I really was interested in a scholarship.

My first eleven years I went to totally segregated schools, but my senior year, we all went to a former "white" school. It was no big deal my senior year because the whole school system changed that year to integration. In '69 they forced it to change, and we all went to the all-white school. I was with my whole class all the way, so it was not as big a shock.

At Alabama, I think things were as smooth as they could have been. Coach Bryant had mentioned, "If you come here and ever have problems, come see me, and I'll make it as easy as possible." No special treatment, but Coach Bryant said he would treat me equally, and he was true to his word.

If you're good in sports, people like you; they perceive you in a certain way. A lot of people were not familiar with blacks, but I was not familiar with whites at that time. They gave me an opportunity, and this in turn provided opportunity for others who otherwise would not have been there. I met people on campus and got to know people. It was a great opportunity.

On progress at 'Bama. From 1969 to 1973 there was a lot of change, but it happened gradually. Going through it then, I didn't notice it. I was the first black player, and when I left I was the team captain. There were nine blacks eligible to vote, so the white players voted for me. What more can I say?

I look back to try to determine a point of reference when the change was happening. I have always been involved with Christianity. It's a good question to ask whether this was the force that made change happen, not just initially but also in terms of the attitudes that allowed my white teammates to vote me team captain four years later. That's hard, because each one is different. My family is conservative. I was raised in the church. I'm not saying I'm perfect. We all fall a little short, but my parents gave me a good foundation, and in public I never strayed. I give you the benefit of the doubt, and even if you do something, then I'll try to understand why you do or don't do what you do.

When integration first happened, I see it as a middle road. I go with "winning games" as being the first motivation of people to begin with. You need the best athletes that you possibly can get to win. If they're black, so be it. A lot of people felt if they could win with all-white players that it would be fine to keep it that way; but over time they needed black players because black athletes were leaving the South. In the beginning, it was just winning games, but out of that came a redeeming quality. As they say, God works in mysterious ways. He picks all kinds of ordinary people to do His work—sometimes sinners, sometimes football players.

As I watch that 1970 game, there was a lot of pride looking at the Southern Cal quarterback, a guy named Jimmy Jones. I'd seen them the year before. Here's a black quarterback leading a major college program that's always playing for a national title, so there was pride in me, sure. But I was still at Alabama, so it was mixed emotions. A lot of people also took pride looking on that field and seeing Clarence Davis, who was from Birmingham originally.

On Bryant's statement. I was not in the locker room, so I didn't hear Coach Bryant say Sam Cunningham was "what a football player looks like." As for the young guys who were players on that team, as opposed to the more entrenched attitudes of older folks, it's hard to say how each individual felt about it, whether the young players were for integration. Let me just say this, if I'd had a bad experience when I was there, I would not have sent my daughter there.

I went to the twenty-five-year anniversary of our 1973 team, and it was one of the best times I've had in a long time. It was a lot of fun, seeing guys I'd not seen in twenty-five years as if I hadn't seen them in two weeks; with these guys we could be talking all night. Yeah, I'm proud to say that my being there in 1970, well, my attitude changed and so did the attitudes of others.

CHAPTER Sixteen

Color Blind

My father was absolutely race neutral.
—*John McKay's son, former USC receiver J. K. McKay*

J im Murray was a press box Shakespeare, a man of such vast talent as to eclipse almost all other sports columnists before or since. Like McKay, Murray was an Irishman with an Irishman's wit. Hailing from Hartford, Connecticut, he had come west to write for *Time* magazine. In the 1950s, he was assigned to the Hollywood beat, which in those days was a combination of glamour and bird's-eye observation of true decadence. It was the era of Frank Sinatra and Ava Gardner, the emergence of the Rat Pack, the rise of Mob-controlled Las Vegas, and the last vestiges of the studio system.

One night Murray had a "date" with movie star Marilyn Monroe. It was an interview, but when a young man dines with the likes of Marilyn, fantasies abound. Marilyn asked Murray if she could excuse herself and leave, not with Jim but with somebody else.

Murray observed that the "somebody else" was Joe DiMaggio, hiding in a secluded booth in a dark corner of the restaurant. "Losing" the girl to Joe D. was okay by Murray. It was not long thereafter that the two were married.

Murray, seeing the interest generated by his writings about Hollywood celebrities, approached Time-Life publishing überboss Henry Luce with an idea for a glossy, color-photo-heavy magazine about the lives and loves of entertainers. Luce told him nobody would read stuff like that. Later, when *People* came into being, Murray received no credit or compensation.

Murray loved history and was known to write something along the lines of "USC wasn't a football team on Saturday. They were the Wehrmacht taking Poland." Or somebody was to "offensive strategy what Napoleon was to artillery." Or a great pitcher was tantamount to a master violinist on a Stradivarius. Mainly because of Murray, the *L.A. Times* had the best sports section in America.

The publishers of the paper were the Chandler family. They ran a conservative ship that catered to the heavy Christian readership that made up disparate L.A. suburbs such as Orange County, Long Beach, and Pasadena. The *Times* had strongly backed the rise of Richard Nixon as he made his name through the House Un-American Affairs Committee investigations of the 1940s, his vice presidency under Dwight Eisenhower in the 1950s, and his presidential comeback in 1968.

The paper had just as strongly supported Ronald Reagan, who in 1970 was in the middle of a successful eight-year run as governor of California, his popularity coming from the law 'n' order conservatives who liked his hard line on campus protestors. By the early 1970s, the decision was made to upgrade the *Times* into a world-class national publication, on par with the *New York Times* and the *Washington Post*. Over time, it toned down its partisan Republicanism. Throughout the 1970s and 1980s, the paper maintained an even approach and had a reputation for digging deeper and more exhaustively into a wider array of political, social, entertainment, local, national, and global stories than any paper in the world.

Throughout the 1990s, the *Times* continued to be one of the real papers of "record," still providing the kind of in-depth analysis and long, detailed stories that few other papers do. But as the paper tilted further and further to the Left politically, at the same time finding itself becoming a subsidiary of, of all things, the *Chicago Tribune* company, its reputation and subscription base suffered.

As the football season got closer, the L.A. sports media assembled for a press conference with John McKay, organized by USC's sports information director, Don Andersen. Among the writers were *L.A. Herald-Express* sports editor Bud Furillo, the venerable lover of all things Trojan, and also of the *Herald-Express*, Jim Perry, coauthor of McKay's autobiography. There was Murray, John Hall, and Mal Florence of the *L.A. Times*, plus young college football beat writers Dwight Chapin and Jeff Prugh.

Hall and Florence were terrific scribes, although today they would be considered too partisan toward their Trojans. Florence in particular assumed the role of unofficial USC sports historian. The passing of Florence and Murray leaves that post begging to be filled, and so far nobody at the *Times* has stepped up to the plate.

Hall and Florence were old school. Bud Furillo was of their generation, but he was ahead of his time. Known as "the Steamer," Bud was a throwback in one regard: he drank, partied, and chased women with the players. Today, it is almost inconceivable that a sportswriter and a Major League baseball player would be good friends, but Furillo was just that with such L.A. wildmen as Angels' playboy Bo Belinsky, the Lakers' Hot Rod Hundley, and other colorful characters. They would meet at a joint in Baldwin Hills called Ernie's House of Surface, which was a denizen of gamblers, hookers, scuffed-shoe reporters, and pro athletes. Furillo would act as unofficial PR man for players, introducing them to important business contacts or acting as their "beard" in order to effectuate various liaisons with the ladies.

These were the days when a player might hold out for an extra grand, where $18,000 was considered good money. Where Furillo was "new breed" was in his New Deal political ideas. He had grown up in Ohio and had seen the effects of the Great Depression. His liberalism was less economic in variety and more social. The New Deal had been popular, and in 1970 the remnants of the Great Society were still being put in place by, of all people, Richard Nixon. Furillo had a heart of gold. He did not help players just to get a story or to sidle close to their female "leftovers." He genuinely wanted to help people, and he had a particular desire to see justice for minorities, who of course were already a major portion of the sporting scene.

Furillo's social ethos was carried forward by his protégé, Doug Krikorian, a talented writer who now pens a column for the *Long Beach Press-Telegram* in addition to sportstalk on TV and radio and occasional forays into Hollywood (*Arli$$*). Krikorian, like Murray, had an eye for more than the Xs and the Os. He wanted to know what made great athletes tick. He also wanted to know what made average athletes tick.

Murray, Hall, Florence, Furillo, Perry, Chapin, and Prugh, along with Loel Schrader and Allan Malamud, were just a few of the talented members of the sporting press with whom McKay had to deal on a regular basis. McKay often engaged them at Julie's, another rather archaic practice by today's standards. McKay is one of the great legends of college coaching, and his record reflects the reasons via cold statistics. But his legend and place in history are very much intertwined with the colorful prose that described him, his commentary, his teams, and his times. It was a marriage made in Heaven, or at least at USC. It might be said that no coach was ever covered by a better group of sports media than was McKay in the 1960s and 1970s.

But there had been others before McKay. In the 1950s, UCLA coach Red Sanders was an extremely flamboyant man. He said the USC-UCLA game was "not a matter of life and death; it's more important than that." When Sanders died of a heart attack in 1958, sportswriters lost one of their favorite sources of quotations. Subsequent UCLA football coaches Tommy Prothro, Pepper Rodgers, Dick Vermeil, and Terry Donahue ranged from businesslike to folksy to boyishly charming, but none had Sanders's flair for "off the record."

USC baseball coach Rod Dedeaux might have been the most gregarious sports figure in L.A., but college baseball just did not generate great publicity. Dodgers manager Walter Alston was a dud, pure and simple. UCLA basketball coach John Wooden may have been a sainted man, but he provided zero color. Rams coach George Allen was too driven and workaholic to give the writers much beyond platitudes.

McKay, on the other hand, was a natural comic who had perhaps the most prestigious coaching job in Los Angeles. He used the press, and they loved him for making their jobs easier. McKay's mood swings suggest that he might have had a clinical imbalance, which in his era was just something a real man shrugged off. He came from the school of thought that the best answer for psychological problems came from football coaches who shouted things like, "Suck it up," "Shrug it off," and "Pick yourself up."

McKay was from West Virginia. His Catholicism formed his conservative view of life; right and wrong; and how to deal with young people, whether it be his sons, his daughter, his players, or blacks.

"I never saw color," McKay said. "I always said, the best man gets the job."

This was a typical "white man's code" among men of McKay's generation. Many chose to abuse this code, often determining that the best man was the white man, using nebulous criteria in decision making. McKay definitely had racial baggage. Issues such as interracial dating, criminal justice, and the like were tainted by his feeling that people needed to know their place, whatever that meant. But as a football coach, it can truly be said that John McKay, from the very beginning, was color blind, at least when it came to playing time and roster space. His son J.K. says, "My father was absolutely race neutral."

When McKay came to USC in 1960, the Trojans were too slow and too white. McKay wanted the best athletes. He wanted speed. He did not recruit for position, to the extent that a football coach can maintain flexibility in this regard. By 1962, USC was one of the most integrated teams in the country—and one of the fastest. This was not a coincidence.

McKay, a man with a glint in his eye, a cigar in his mouth, and a shock of white hair on his head, also adapted to his Los Angeles environs. It would be an exaggeration to suggest that he ever "went Hollywood," certainly not in the manner of later Dodgers manager Tommy Lasorda, but he had flair and a style that suited his environment. It also suited the style of the L.A. writers who covered him.

There was little beating around the bush when it came to the racial significance of the game at hand. USC had traveled to various parts of the country for years, since before he was the coach. The 1956 game at Austin, Texas, for instance, had featured black running back C. R. Roberts.

"The question was inevitable," Jeff Prugh wrote as part of his pregame "Notes" column on the game. "Somebody in a group of newsmen wanted to know how USC's black players felt about playing against the all-white Alabama team this weekend."

"Well, I don't consider players as to whether they're white or black," said McKay. "We think of all of them as student-athletes. . . . We've never really discussed this before—and we've played teams such as Georgia Tech, SMU and Georgia. But I do think it's good that we can show everybody we have various people, not just one type, playing for us."

"My father tried to raise us without prejudice," McKay wrote in his 1974 book, *McKay: A Coach's Story* (with Jim Perry). He had been a victim of it. The KKK once burned a cross on the McKay family lawn because they were Catholic. The family became very poor because of the Great Depression. World War II probably saved him from the coal mines. He played at Purdue first before transferring to Oregon.

"As far as I know, we have escaped black-white problems on our team over the years, because I think the great majority of our players—and that's all you can go by—believed we were trying with all our power to do what was right. . . ." McKay stated. "When I got into coaching, I think I was perceptive enough to realize that some black players have certain disadvantages, because of school or family background. In lower-income families—and this applies to both blacks and whites—the parents may not have gone to high school and there might not be any books or newspapers in the house. So how can the young man have a fair chance to learn to read? This is a particular ghetto problem."

One father of a black player advised his son against going to USC because he felt McKay was prejudiced, but "I got letters from other people who said I had too many blacks on my team. But I ignore all those people. . . . There's no way to convince the cynics."

McKay instinctively felt the need to protect his friend Bear Bryant should the West Coast writers begin to accuse the legendary coach of racism. McKay, the master of deflection, preferred to keep the conversation centered on football. He made it clear that he had no worries about the health and safety of his players, but in a candid aside he allowed that he would not be displeased to see black athletes play for the Crimson Tide.

Commentary much beyond that would have elicited some concern from Bear and no doubt bad press in the Southern newspapers. Today, the media would have eaten McKay alive for his "failure" to address the issue of segregation, but 1970 was an entirely different era.

Other Voices: Wendell Hudson

Wendell Hudson, an African American native of Birmingham, signed on to play basketball at the University of Alabama before blacks played football. In The Herschel Walker Story, Jeff Prugh described the atmosphere that early black basketball pioneers in the SEC endured. Basketball, because of the intimacy of the arenas and closeness of the fans, offers more opportunity for verbal and physical abuse than does football, with its huge stadiums and protective gear. Hudson offered no bitterness. After graduating from 'Bama, he played in the American Basketball Association, and today he is Alabama's associate athletic director.

There was no reason to think I'd be at Alabama. I went to Parker High School in Birmingham, graduating in 1969. It was tough being black, playing in SEC arenas. We'd visit some places, like the Mississippi schools in particular. Those two stand out in terms of racially derogatory worries.

That said, change was occurring. How did it change? "All of the above." I don't want to put too much emphasis on the reasons it happened as it did. Right off the top, I think about that USC-Alabama football game. *That* was the big thing that happened. The way USC came into Birmingham with black athletes on their team changed the whole outlook of football, and football is very important in Alabama. Nobody wants to lose, to keep getting beaten by these integrated teams. Do they hold on to that whole old deal—segregation?

On Bryant's intention for the game. Now I want to give Paul "Bear" Bryant the credit, because I think he knew *exactly* what he was doing. I knew him as a basketball player, not as a football player knowing him as a football coach. He was making a point.

No, he did not schedule that game to lose it. He scheduled it to see where we all were in the national market, as the world was changing. He knew John McKay well. He knew other coaches were winning. He had other problems, too, and he knew it was time to do something drastic or most of what he'd worked for was going to fade away. So here we are, thirty-five years later, talking about his place in history. Had he not changed, he'd be just a name in a book. Instead, he's a legend. There's a reason for that.

Now, I don't think the McKay connection was an issue with the average Alabama fan. They all thought Alabama would beat USC; so looking back on it, the thing I don't want to do is to start reading too much into it. There were too many reasons. I don't think any 'Bama fan was thinking, "Well, it's USC and John McKay, and Bear likes McKay; so to prove a point we're gonna get beat by USC."

On recruiting blacks at Alabama. Wilbur Jackson was recruited one year after me. I was hearing about how he was being recruited in the spring of my freshman year. That's 1970. I can remember when we played that game [against USC], which was the fall of my sophomore year. All kinds of emotions were going through my mind. When it was done, you can't judge the mental state of our fans, thinking that what they just saw would turn our program around. It wasn't like, "Hey, let's integrate," and we see all this effect that we see today.

From my perspective, I watched USC and UCLA on TV. They had integrated teams, so if I'm thinking about other schools, I'm thinking I'd be accepted there. I can tell you that in the black community there was no question that the Sam Cunningham game was seen as an event that would usher in change.

Sports is egalitarian. When I came here I was the only black in my dorm, on my team. All of a sudden we're in a position to have two white guys on the team from Selma. I don't need to tell you what the word *Selma* meant to black people in Alabama. [Selma, Alabama, was the notorious site of some of the most violent confrontations of the civil rights struggle.] They'd just played the first integrated state tournament.

Well, these two guys from Selma, the fact is we all sweated together. It's not like the old practices we're all used to anymore. These guys are sweatin' more than you did, but we're together, practicing, competing, winning, and losing together. All the myths are going down the drain like the sweat after you shower. Now I'm close friends with these guys.

You know, women's sports have created opportunities too. Sports are so great, and I really appreciate what you say, that the opportunities are not created just for blacks, but that whites benefit from the experience too. So true.

On the crowd's response at the game. I was not at the game. I didn't see all that stuff about black folk carrying Bibles and candles, like Moses had come to Legion Field. You have to understand, Legion Field's in the middle of a community that's not too far down the street from what was my high school. A little more west, the community is more desegregated. My school was six or seven blocks from there. It's a diverse community. When the game was over, some people are thinking, *Change is in the air,* but it's not the end of racial tensions. Three or four years before I got to Parker, I'm hearing George Wallace while he stood in the schoolhouse door. So we had to be realistic.

On the game's effect on him. For me, it made me more open-minded. I was eighteen years old. I never thought about not doing anything different when it came to integrating an athletic department. But in those days, there were black students who needed National Guard protection. I signed a scholarship to play for Alabama. I was in my neighborhood, and it was a big day. But my first day I came here, it was like hearing the proverbial pin drop. Everybody just stared at me when I came in there, in the cafeteria. I realized it was different. I was uncomfortable, but I *never* felt I should not be there.

No civil rights leaders approached me. It was a totally different situation for me. But I got support from important people who said, "We're with you." C. M. Newton, the basketball coach then, he talked about this a lot, and I agree. He said the integrating of the state was a struggle, but once the Alabama athletic department integrated, the world moved faster. We play and win; if we can do it here, then the rest of us ought to be able to move along.

On racism now. Thirty-five years later, the world has changed some. I don't see the same world, but some people think in those thirty-five years we've covered more ground than we really have. People want to feel better than it is. We still need to make progress; we still need to change. But talking to people in Alabama here, I moved to Texas twenty years ago. There are problems in Texas and still problems in Alabama. More so, I lived in Houston, which is a melting pot compared with Alabama. But there's still black and white problems. But I sure could see good change when I came back here.

On Bear Bryant. Being around here when he was here, there's one thing I can say about my relationship with Coach Bryant. He knew exactly what he was doing. He didn't treat anybody differently. I was a spectator in football practice, and I enjoyed watching him work. I helped recruit Wilbur and Mitchell, and I can tell you from day one, never once did I ever see him behave poorly. I remember his ways, his kind nature.

Here I am, I'm a basketball player. I'd be in Bryant's office after I was coaching here, and I tell you something: he doesn't hire you if he's a racist. I'd know it. I'm telling you, he was in all the team meetings; Sylvester Croom was, too, and so was Mitchell. Something's going to happen. Somebody's going to get mad, under pressure, daily, hundreds of practices; *nothing* came out there the wrong way. I don't know what was said and done before the changes I saw, but in the athletic dorms, dealing with personnel—if Bryant was racist, it would have been known.

This goes to Bryant's background. He had two black guys who had been his chauffeurs, who cleaned rooms; but when they went to bowl games, they got a bonus like everybody and were treated well by Bryant. Maybe it was a different relationship, but they took pride in taking care of that facility. That's a reflection of Bear Bryant!

There are so many stories. I told people since I got back here about Bryant and what I remember, like when he came over at 10:00 p.m. we'd have a snack, peanut butter and jelly or something. One time he came in. I'm waiting in line with my basketball teammates, and we let him in line. Bryant asked me if he can sit down at my table. I say, "Yes, sir." The rest of that meal, none of the other athletes would sit down with Coach Bryant. I felt such great respect, and the other athletes out of respect felt it wasn't right to impose on his space, but here he's askin' me if it's okay if he sits next to me!

On the USC game. I can tell you that USC game was one of the toughest games for me. My observation is I had cheered for USC before, but now I'm at Alabama. I thought about USC. A young man from Parker went to Washington or Washington State. Going west meant something for me; it meant you'd made a transition. I'd chosen not to do it, I'd chosen a tough path to stay, but it paid off in the end.

Other Voices: Coach Jack Rutledge

Jack Rutledge had a career at Alabama similar to Marv Goux's at USC. Today, assistants consider most jobs as stepping-stones. The path to coaching ascendancy usually involves coaching different positions, often offense and defense, at a variety of colleges, with some professional experience mixed in, all leading up to a "big break" as a head coach at the college level or in the NFL. Rutledge played for Bear Bryant at Alabama and was a member of his staff from 1966 until Bryant's 1983 retirement. Today, he is still close to his alma mater.

I played for coach Paul "Bear" Bryant from the time he took over until 1961 and began coaching under him in 1966 until he retired in 1983. We should have won the title [in 1966], but the voters took it from us. In 1967, he'd won all he could win in college by that time, so Coach Bryant was offered the Miami Dolphins job.

He always said if he retired, he'd die and go straight to the Lord; and you know what, maybe there's some truth to that. He traveled with his mother, you know, who was a lay preacher, and a lot of that stuff that he said came indirectly out of the Bible.

Now, I'm not sayin' he was a straitlaced, Bible-preachin' type of guy. Coach Bryant was a man's man. What I'm sayin' is he didn't talk about the Bible a lot, but I used to look at the Bible a lot, and I'd find verses and things from in there that found their way mixed into his speeches. The best speech he ever made was at Tennessee, and it had Old Testament overtones about "We chose you, you chose us, and today we become one." He was intimating that in a football sense his team was the chosen people, and he'd lead 'em to the promised land, yes sir.

On Bryant and McKay. Coach John McKay was always with Bryant. Coach Bryant had the same relationship with other coaches; they'd see each other at speaking engagements and the like. He had a similar kind of close friendship with Bobby Dodd and stayed in touch with other head coaches. He'd call around and get all kinds of opinions.

Now John Wayne and McKay were friends, and that's how it came about that Bryant knew him. He picked up on that Wayne walk; he knew he needed certain things to make himself stand out, and that was one of 'em.

Coach Bryant loved football, and that was all he thought about durin' the season. But after the season, if you played or worked for him, you weren't personal friends. Sam Bailey was his top administrative assistant. Coach had key individuals, in recruitin', in life, and in investments, but assistants and team players were not that close. But after they graduated, he would write telegrams, letters, stay in touch. So if he met you, he knew you.

Now, because of this relationship, it is possible, you see, that some of what the Southern Cal folks say is different from what we heard or say. We saw a different Paul "Bear" Bryant than, say, his friend Coach McKay saw, huntin' or drinkin'. So what you're gettin' after, about how he planned that game, well maybe it's as you say, but I can't say 'cause I saw the Bryant I saw.

On 'Bama players. Wilbur Jackson was somethin' else. We'll never really know how great he really was, but what I remember was him sittin' in the den, and he bought a car for his mom.

On the controversy surrounding Bryant's statement. This story you're talkin' about, how Coach Bryant was supposed to have said, "This here's what a football player looks like," well, it's typical of his relationship with Coach McKay. It was typical of Bryant to honor him, to go to their dressing room. I know he did that, and he may have said those words, but I cannot remember or don't think Coach Bryant would have brought Sam Cunningham into our dressing room. I would have remembered. I do remember Bryant comin' in. He was down, disappointed. . . . I think he said maybe, "That's what a football player looks like"; I don't remember exactly. I would have remembered if he did it the way some say it happened, with Cunningham on a stool or whatnot in front of the gathered team.

I don't know where the story comes from. Maybe a certain person was going to write a book or make a movie. I can see that picture in my mind, the right side of that dressing room. I'd remember him being in that dressing room; he probably said something about Sam being what a football player looked like or was supposed to be. . . .

Jerry Claiborne said, "Sam did more for civil rights in sixty minutes than Martin Luther King did in twenty years." I heard some of that. He was here by Bryant's side since 1958, and he was close to Coach Bryant; through his career he took the plays. Claiborne was going to be the head coach; that's what the plan was until Jerry left. He was Coach Bryant's man through and through, his most trusted assistant.

On Bryant's plans to integrate. I've heard things about that situation regarding Coach Bryant's plan to integrate. As I say, I lived in the athletic dorms for eighteen years and was there when Wilbur was signed. You remember Condredge Holloway? I recruited him. His whole family wanted him to come to Alabama. In the process of recruiting at the end, Coach Bryant brought him in the office, and he told him he couldn't sign a black quarterback because "his people" [Alabama administrators and alumni] wouldn't let him play. Bryant never differentiated between black and white.

We never had racial problems at Alabama all the time I was here. We let all our players choose their roommates, and sometimes blacks and whites chose to room together.

Bryant wanted change. Why? Well, sir, as I say, there were people close to him whom he talked to about stuff like that, but his assistants and players were employees, and he kept them at arm's length. You can speculate that he was thinkin' he couldn't recruit black athletes [in Alabama], but he could have anybody he wanted play for him in the pros; plus there were a couple years around 1970 or so when the alumni were saying the ol' Bear was past it, and he might've been tired of dealin' with that.

Lookin' back, from my perspective, the problems we had, it's not racial; it's the environment you're in. A lot of folks lived in the country; they all worked and were equal. Now all of us are able to get the same education. A lot of people out in the country could not get into college; now they all get an equal education. No one should be held back. So many of us saw grandparents who had their first car or TV. As society modernized, people could see and hear about so much more, and that's how we set aside our differences.

On 'Bama's national championships. Now, comparing 1966 with 1978, well in '66 Coach Bryant had won three titles and was dominating football. A lot of people hate trophies and want 'em shared around. They'd given him the title because he'd been so strong, so maybe they wanted it to go to somebody else. Then we'd gone down, and in the 1970s we were back winnin' or almost winnin' titles almost every year. In 1977, we were 11–1. I think we should have been national champions, but we lost to Joe Montana and Notre Dame, who came from fifth to first after beating Earl Campbell and Texas in the Cotton Bowl. We should have won titles in 1976 and 1977, and in 1978 and 1979 we had a tremendous team, just a great team.

In 1970, I didn't see the change comin' via the USC game. Coach Bryant would never talk about it like this, about society. He never complained, like when Notre Dame won the national championship instead of us. He never wanted to hear negatives. He never complained to officials about a call. He always said he wanted to be sure, so he'd never have to second guess.

On Bryant. I recall Buddy Brown; he played up in Canada. They had a day for Wayne Hall, one of Buddy's friends. Bryant went up to ol' Buddy, and, why, he apologized to him for movin' him to the offensive line. "You could have been a great defensive lineman," he told Buddy. He said he was sorry, that was what he needed Buddy to play on that team. . . . Coach never forgot stuff like that.

In life, he never forgot anything. He still has a scholarship for the children of all his players. It started with Pat Trammell, his quarterback in 1961, and he had cancer and passed away. He'd never gone pro, he became a doctor, and the coach set up a scholarship for the needy ones, but now it's for all his former players. There's a grant set up with interest for all of them.

In Junction, Texas, he was brutal and hard. Bryant's theory was that he had doctors trained to fix the hurt, and he was fixin' to do our business. Bryant was not about makin' money but making things happen.

Coach Bryant was a team man; he didn't like single individuals as it related to his football team. I was on the freshman team when he came in from Texas A&M. Gene Stallings had been in Junction. Five or six guys came with him at 'Bama and put us through three months of that thing. We had great players here. A lot of those athletes were tremendous people who still could not put up with it. Bryant wanted to know who wanted to play. I was one of fourteen who went through that.

Coach Bryant didn't want married men on his team, but Coach Bryant tells me he and I had an agreement, because I was to get married. So I talked to Thomas Helling, and he told me I could play as a married man. On the sideline in 1958, I asked Bryant could I be red-shirted, and he said yes. So I started sixteen games between Lee Roy Jordan and those guys.

Now I'm going back [in time], but the players, they accepted Bryant because he was tough but in a fair way. The only guy who complained was Steve Wright, who was not his type of player. He played pro several years.

Coach could change with the times. Hair, for instance; they started growing it longer. Coach Bryant looked through a book and marked the styles of what he would or wouldn't let them do. He wanted them clean, but some of the black players, if they shave too close it causes in-grown hair, so he changed and let them not shave so close. These were the little details he attended to.

He was the kind of person who could pick out any individual's full potential, and he said he needed 110 percent out of them. But he wouldn't ask people to do things they couldn't do. But it didn't matter who you were, if you followed the rules, if you gave the effort, Coach Bryant was with you. In the early years he dismissed guys, but in later years he put players on the second or third team. He'd tell the players what they needed to do to get back in his good graces. He gave you a chance. If you overcame that, all was forgotten. If you didn't, then at the end of the semester, they quietly didn't report back. They all accepted it, what he did for them.

There were these social changes, but he saw them. This is why he's so great a person: he was totally abreast of all that was happening. He had certain people he respected in different subjects who would know in-depth the situation, and if he had a problem in that area, he would call the person.

He was on top of stuff. If change was going to happen, he had the loyalty of people and it never leaked out. He kept the secret of the wishbone all through two-a-days. We'd not practice the wishbone. We'd practice the old offense, then the writers would leave, or he had canvas put all around and installed a new secondary; we'd work on it and have a twelfth man out there.

I'm sixty-six years old. I have tractors and dump trucks; that's my hobby. Now I have a computer, and so I'm archivin' what people are doing. You just verify what I say, when you call around and ask about Coach Bryant, in that he was always on the phone gathering a lot of information about the world.

In my life, I lived with the strongest, the best chosen, the most physical people. I've lived a life of roughhouse, but Coach Bryant taught us about life, how things go on a curve, and you get down but you fight and get back up. If not for Coach Bryant, I don't know what I'd have been. But I'm set up now because Coach Bryant taught me the way to live life.

I've dealt with cancer surgery a few times over the last years, too, and I keep fightin' it off, and I thank the Good Lord, Jesus Christ. He's come into my heart. That's how I look at racial issues, through Him. I lived in certain times, but I've come to know that all people, of all colors—there ain't no difference between races—are all people under the Lord.

CHAPTER **Seventeen**

Pattonesque

Americans, real Americans . . . love a winner and
will not tolerate a loser, because the very thought of
losing is hateful to Americans.

—*George C. Scott in* Patton

In 1970, with no metal detectors at airports, courthouses, or many other places, for that matter, Angela Davis was able to smuggle a gun into the Marin County Civic Center, where George Jackson was able to use it to blow the head off of Judge Harold Haley before finally being shot and killed himself.

As a result of this incident, and with the rise of terrorist hijackings, metal detectors became commonplace at airports and public buildings. In an egregious example of political correctness, Angela Davis never stood trial for her complicity in the act of terror, murder, and mayhem. Instead, she was allowed to become a university professor, indoctrinating college students with her Communist garbage for years. She became a symbol of the kind of anti-American ideology that has become rampant among the tenured ivory-tower cult that passes itself off as academia in modern America.

Controversial modern professors such as the University of Colorado's Ward Churchill, who faked an Indian heritage in order to become the head of CU's ethnic studies program (a code word for the "hate whitey" wing of many college campuses), are the natural by-product of the Angela Davisification of so-called higher education. In 2005, it was revealed that

Churchill was "rooting for" Osama bin Laden, finding justification for the World Trade Center terrorist acts. Churchill's commentary was the most incendiary, but many leftist professors have made and written similar statements.

Despite the violence at the Marin County Civic Center, when USC flew to Alabama, Tody Smith was free to pack heat in his briefcase. Smith's older brother, Bubba Smith, would go on to an acting career, including comic turns in the *Police Academy* franchise, after a superstar career with the Colts. The Smiths hailed from Beaumont, Texas, where racism was rampant. Tody had transferred to USC from Michigan State because he heard it was the best place for black athletes to play. He considered it ironic that the very thing he had left he was being brought back to by the very program he had "escaped" to.

Jimmy Jones, from Harrisburg, Pennsylvania, had not seen the kind of widespread racism that Tody Smith had. He preferred the peaceful, nonviolent approach to solving problems. But most important, he was the *team* leader, not just the black leader. He told Smith to leave the weapon at home. A potential tragedy lay in the offing because Smith chose to ignore this.

Marv Goux liked to quote George Patton. Patton and Goux both used militaristic language, invoking the sense of honor inherent in warfare, whether on the football field or battlefield. That language was coarse, filled with swearwords, brutal, and violent.

But Patton was a Christian who prayed on his knees and wept like a little boy. He was a walking conundrum. In Patton, we have the essence of man's duality. The American military is a profession that specializes in breaking things and killing people. But within its branches exists a devout Christianity. No service division makes more regular reference to God than the most violent of them, the U.S. Marines.

The movie *Patton* opened in February 1970. It was hugely popular, especially in the South. *Patton* won eight Oscars, including best actor for George C. Scott and best picture. 1970 was the least likely year such a film might have been successful, or so it would seem. Its success demonstrated that the country was not as antiwar or liberal as the TV broadcasts made it seem. There was a real and genuine "silent majority," as Richard Nixon called the conservative and Christian voting block. The success of *Patton* demonstrated the continuing power of conservatism in a world seemingly gone mad.

Football players such as John Papadakis, Sam Cunningham, Dave Brown, Scott Hunter, and Johnny Musso—whether they are black or white, from the city or from the country—tend to be conservative and often Christian, because football demands it. It is a game of self-discipline, sacrifice, hard work, and personal responsibility in the service of others, qualities that play to Republican principles and religious austerity. While they may "play" after the game, the week leading up to it requires a commitment of time and physical hardship.

Athletes in general tend to vote Republican. A look at athletes and other "entertainers," such as actors and rock stars, reveals stark differences. Actors and rock stars are usually Democrats, often using their platforms to push leftist causes and candidates.

Furthermore, actors and rock stars are much more likely to lead immoral lifestyles. They are prone to alcoholism, drug addiction, and wild sexual excess. An enormous number of Hollywood actors and directors lead flagrant homosexual existences, then make movies promoting that to do so is acceptable.

Athletes, on the other hand, are much more likely to be straight arrows. Of course, some of them do drugs, whether it be steroids or recreational narcotics. Many drink. However, the physical and mental demands of everyday athletic competition make it much less likely that an athlete can get away with this kind of thing the way a Hollywood actor can.

Perhaps the most telling difference between the athlete and the actor or singer is in their women. First of all, most athletes are heterosexual. Statistically, there are gays in sports, but the social factors that drive men into team endeavors such as baseball, basketball, and football produce a larger-than-normal amount of straights from the talent pool.

Second, the *kind* of women that athletes are seen with is indicative of the differences. Many in Hollywood openly cavort with Heidi Fleiss–style escorts. Many rock stars are even less discreet, traveling and partying with highly promiscuous porn actresses.

Athletes like to party, and they love beautiful women, too. They go to strip clubs and have sex with those girls. They have groupies who seek them out in hotel bars and the trendy clubs they hang out at, mostly on the road. Especially in cities such as L.A., Miami, New York, Dallas, and New Orleans, the same kinds of scantily clad bombshells seen backstage at a Van Halen, Aerosmith, or AC/DC concert throw themselves at big-league ballplayers, NBA stars, and pro football players.

The big difference, however, is that while the rockers travel with them, for all practical purposes subsidize them, and in many cases actually *marry* them, the athletes keep their relationships with these women distant from their professional and personal lives.

At the ballpark, an athlete's parents and family congregate outside the clubhouse after games. It would be unseemly for some girl whose boxcover photo can be found in any nearby video store depicting her servicing the "Trojan Army" to be standing next to Mom and little brother Johnny, "hanging out" in her halter top while waiting for the .300 hitter in question to emerge and take the whole "family" out to dinner.

Athletes, while often seduced by the temptations of money and the women that flock to it, still must maintain a degree of discipline in order to meet the demands of the sport. Growing up, they always had to toe the line: demanding coaches, tough opponents, competition for the position they covet, all forcing them to be their best. Parents of athletes are usually part of their lives, sacrificing their time to coach, drive them to practice, and support them in their efforts.

The "family values" that are so much a part of most athletes' backgrounds tend to lead to a certain amount of religious tradition, especially in the South. Athletes may enjoy the company of strippers and porn chicks, but when it comes to committed relationships—wives and kids— they are far more likely to marry the "kind of girl who married dear old dad."

The wives and kids of professional athletes can usually be seen waiting in specially designated rooms adjacent to the clubhouse at most stadiums. Members of the media, given access to their sanctuary, see the women who marry pro athletes. They are struck by the fact that, despite the players being physically attractive and worth millions, their wives are often "plain Janes." Not ugly, but not the kind of flashy "baseball Annies" who troll for them in nightclubs and hotel bars. The athletes more often than not reject that kind of "showy" girl for somebody they will feel comfortable raising their children with.

There may be some hypocrisy in all of this, but down deep it is reflective of a more conservative approach. Along these same lines, athletes are much more likely to be patriotic and supportive of the military than are the Hollywood crowd.

Furthermore, fans of a film like *Patton* (including John McKay and then-president Nixon, who saw the movie four times before invading Cambodia in the spring of 1970) tended toward football as a metaphor for life. Football is a small-scale version of *Patton* and warfare: capturing and holding real estate in order to reach a goal that, in the end, is about conquest. Casualties are accepted if glory is attained.

Marv Goux was the George Patton of USC football. Goux was a legendary figure whose father died fighting at the Battle of the Bulge, the December 1944 to January 1945 German offensive in which General Patton saved the Allies from disaster when he rescued the 101st Airborne Division defending Bastogne. Had Goux not been a football coach, he might have been in the U.S. Army Special Forces or a CIA agent. He had the persona of Watergate conspirator G. Gordon Liddy—brash, outspoken, the walking embodiment of manly courage and machismo.

Despite being undersized, Goux had twice been voted USC's most inspirational player when he starred for the Trojans from 1954 to 1955. His specialty was the pep talk. He took it seriously, inflecting his loud, overbearing speeches with references to wars, gladiatorial conflict, pride, honor, and bloodlust. He may have been the most politically incorrect man in football, but he was fair to the extreme.

When Goux came to USC, the school had gone a number of years without a lot of black football players. There was Brice Taylor, their black All-American of 1925, but in the intervening years, however, a "gentlemen's agreement" of sorts had taken effect. African Americans were not prominent in campus life, whether in sports, academics, or the stuffy all-white fraternities that are so influential at USC.

"I played with C. R. Roberts," Goux recalled. Roberts was a man ahead of his time, a talented black running back who had accompanied the team to Austin, Texas, in 1956. "I had graduated, and that was the one year I wasn't at USC," recalled Goux. "But I know the story. They checked into the hotel, where they told [coach Jess] Hill that C.R. couldn't stay. Hill had a real problem on his hands, man. He wanted to get the team ready for the Longhorns, and now he's got a racial situation in his lap. A few of the guys told him, 'If C.R. doesn't stay, we don't stay.'"

Hill did the right thing. He moved his team from the hotel, at great expense and logistical difficulty, to other lodgings.

"I'm a competitive son of a gun," said Goux, "and so was C.R. You take a competitor and make him fight for what is his, for what he's already earned, for what he deserves, and he will fight! That's what he did. You might think being forced out of the hotel, out of our routine, would've set us back. It just made us angry, and C.R. went off like crazy. Not O.J. [Simpson] on his best day ran with such abandon as C.R."

Roberts ran over and through the Longhorns, despite vile epithets delivered by players and fans alike.

"That game could have changed the South," said Goux, "but it didn't. Why, I'm not sure. The time wasn't right."

Goux did not have what it took for the NFL. He knew he wanted to be a coach and took over at Carpinteria High School, which is located near Ventura. Cunningham is known to be from Santa Barbara, located about an hour's drive north on Highway 101 from Ventura. However, he only moved to Santa Barbara when he got to high school, having grown up in the Ventura area. Both Goux and Cunningham are graduates of Santa Barbara High School.

This stretch of southern California strand is famous for its residents' laid-back attitude. Today, they are reliably liberal Democratic constituencies who put environmental concerns above most others. Even in Goux's day, this was a relaxed atmosphere. It might be the last place a man like Marv Goux would be expected to hail from. When he took over at Carpinteria, all the parents were aghast at how he tried to turn the football program into Patton's Third Army.

According to legend, Goux attempted to put up a duplicate of Tommy Trojan, the famous statue that is the centerpiece of the USC campus, in front of the basketball gym at Carpinteria High School. Not everybody in Carpinteria was a Trojan fan, which seemed entirely un-American to Goux. To him, rooting for a team other than the Trojans meant you were the enemy. This was the world he lived in.

Goux's football talks were filled with war metaphor. Goux liberally borrowed from George C. Scott's incendiary performance. He mixed football with Scott's indelicate references and morphed gridiron jargon with phrases such as "We're gonna use their living guts to grease the treads of our tanks."

Final pregame meetings were held in the stuffy basement of the gym next to the practice field. Players and band members mingled in a show of unity. Goux, the defensive line coach, used these occasions to urge his charges on with fiery rhetoric, often citing his own exploits, such as when he had played the second half of his senior year with a broken back.

The McKay-Goux relationship was the perfect "good cop, bad cop" combination. McKay was often moody and hard to get close to, but Goux befriended his charges the way a drill sergeant bonds with his recruits after basic training. Goux had the fiery look of a movie bad guy, the kind one finds in *noir* movies depicting Raymond Chandler's Los Angeles. He was one of the gladiators in the 1960 Stanley Kubrick classic *Spartacus* starring Kirk Douglas (also featuring former UCLA football star Woody Strode as the black gladiator who dies so Douglas may live), and he "blended" whites and blacks. Some white players felt cheated when a black player took their position. Goux told them that the team colors, cardinal and gold, were more than just clothes.

"Cardinal is the color of blood," Goux told the players, "which we all are on the inside. Gold is what every man wants to be—rich—and will shed blood for." This kind of statement, idealistic or corny as it may sound, had the ring of truth when Goux spoke it because he meant it. It assuaged the egos of athletes, white or black, who found themselves benched or moved to a secondary position by a rival teammate. It was Goux who taught the Trojans to see their teammates not as rivals but as brothers. These speeches of his would be repeated, sometimes verbatim, by Papadakis and other Trojans speaking at public gatherings, for the next thirty-seven years.

McKay was renowned for recruiting great athletes, not merely position players. The benefit of this style was that a top running back like John Papadakis, if beaten out for his position by a better running back like Sam Cunningham, often was able to compete for another starting position. In Papadakis's case, that position was linebacker. A fast quarterback could become a cornerback. A running back could be a wide receiver. A defensive lineman could switch to offense.

Bear Bryant had noticed the way Goux and McKay created the togetherness and teamwork of blacks and whites. He longed to figure out how to create a Southern version of what the Trojans had.

At the team meeting prior to the departure for Birmingham, with the USC anthem "Conquest" playing in the background, Goux told his charges, "No team has gone where we'll go; no 'real' team can do what you will do.

"Gentlemen," Goux went on, "a conquest is the act of going into another man's stadium and destroying him. On Saturday, we will conquer the Tide! Right there on Legion Field, we'll take all that they hold dear, everything that the Crimson Tide has! We will use their living guts to grease the treads of our tanks. We'll crush their will to live! Their faith in themselves will be taken from them on their own field. We'll rob them of their pride! Why? Because *we are* the University of Southern California Trojans. *We are!* SC! *We are!* SC!"

He had tears in his eyes as he told the Trojans it was their "destiny" to "rape, pillage, burn," and "take no prisoners." He told them that after the game, if Alabama still had anything left, they would beat them in any other setting available.

This speech, like most of Goux's speeches, was met by wild exuberance. The Trojans were now ready, like Generals William T. Sherman and Ulysses S. Grant more than one hundred years before, to enter the South on a mission of conquest.

Wearing coats and ties, the Trojans were screaming with confidence. But amid the hoopla, eighteen black players had an uneasy feeling.

Other Voices: John Vella

John Vella was an All-American at USC in 1971 and Tody Smith's roommate during the 1970 road trip to Birmingham. He was drafted by Oakland and starred as a lineman for some of John Madden's greatest Raiders teams, including the 1976 Super Bowl champions. Today, Vella is a successful entrepreneur, the owner of a chain of San Francisco Bay Area sporting goods stores called Vella's Locker Room.

I played at Notre Dame High in Sherman Oaks. Growing up in L.A., you automatically rooted for the Trojans. We didn't have any black players on our team, but I played in the old Catholic league, and competing against blacks was commonplace. Mount Carmel and Loyola had black players, as did other teams. When I got to USC, it was just not an issue.

On tension before the game. It wasn't until we got to Alabama that these kinds of things came up, and it caught me by surprise. Tody Smith, my roommate, had brought a gun. I questioned Tody at the airport, or maybe on the plane. He had a briefcase, I think, which was not like him. I just thought it was odd, so I asked him, "What is that? What have you got?"

He just played it off, but in the room at the hotel, I asked him again. The briefcase was on the bed, so he finally admitted that he'd brought a gun, which really took me aback. I asked him to show it to me. I just asked him, "What do you need that for?"

I don't even think there were metal detectors at airports then. We'd taken a charter plane, and nobody'd gotten wind of it. He just told me he needed it for protection. That was the first time I'd realized how the black players felt about that trip. Tody just said he didn't feel comfortable. I was much more aware of everything the rest of the weekend after that. The other players had the same feeling. There was real fear in the air; it wasn't comfortable.

I guess at the hotel there'd been some words exchanged. Tody had heard it and just felt really defensive. Now I became more aware of the cat-calls after seeing Tody with that gun in his room. I became aware of the interaction between the black players. Everything just became clear; it opened my eyes.

I heard a story for the first time that Fertig said. At bed check, he knocked on the doors; he would wait a few seconds then enter. He saw Clarence Davis in his room, and he could tell he was hiding something under the covers. He said to him, "I saw something," and Davis just said he didn't have anything. But Fertig said, "Come on, Clarence, whaddaya got under there?" and Davis lifted the covers, and he had a knife. So Fertig saw that Clarence was concerned.

As for the meeting in the room, other than to know there was a meeting, I didn't really know anything about it. I knew things were calmed down, but not details. John Papadakis and I were close, so whatever I got came from John. I guess he calmed down the black players by relaxing them and showing no fear.

On fellow teammates and coaches. I played from 1969 to 1971 and was All-American my senior year. Marv Goux coached me on both offense and defense. He was an inspiration and handled the role of motivator really well. He *was* the face of the Trojans. Nobody loved USC more than he did. I remember the speeches he gave down in the old "dungeon." When you heard Goux give it to us down there, if you weren't ready to play after that, you never would be.

Goux really was like Patton. He would talk about war, about going into somebody else's city and taking what was theirs. He made that comparison between football and war all the time. But he held the team together; he made sure we watched each other's backs. He would say stuff like, "It's us against the whole state; we gotta stick together if we want to win."

John Papadakis was brilliant. When we beat Notre Dame, John knew the press would come to us, and he told me to tell the reporters when they asked me, "How did you beat Notre Dame?" to answer, "With the glory of Greece, the grandeur of Rome, and the undying pride of the Trojans!"

Tody left Michigan State for whatever reason and was a Trojan for two years. This was his second year, his senior year. As far as the game—being black, having the gun—none of that played a part in the game that I could tell. He never showed anything toward me to warrant any confrontation that he was having with Alabama, not that he'd avoid confrontation, but it was not part of our relationship, which was about mutual respect. We were not close off the field, although we did live in the same apartment building. We didn't have a lot of dialogue; it was a matter of being friendly but not really friends.

But we were both defensive linemen, and Goux wanted to room whites and blacks together. I'm sure there were a handful of other situations where coaches put players together not knowing about whether they were close off the field, but they thought it could help the team. Players tended to room by position anyway.

We could handle it. It did help on the field. Maybe you learned something about your roommate that you hadn't known, maybe one or two things, like seeing the gun, which gave me understanding and opened my eyes. I was naïve before that, but I was also centered on John Hannah; I had blinders to all else. I had heard about all this stuff, but to see that gun was reality.

On racism at USC. Regarding the whole issue of whites and blacks, as I said, at USC it just wasn't an issue. We'd all pretty much played integrated football all through high school in California. I think Goux might have been dealing with our black players in anticipation of the Alabama trip, but the whole thing kind of caught me by surprise because, from my angle, we were so far from any of that. I'd been recruited with, played against, black players; I'd been with and next to black players. It was accepted, so I have a hard time really remembering any racial incidents on our team. We were about competition, and if you were good enough you were accepted.

On his new position in the game. Shoot, we were going to play John Hannah. I'm on my first game on defense. I was on offense before; I played tackle in 1969, and in '70 I got moved to the defensive line.

McKay's secretary had called me at home; he wanted a meeting. It was very unusual. He walked around that room, made some small talk, then all of a sudden it was, "What do you think about playing defense?" He gave reasons—others were not progressing at their positions enough, and Pete Adams could handle my old spot.

So I knew I'd be up against Hannah. Everybody knew all about Hannah. Later, he became an All-Pro, and we faced each other over the years, with me on the Raiders and Hannah with the Patriots (he was a teammate of Sam Cunningham's).

On the game at Legion Field. I do remember the crowd at Legion Field. Crowds in the South can make a decisive difference. They had a national reputation, the place was all red, there were seventy-thousand-plus, and the place was packed. You knew you were the visitor. What I also remember was that it was an easy, one-sided victory. Sam was playing his first game, and he rumbled for more than a hundred yards and two touchdowns, but lots of our best players dominated.

As for the psychology at play, sure—Goux and McKay gave their standard speeches, the motivation before a game; but if you weren't ready, hey, I didn't need to hear a speech to get ready. I downplay the effect of that. I felt as if I'd been preparing my whole life to be in that situation. Maybe it gave us a little boost, but in the first game you just don't need it, and it was my first game on the other side of the ball, so, no, I didn't need it.

As the game went on, Hannah was great. I'm lined up, and he was not afraid. He was a great player.

The crowd was taken out of the game. It had been deafening, and now in the second half, the crowd was silenced. They were in amazement.

On USC's reputation. As for Alabama being intimidated by us, I don't buy it. It's true we were undefeated in 1969 and won the Rose Bowl, while 'Bama was down, but when you play for a national program, you don't feel you're ever supposed to lose. We beat Notre Dame when we were 2–4 and they were 5–0, there was the Joe Theismann game in the rain, and we were always confident. At a big program, if you played at that level you had confidence, so you expected to win. I was confident. I felt we'd win every game, and so I would think that a national program like Alabama would feel the same way.

But the crowd was stunned. I'm sure it had to be a combination of things, in terms of both how USC was good and we had good black players. You had to be blind to not see that a lot of our best players were black and they had none, so it was no surprise when Bryant recruited blacks the following year.

After the game, it was just a big crowd everywhere—family and friends who were in attendance. As I said, I didn't realize the importance of it all until I saw Tody's gun, when they called that meeting. So many of the blacks were upset, and they might have had trouble concentrating, which is when I became aware of its significance.

I don't remember McKay hearing about that meeting. Not everyone was invited to it, so to McKay it seemed like it was business as usual. When coaches get word of something like that, they get concerned if there's a meeting. I guess it was called to calm the players down. Preceding a game, it's normal to be jittery anyway.

McKay had the power to create fear, for everybody knew there was one boss. Late in that week, Sam learned he would play a lot. Sam was not a star before his first game. McKay influenced my success and so I had some fear, but overall I was a little different; I knew I was playing.

Goux was not about fear but about mutual respect, as well as McKay. My feeling toward the coaches was once I had their respect, then it was vice versa, not to let this guy down. Goux was my coach, I was a defensive lineman, and I'd gained the respect of these guys.

On being a Trojan. Being a Trojan, it's definitely a proud tradition. There are not too many places where you have the confidence that you are superior as a team, as a program, as a tradition, so you want to live up to it. At USC I never lost confidence for even a play.

I never ever remember losing confidence in our tradition to be part of a Trojan team; it's something that stuck with you. I carried it into the pros. I'd say the same thing about the Raiders: we never felt we'd lose. It makes a big difference.

Other Voices: John Hannah

John Hannah was a sophomore offensive lineman on the 1970 Alabama team. He blossomed into an All-American, became a perennial All-Pro with the New England Patriots (where he blocked for his teammate Sam "Bam" Cunningham), and in 1991 was elected into the Pro Football Hall of Fame. A longtime New England resident, Hannah recently went back to his Southern roots, taking a job with the football program at the Baylor School in Chattanooga, Tennessee.

In New England, I think Sam "Bam" Cunningham was a class act. I enjoyed blocking for him. He was a hard runner, a fine gentleman, and a great teammate. We hated to lose him. He's a leader.

John Vella was my opposite number that day against Southern Cal. He's a great player. Tody Smith was also opposing me in that game, and he tore me a new one. He's a senior, and I'm a sophomore. He ate me up that year. Who was that other guy, Charlie Weaver? Man, I'm telling you, he was a great player too.

I was familiar with Southern Cal football because my uncle was a coach in California. He'd been at San Bernardino Junior College and was at Cal State, Fullerton. He found I was thinking about going someplace other than Alabama, so he had the Southern Cal coaches call me, but I stayed at home instead. My uncle, he was one of those guys who died in that Fullerton State plane crash in 1971. My junior year, six coaches died on a scouting trip prior to some play-offs. He was on his way up to scout opposition. They hit a wind current, and the plane went down.

On the game against USC. I saw a little game film from the year before, so I knew we were in for a handful. We had a bunch of sophomores playing, and I saw their size relative to our team. They were bigger than we were. Compared with them, we were runts.

They were a bunch of ball hawks on defense, they ran the ball out of an I [formation] on offense, and they were going everywhere. I was impressed with what they did and how physical they were.

There wasn't much going on in my mind [about political issues], to be quite honest with you. I did know about the world going on. If I got selected in the draft, I'd go; but I wasn't worried about it. I guess I was very patriotic; I wasn't one of those guys protesting the war or anything like that. I was a typical young Alabamian. In 1970, I was nineteen. One time, a couple of our guys were walking through the student union when those protests hit, and they tried to take down the flag. A few of us surrounded that flag and wouldn't allow it to happen.

On Bryant's statement. Coach Bryant was supposed to have said of Sam Cunningham, "This here's what a football player looks like." I don't remember him doing that. He didn't need to bring him in the locker room. I saw what it was supposed to be like on that field. Sam was six foot three, 212 pounds. He overpowered people. You can't deny what he did. I was busy licking my wounds, because I had *witnessed* what a football player looks like.

That being said, it was a long time ago, and the way the lockers were at Legion Field, he could do things in part of the locker room and we wouldn't see it, or maybe I was in the training room. He might have brought him in that locker room, but I don't know exactly what happened.

I *do* recall Jerry Claiborne saying, "Sam did more for civil rights than Martin Luther King."

On the media after the game. I'm sure there were media in there. They'd all come in, and that's when I headed into the locker room, especially after the game when the emotions were still flowing. I was afraid I'd say something stupid.

Bryant had a select few writers he'd let in because he knew they wouldn't do anything detrimental to the team. It was not an open door, but he knew who he wanted in there. The newspapers knew if they ever wrote anything crazy, they'd not be allowed in again. He'd do most of the talking. I'm just a dumb offensive lineman, a sophomore—heck, they don't want to talk to me.

On USC recruiting at the game. I don't know if Southern Cal had five black recruits from Alabama at that game. I can't recall all that much. Our family wasn't racist; it was not like they depict us on TV. The whole state was not racist, but that loud few, unfortunately they got all the attention. I played with a lot of black guys when I was a kid. I don't remember any problem with blacks. John Mitchell came over, and we hung out all the time. Wilbur Jackson and I weren't close, but that had nothing to do with race. I didn't think that much about it.

I was glad to have [black players] John and Wilbur on the team beginning the next year. It made my life easier. Alabama fans, a lot of 'em, whether they admit it or not, I think, were prejudiced. George Wallace was still there. I think it would have been hard for a lot of blacks to come to Alabama if not for Sam. He gave us that shellacking.

On Bryant's intentions with the game. Now the question you're after is whether or not Coach Bryant "planned" it out. In other words, was this just a nonconference football game, or was it supposed to open doors for black recruits? You know what, I think Bryant planned it to open doors for blacks.

Let me give you an example. Just a week before the Southern Cal game, Bryant had one of those old-fashioned "gut check" practices, like they depict in *The Junction Boys*. Six or seven guys dropped out on account of dehydration cases. It's hot—late summer in Alabama. Oh, man.

I'm not sure about "the Pit." We had "the Cage," which were blocking chutes that pitted offensive linemen on one side and defensive linemen on the other. It was meant to determine who could push the other man out of that cage. It was pure mano a mano, and if you raised high up or gave in, you'd get your head nearly torn off; it'd get caught in that cage, and all the guys are screaming and yelling. It's intense, and if Coach didn't like the way you did it, he'd have you do it again or put somebody else in there.

The point is, he never had that kind of practice so close before a game. Something was up; I just didn't know it at the time. Now, the Bear schedules this game. I know his assistants all say he didn't set us up, whether it was to lose. But was there a larger plan other than just preparing for this game? Yes. I think he did plan an event that would lead to integration. I believe Bryant realized, if you think about it, that we were starting fifteen sophomores, and juniors who were inexperienced, and just a few seniors.

Why else, a week before this game, would he go and put us through the "death camp"—I'm telling you, people were fallin' out like flies—*then play Southern Cal*? I think he felt we'd be okay over the next ten games; it was a young team he wanted to get ready for greatness in our future. This game was for our future. He knew we were not getting the best blacks out of Alabama, so I think he had that in the back of his mind. He was good friends with John McKay; it was easily doable. So, yes, I'm just convinced that Bear Bryant accomplished several things in losing at home to Southern Cal. He accomplished the task of toughening up a young team, and at the same time he opened people's eyes to letting blacks into the program. The fact he did it quietly, was sly about it, didn't brag it up or talk about it a whole lot, was pure Bear Bryant—but he planned it, no question. Look how successful it all worked out!

I think, in the back of my mind, no coach in his right mind would bring in a team the caliber of Southern Cal as an extra game, knowing the inexperience we had, plus the "meat grinder" the week before—ask anybody if he remembers what it was like the week before that game. We had a guy named [Tommy] Wade, a starting defensive back, who broke his leg; six guys ended up in the hospital. I never want to go through another practice like that. I wanted to go home so bad, so instead of eating I fell asleep on my bed. I'm not lying, if I'd not fallen asleep, I'd have quit Alabama that day and gone home.

The next day, Bryant says, "Y'all learned a big lesson yesterday. You find the human body is an amazing machine that passes out before it dies!"

So, based on all these factors, yes, Bryant was willing to sacrifice a loss in the 1970 season opener in order to make his program successful over the long run. He didn't want to lose that game. He wanted to win, but he knew that a loss had the potential of accomplishing his larger goal.

That was the game. I think that one game did more for social change in Alabama than anything that ever transpired. You lead by influencing people to *want* to do something, you don't stuff it down people's throats; that automatically causes total resistance. Now here's Bryant, a leader, and he's saying, "Let's be leaders; let's make people *want* to integrate." All of a sudden, everybody wanted to integrate the schools. You don't stuff it down people, absolutely not.

George Wallace called Bryant weekly. The reason was he was scared that Bryant would run for governor, because he'd win. Auburn people would vote for him, too, so he wouldn't coach anymore. The South, if you think about it, it's all Scots-Irish, and we're tribal people. Scots-Irish aren't feudal; they don't like government interfering with their rights. The liberal media never believes this, they never gave us a chance, but we would have done the right thing on our own given the chance to do it our way.

I'm tellin' you, we were going to integrate and do the moral thing on our own. That said, yes, it needed a push, and this game was that push. But it happened the way Bear Bryant planned it—quietly, smoothly—not because of a protest march. This is the best evidence, I think, that what I'm saying is right.

Again, don't get me wrong. There were "rednecks," and they took it as integration instead of a federal versus states' rights issue. Blacks took the fall throughout the South. But through Sam, Lynn Swann, guys like that, they refocused the issues again and made people understand that when it came to black athletes, we needed 'em.

Some Alabamians and other Southerners basically just say they need blacks to have a winning team. Others see the money perspective because football is huge business. Coach Bryant never had to take money from the school for scholarships. We built the law school, we built the student union—football built that school. Money was important to the administration. But an overwhelming number of people in this region of America do believe in the divine Trinity. There are a lot of good Christian believers who realized the color of a man's skin is not what he is, but rather, it's his spirit, and that's what he is as a person. So all three of those issues—democratic freedom, money, and religion—help us get to the right conclusions.

One last thing: I'd not heard from Sam Cunningham in a long time. He left the Patriots in 1982. It had been fifteen, sixteen years, and I didn't know how to get hold of him. Finally I saw somebody, and that person called me and gave me Sam's phone number. So I called to see how he had been, not knowing how he'd been.

I don't know if you know this, but his mom passed away around 1982. He was the eldest, so he came home to take care of things and had to stay away for two weeks. Sam felt so bad about leaving the Patriots, but it was Ron Meyer who cut him when he was away taking care of his family. He thought the players were mad at him for leaving them "high and dry," but we all knew Ron Meyer had mistreated him, and I told him how much I admired him and the way he played. Of all the guys, I loved blocking for Sam.

The next year, after Meyer cut him, he decimated the team up here. For Sam, who I think did what was right for his family, because of the coach unjustly cutting him, Sam thinks he let us down and he felt bad. It was the other way around, and we thought we'd let him down. Which is why he didn't come around—that's the kind of guy he was—but nothing could be further from the truth. So I talked for two hours with Sam, and it was a great talk. I think the world of Sam.

He's the kind of man I look at and say, "I want to be somebody like him."

CHAPTER **Eighteen**

The War of
Northern Aggression

Coach, I know about war. Football's a sport.
—*Father of Bear's injured Texas A&M player,* The Junction Boys

Tody Smith did bring his gun, which he kept in a briefcase. Throughout the flight to Alabama, he kept searching his soul, asking himself what he would do if forced to defend himself.

USC's players deplaned at the Birmingham airport. They were met by a much friendlier reception than either Sherman or Grant had faced. Thousands of people met the Trojans. The late summer air was hot and humid. As the Trojans began to leave, they saw black folks waving at their bus, holding signs exhorting the Trojans. Clarence Davis's Uncle Claude had told him this was a big deal, but he had no idea it was *this* big a deal. The entire scene awed the Trojans. As they got on the bus, "you could hear a penny drop on the ground," Papadakis told the *Mobile Press-Register*. "When we got on the buses, there was absolute dead silence and the guys staring every which way, just looking deeply."

The ride from the airport was revealing. First, the team noticed a billboard showing Coach Bryant sipping a Coke while *walking on water*. As the bus continued, it rolled through the poor side of town. Dave Brown, the team's Athletes in Action representative, was struck by what he saw.

"God help them," said Brown.

Papadakis, who had grown up in Los Angeles, was also struck by the poverty.

"In L.A.," he said in a 2005 public conference call, "our 'ghetto' is Watts. But if you drive through Watts, there are a lot of single-family dwellings. Most of the houses have a front yard. It's not tenements by any means. But on that ride I saw real poverty, people just living on top of each other. . . . It was real squalor."

This experience caused a quiet discomfort in the bus. The boisterousness and the smiles disappeared. The team arrived at a Holiday Inn in an upscale Birmingham neighborhood, and there was commotion, albeit different from the airport commotion. Many of the people at the hotel and in this suburb were looking at "free" blacks in their neighborhood for the first time. The hotel and the surrounding businesses employed blacks as waiters, janitors, and other low-level jobs. Yet these were well-dressed, college-educated West Coast athletes who carried themselves like Roman gladiators. White customers and teenagers strolled over from the shopping plaza across the street to see these new "Union soldiers," here to "invade" Legion Field in the most aggressive manner possible.

"The [hotel] marquee said, 'Welcome, USC Trojans.' Well, it could have just as well said, 'Welcome, USC N--rs,'" Papadakis said. "There were crowds of people there waiting for the team and gawking, pointing at and almost being in shock at seeing these black players come off the bus in coats and ties and going into that hotel."

As the team checked in and began to roam about the hotel, the black players, as they had planned, traveled in packs. The sight of huge black athletes in large numbers had its effect on the local gentry.

"One little boy noted that there sure were 'a lot of n--rs on this team,'" said Dave Brown.

When Brown heard that, he turned to his black teammate Bill Holland and apologized. Holland told him that he heard that kind of talk in L.A. Tody Smith made a mental note of it and felt the bottom of his briefcase for something hard.

Innocent white folks who knew nothing of the USC team were shocked. The team gathered to collect room keys, then headed toward their rooms.

"The black players themselves weren't loose and fluid in their motion," Papadakis said in the *Press-Register* interview. "They were huddled together like Japanese tourists in Disneyland. They got their keys quickly, and we started going across a pedestrian bridge that went over a pool. There were kids playing in the pool and the kids started screaming, 'Look at the n--rs! They're coming into our hotel!' A group of black players were said to have run at a sprint to their rooms."

The unmistakable Southern drawls and epithets droned into the consciousness of the USC players, white and black. The inquisitive suburban white kids were on a mission. Some went knocking on the players' doors. They wanted to get a close look at blacks dressed in shirts and ties. Papadakis roomed with USC's black outside linebacker Kent Carter.

"We get three kids knocking on our door, and they're just wanting to take a look at the black players," Papadakis said. "I go to the door and it's time to go to the field for a workout and I think it's a coach reminding us to go and there's three kids there. One's really small. One's sort of middle [sized] and one's larger, maybe ranging in age from six to 10. They say, 'Are there any USC n--rs in there?'

"So when they come to the door, I say, 'Yeah, I got one in here. He's right over here,' just to rib my teammate, right? He and I are very close. I said, 'Go over and see him. Touch him.' The two older kids kind of stayed behind, but the young one was brave. He just walked right up to Kent. I said, 'Touch him.'

"He put his hand out and you know what Kent Carter did? This was a great moment. He picked the kid up, took the kid's hand, and ran it down his face. The kid was shaking. He was making contact, skin contact with a black man.

"Kent said, 'Black is beautiful.' The other two kids were shocked. They said, 'What am I gonna tell my parents?' I said, 'Tell them the truth. You came looking for a black man and you found one.'"

That night, the Trojans attended a movie in Birmingham, *Two Mules for Sister Sara*, starring Clint Eastwood. Marv Montgomery, a six-foot-five, 255-pound All-American black offensive lineman, was standing with Tody Smith, who was just as massive—the "little" brother of Baltimore's monstrous Bubba Smith. A lady walked by. "God, those are the biggest n--rs I've ever seen in my life."

Her date rushed her out of the theater as if in great fear for his life.

Tody Smith roomed across the hall from Carter and Papadakis. His roommate was a huge white defensive/offensive tackle named John Vella. Vella would become an All-American and later star for the Oakland Raiders. He had heard Smith boast that he would bring a gun, but he did not think he was serious—until he saw the revolver.

Despite Vella's combination of shock and revulsion, Smith clutched the gun, oblivious to Vella's reaction. He aimed it at imaginary enemies. The taunts from the lobby and swimming pool still reverberated in his ears. Fear is the first cousin of violence.

* * *

Alabama engaged in their pregame "walk-through" on the day before the game. They stayed at the Bessemer Hotel. Their tradition was to see a movie after dinner. It was during this time that Bryant hosted a reception for McKay. The meeting was replete with cocktails and stories. The social significance of the upcoming game hung in the air, the unspoken words being that if USC won, it could "end" segregation. If 'Bama won, it would be harder. Wilbur Jackson was coming, that was already a done deal, but the smooth or not-so-smooth transition of this planned event could very well be decided this weekend.

The subject of great homegrown black talent was brought up. McKay had told Bryant about a defensive end out of an Arizona junior college who had grown up in Mobile. Mobile's black population may have been the greatest hotbed of African American athletic talent of all time within a small population. Willie McCovey and the Aaron brothers, Henry and Tommy, were from Mobile. So were Tommie Agee and Cleon Jones, who had helped lead the Miracle Mets to an amazing world championship the previous year. Willie Mays had grown up in Fairfield, Alabama, closer to Birmingham.

McKay told Bryant that the black recruit's name was John Mitchell. As it turned out, Bear had already been courting Mitchell since the previous Christmas vacation.

While this was going on, safety was a concern for some of USC's black players. But not all the black athletes were worried.

"I didn't fear for my safety," Sam Cunningham said in a phone interview with Neal McCready. "I was just a sophomore. I wasn't a leader. I understood the racial climate at the time. If I'd have known it would be as historic as it was, I would have paid a lot more attention. . . . I was looking forward to that game because it was my very first varsity football game. My only concern was if I got a chance to play, I wanted to play well enough to play the next week. I was blessed to have a good game."

While McKay and Bryant were drinking whiskey, a meeting was taking place for black players who *were* concerned. Smith, Jimmy Jones, and Charlie Weaver were supposedly among those in attendance. The atmosphere, it is said, began to take on the tone of an alternative NRA rally, complete with loud music and semiconstitutional admonitions that they had the right to protect themselves. Jones, who today is a Christian minister in his hometown of Harrisburg, Pennsylvania, reportedly tried to talk his teammates down, telling them they had a responsibility not just to themselves but also to the black folks in Alabama.

According to writer Don Yaeger, Tody Smith declared that he was going to "shoot first and ask questions later. . . . I'm not taking any chances. If they get me, I'm taking some with me." Jones reportedly was shocked, declaring, "I'll be damned. I can't believe you really brought a gun." Smith supposedly said, "When one of those rednecks tries to string your ass up, you're going to wish you had this."

This story was related to Yaeger by John Papadakis, but Cunningham, Vella, Sam Dickerson, and many other Trojans interviewed for this book do not recall the incident.

Clarence Davis did bring a Cub Scout knife, which was discovered by assistant coach Craig Fertig, but that was more a source of laughter than anything else.

The exact details of the meeting, reportedly held in Jones's room, are cloudy. Papadakis has spoken of this incident in interviews and other public settings, but his story, which centers on his personal intervention to prevent guns from being taken to Legion Field, cannot be verified. Papadakis once described being called in to the meeting; reaching back some two thousand five hundred years to Plato, Socrates, and Aristotle; and using Greek philosophy with his black teammates to "talk them down" from using guns. Tody Smith died almost a decade ago. Jimmy Jones would not elaborate on John's behalf or against him.

Many Southerners at that time wanted to believe the myth that blacks, while physically impressive, lacked the *moral* strength to compete when the going got tough. If the black players made their guns public, then it would only confirm the Southerners' belief.

Cunningham has made it clear he felt no fear and was not aware of the significance of the event at the time. Interviews with black players such as Clarence Davis, Sam Dickerson, Manfred Moore, Rod McNeill, and Charle' Young also failed to confirm John's account. Most of these men say they do not remember it or they were not in that room, although none flat deny that the meeting happened.

John Vella and Dave Brown were close to several of the blacks as well as to Papadakis. Vella confirmed that his roommate, Tody Smith, had a gun; but he could not verify that the others did. He says a meeting took place, but his knowledge of Papadakis's Platonic efforts is either hearsay, nonexistent, or based on John's version over the years. He did not hear of John's "heroic efforts" in the immediate minutes after Smith returned to their room. Brown was an underclassman and not yet a leader. He could not verify the incident as depicted by his teammate, either. Assistant coach Craig Fertig had no clue that guns had played a part in the trip.

The media covering the game debated the meeting as well. Loel Schrader of the *Long Beach Press-Telegram* was unaware of it. So, too, was USC's sports information director at the time, Don Andersen, as well as his successor, Jim Perry, who was in Birmingham that weekend, also with the *Press-Telegram*. USC's announcers, Mike Walden and Tom Kelly, were ignorant of the meeting as well. But Kelly and assistant coach Dave Levy were cognizant of racial tensions.

"I have suspected for decades that the team was divided along racial lines," said Kelly. "I never could put my finger on it, but that team was loaded with talent, yet they ultimately played well below their abilities."

When Kelly heard the gun story for the first time, he placed it into the larger context of the "controversy" surrounding a black quarterback (Jones) playing ahead of a heralded white blue-chipper (Mike Rae). He now feels it explains how teams that should have competed for national championships, such as the 1967–1969 Trojans, could instead lose two years in a row (1970 and 1971) to talented but inferior Stanford teams, en route to barely .500 records.

Levy, while also unaware of the gun incident, was particularly attuned to the racial situation, more so than Goux or McKay. Levy had been Willie Brown's coach at Long Beach Poly High School.

"I remember having a long conversation with Willie," recalled Levy, "in which he informed me how much racism he was dealing with in Long Beach. This was the late '50s, maybe early 1960s. Long Beach was already a multicultural city, Poly was a diverse school, and I was surprised to hear Willie say this. I was unaware prior to that. I just told Willie that he needed to take advantage of his athletic ability to make a better life for himself."

Sam Dickerson said the team was divided in part by their reaction to a "cowboys 'n' Indians" movie they watched as a team. In typical fashion of the era, the cowboys annihilated the Indians by the bushel. Afterward, the white players expressed the view that it was a great movie depicting America's inexorable "winning of the West." The blacks, on the other hand, were horrified at the violence done to the Indians, whom they identified with and saw as kindred spirits in a racist America. When the two views were aired, strong arguments ensued.

"That split us apart," recalled Dickerson.

What is agreed on at USC, by almost everybody—black, white, coaches, and media—is that there was dissension in the ranks and that it was Christian fellowship that converted a 6-4-1 team into the 1972 "all-time greatest" national champions. With little prompting, this theme was echoed, in one form or another, by Tom Kelly, Dave Brown, Manfred Moore, Charle' Young, Rod McNeill, J. K. McKay, Pat Haden, Craig Fertig, and most everybody who was there during the two- to three-year transition period that marked the difference between McKay being a successful coach and a legendary one.

Coach McKay and Marv Goux granted interviews in 2000 in which they spoke in detail about the 1970 USC game at Alabama, but neither brought up any gun incidents or offered insight into racial tensions among the Trojans. However, interviews with Willie Brown, along with USC's black players, then juxtaposed with white teammates, coaches, and media (not to mention the perceptions from the 'Bama side), reveal an interesting dynamic. The entire story—the meetings in L.A. and Birmingham; racial problems; the alleged gun incident; Papadakis's involvement; the bus trips in Alabama; the reception at the airport, the hotel, and the stadium; the reaction of black fans inside and outside Legion Field; Bryant's "this here's what a football player looks like" statement; and the aftermath (national championships for USC and Alabama in the 1970s, integration in the South)—is described in widely different ways, mostly based on whether the storyteller is black or white.

For whites, the lesson of this is that sensitivity for and understanding of African Americans *must* be seen, as best they can, through the prism of African Americans' perspectives, their historical experiences, and their communications with each other.

The lesson for black people is more difficult to discern, especially when the discerner is white, but common sense lends itself to the notion that they need to understand that well-meaning white folks occasionally see things differently and that the best way is for everybody to merge their understanding into as common a knowledge as possible. It is in coming together that we all learn and benefit from each other.

As for the gun incident, it should be true. Did John Papadakis really reach back 2,500 years to channel the wisdom of his Greek ancestors and turn disaster into triumph? Whatever the case, John's teammates *do* remember him as brilliant and Socratic—regardless of the accuracy of what may or may not have happened that late summer of 1970 in a Birmingham hotel room. Whether his charisma can be distilled into a single meeting in a Birmingham hotel room is less important than his positive impact on teammates of all colors during his USC career.

What is *not* in dispute, and everybody associated with this game agrees, is that it would have been a nightmare to deal with McKay and Goux if they had been called to bail the players out of a Birmingham jail. This scenario was more horrible than any possibility. Regardless of motivation, the guns were put away. They would not reappear.

Other Voices: John Mitchell

Wilbur Jackson may have been the first recruited African American scholarship football player in Alabama's history, but John Mitchell was the first to actually play in a varsity game. After graduate school, he went on to a long coaching career and today is the defensive line coach with the Pittsburgh Steelers.

I grew up in Mobile, Alabama, graduating from high school in 1969. From there I played at Eastern Arizona Junior College from 1969 to 1970 and lettered two years on the Alabama varsity football team, 1971–1972. I graduated six months ahead of my class, the fall instead of the spring.

I wanted to go to graduate school, so in order to finish that fall, I took a job at the university and took six months of grad courses at night and in the summer. I called Coach Bryant about a job in the athletic department. He said this was something we should talk about face to face, so he asked me to come to talk with him. I drove to Tuscaloosa, and he offered me a job. I was twenty-one years old. This was not a graduate assistant's job, but a full-time staff job.

I coached at Alabama for four years, right through a bowl game against UCLA in 1976. Then I went to Arkansas with Lou Holtz, where I was on the staff with Pete Carroll. You could see he had a bright future in front of him.

I was at Arkansas for six years, 1977–1982, then I coached at Birmingham for the United States Football League, which lasted three years. I took a job at Temple for one year, then LSU for four years, first as a linebacker coach and then as their defensive coordinator. I was the first African American coordinator, defensive or offensive, in the SEC. I was at LSU from 1986 through '91. I was with the Cleveland Browns for three

years, 1991–1994. I have been with the Steelers since 1994, all the years that
Bill Cowher has been their head coach. I coach the defensive line.

I'd agreed to go to Southern Cal. John McKay recruited me. I played
against Arizona Western J.C. in Yuma. They had a number of players who
went to USC, including Charlie Weaver. The Arizona Western coach recommended me. I had a great time on my recruiting trip to L.A., and I was
at home when Alabama recruited me. McKay and Bryant were friends, and
McKay did tell him he'd signed a young man from Mobile. Bryant excused
himself and called Clem Gryska. They were playing in the Bluebonnet
Bowl a couple of days later. This is December 1970.

In 1969, Alabama hadn't recruited African American football players.
However, five blacks had won a science fair in Mobile and then the state
science fair and competed in the national science fair. All five had academic scholarships to Alabama and Auburn based on a science fair at South
Carolina. A lot of schools were beginning to recruit us as students; this was
the cream of the crop. They wanted students who offered a lot to the university. Some of these students were classmates of mine, and I had a good
showing in the science fair. It demonstrated that African Americans were
on to something academically.

Clem Gryska and Hayden Riley came to the house a couple of days
later to speak with my mother and father. They gave us the whole spiel
about Alabama football. As an African American kid growing up, I knew
all about their three national titles, so a player of any kind of color would
want the opportunity to go to the University of Alabama during that time.
You're gonna do that if you get the chance. I'd been in Arizona for a year
and a half, and I wanted my family to see me play. That's why I chose not
to go out to L.A. and instead stayed home in Alabama where they could
just drive a few hours to watch the games.

Wilbur Jackson was the first recruited player, but I was the first one to
play in a game. It was against Southern Cal in the 1971 season opener at
the L.A. Coliseum. I was on the kickoff team, so yeah, McKay would have
turned to Craig Fertig and said something about it.

Coach Bryant told me he was sure I'd have some problems, but if I
have a problem come to him first instead of going to the press. I got to my
dorm a few days early, and that night I met my roommate, a white guy
from Georgia named Bobby Stanford. We were the school's first black-
white roommates ever. Now we're more like brothers than friends. We've
been best men in each other's weddings.

Southern Cal had played extremely well against Alabama, so people thought 'Bama'd fare better with black players. They wanted to do what they could to have a good football team, and they needed African American players.

It was as smooth as it could have been. Coach Bryant treated all his players alike. We played Texas in the Cotton Bowl in my last game, and my mom was outside the dressing room. Bryant comes outside, and one of the reporters asked how many black players he had.

"I have no black players," Coach Bryant told him. "I have no white players. I just have ball players." My mom loved Coach Bryant for being so straight up and fair.

They ask me to come back from time to time, but my team's always playing at the same time, so it's hard for me to get back there. In the summer I'll drive to the campus to see what changes have occurred, and I have friends in Tuscaloosa who invite me to come back, but the timing's not always been good.

On Bryant's alleged statement. From what I know of Bryant, I totally doubt he would do that big demonstration with Cunningham. It's out of character. I heard that story. I know some of the people who would know, but I think because Southern Cal won, a lot of stories—from writers and people who watched at the stadium or on TV—said Sam Cunningham did more for integration in sixty minutes than all that had taken place before that. As for what happened, I still don't think even the hallway story happened; from what I know it's not in Coach Bryant's character.

When I was recruited by Southern Cal, Cunningham and Charle' Young were my hosts, and I got to know them pretty well, but they shed no light on that story. I know Scott Hunter well, and if it happened they'd have said so.

The only thing I wanted to do [at Alabama] was get a good education, which I got. I wanted to see if I could play with the best. I think any young boy would want that challenge. That's the only reason I went there.

On progress in Alabama. I think the change is all for the good now. They've had a black mayor in Birmingham, black city councilmen elected across the state, mayors in other cities. There were only a small number of African American students then, but now there are many more, and it's opened a lot of doors for people who might have migrated out of the South. They could make a living without leaving. We've hosted the Atlanta Olympics, and looking back now at Montgomery, Birmingham, Atlanta, the hot spots of integration—why, things have really changed in terms of race relationships.

The legacy of Martin Luther King is felt today. He went everywhere he thought injustice was: the Carolinas, Mississippi, Kentucky, all over the South. There were many other ways they thought integration would take place. A lot of people lost their lives during that time, but here's a man who says, "We're gonna march and do it in a way without hurting people." He did it with class; he thought it out thoroughly, the way he went about it. He was slapped, jailed, beaten, but he turned the other cheek. He made it better not just for black people but for anybody.

On the influence of religion. Christianity was very influential. Growing up in Mobile, mine was a very religious family. That's what we had. It was faith in our religion. My family had for generations been telling stories about faith, about believing in yourself despite great obstacles, that there's a greater spirit than you. People's feelings can change. A great example is George Wallace, who stood in the doorway to prevent Vivian Malone and James Hood from entering the university, but over the years his heart got soft and he admitted his mistakes.

People who'd never been around different folks, in the '60s a lot of whites and blacks never interacted. Both parties didn't know anybody else from their kind. But you saw slowly, as integration happened, people saw that another person is no different from them. Others have differing opinions, and there are black racists too.

But I think this question of whether football integration happened to cynically win games or because of a larger morality, I think a little of both happened. I don't just take the cynical view; I also believe morality eventually allowed black players at Alabama and other schools. I'll say this: When I played, Ole Miss had none, LSU had none, Mississippi State had none. I played in stadiums in which I was the only black on the field or maybe in the stadium. I've seen it go from when Bryant hired me, and no school had black coaches, to when I got hired as a defensive coordinator at LSU, to where this thing has mushroomed.

We've a long way to go, but we've made strides. Our foot is through the door, yes.

Other Voices: Anthony Davis

Anthony Davis came to USC the year after the 1970 game at Birmingham, but as a "young brother" he heard all the stories of this event, told to him in "barbershop style" by Tody Smith and other veterans. A. D. became one of the all-time great Trojans; an All-American, he should have won the 1974 Heisman Trophy, and his legendary performances as the "Notre Dame killer" are considered to be among the finest games ever played by a collegiate football player. His views of the events surrounding the trip to Birmingham differ from those of many of his teammates. He is a producing partner of mine in the project to depict the events of the 1970 USC-Alabama game as a major motion picture.

Basically, historically, from the turn of the century, since Reconstruction, there were rules about what blacks could and could not do. As a young African American, I saw old clips of Jack Johnson and marveled at how a dark man could do what he did.

Johnson became a money machine for white promoters, building them up. My whole thing for anybody to understand about the summer of 1970, USC versus Alabama, was that it was a segregated country. Being fifty-three now, the only way to demonstrate my talents was through physical talent. We looked at it like we couldn't be doctors, businessmen, industrial leaders. We did hard labor. We knew we had physical tools to play sports. It was a struggle.

As I say, I always admired Jack Johnson. They pulled the Mann Act out of mothballs to get Jack Johnson. For twenty years after that, they did not want blacks. Until Joe Louis came along—he became an American symbol of the anti-Nazi movement. He and Jesse Owens. Louis beat Max Schmeling, and society started opening their eyes and understanding athletes can be profitable. Owens could win four golds but could not get a job back in the United States. Louis was a functional illiterate, exploited throughout his career. He went in the Army, he was abused, he was hit for tax evasion.

* * *

Historically, what I've known with white and black athletes over the years, an example is I was able to have an autograph session with Ted Williams, and he said, "My only regret is I never knew how great I could have been because I never really competed against black athletes.

"I knew something was missing," he said. "Coop Papa Bell, Josh Gibson, guys we never heard of, denied by color." Jim Crow in society is denied. Just think, women could not vote until 1924, but imagine the black man's plight.

I never forget a meeting I had with Don Newcombe. All the published reports were that he loved the Dodgers organization, but Newcombe said this was not really true. The story of Jackie Robinson staying in a bus, he's gotta get food from the back of the restaurant; a lot of those guys really carry this chip on their shoulders.

There's a slogan you hear in barbershops, nationwide. Tiger [Woods], [Michael] Jordan, no matter what you do financially, no matter what you do you're still a n--r. Tiger was the one who knocked down all the walls. Jordan might play in the house, but he won't *own* the house. Willie Mays carried the chip on his shoulder to Barry Bonds, which is how I handle it in my own situation.

The 1960s were a boiling point. Civil rights leaders established King, Evers; this was the nucleus, there was a pressure cooker, a boiling point. The South was oblivious, but this was happening all over. I came from an educated family, but I'd go to Agoura, Granada Hills, Sylmar; people'd say s--t. It's like, hey, if you get mistreated there, imagine what it was like in the South. If you saw a white person you had to tip your hat. Before integration a lot of stuff was out of line. We were "nigras."

With all that going on, how do you get an education? You can't get to first base on social or political acceptance. Through the turn of the century, blacks could not read; they were functionally illiterate.

I was one of the fortunate blacks, one of those whose father's side was educated. There was fear on the farm—this was the white man's plantation. It was a security blanket, just like the Negro Leagues. Blacks marveled that these guys stepped up and established, barnstormed with, and beat Major League teams. Back to Ted Williams, you could always tell what a man's socioeconomic background was. A white guy like Williams, who understands people who grew up poor as he did. This was major; you can develop backdoor friendships. You can't go out and promote it in public. Sinatra finally promoted Sammy Davis Jr.

In the '60s, blacks could not go to 'Bama, Mississippi, Texas A&M. They could go to Southern, Florida A&M; they could go north. You'd still see bits and pieces of Jim Crow even in the North. Jim Brown was fifth string, but he played when all the others got hurt.

I couldn't go to Sylmar High. My dad couldn't go to Glendale. These are examples of the Deep South. Use your imagination. So here I am in the '60s. In '61, '62, and '63 I went to Texas with my parents. We're in the station wagon with my grandfather, and he forgets he has two grandsons from the liberal West Coast. You had to have a certain demeanor. I started yelling, "Watermelons." This guy comes out and says, "If we want watermelons, we'll tell you." I'm just jokin' around, right.

My grandfather just says to me, "Son, you don't understand. . . . You could be hangin' from that tree."

Back in California, I'm now more aware of color. I saw signs: "Whites only." I saw the plight of black survival. It was deplorable. But I look back at the West Coast, I look at the rosters, and there weren't that many blacks on the West Coast. There was C.R. [Roberts], Brice [Taylor], Willie Brown, Mike Garrett; there weren't that many at USC until my class, the '71 USC freshman class. So I'm a young black man, and I realize there's a difference in society. I was considered an aggressive black. I remember I liked white girls.

Jeri Gibson, she was a beautiful girl. She was smart enough to say that there are good whites and bad whites. On a segregated campus, this university likes only certain blacks. If you're a pretty boy or a radical, you'll pay a price for that. I call Charle' Young; he was part of the "underground railroad" at that time. He'd deliver a "message." He and other blacks such as Edesel Garrison, they kept it underneath, but I wore it on my sleeve, so if I can't join a frat then it's segregated, but it's because I wasn't part of the "mainstream."

There was a big frat fight. I knew Tody Smith for years. Tody was flamboyant. He got around. If he saw a female, he was the kind of guy who'd talk to black girls and white girls the same way. Guys were jealous; it was a jealousy thing, and this white dude, he loses control of his girl. Tody was part of the Wild Bunch, so he was a popular character. Nobody wanted to tangle with these guys. They carried a gun; he'd cut your head off. He was smooth but he had rough edges, but he was smart and fashionable, intimidating to these guys. We were ahead of our times. He couldn't live in Texas. I couldn't, either; they'd call me an "uppity n--r."

When I was at USC, the thought process of what I knew in this country, I was aware of that, my being a pretty boy, "high yellow." I didn't fit the stereotype, but I was a combination of both; decent looks and a great athlete. If I saw a woman, I went after her. Blacks I knew went with either black or white girls, so they'd remind me of Ty Hudson, who'd gotten in trouble with white girls, with McKay's daughter. I said, "They brought me here, this is my school, so I'll do what I want." So I'd go for girls with blonde hair and blue eyes.

"They gonna get you," they said to me.

Dr. Don Wildon started a curriculum of black studies. Half the class was black, and he marveled over my sports accomplishments. I was a new breed of '70s guy; things I did on the West Coast I couldn't do in the Deep

South. They'd say, "Boy, they gonna get you for that. Black boys down here can't do that."

I said, "I'm at USC. As long as I win titles, there's nothing I can't do." They couldn't get rid of a talented guy.

* * *

What Tody Smith told me over the years, about the guns in Alabama . . . Bubba Scott was no longer there; Tody took me under his wing. He said it was a volatile situation. He said, "I was packin', Jimmy Gunn was packin'." People were calling John Papadakis a Greek bigot because he was trying to keep these blacks from protecting themselves. There was fear in 'Bama—snipers, assassins. For John to sit up and take credit for not having guns was b--t. They knew the mind-set down there. There's a disconnect between open and silent racism, the liberals, the melting pot, but these guys—Tody, Gunn, Weaver—they weren't into that. They knew. Liberals could argue, "Don't do nothing, it's cool," but they knew they wouldn't protect them when the time came.

On the day of the game I was in my house in San Fernando, with my teammates. I was a senior at San Fernando High School. They were excited because they knew these brothers would go down there and kick their asses. White boys never faced blacks like that with killer in their eyes. You got a feel for the blacks going after your ass.

Professor Cockeroo was a history professor at USC. I asked him what was going on in their minds, this is before the game. He said there was some fear, some anger, some get-back time; they were looking for superior play in this game. The astute ones who knew about the racial situation, about seg-regation, who knew about King, who knew socioeconomics, knew this was a historical game. There were some of us who knew what it meant.

Professor Cockeroo said that all the blacks on this team had to create fear in the eyes of 'Bama, that they did not realize USC had some serious players to face. I knew USC would beat 'em, this was a major impact to me. I'd get letters from the South, and they went right in the trash. John Mitchell was just an agent for change but not change right away. What happened in 'Bama in the South was like after slavery; there was still dis-crimination everywhere else.

* * *

There's a disconnect about all this stuff. I was conscious of and understood bigotry. McKay was a slickster; Bryant was a straight-out bigot. There were two types of whites at that time. Bryant was perceived as a man who didn't like blacks but needed 'em to win. I heard stories. McKay said you don't have to like 'em to play 'em. This is what we were dealing with, what McKay was dealing with. I had conversations with recruits. They asked, "Does McKay like blacks?" I said, "Take the fruits of what you can get," and it was monumental just to be at USC. We had few choices. You'd try to pick a school hoping this white coach likes you; even if McKay was not a devout bigot in certain ways, we had bigots with deep pockets. I knew he was getting that about me because of the way I carried myself. I was open.

I was a loner. I gravitated to Tody Smith, who was straight out, but we had guys like Clarence Davis who grew up in 'Bama, and it's like, "How do you entertain going down there to play with bigots, with what George Wallace was saying at the schoolhouse door?"

Why would you even think of going to play with perceived bigots? Why'd we put ourselves in harm's way to *help them*?

With Martin Luther King, blacks were divided even with him, but he was passive to white men. Some saw him as self-indulgent, with J. Edgar Hoover who was investigating him, reporting to Bobby Kennedy, reporting things that were true about Communists, womanizing, this kind of thing.

* * *

Manfred Moore told me that at the end of the day we're both dead, that we're not "advanced as a people yet, not advanced enough to follow me or you." He saw it like "forgive and forget."

Tody said this was the "wild, wild West," they don't care here in L.A., so smart blacks said, "I'll take what I can take and move on." Then there was Step'n Fetchit. I told 'em at the end of day, they're all still n--rs.

Sam Cunningham was middle of the road, a passive sophomore. Tody was "Butch Cassidy"; he was smart, he was a leader, comin' from the South. McKay knew. McKay said if he can play, "I'll play him." But it was McKay the bigot versus Bryant the bigot, subtle versus overt.

Talking about Bear, Bryant was saying no n--rs. But he needed 'em. There were all these blacks around Legion Field; the key was Wallace was out of office. The locals all said, "Ain't never gonna happen. Them brothas ain't like you down here." But they looked at USC; these are gut-wrenching brothers, high-powered brothers who can kick asses.

Bottom line is when they saw the size of USC's blacks they had fear in their eyes. They saw all this meanness in these guys' eyes. They saw the killers in these eyes, these ancestors of caste and slavery. They wanted to legally kick their asses.

Tody said, "We're gonna give you a taste of your medicine. We're gonna give you a piece of it." Tody was talkin' trash on the field. We were bigger, faster. What people don't realize is some of these things going on outside the stadium. The payback was about the general public. Some had fear of riots, retaliation. Some hoped that USC would be beat, thinking there'd be backlash against them, people left behind. But the opposite happened, and the crowd just said, "*Man!*"

Tody was packing anyway. He's goin' back regardless; there's not even a matter of fear. His father was a legend in the South for coaching Gale Sayers. Tody was looking for the challenge. They were all very wary of white men of authority, men such as McKay. He could still screw me at the end of the day.

Tody was not on that team I was on, my team in '74. He was older than I, but he passed it down to me. I don't care about Papadakis or Allan Graf, these guys who think they're the story. It didn't matter if you were black or white, you played to kick ass on the field. Marv Goux: he and Tody clashed, but at the end of the day they respected each other. It was just a game, what you feel with a group of people. You can visualize what happened after the game. I knew a buddy who grew up in Gaston, Alabama. People were walking around saying, "We felt they're gonna get you anyway. At the end of the day, win or lose, you're gonna be a n--r."

They didn't know what would happen in 'Bama, the aftereffects. Tody was confused about McKay; he defined his thought process. Those who were astute of it, if you were not a certain kind of black guy, McKay would not play you. Ballplayers had this perception. After all, the game's not changed a lot of guys' attitudes. Some blacks thought it would not change anything. Whites knew blacks were physical. What they didn't realize about that game is it did not turn it around right away. It didn't see Tennessee, Auburn, Florida change, just like with slavery—blacks didn't know they were free until 1877.

It didn't change recruiting. If not for Bear Bryant then it never would have happened, not even Bobby Mitchell. It didn't change. McKay persuaded him, Bryant went to his superiors, but from people I talk to he was a straight bigot. From people I talk to, there was more anger with whites about playing games against blacks than there was fear. It was a carnival. I never thought it would be historical. To me it was barnstorming; there was nothing set in gold.

* * *

Joe Namath's roots are from Eastern Europe. This was his personality, loose, flamboyant, and it got him in trouble at 'Bama. If Namath grew up in the South, then he never would have ventured into those neighborhoods to talk to blacks. He saw things he could not understand. He refused to fall to the pressures of society at that time.

* * *

I would think John Hannah had a serious challenge ahead of him. I consider him the best pulling guard ever. He knew they didn't have anybody comparable. But people did not perceive.

* * *

The Vietnam War . . . all the colored stuff went out when the VC were shooting at them. War is the biggest liberating factor. When you go to other foreign lands, this is a liberating factor.

I didn't think the antiwar protests had anything to do with football, with the streets and the football game. Sports when it came to the black athlete did not make a big breakthrough until the 1980s. To the astute of the time, they saw a turning point in American society. Bear was not into social change. McKay did not think like that, but he was not sophisticated in societal issues—most coaches aren't.

When I scored six TDs, I predicted, I could see it in McKay's eyes, there was a change in his attitude toward me. When I did it, [Muhammad] Ali wanted to meet me. It was arranged for me to meet Ali at LAX [Los Angeles International Airport]. Ali turns to me and says, "I was recruited by the Nation of Islam, I was torn by two worlds."

* * *

Fertig just did what McKay asked of him. Goux was a dominating figure on defense. I represented the new breed of black that you talked about. You could not be intellectual and be an athlete; you were either a stupid n--r athlete or one of the nerd students.

Tody would say, "A.D., watch your back, and even here they watchin' your ass." I met John Carlos [1968 Olympian who gave the controversial "Black Power" salute in Mexico City]. They had problems with that.

The key was the brothers had to be good enough, to stay healthy. I was competing with three black running backs. I knew I had to do something special. When I scored six versus Notre Dame, when I came off the bench versus Oregon, broke a 0–0 game, I knew people marveled at how I scored 206 points.

If I don't do what I do, we don't win the national title. Throughout history, "the Man" was always screwing me; these were little subtle things. This is a sociopolitical statement. This game, this story, it must have all the dramatic points. But I'm sayin', at USC there were "house n––rs" and there were "field n––rs." The field n––rs thought McKay was puttin' them in harm's way going back to Alabama, for what, to help Bear Bryant? McKay put them in harm's way to help Bryant.

CHAPTER Nineteen

Game Faces

I think that one game did more for social change in
Alabama than anything that ever transpired.
—*John Hannah*

On the morning of the game, the Tide ate breakfast at nine. After
sitting about the hotel lobby watching TV (the team had stayed
the night before in a hotel), they finally roused from their day-
long lounge act, arriving at Legion Field ninety minutes before the night-
time kickoff. Quarterback Scott Hunter strolled alongside Coach Bryant
in the walk-through. The Tide was confident. Bryant was not, but he did
not let on.

The Trojans arrived by bus, and to everybody's surprise were met by
hundreds of revelers. Half-drum grills put forth huge plumes of smoke.
Confederate flags flew as if the scene was a reenactment of Bull Run. The
state seemingly had banned all colors except crimson. These were white
fans, and the place was crawling with white cops. *Roll Tide!*

A huge ovation met the Alabama Million-Dollar Band, which created
an electric feeling as the team approached the stadium. They were not playing "Fight On!" as they had done at the airport.

Just like at the airport, the Trojans noticed the black fans last.
Normally, they were nowhere to be seen at Legion Field on game day, but
on this night they were emboldened to push forward, making their presence known to the USC players.

People held Bibles in their hands and had tears in their eyes. As far as these folks were concerned, the Trojans were a collective Moses. The new Red Sea was Legion Field, and the team would "part it" with their speed and strength, leading these people to their promised land.

The Bible toters approached the black players, telling them they had prayed for this day. Tody Smith no doubt realized what a mistake it would have been to bring the gun. Since the team was leaving straight for the air-port after the game, he had it at the stadium, but it was tucked away with his luggage, not available to him on the field or in the dressing room. The attitude in the dressing room could only be described as intense to the extreme. McKay's team dressed quietly, like soldiers before battle. Then they took the field to get the feel of the lights; the artificial turf; the sights, smells, and sounds of a stadium that was quickly filling up with seventy thousand fans. Then they heard them. Distant. At first hard to discern, then louder and more distinct.

Racial slurs. Catcalls.

Deep in the end zone, however, almost hidden from view, a small group of black fans was supporting USC.

Coach Bryant, who normally observed pregame rituals from the goal-post, moved to midfield. He was in his late fifties, with the weathered face of experience. The crowd cheered his every move. At the fifty-yard line, he met his good friend John McKay. McKay had the look of a field general in full command of strategy and troop strength. He had a full head of white hair. Both coaches were dressed in coats and ties. They shook hands.

Platitudes were exchanged about how good each team looked to the other. McKay tried a little psychology with Bear. His team was too wound up, too tense. Goux had assured him that this tension was just an uncoiled spring ready to explode all over Legion Field. McKay told Bryant that USC was as ready as they would ever be, and the Alabama coach again thanked him for making the trip all the way from California, which produced a wry look from the USC head man.

Sam Cunningham and his teammates refused to be baited by catcalls from the stands or taunts from the Crimson Tide, who still thought of themselves as the mighty powerhouse that had dominated the game. The Trojans feared no team, but as Craig Fertig pointed out, they *did* fear John McKay!

* * *

Jimmy Jones, wearing number 8, was nervous. He felt as if the whole world was on his shoulders.

The fiery assistant coach Marv Goux was in his element.

The six-foot-five, 270-pound black defensive tackle, Tody Smith, wearing number 73, had made it this far without coming unglued. He acted loose, but he was a bundle of insecurities. Goux could read his players like a book. He knew that all the Trojans' pent-up nervous energy would explode like a "Wrecking Crew," which he called his linemen. Goux had done his job, fine-tuning his team with just the right mixture of fear, confidence, hubris, challenge, and waiting! His confidence soared.

A few yards away, Clarence Davis had that ongoing pressure on him. He had the pressure of coming through for his extended family, still living in Birmingham. Davis came on the scene as a junior in 1969, replacing the great O. J. Simpson. USC was already Tailback U. Simpson had led USC to the 1967 national championship and won the 1968 Heisman Trophy.

Simpson had completed the greatest collegiate running career ever up to that time. He had done it in only two years. A native of San Francisco, Simpson had played at Galileo High School. Galileo is a legendary sports school that has produced athletes such as Joe DiMaggio and Hank Luisetti (inventor of the jump shot), who at one time or another might have been considered the best or close to the best of all time in their respective sports.

Simpson would break Jim Brown's single-season rushing record with Buffalo in 1973. In his heyday, Simpson was on a very short list of "the greatest football players ever."

Simpson broke all the records as a City College of San Francisco freshman, attracting the attention of every college in the country, including USC. He fell in love with USC's mascot, the white horse Traveler, whom he had seen traipsing around the Rose Bowl field while watching USC's 1963 Rose Bowl victory over Wisconsin. But Simpson still did not have the academic qualifications for admittance to USC.

Arizona State and Utah were willing to let him into school. Simpson, itching to play four-year ball, was ready to go. Marv Goux made an emergency flight to San Francisco, telling him that if he wanted something bad enough, it was worth it to wait. Simpson agreed to stay at CCSF for one more year and then transfer to USC as a junior. What is little known is that a cadre of "wise men" at City College also mentored Simpson, advising the same thing as Goux. Among these faculty members were Louis "Dutch" Conlan, the president of the college, and Donald E. Travers, my father, who taught business law at CCSF at that time after having been a legendary track coach at San Francisco's Lowell and Balboa High Schools.

The rest is history.

USC has easily produced the most first-round NFL Draft picks. Five Trojans from Simpson's 1967 national championship team went in the first round. One year later, Simpson himself was the league's number one pick.

The media had pressured McKay to find a comparable running back to replace Simpson. What he produced was an undersized junior college transfer. In 1969, Clarence Davis became USC's second straight juco transfer to make All-American. He does not go down in Trojan lore as Simpson's equal, but he certainly rates among the school's legendary runners.

Davis, however, was no second-class citizen. His family had moved to the Golden State to avoid just such status. After leaving school, he would play for some of the greatest Oakland Raiders teams ever. In 1974, he caught a game-winning pass from (Alabama alum) Kenny Stabler amid a "sea of hands" from the Miami Dolphins, literally draped over him, in the AFC play-offs, a play that rates high in Raiders legend and lives forever on NFL highlight shows. In 1976, he helped Oakland win the Super Bowl.

Davis's All-American status in 1969, his successful continuation of O.J.'s standards, and his bright future, was all in the backseat on September 12, 1970. The pressure he felt went far beyond just performing well and winning the game. He wanted to uphold the honor of his family and his race, right here in the town of his birth. Playing in front of seventy thousand "hostiles" made this an uphill battle. It certainly was not the kind of homecoming he would have preferred.

In many ways, every black person in Alabama was, at least that night, a member of Clarence's "family." Clarence would play the game, then fly home for more football, school, and a pro career. But the local black citizenry was stuck here. The community would be forced to deal with the aftermath of what happened. There seemed little compromise in this scenario. Either the Trojans would win and things would change, or God forbid Alabama would dominate, thus reinforcing all the old stereotypes. Outsiders could spin it any way they felt they wanted to, but as former House Speaker Tip O'Neill once said, "All politics is local."

A 'Bama victory would be a political victory, vindication for the white man. Alabama blacks wanted a victory for the black man. Such things were few and far between.

What these people did not know, never could have guessed in a million years in fact, was that what they wanted was, in a strange way, what Coach Bryant wanted. It would be imprudent to say that Bear Bryant *wanted* his team to lose that game. It would not be imprudent to say that he *expected* them to and felt that if indeed they did lose, then his vision of the future was one he might have shared with Clarence's "family."

Most Southern blacks were Christians. Most Southern blacks were also realists. Christianity had always been the bulwark that blacks leaned against in times of despair. Black Christianity had always centered on the afterlife. It was after death that freedom would ring. To expect much in this life was not realistic. Too many black men had been disappointed too often to expect much to change.

This game aroused contradictory feelings in these men. On the one hand, it was an opportunity for men of their race to demonstrate what they were capable of, like the Tuskegee Airmen, trained in Alabama of all places, who had flown with distinction in World War II. But the Tuskegee Airmen, while arousing pride among blacks, had not really changed attitudes, at least locally. That was, to note Tip O'Neill's words, all that mattered in Alabama.

The Tuskegee Airmen had never gotten real national publicity, either. Not like college football. Sports were the heartbeat of America. This game would have national implications. When two football powers like USC and Alabama meet, in almost any year over the past seventy seasons, the game is likely to have national implications for somebody.

This, however, further worried many black folks. With all the attention, if Davis's team, if their people, if *Clarence* flopped, it would be a disappointment too hard to bear. It would set their people back for years, maybe a decade—or more.

Southern blacks loved football, too, and on this night they bled cardinal and gold as much as Marv Goux did, but if the outcome was dismal then the future seemed dismal. Some were almost angry that they were faced with such a situation. Coach McKay had seen the opportunity and taken it. Eventually, it would be seen that Coach Bryant's motivations were the same as black motivations. The black players would have the chance to shine. But everybody else—McKay, Bryant, Clarence, his teammates—they could all go back to their lives even if things went badly. USC's black athletes would have college degrees, pro contracts, and bright lives. Birmingham's blacks would be left to pick up the pieces.

It was not fair, but then again, the men in Birmingham's black neighborhoods surrounding Legion Field had rarely been treated fairly by life. Some of them on this night looked angry. Their wives could see their husbands' expressions and were not happy with them. Many women in black America often found themselves forced to be the "strength" in their families when their men were too drained by circumstance to rise above the occasion. They knew that if Clarence and the Trojans lost, it would be a setback, but they girded for it. They knew they would need to be the strong ones. They were not pleased at this prospect, but they expected it nevertheless.

In the backyards of Birmingham's neighborhoods, small children played noisily, unaware that something was happening a few miles away that would change their lives profoundly. They lived in typically poor surroundings, but their homes were usually well kept. Inside many of these homes, a picture of number 28, Clarence, hung on the wall. "Extended family" listened to the game on a radio. The women served barbecue. Palpable tension hung in the air.

At bars near Legion Field, in rundown sections of town, beer and whiskey were served to these men. The radio was tuned into the local Alabama game broadcast.

Inside the stadium, shirtless fans spelled T-I-D-E while making intemperate remarks. They normally growled, "Bear meat," or cruder variations on the theme. USC's black players could see that the stands were not exactly filled with brothers. No, this was definitely not L.A. A typical USC game at the Coliseum may have been the greatest melting pot in America.

There were, of course, the alumni. The younger ones might have been described as yuppies, except the term had not been invented yet. They came in their sweaters, tailgating before the game, the corporate types and their trophy wives, their perfect children in tow. The students were just a younger version of their parents: rich and confident that the axis of the earth was spinning around them because they were the future "masters of the universe."

But the crowds in South Central L.A. always included a heavy mix of local citizenry, the black and Hispanic populations that surrounded the Coliseum. Despite the school's wealth and its rich, conservative reputation, the football team and its black stars had succeeded in making the Trojans the "people's team" in Los Angeles. It was an eclectic demographic any politician would die for, as coach John Robinson pointed out.

But at Legion Field the players were getting their "game faces" on. The Tide fans were standing, getting rowdier by the minute. The black players looked at them with some trepidation.

"Just *stay* in those seats," their looks seemed to be saying.

CHAPTER Twenty

Conquest

Fight on and win
For ol' SC.
Fight on to victory.
Fight on!
—"Fight On," USC's official fight song

Number 67 for the Trojans was first-time starting middle linebacker John Papadakis. He had come to USC from Rolling Hills
High School, one of the wealthiest, most prestigious schools in
the state. A multisport athlete, John's baseball coach at Rolling Hills was
Mike Gillespie, who would become USC's head baseball coach in 1987 and
coach the Trojans to the 1998 College World Series championship.

"Papadakis?" Gillespie said with a laugh when asked about his old
player. "Now there's a piece of work."

Papadakis always had that effect on people. One does not meet John;
one *experiences* him! Papadakis came to USC full of vim and vigor, convinced of his own talents. He was a star running back. Then he met up
with Sam Cunningham.

"Anybody involved in athletics in southern California knew who Sam
Cunningham was in high school," John said over the phone. "I knew all
about him. I still thought I could beat him out, until I saw him on the
practice field."

Despite being a year younger than Papadakis, Cunningham did beat him out for the starting fullback job, although keeping that job was still very much up in the air prior to the Alabama game.

However, Papadakis was not given a bench to languish on; he was given a chance to compete for the middle linebacker position, and with it a place at the table. Like all competitive men, if he saw an opportunity, he assumed ownership of it, took what was his without asking, and insisted on keeping what he had earned through hard work.

Papadakis would earn his spurs at USC. He would graduate a year ahead of the great 1972 national championship team that many insisted was the best ever to lace up cleats. He would not go on to pro football but instead would make his mark as an entrepreneur. He opened Papadakis Taverna, a Greek restaurant in San Pedro, which to this day is the best of its kind in Los Angeles.

Papadakis Taverna is pure John Papadakis—loud, boisterous, and full of life. Dining there is a party, filled with dance and music, all wrapped in great family fun. Papadakis is now, just as he was when he played football at USC, a walking embodiment of three thousand years of Greek culture. This was what made him such a unique teammate—and leader—on the 1970 USC football squad.

Eventually, the handsome Greek man about town married and started a family. His son Taso played football at USC too. His other son, Petros, was one of USC's four football captains in 2000 and today is a modern, boisterous version of the old man. He hosted a successful sports talk show in L.A., filled with references to pop and literary figures ranging from 50 Cent to Shakespeare to Dostoevsky to Robert Towne. In addition, Petros broadcasts football games for Fox Sports.

Some time around 1999 or 2000, Doug Krikorian of the *Long Beach Press-Telegram* interviewed Sam Cunningham. Krikorian asked who hit him the hardest in his career: Dick Butkus? Mean Joe Greene?

"John Papadakis," was Sam's answer. The man he beat out earned his respect with his no-holds-barred hitting in practice.

McKay wanted to get his charges into the locker room to settle them down. He and Goux had built them up with just the right pace and momentum. Such is the balancing act of coaching psychology, a little-understood aspect of sports that few writers, who were rarely good athletes themselves, truly grasp.

It was perhaps McKay's greatest attribute, and nobody balanced the act like Goux. In the locker room just before heading out to the kickoff, the Trojans had the look of determination that members of the 101st Airborne Division described upon flying into D-day. That was the look Marv Goux was paid to deliver.

USC was inculcated by Plato's legendary "warrior spirit," which Goux had expanded on, making reference to most of the military heroes since the Peloponnesian War. It did not matter to Goux whether he was talking about Roman gladiators, legionnaires, or Patton's Third Army, as long as they fought and won. His fierce side was not tempered by Papadakis's Greek sensibilities.

The last word, as always, was left to Goux. He had said it all a million times. He knew that if he had done his job, now was not the time for a lengthy talk. The coach just told his charges to remember what they had come to Alabama for. Then he finished strong and used the theme borrowed from USC's "other" fight song: *Conquest!*

Sport—as well as politics, war, and most anything else, for that matter—is too often marred by overripe hyperbole. Still, it might just be said with some real truth that the USC football team that left the locker room to take the field on September 12, 1970, might have been as ready to win as any in football history. At least the players who were there that night think so.

On the other side of the field, Alabama looked cocky. So did their fans.

McKay maintained calm before the storm. He knew his team was ready. The atmosphere was all the firing up they needed. Calmly, McKay simply told his charges that the game they were about to play would mean more to college football than any they would ever play. He never mentioned race. McKay was like Ulysses S. Grant, his team a modern Army of the Potomac.

On the other side, Bryant warned his still-confident players that USC was the fastest team they had ever played. He did not speak of color, but *speed* could have been a code word for *black*. In the six months since the game had been scheduled, the coach almost never mentioned race. Bryant was like Robert E. Lee, his team a modern Army of Northern Virginia.

The second civil war was about to begin. Both sides were convinced they were the good guys.

CHAPTER Twenty-One

Student Body Right

My football career ended thanks to a few hits courtesy of
Sam "Bam" Cunningham.

—*Former USC football player and Major League All-Star Fred Lynn*

Like many tense confrontations, the 1970 USC-Alabama game started with tentative offensive efforts met by a hard-hitting defense. Alabama got the ball first and tried to run out of a slot left I formation. The talented Hunter had trouble adjusting to USC's defensive alignments. USC's defense gave them nothing. Five blacks started on defense, and several more came off the bench. Hunter and running back Johnny Musso were shut down totally. When Hunter handed off to Musso, USC exploded off the line; Musso was met by Papadakis and Charlie Weaver, who laid waste to him.

On a third-down pass attempt, Willie Hall hit the receiver hard enough to force a drop, setting up the punt.

In later years, Hunter would say that he wished he had not seen the game films from the 1970 Rose Bowl between USC and Michigan, as it gave him a false sense of security. USC had played conservatively, which strangely foreshadowed USC's low-scoring Rose Bowl wins over Michigan in 1977, 1979, and 1990. The 1970 Rose Bowl had not revealed the size and speed they displayed in Alabama.

Jones still was battling an understandable case of the nerves during USC's first possession. In games like this, the defense often has an advantage in the first quarter. A jumpy team can more easily explode out of the box early, defenders laying wicked licks on ball carriers who have not yet developed their sea legs. Plus, the offensive players are still dealing with crowd noise. They must try to pick up the count and the audibles. They have to deal with bone-jarring tackles and blood trickling out of their noses, all the while trying to incorporate the "finesse" part of football. This includes reading defenses, looking over massive rushing linemen, throwing tight spirals, and making catches surrounded by the enemy. Jones found himself off-key, missing Davis on a first-down pass. But Jones was not the only part, maybe not even the most important part, of USC's offensive scheme.

* * *

McKay had instituted the Student Body Right offense, which had been so effective using Mike Garrett, O. J. Simpson, and, in 1969, Clarence Davis. Student Body Right, however, was not to be confused with the (later maligned) "three yards and a cloud of dust" offenses that Bo Schembechler at Michigan and Woody Hayes at Ohio State had created as staples of Big 10 football.

Both Schembechler and Hayes were scared to throw the ball. Both were often quoted on variations of the statement "When you throw the ball, there are three things that can happen, and two of them are bad."

McKay did not share this fear of the forward pass. True, USC was a running school, but McKay had coached good passing quarterbacks in the past. His 1962 national championship team featured a rotation of Pete Beathard and Bill Nelsen, with Fertig in a backup role. Beathard and Nelsen could both throw and would be outstanding professionals. Fertig had been forced to pass in come-from-behind situations in 1964. His crossover toss to Rod Sherman with 1:33 left in the fourth quarter had wrapped up a come-from-behind victory over Notre Dame.

Toby Page and Steve Sogge mainly handed off to O. J., although they occasionally threw the screen pass to him, as well. But Jones had added a new dimension to the position and the offense.

Jimmy Raye, a black quarterback at Michigan State in 1966, had used his athleticism. He ran liberally, drawing in defenders and allowing him to utilize a short passing game.

What McKay and Duffy Daugherty of Michigan State were doing in the late 1960s was in some ways a throwback to an earlier era, which was dominated by single-wing football. Red Sanders had utilized the dual-threat skills of Billy Kilmer at UCLA. A quarterback could also be a running back, even a receiver.

Red Hickey had instituted an early version of the "shotgun" with the 49ers, using Kilmer and John Brodie. The quarterback had several options, although in Hickey's offense, the pass was the preferred option. The NFL was unprepared for Hickey's schemes but eventually caught on. The NFL and the colleges then settled into a period of stability. Quarterbacks such as Johnny Unitas of Baltimore, Bart Starr of Green Bay, and Daryle Lamonica of Oakland were pure drop-back-in-the-pocket passers. The results could not be argued with.

Still, the running quarterback never truly went out of style. Navy's Roger Staubach could run when flushed out of the pocket. After his military service was completed, he would use that style to lead the Dallas Cowboys to two Super Bowl victories in the 1970s.

Alabama's own Joe Namath was a great runner. "The best athlete who ever played for me," according to Bryant. But he had injured his knee in 1964. As a pro, he was strictly a passing threat because of it. Namath was seen as a cautionary example: *don't let your quarterbacks run.*

However, some offenses were not designed around passing quarterbacks. Oklahoma's Bud Wilkinson had won forty-seven straight games in the 1950s, mainly on the ground. Darrell Royal of Texas had learned from Wilkinson. He played the Sooners at the Cotton Bowl every year. Royal designed, or at least perfected, the option. Theoretically, the option featured the quarterback taking the snap and running to one side or the other, blockers in front of him, one or two running backs trailing him. He had the "option" to keep, lateral, or pass.

In Texas, quarterback James Street rarely chose the pass option. Longhorn fans had taken to calling Royal's offense the "wishbone." Street could and did run. If about to be tackled, he would lateral to running back Steve Worster. Fans in the stands often did not know who had the ball until a tackle was made—upfield. In 1969, Texas went undefeated using these tactics.

McKay was more innovative than Darrell Royal. When Simpson left and Jimmy Jones came in, McKay decided to turn crisis into opportunity. Jones would hand the ball off plenty—to Davis, Cunningham, and a host of other talented backs. He could drop back and throw too; but unlike Page, Sogge, or Fertig, if flushed out of the pocket—or even in a planned play—he could run, or he could throw on the run. Jones may not have been a revolutionary quarterback, but his style was a relatively new thing in 1969.

Despite media criticism, USC did *not* go undefeated in 1969 based strictly on the defense. Jones had a highly productive game, leading the

Trojans to a 31–21 victory over Bob Devaney's Nebraska Cornhuskers at Lincoln. USC defeated Northwestern and Oregon State resoundingly, 48–6 and 31–7, respectively.

Jim Plunkett's Stanford Indians played USC even up, forcing Jones to mount an impressive late-game drive. He threw and ran under pressure. Ron Ayala's field goal won it, 26–24. Down the stretch, USC played a series of conservative games; but against UCLA in the season-ending rivalry contest, Jimmy Jones made history.

With almost no time left, his incomplete pass seemed to signal victory for the Bruins. A pass interference call, disputed to this day in Westwood, gave Jones one last chance. He hit Sam Dickerson in the end zone for a thirty-two-yard game-winning miracle touchdown to break UCLA's hearts, 14–12. That is why the Trojans were called the Cardiac Kids.

In the Rose Bowl, USC's defense stuffed Michigan. Jones hit Bob Chandler for a long touchdown but played it close to the vest in the 10–3 win, which served the dual purpose of lulling Scott Hunter into thinking USC was not as "wild" as their Wild Bunch reputation might have indicated.

Hunter and his Alabama teammates thought USC was "Hollywood hype." The 1969 defensive front had been nicknamed the Wild Bunch, in reference to Sam Peckinpah's groundbreaking Western film of the same name. Hunter and his mates were about to find out just how wild this 1970 bunch was.

* * *

Their first lesson came when Cunningham took a snap and literally ran over his man, rambling in for a touchdown. In his first two carries, he had thirty-nine yards already.

On the Alabama sideline, coach Mal Moore was asking how in God's name a sophomore in his first game could just roll over the Tide defenders in such an easy manner. Black-and-white footage of Cunningham's first touchdown shows a man seemingly knocking down boys.

Up in the press box, assistant coach Craig Fertig told Jones by phone to keep giving the ball to Sam.

Great players can make coaches look mighty smart, a fact that McKay himself liked to remind everybody. After capturing the 1962 national championship, McKay quipped that he was "not so dumb after all."

He was a genius on this day. After Musso gained a first down, the Trojan defense forced a few overthrows from Hunter, who was obviously not up to the task. A talented youngster who would go on to big things, he was struggling to make do with a largely immature team at his disposal. USC was in his face on every try. 'Bama was forced to punt.

After USC was held and punted away, the defense, still literally exploding off the ball, stuffed the Tide. Through the process of acceleration over a series of possessions, USC was winning the war of field position. Fertig's advice was good. Cunningham kept getting the ball. When he carried three defenders into the end zone, USC led by 12–0.

The raucous Legion Field throng was utterly silent, except for a few lackluster jeers. The USC players were beginning to celebrate. The sight of the blacks from California was starting to rub some of the Alabama faithful the wrong way. Some fans started to openly call them "n--rs," admonishing the players for their cocky attitudes.

The Trojans had every reason to be cocky. They harassed Scott Hunter all the way to the bench. Neb Hayden was brought in to replace him. Hunter's shoulder was bothering him. Being attacked by 270-pound black defensive linemen was not proving to be the best thing for his health.

Hayden was no more effective than Hunter. USC regained the ball and the offensive, drove for field position, and went up 15–0 on Ron Ayala's field goal. The crowd lost the last vestiges of its surly edge. They were not even petulant. They just sat there and looked. Something was going on at Legion Field.

A white man expertly coached the University of Southern California. Another white assistant spurred them on. They had numerous talented white stars. But they also had a cavalcade of superbly talented black athletes and a black assistant coach. The blacks were making spectacular plays, left and right. What the fans were seeing was truth. Not just the kind of truth that makes up everyday life, but a different kind of truth—the kind that, as John Papadakis said, when witnessed in an American arena, is never misunderstood. The truth was not being misunderstood on this evening.

But this truth was not just a realization that black football players had talent, could compete with their "boys," and were tough as nails. The existence of McKay and Goux orchestrating their efforts, of Bob Chandler, John Vella, and Papadakis working in tandem with them, was creating the first vestiges of what in their *hearts* was a new reality. A new truth!

These were not Jewish college students coming to Mississippi to organize Freedom Summer. These were not Northern radicals, liberals, or agitators. These were football coaches and football players. Big, strong, macho men. American men. Every bit as American as they were. *My God, maybe more so!*

They were not taunting the Alabama players or their fans. McKay never tolerated that, anyway. Auburn and LSU players acted crazier when they beat the Tide than these Trojans were acting. So what in the wide, wide world of sports, as Slim Pickens might have said, was goin' on here?

* * *

John McKay, another "good ol' boy," was Bear's friend. Most 'Bama fans knew they liked to go duck hunting together. Heck, McKay was not even from California. He was from West Virginia. *West Virginia?* That place is America through and through.

Then there was Marv Goux. He *was* from California, and he already had a national reputation as one of the most respected assistant coaches in the country. California? Come to think of it, General George Patton had come from California. Nobody was a tougher son of a gun than Patton. What about John "Duke" Wayne? He had *played football for USC*, for God's sake. 'Bama's fans may have thought about California's governor, Ronald Reagan. This guy was a law-and-order man. People were talking about him for president someday, and he certainly was a man they could support. He had put down all those Communist protests at UC Berkeley, trying to take our colleges away from us.

Then there was the current president, Richard Nixon. Nixon had catered to Southern voters two years earlier. Alabama, and the rest of the South, was still solidly Democratic; but some of these Republicans sure looked better than the poet-socialist Democrats. Hubert Humphrey? George McGovern? *Teddy Kennedy?*

Nixon had moved just enough of the Wallace supporters to sway Southern electoral votes away from Vice President Hubert Humphrey in 1968. The liberals called his "Southern strategy" cynical. His admirers called it brilliant. He was fighting Communism in Vietnam and, as far as these people were concerned, in Berkeley, Columbia, Kent State, and all points in between. He was *palatable*.

Where had Nixon been born? Orange County, a suburb in southern California, near L.A.—the home of Disneyland. You can't get any more wholesome than that. The place had gotten a lot of attention in 1964. Nelson Rockefeller, a man the Alabamians had little regard for, was supposed to win the Republican nomination that year, but along came this ex-fighter pilot, Barry Goldwater. Goldwater was from "out West," as they thought of it. Wide open spaces. People who really understood freedom. Real freedom, tribal freedom, as John Hannah would put it, not a feudal, city-style serf freedom as practiced in the Northeast, where the labor unions told you how much you would make and when you would work, except you'd never *own the company*! Goldwater seemed to be a long shot, but at the convention in San Francisco, he had captured the big delegate prize: California. The reason he had taken California was because he had won Orange County by a landslide.

What about Orange County? It was just a freeway commute from L.A. Many of these Trojan players had played high school ball there. It was said they had a huge alumni base. Orange County was virulently anti-Communist, and any place that was anti-Communist had a lot to praise about it. The John Birch Society was said to be really big there. So a lot of USC alumni lived in a place where the Birchers were popular.

These kinds of thoughts, whether Dr. Culpepper Clark would admit it or not, began twirling around in the tiniest recesses of the minds of some of the Alabama fans as they watched USC's brilliant performance. A realization, maybe even an epiphany, was taking place. No, they did not understand it, in one lump sum, in the first half of this football game. Rather, seeds were being planted. California, at least some of what was going on in California, was not so bad.

Many of these people had come into Legion Field thinking that everybody in California was like Dennis Hopper and Peter Fonda, those "freaks" who had starred in *Easy Rider*, the big independent sensation of 1969. The film had affected a lot of people in a lot of ways.

At Ohio State, Woody Hayes almost had a heart attack when two of his players informed him that they had seen the flick the *night before a game!* What was wrong with *Patton*?

A lot of black and white football players at USC had seen *Easy Rider*, too. They could not help but make the connection. Hopper and Fonda had been killed by a redneck in some redneck state, probably Alabama or Louisiana, because they were different and they were going through the South, where they were *really* different.

But a few of the Alabama players had also seen *Easy Rider*. So had some of their fans. There was a schism going on, between older people and younger people, and all the players on the Tide were younger people. A few of them had thought *Easy Rider* was kind of . . . groovy. Good music. Something new.

The players on the field and their classmates in the stands were making note of their surroundings, at least when the players were not getting the breath knocked out of them. The world was changing around them. These guys were not hayseeds. They were college students, the future of America. They were among an elite class of citizens who would make up future leaders—coaches, teachers, politicians, and judges. They knew what was going on in Vietnam; and while they loved their country, they had no desire to die in some far-away rice paddy. They had heard King's speeches, the protests, and the demonstrations. Hey, they had heard the old codgers talk on the porch or at the feed store or in the barbershop.

Then there was the coach, Bear Bryant. Bear never put down the blacks. Maybe—although most close to him insisted to the contrary—he used the word *n—r* every once in a while; but in Alabama, especially among men of a certain age, that was as common as "ma'am" or "sir." There were rumors too. Why had Bear scheduled this game? He had in his desk a list of names of the best black high school football players in the state. Alabama had black walk-ons. Wilbur Jackson had a scholarship and would be on the varsity *next year*. John Mitchell of Mobile was rumored to be thinking twice about his decision to go to USC in 1971. Could it be . . . ?

And Clarence Davis. *That boy was born in Birmingham*, some of the faithful were beginning to think.

He's the best running back in the state, truth be told.

And he's not even the best running back on this USC team. Cunningham's better. And they're both with them, not us.

All of these—maybe not actual statements, but thoughts that eventually would become ideas—began to twirl around in the minds of the Alabama fans and their players. Patton, Duke Wayne, Reagan, and Nixon. Clarence Davis and Sam Cunningham.

Wilbur Jackson was a heck of a player. With Jackson and Mitchell, plus Musso and the other players coming back . . . maybe 'Bama could be a national power again. Did Coach Bryant *expect* them to lose? The old man was as wise as Moses. Was this part of the plan?

But something else was happening, not in their minds but before their very eyes. It always came back to the white-haired coach, his seemingly possessed assistant, and the teamwork they had orchestrated, like a perfectly choreographed musical, on Legion Field below them.

White coaches, black coaches. White players, black players. All working together. In harmony. *They're kicking our butts!*

The USC Trojans were demonstrating, right in front of them, that people of different colors could mix together, sweat together, shed blood together, work together, and win together.

Maybe we could do this too!

"Mine eyes have seen the glory of the coming of the Lord." When you believe in something as much as these fans believed in Alabama football, and you're getting your hat handed to you, there is time to reflect on these kinds of issues and do a little soul-searching. A good beating on the football field *can* have that effect. But wait. . . .

The boys, *their* boys, just recovered a fumble. Maybe 'Bama could get back into this game after all. Maybe the South *would* rise again. Maybe the 'Bama fans wouldn't need to rethink all their dearly held values after all. If only the Tide could pull this game out, hold the barbarians, or in this case the Trojan Army, from storming the gates.

* * *

A little break can go a long way. With Scott Hunter back in the game, the Tide was determined to make the most of this one. Hunter began to see a few new holes in the USC defense. Musso was determined to get every yard. The Tide managed to work their way into scoring position, with Musso bulling his way into the end zone on the strength of sheer willpower. The Tide advanced forty-nine yards on seven plays, 15–7. *Roll Tide!* USC's kicking problems on extra points might just come back to haunt them.

The Trojans were starting to show a little bit of the pressure they felt. The game was now entering the phase where emotion and early hard hitting are replaced by strategy, breaks, fatigue, and mano-a-mano ability. Davis took the kickoff all the way out to the USC forty, but he fumbled. Luckily for Clarence, Holland recovered it.

Give the ball to Sam.

Davis's fumble certainly did not deter Craig Fertig from his earlier strategy. Cunningham rumbled for five yards. A few runs and play-action passes later, Troy was down at the 'Bama twenty-four. Then Cunningham broke for twelve yards to get his offense into the "red zone." After that, the Tide was broken. USC was just too good. Staying on the ground, USC moved it down inside the ten-yard line. Evans took it in from the seven over the left tackle. This time, Ayala made the kick, and USC was up 22–7.

For Sam Cunningham, his life was changing minute by minute, but not because he was becoming a civil rights icon. Sam would not have any idea that this had happened for years after the game. No, Sam was now firmly ensconced in the starting fullback job over Charlie Evans. Evans would "hold on to that" for years, according to tight end Charle' Young. A white recruit from Gardena, the talented Evans would never regain the spotlight from Sam, and when contacted for this book had nothing to say one way or the other.

Now all that pressure was being replaced by accomplishment. All the pent-up energy and nervous anxiety were now channeled into what athletes call "the zone," which is a point at which they can seemingly do no wrong. Nobody knows how long "the zone" will last. It can be taken away as quickly as it is rewarded by the "sports gods." Only focus can keep it alive. Sam was focused. Sam was earning his nickname, "Bam," by knocking players from here to tomorrow.

Fred Lynn was, like Sam, a great multisport high school athlete in southern California. He had come to USC the same year as Cunningham, to play safety for John McKay's football team and center field for Rod Dedeaux's baseball team. Early on, he had found himself one on one, trying to tackle Sam. Sam knocked Lynn all over the field.

Lynn was helped up and off the field. Shortly thereafter, he went to Dedeaux and asked if it would be okay if his scholarship could be transferred from the football budget to the baseball budget.

"My football career ended thanks to a few hits courtesy of Sam 'Bam' Cunningham," Lynn said.

Lynn would be an All-American on three consecutive Trojan College World Series champions, then earn American League rookie of the year and most valuable player honors with the 1975 Boston Red Sox.

When a team trails 22–7 in the second quarter of a home game against a team the players know is great—a team coming off an undefeated season and a Rose Bowl win—then the trailing team is compelled to evaluate the battle. Dwight Eisenhower once said that before the fighting starts, battle plans are of the utmost importance; but once it begins, plans go out the window. The same philosophy applies to football. A gridiron general like Bear Bryant, along with his staff and his "soldiers," was evaluating this battle in all of its disaster, chaos, and glory.

A score of 22–7 is not an impossible deficit to overcome. The mind-set is often determined by *how* the score got that way. Luck? Turnovers? Fluke plays? In this case, none of those factors were in play. This was the kind of 22–7 mind-set that was leading Alabama's fans and players to the inevitable conclusion that the score was only going to get bigger on the

Trojans' side. The idea of holding USC's offense down while Alabama engineered comeback drives seemed to be a distant impossibility.

Those feelings? USC's black-white harmony. The white field general directing his integrated team, each player giving him everything he had. What was going on out there?

Silence. The crowd was utterly quiet. The fans could hear the USC players cheering each other on. They could hear Bryant and his coaches droning from the sidelines, trying to instill anything they could into their team. Jones said he could see in their eyes that Alabama was beaten, something the fans failed to pick up.

While various self-evident truths twirled around in the minds of seventy thousand people, many of whom would be in church on Sunday, the rest of the first half played itself out with no further developments.

As the teams ran off the field, some of the Alabama fans began to show some anger. It was directed not at USC or the black players but at their own team. The mighty Crimson Tide felt two emotions: shock and embarrassment. They were being schooled. Their locker room was as quiet as an empty church.

CHAPTER Twenty-Two

The Turning of the Tide

[Bear's] just gotten his a–s kicked, and
he's thanking McKay for the favor.

—*USC assistant coach Craig Fertig*

Bryant has been deceased for years now. The cagey old Bear never really let on what he truly had planned for that night. Like any good general, he knew that his plans would have to change. To think that the man wanted his team to lose goes against everything we know about him. He was a winner, through and through. He played to win, coached to win, and accomplished this feat as much as any coach ever. When he retired in the early 1980s, it was as the winningest coach in college history.

Had his team played well and won, or come from behind to triumph, Bear no doubt had a plan for handling this scenario. He already had black walk-ons and a black freshman on scholarship, and he had secretly been going after John Mitchell, or was about to start. An Alabama victory, in his mind, was not going to make the transition of these new players into his program less smooth. But he also had a plan in case his team did lose. He understood the nature of the worst-case scenario. The real question is whether, in his mind, a defeat *was* the worst-case scenario.

As a football coach, he had a responsibility to his players, coaches, school, fans, and state. That mandate was to win. His approach in the locker room centered on this mandate. He told his silent team that they had indeed been outplayed. There was no denying this. But USC had given them just a little bit of hope by missing two point-afters.

Bryant understood the Southern culture and how football was intertwined with God, family, and patriotism. These boys had grown up in the unique world of high school football south of the Mason-Dixon Line.

Bryant understood his players and what made them tick. He understood the notion that America wins its wars, in part at least, because of high school football. He knew that his players were "soldiers." So the whole "soldiers entering battle" theme; the community coming together to rally the "troops"; the interceptions, fumbles, and tackles for losses as a form of espionage, all were designed to take away from the "enemy" what he holds dearest, as Marv Goux liked to remind his team. Bryant knew when to play to this form of psychology and when not to.

Football, particularly in the South, was one area where people could still display what Plato had called the "warrior spirit" without having the Jane Fonda crowd breathing down their necks. In the South, this was the world that fed and nurtured Alabama's young men, now sitting glumly in front of a man who represented a godlike figure for every football player in the region.

It was with all of this in mind that Bear Bryant addressed his team. He sensed that the warlike pep speech was not appropriate for this particular time. Rather, the thing that stuck in his players' craws the most was the fact that they were playing, and losing, right in front of their families.

As a younger man, Bear had taken over a moribund program at Texas A&M. In his first season, he had taken his new team to Junction, Texas. They had endured torturous two-a-days, even three-a-days, in hundred-degree heat, on a field of stumps and sharp prickly spikes. Several players were hurt, many quit, and others were almost overcome with heat exhaustion. One of the parents came to see Bear, who apologized about the rough treatment, stating that he was preparing his boys for "war." The father reminded Bear that a decade earlier he had personally *seen* war and that this was just a sport.

The Junction experience changed Bear. He softened after that, was never the iron-fisted disciplinarian that he had once been. In that Alabama locker room, he told his team to keep their heads up and stay proud. To quit would be the real shame, and if anybody felt that urge, now was the time to say so.

Bryant's halftime talk was pregnant with what he did not say. He never said anything about losing to a team with "colored" players. He never insulted his team's manhood by insinuating that they were less than complete if black players outplayed them. In so doing, he gave credit to the black players—and all the white coaches and players—who had come out from California and were playing so well on this night.

"No listen, this just makes it perfect," he told his team, trying psychology. "We're behind, they're all fired up. . . . If we got class, we're gonna find it out. We got class and I know we got it."

Over in the USC locker room, the Trojans were excited but acting as if they had done this before. Sam Cunningham thanked his line for the huge holes they had opened up for him. This was typical of Sam. A humble man, he was not bathing in glory but handing out credit. A replay of the game footage shows that some of his best runs were not just because of the big holes he was getting. The man had truly bowled over several defenders. This was his trademark. McKay had two halftime approaches: wry humor or hubris in the face of disaster, such as his 1974 speech with the Trojans trailing Notre Dame, 24–6.

On that day, he told his team, "If Anthony Davis returns the second-half kickoff for a touchdown, we'll win this game." A.D. did just that, and legend revised McKay's statement from "*if* Davis returns" to "*when* Davis returns the second-half kickoff for a touchdown."

But with his team ahead against Alabama, he maintained quiet confidence.

McKay could see that his charges had not lost an ounce of their pregame explosiveness. The only thing to do was remind them they were still in Birmingham, Alabama, playing a team that had won three national titles in the past decade and was coached by a man who, at least according to the Coca-Cola Company, walked on water.

McKay's staff was not congratulating the team but staying on them, but the staff did not need to. USC's players were focused and aware that the task was only half complete.

Sport is a very psychological business. Whether it be self-fulfilling prophecy, irony, or attitude, the "big lead" can wither away in sports; and when it does, the team coming from behind is ahead of the team that had the lead even when they are tied. In 1969, when the New York Mets came from nine games out in August to tie the Chicago Cubs by early September, the momentum was all in favor of the Mets. The Cubs were done, and the rest of the season was a Mets parade.

A great coach does his best work not in coaxing a team from behind but in keeping them in front. The key is focus. McKay was a master at it. His players practiced it as a sixth sense.

A lot of college football teams would have blown a 22–7 halftime lead to a Bear Bryant–coached Alabama team in 1970. If the University of California, for instance, were in USC's position, the players would have been jumping up and down at the half, not believing their good fortune. They would have blown the game. But McKay's guys acted, as coaches like to say, as if they had done it before—because they had.

At all the black bars in all the black neighborhoods, around the corner from Legion Field and throughout the state, black patrons were jumping up and down as if it was Christmas, Mardi Gras, and the Second Coming all rolled into one.

In the stands at Legion Field, a member of Clarence Davis's real family, his Uncle Claude, the minister, was daring to ask if some kind of miracle was taking place on the field below him. Hope springs eternal, and there was a lot of hope in the air that night. Black fans were hoping USC would keep pouring it on in the second half. White fans were hoping against hope that Bear could pull out a miracle. They had seen the great Joe Namath engineer stirring victories, and Ken Stabler was a master of the two-minute drill. Maybe, just maybe, Scott Hunter would etch his name in their memories tonight as those heroes had done.

* * *

USC got the ball to start the second half. After Davis returned the kick to the thirty-four, where he was tripped by a teammate, Jones engineered a beautiful thirteen-play sixty-nine-yard drive. Everybody got the ball: Davis, Evans, Cunningham, Jones for thirteen himself; and then a few passes were thrown to mix it up. When Jimmy hit Davis alone in the back of the end zone to make it 29–7, they knew that not Hunter, Namath, or Stabler could save them now. Nobody could.

Alabama found themselves in fourth-down desperation mode. They got the ball into USC territory, but on fourth and three at the forty, Hunter's pass was knocked out of the air. The Trojans drove to the Alabama six, were held, but then converted an Ayala field goal from the twenty-five to make it 32–7.

Neb Hayden went back in to replace Hunter for the second time amid more stony silence. Hayden was up to the immediate task, leading a seventy-five-yard drive for a touchdown with barely a minute left in the third quarter. But it was too little, too late, and the Alabama cheers rang hollow in the humid air.

USC was relentless. Eleven plays and seventy-one yards later, Ron Ayala made up for the missed extra points by making a team-record third field goal to make the score USC 35, Alabama 13.

Then, after Hayden's pass was swatted away by John Vella, Bear sent Hunter back in; but his third-down try fell incomplete. The Alabama fans watched as the final act of humiliation was applied: McKay went to his substitutes, and as many people have said over the years of his teams, the second string might have been better than the starters. In those days of unlimited scholarships (although McKay called this notion "baloney"), McKay would recruit high school superstars he knew would not play right away, sometimes never, just so they would not be playing against him wearing the uniforms of UCLA, Stanford, Notre Dame, or other rivals.

His second string was indeed talented, but they were also hungry and eager to show what they had. Against Alabama, in this place and under these circumstances, they had a little more to prove.

Sophomore Mike Rae took over. In retrospect, Rae probably *was* better than Jones. It was Rae who would lead the 1972 Trojans to a wire-to-wire number one season and later play for the Raiders. When Rae connected with Holland sixty-one yards later, it was 42–13.

USC's team could not contain themselves any longer. Papadakis was doling out the tributes like Alexander the Great. Clarence Davis, the All-American, deferred to the "rookie" who was no longer a rookie, Sam Cunningham.

Davis rushed for 76 yards on thirteen carries. Sam Cunningham rushed for 135 yards and two touchdowns. Jones, Smith, Charle' Young, Charlie Weaver, Skip Thomas, Willie Hall, and Kent Carter all contributed. The final score was 42–21.

The crowd truly knew it was all over but the shouting. That was the eeriest part of the night. Amid the shouts of USC's players, off in the distance beyond the piney woods you could hear the whistle of a distant train. Then people started to cock their heads, to hear something else.

In the corner of the stadium, a small group of black fans was cheering for USC. 'Bama fans could not hold it against them. These people were not "traitors" for rooting against the home team. The truth was not misunderstood. But this small group was not all they heard. It was something else.

After adjusting, the people in the cavernous, near-silent Legion Field could hear black fans cheering outside the stadium. There were at least 1,500 cheering, and that number was growing every minute. The meaning of this game, to black people, and, yes, to white people—*to America!*—did not go unnoticed.

The sound of those cheers was the demarcation point in American history. In the annals of civil rights—slavery, abolition, Reconstruction, Jim Crow; then Jack Johnson, Jesse Owens, Joe Louis, Jackie Robinson, Texas Western, John Carlos, and Tommie Smith; the words and actions of Frederick Douglass, Booker T. Washington, Martin Luther King Jr., and Malcolm X—it had all come down to this moment. Approximately 10:00 p.m. Eastern Standard Time on September 12, 1970. This was the tipping point. *One night, two teams—Alabama versus USC—and the game that changed a nation.*

There were two black Americans who stood silently while their brethren cheered. One was Wilbur Jackson, a college freshman on scholarship at the University of Alabama, seeing visions of himself wearing the Crimson Tide uniform on Legion Field in 1971, 1972, and 1973. He had watched the game, keeping his feelings to himself. On one hand, he rooted for his team to beat USC. On the other hand, as he heard the cheers, it began to occur to him that the door, which had just ever so slightly opened for him, had opened a little bit more.

The other black kid was John Mitchell. The Mobile, Alabama, native, still at an Arizona junior college, was back home for the weekend. He was one of those "five black kids," according to Craig Fertig, who were being recruited by USC and were in the stands as guests of the Trojans. But after this game, he had some thinking to do. McKay thought he was in the bag, although he was not yet signed. Mitchell had visions of Los Angeles dancing in his head—Hollywood nightlife, girls in bikinis, beaches, and plenty of socializing. In his mind, McKay had Mitchell starting next year, but Mitchell had seen just how good USC was. Their substitutes looked to be as strong as their starters. As a junior college transfer, he could not afford to sit on the bench waiting his turn for a year or two. Yes, it would be nice to be in L.A., playing for national championships and Rose Bowls, but he knew that change had washed over the Legion Field stands like a wave, just as everybody else had. If Bear Bryant were to call him, Mitchell would think seriously about changing his mind and joining Wilbur Jackson at Alabama the next year. As he left the stadium, Mitchell overheard white fans stating the obvious.

"Bryant needs some blacks of his own," they could be heard murmuring to themselves.

"Holy cow," Mitchell thought to himself. "This is a *big deal!*"

When the game ended, players from both teams were cordial and respectful. McKay and Bryant greeted each other at midfield, walking off together.

"Damn, John, we just ran out of time," McKay said Bryant told him in his autobiography, *McKay: A Coach's Story.*

McKay did not rub it in. Bryant thanked him for the whipping, to the surprise of Craig Fertig, who was walking with McKay.

"He'd just gotten his a–s kicked," said Fertig, "and he's thanking McKay for the favor."

A football game had been played, fairly and competitively. Any bloodshed on this night had come not from nightsticks and police brutality but from the unrelenting artificial turf. But football was merely a metaphor for a changing America. Hearts and minds were changed, softened. Pride replaced shame. Hope replaced hatred. Sam Cunningham and his teammates were vessels who did God's work that night. They deserve their share of the credit; but what these strong, virile young men did was simply to get together and push the rock the last few yards over the mountain—the same rock that people of good conscience, of all colors, had been pushing for two centuries. People too tired to persevere any longer, who needed younger, stronger men to pick up where they left off.

Martin Luther King Jr. had been pushing that rock for more than a decade, and he died for his efforts. For two years, there were very real questions as to whether anybody could replace him. Robert F. Kennedy had seemed to be a good possibility, but he had met the same fate as King. The civil rights movement had slipped into chaos, the Christian nonviolence of Dr. King replaced by the Black Panthers, Stokely Carmichael, and the voices of rage.

Any coach can tell you that strong competition for positions on a team makes for a better ball club. What this game would demonstrate over the succeeding years was that the power of competition was a driving force, combined with Christianity, capitalism, and American-style freedom, which pushed Southern citizens into the mass belief that their college football teams needed to integrate.

The USC football team that went to Alabama in 1970 certainly had to contend with competitive rivalries within its own ranks. An excellent example is the case of John Papadakis losing his fullback job to Sam Cunningham, then the two eventually coming together for the benefit of the team, with the subsequent result of a lifelong friendship.

What football did was give whites and blacks real middle ground in which their respective goals could be the same. This was the job of Marv Goux, who taught his charges to fight like gladiators, each protecting the others in an effort to achieve a common purpose. This sense of common purpose would transcend football, carrying on well past each man's playing career, inculcating their private lives, their efforts at business, and their approach to all they would endeavor to achieve.

What Sam Cunningham, Jimmy Jones, Clarence Davis, and their team—and the credit is deservedly shared with whites such as Papadakis, Vella, Chandler, McKay, Fertig, and Goux—had done was an extension of the work that came before them. The stage had already been set, waiting for just the right man, or team, to make the most of a situation. In this regard, it is not appropriate to overstate the contribution of the USC Trojans. But this game put a face and words to history. It will be remembered because it should never be forgotten.

CHAPTER Twenty-Three

"This Here's What a Football Player Looks Like"

It was like one of those forest fires they get when the land is dry out in California. Boom! And that fire just spread.

—Former University of Alabama assistant coach Christ Vagotis

USC's players were utterly drained, physically and emotionally, by the pressure valve being lifted, the turf, and the late-summer humidity. Outside of surgery, military training, and, of course, actual combat, they had just engaged in one of the most debilitating human exercises imaginable. They celebrated in fits and starts and were doing so when Bear Bryant entered.

Bryant's appearance caused more than a few eyes to follow him as he made his way into the room, but it was not unusual for Bear to enter an opponent's dressing room. Bud Wilkinson had done the same thing, congratulating Bryant and Kentucky after Oklahoma lost the 1951 Sugar Bowl to Bryant's Wildcats. Bryant admired Wilkinson.

Craig Fertig saw Bryant, shook his hand, and welcomed him. The two spoke for a few moments. Fertig had an expression on his face that said, "You want *what?*"

The players watched this exchange.

"What's goin' on?" a few asked.

Then Fertig straightened up. Bryant hung back as Fertig walked over to where McKay was. Something *was* going on. A small drama of some kind.

"Coach Bryant wants to borrow Cunningham," Fertig told McKay.

"What do you mean, 'borrow' him?" asked McKay. Then Bear approached McKay, as the Trojans looked on.

"Coach, could I borrow Sam Cunningham?" he asked.

"You mean for the remainder of the season?" quipped McKay. "Go ahead and take him."

Bryant smiled as if to say, "Just give me an inch, Coach, and I'll take a mile."

McKay summoned big Sam Cunningham. He introduced Bryant to Sam and told him that the Alabama coach would like for Sam to go with him for a few minutes. Cunningham had no idea what was going on, either, but it seemed on the up and up.

Bryant thanked McKay and left with Cunningham. On McKay's instructions, Fertig went with them. Cunningham, bare chested, followed Bryant out the door.

Bryant thanked Cunningham for coming with him. Fertig accompanied them, thinking that maybe some kind of sociological history was about to be made. The fact that Sam was black could not escape Fertig's attention.

What happened next is in dispute. Some say they entered the Alabama locker room. Some say the exchange took place in the crowded hallway between the visitors' and home lockers. Some say it never happened. The following story, which may not be 100 percent accurate, is rooted, like most myth and lore, in truth.

They entered the Alabama locker room. The mood was one of utter demoralization and despondency. Cunningham was instructed to stand on a bench. He towered above the all-white Crimson Tide. He was still sweaty. He had deep bruises. There was still blood on his pants.

Bryant allegedly started off by referring to Sam as "this ol' boy" but corrected himself by changing his description to "this man," or, according to others who claim to have been in the room, he gathered his team's attention by starting off with "Gentlemen."

"This is Sam Cunningham, number 39," Bryant told his team as they sat and looked *up* at Sam. "This man and his Trojan brothers," a term Bryant believed in and did not use lightly because he knew and understood Marv Goux's sincerity when he talked about "Trojan pride" and loyalty, "just ran us right out of Legion Field," he said—just as Goux had said they would.

Bryant is said to have told them to "raise your heads and open your eyes," because "this here's what a football player looks like." Those words would symbolize everything that had happened. It would be what everybody remembered about that night.

The coach instructed every one of his players to shake the stunned Sam's hand. There was no hesitation.

Scott Hunter, who had been humiliated but would come back strong like the champ he was, led the way. "Sam, you're a heck of a running back," he (allegedly) said.

As Cunningham stood shirtless in the middle of the room, he was the perfect example of grace, pride, and class, at that moment a vessel of God. Each player shook his hand, most looking him in the eye. There were smiles, gentle ribbing, and a lot of congratulations. Bryant had *sanctified* this moment, and as the billboard on the highway had demonstrated, the man walked on water around this neck of the woods. The Alabama players did not feel humiliated anymore. Many began to understand that they, too, were part of something.

Papadakis, a close friend of Cunningham's to this day, was not in the room, but he has publicly described it in vivid terms many times in interviews and in numerous conversations.

"You have to understand," said Papadakis, "that Sam Cunningham was a *beautiful*, and I mean a *beautiful* black man. You know the term 'black is beautiful,' which is what a lot of blacks were saying in those days? Sam was beautiful. He had been a decathlete. He was an Adonis. I'm Greek. The Greeks have always admired physical beauty and competition. It's part of the Greek ideal. Sam embodied all of that.

"He was bare chested, still glistening with sweat. The very picture of a warrior, a Trojan warrior. He had muscles that just *bulged*, a big barrel chest, tight stomach. He was an absolute physical specimen. But Sam was naïve, too. He was a sophomore from Santa Barbara, fighting for his job three hours earlier, and now here he was being held up as the symbol of football to the pride of the South.

"History was being made, and he didn't realize it. He had just destroyed the Crimson Tide. You can't believe it—watch the tape—he just went right through the best that the state of Alabama had to offer."

Athletes have a code of respect, which is an important point. In 1956, after C. R. Roberts had done the same thing to Texas at Austin, the Longhorns congratulated him, but the fans continued to catcall him all the way off the field. A lot had changed in fourteen years, however. If one were to analyze American history, and maybe even human history, the fourteen years that separated C.R.'s game from Sam's saw some of the greatest social change ever.

From the mid-1950s to 1970, and especially in the ensuing years, *people*, not just politics, governments, and militaries, had changed. It was a truly societal revolution, which despite the many good things that emerged from it, some argue had happened much too soon. There was official school desegregation, followed by John Kennedy's assassination, the civil rights movement, the Great Society, Vietnam, the antiwar movement, the free speech movement, the Black Muslim movement, the feminist movement, the gay liberation movement, the beatnik movement, the hippie movement, and the black militant movement, and now the *actual* desegregation movement was about to happen. Not a Supreme Court ruling, as in *Brown v. Board of Education*. Not National Guard protection. Not President Kennedy ordering Governor Barnett to enforce federal legislation in Mississippi. Not a speech or a protest march.

This was something everybody could believe in. Real change. Change of the heart. The best kind of change.

So what had happened in those fourteen years? The 1960s had happened.

The athletes who have a universal "code of respect" for each other had lived through the 1960s. They had been eight, nine, or ten years old when the decade started. In 1964, many were in junior high school, old enough to understand the world around them. Their high school and college years had paralleled years of enormous unrest. They lived in a new age of television and mass communication. They lived in a brave, modern new world, the South having been transformed by federal works projects instituted by Franklin Roosevelt, such as the Tennessee Valley Authority, since the 1930s. They were college-educated leaders of the future, not backwoods hicks, and they respected Sam Cunningham.

"Since the Alabama team could relate to Sam as a football player," Papadakis said, "they could understand the context of Sam as a man, because they were all football players. We all strive for the same thing on the field. Competition, especially in America, is where we determine what the truth is, where we separate the men from the boys. These white players could never relate to protests or speeches. But they could relate to football." God works in mysterious ways.

This scene has been touted as Holy Grail within the Trojan family for decades and by many others, including Papadakis and possibly Cunningham, who has remained somewhere between vague, coy, sure it happened, or sure it did not, depending on whom you ask (and this includes Southern sportswriters and former USC teammates).

Hunter, who allegedly complimented Sam in the locker room, insists none of it happened—not the Bryant speech and certainly not his hand-shaking. Hunter's attitude, some contend, is "negative," but a lengthy interview with him revealed that this is entirely untrue. Hunter says the event did not happen, but "it should have." He had been to Vietnam on an all-star tour with black players, was happy to see integration, and expressed great admiration for Dr. King because he recognized that Bryant's words mirrored the civil rights leader's.

"If I admired this man [Bryant]," Hunter says, "and he's saying the same things as Dr. King, then do I pick and choose and not admire King? No."

Told this, Craig Fertig, who previously thought of Hunter as "negative" and "sour," could only say, "Wow, that changes my whole interpretation of Scott Hunter."

Nevertheless, as Hunter expressed, just like Papadakis's claim that he used Greek philosophy to "talk his teammates down" from bringing guns to the stadium—whether it happened exactly that way or not—*it should have*!

Talking to the Alabama players and the coaches, sportswriters, others—nobody remembers this Bryant speech about Sam Cunningham being "what a football player looks like." The *Mobile Press-Register*'s Neal McCready tried to clear this up. As for Cunningham, Sam told McCready, "I don't want to be the one who said it didn't happen."

Craig Fertig was not in the Alabama locker room. A couple of coaches said it didn't happen. Clem Gryska, an honorable man, had a very good point, and so did Scott Hunter. They both said, "The players were ready for integration." Kenny Stabler said that as far back as the 1960s, the *players* had no objection. But what would have been the point of bringing Cunningham into that locker room?

"One of the great mythological stories" is how longtime sportswriter Allen Barra referred to the incident. "Something happened, but not in the way it is described. . . . Generally something is there on which the legend is based, but it is almost never exactly that way. But there is always a nugget or kernel of truth. Why would not a single Alabama player say it happened? Somebody would say it happened.

"If it happened to make such an impression, why did it not make an impression, at least on the Alabama players who it was purported to have been for? Why didn't Bryant talk about this? Bryant biographer John Underwood did not recall him saying anything about this story. All that being said, under the category of double hearsay, journalist Al Browning of the *Tuscaloosa News* was a good friend of Bryant's who may even have worked for Bryant and wrote a book called *I Remember Bear Bryant*.

"In the 1990s—Al died around 2000—Diane McWhorter, Browning, and I were at a bar. Browning told us that the lockers at Legion Field were really close, cramped, and right next to the hallway area, which led straight into another locker room. Browning thinks what happened is there was a bunch of people from the university administration, who really needed an object lesson, and who got it with this game.

"In all this tumult, and McKay said this in his biography, Bryant went in the locker room. It was known to have been set up by Bryant, and he knew what would happen. Bryant idolized Bud Wilkinson. Bryant's Kentucky team had played Oklahoma in the Sugar Bowl. After the game, Wilkinson went in the 'Bama locker room to congratulate Babe Parilli. Bryant determined he would do that in the future when the time was right and make the best possible impression. Tom Clements said he did the same thing after the Sugar Bowl following the 1973 season, in a game that determined the national championship for Notre Dame.

"Bryant most likely went up to Sam and said something complimentary, but if he brought Sam into the Alabama locker room, they would have remembered it. There would be no reason not to. Browning said there were guys in the hallway, including some old World War II guys who had resisted.

"A couple of guys in the Alabama administration were openly against change. Browning said they were in the hall. Bear grabbed Sam, put his arm around him, and might have taken him *in the hall*, not the Alabama locker room. The fact that Sam may not remember it exactly as it is described—on a stool in front of the Alabama team—that is not unusual. If he put him on a stool, that is too eerily close to a slave market. If they stepped ten or twelve feet into that hallway, next to and in front of men he does not know, there may be no way to prove it, but when a story like that happens, this is plausible. But in the locker room before the players? If he were in that hallway, and if the door to the locker is open, then he can see Alabama players undressing a few feet away. But it is crowded; it is loud.

Think about being in a crowd, at a game, a rock concert. You cannot tell what somebody is saying just a few feet away."

"I talked to Sam about it, and he said it *kind* of happened, but not the way it was explained," said Sam Dickerson.

"There's a lot I don't remember about some of those early days," Cunningham says of the event and its immediate aftermath. "It was thirty-five years ago, remember. But I really think I would remember it if it happened."

Papadakis, despite mountains of evidence to the contrary, claims he *witnessed* the event that Cunningham, the central player in it, cannot recall. He wrote a film treatment filled with colorful verbiage of the supposed happenings in the 'Bama dressing room, none of which was remembered by Sam, the Alabama players or coaches, or even Craig Fertig. Fertig escorted Sam when Bryant came to "borrow him," but he did not actually see it or claim to see it. It is possible he was schmoozing in the hallway, which was his wont.

Loel Schrader swore that he saw it, but in 2006 when reports of its mythology became increasingly obvious, even he backed off his original assertions. Papadakis claimed to Don Yaeger that the legend was "on Alabama's shoulders. It didn't come from us." This does not particularly make sense. Bryant never mentioned it. The players are as adamant that it did not happen as they possibly could be. It really appears that it was McKay, probably exaggerating in the manner of an Irish storyteller drinking whiskey on the banquet circuit over the years, who told it so many times that he believed it. He certainly told Papadakis that it happened that way, and John understandably chose to believe his coach. J. K. McKay claimed to have heard the story many times from his father, indicating it got better over time.

Bryant knew how to lose. He talked to Cunningham; no one denies this, but there are not many witnesses. If it was anybody, it was some California sportswriter. Fertig says he was *outside* the door. Loel Schrader says he was *at* the door. Somehow, could it be they were at the door to one of those locker rooms and saw the hallway scene, remembering it for a locker room scene? There is some discrepancy between Schrader and Fertig, one being outside the door and not seeing it, the other at the door and witnessing it. Some saw it from a distance and thought it happened that way. Add to all this the excitement and adrenaline; the passage of time; faulty memories; a crowded, loud hallway that could be mistaken for a locker room; a door that might have looked into a locker room . . .

"If one walks out of the visitors' locker room, one can see right in that other locker room," continued Barra. "It is so crowded, that might be exactly what happened. The Alabama people 'in the know' cannot conceive that Bryant would have humiliated his players and coaches, but rather he was doing it for the administration. He was not going to just write them off to Governor Wallace. But why did Bryant not talk about this? He was sticking it to the reactionaries, but he would not brag about it.

"One cannot underestimate the importance of this game and of Bryant's opening up opportunities. This was just one of many signs of change throughout America, directly attributable to Bryant, the 1970 game, and his policies. Everything was influenced by Paul 'Bear' Bryant."

The exact details of this event remain a mystery to this day. John McKay repeated the story for years, probably embellishing it, but of course he was not in that room. Nobody ever disputed him or told him that what he was saying might not be 100 percent accurate. Over time his message became an accepted fact. He never had any reason to doubt that the essential story, embellished or not, was true. Many, many others associated with USC repeated the story, most notably Marv Goux and Craig Fertig. Writers such as Loel Schrader of the *Long Beach Press-Telegram*, who would later create the *USC Report* newsletter, spread the message. USC's sports information director at that time, Don Andersen, and broadcaster Tom Kelly enthusiastically repeated the story in many venues.

It is important to note, however, that this mythological event did not gain major public credence for years, maybe even for more than a decade. Many did not hear the story until Tom Kelly repeated it in the 1987 *Trojan Video Gold*, documenting USC's football tradition.

Oddly, Sam Cunningham distanced himself from the event and his school. He went to New England, where he played for a decade. He never spoke to John Hannah about it, even though the two then teammates had opposed each other in the 1970 game. Cunningham was miffed at USC when they told him his younger brother, Randall, would not be the starting quarterback in the early 1980s. Coach John Robinson invested his hopes in Sean Salisbury, a major blue-chipper from the San Diego area, instead. Randall chose UNLV, where he became an All-American and later an All-Pro in Philadelphia. Salisbury was a bust, or close to it, and his failures ushered in a long down period in USC gridiron annals.

Sam faded in memory as a Trojan legend. Many others, such as O. J. Simpson, Marcus Allen, Anthony Davis, Mike Garrett, Pat Haden, and Lynn Swann, along with Tom Seaver, Tom Selleck, and John Naber, maintained far more colorful public personas. Many would achieve a high profile in broadcasting or acting, a tradition at a place long considered "Hollywood's school." Before the NCAA came along to regulate such things, USC football players had made extra money as Roman soldiers, gladiators, Napoleon's Grand Army, and Biblical legions in the classic epics of DeMille, Huston, Ford, and Mayer. According to *Los Angeles* magazine, 1920s "it girl" Clara Bow had satisfied her insatiable sexual appetite in wild orgies with the USC football team, which included Marion Morrison (later John Wayne). Access to beautiful Hollywood actresses and opportunity had played no small role in Howard Jones's recruitment of the players who made the Trojans a major power. By the 1960s, USC was making its mark in Hollywood through more legitimate means. Their film school became the best of its kind in the nation, and it remains so to this day.

Sam Cunningham was a quiet type who receded into private life after a career three thousand miles removed from his college exploits. Anybody who looks back on their own lives—ten, twenty, thirty-five years—is generally unable to recall events in crystal clear detail. It is highly possible that Sam's memory is not clear or that people's descriptions of what happened have been impressed on his mind as actual events. There is no reason to believe Sam has made up any of this; and it appears that now, with disputes coming from the 'Bama side, he is unable to give a more certain account than his vague memories. In media interviews with those who simply assume the story is true, Sam agrees with the premise. But whether this is actual memory or posthistorical editing is unclear. His friend and former teammate Rod McNeill got wind of the 2003 *Mobile Press-Register* interview with Sam, in which he stated, "I don't want to be the one who said it didn't happen."

"I asked him if it happened," McNeill said. "He says it never happened."

None of the Alabama players and coaches who were in the locker room said it happened. Alabama football historian Allen Barra offered the highly plausible explanation that it may have happened in the hallway, not the locker room, allowing for Sam to recall Bryant's speech, an object lesson not for the team but for the reactionary old racists who made up alumni and administration and who were crowding that hallway. Sam very well may have seen Alabama players dressing through the open door a few yards away.

But none of this really matters because, as Scott Hunter said, "It should have happened." The fact that such a famous public event, so publicly quoted and now publicly disputed, could occur almost lends a spiritual quality to it, in that religious visions and epiphanies throughout history—events that supposedly happened—are seen differently by different people, making one wonder whether the hand of God was at play in that locker room, transforming it into a Pentecostal vision of some kind.

After all, the South, as University of Alabama professor E. Culpepper Clark said, was a place in which the "blood was hot." Violence, hatred, and real terror had engulfed the region and had shown very little sign of abating prior to September 12, 1970. Professors, sportswriters, historians, and political pundits can try to put their spin on it, but the breathtaking change that occurred after that night has a Biblical feel to it. It is in this theological analysis that one begins to see that Sam—naïve, beautiful, wise, a human man of faulty memory—may just have been a vessel, not merely a fullback.

The Bible describes all sorts of people as being God's vessels. These include sinners, tax collectors, and prostitutes. Two thousand years later, it certainly seems plausible that He would have chosen a fullback. However, Sam's former teammates—pro and college—do not describe Sam as an average, sinful college athlete. To a man, they describe a remarkable young individual. Young athletes are notoriously narcissistic, vain, and hedonistic. The world is theirs for the taking, and they take without asking a lot of questions or extending a lot of gratitude. As they say, youth is wasted on the young. When speaking to these people in later years, it is clear that maturity and life experience gave them a sensible quality that they too often did not have in their youth.

But over and over again, teammates of Sam Cunningham's—black and white, from USC and the Patriots—describe an incredible young man. Words such as *wise*, *Christian*, *loyal*, and *hero* abound in almost endless praise. Cunningham hung out with a group of young black athletes at USC called the Big Five, which included Manfred Moore, Rod McNeill, and Charle' Young. Conversations with these men, more than thirty years later, reveal guys who sound more like prophets than former football players. Moore and Young, in particular, speak in a highly spiritual manner. Each man, who offered the same perspective without prompting, backs up lineman Dave Brown's descriptions of a racially divided team that came together through Christian fellowship to have a perfect season in 1972. These do not sound like the kinds of scholarship athletes who too often make their presence known on college campuses with oversized bodies, undersized brains, and overactive glands.

The events of 1970–1972, starting with Cunningham's game, the racial inclusion in the South that followed it, and the moral fellowship that overcame suspicion at USC, begin to reveal a mosaic that is faith centered. On the field, the Trojans were average in 1970 and 1971, but they posted a 12–0 record in 1972. Alabama was average in 1969 and 1970, but in 1971 they were 11–1. By delving deeper into the events that surrounded them—the game in Birmingham, their young lives, and the destinies of their units—a religious man very well might make the connection that Cunningham was not the only vessel of God's work. When Dave Brown emerged as a leader presiding over Bible studies with increased attendance, the team went undefeated in 1972. As McNeill said, "His wonders never cease."

Of those interviewed for this book, there are mixed interpretations of religion as it relates to this game and its effect on desegregation. Dr. Culpepper Clark wouldn't say that the hand of God guided the civil rights struggle, but he did use the term *miracle* when mentioning that, despite "the blood being hot," a relatively small number of blacks were killed in the years since Emmett Till's death in the mid-1950s.

However, Sam's teammates, Manfred Moore and Charle' Young in particular, sounded like tent revivalists in their descriptions of their friend, stating that he had been "chosen" by God. Despite Sam's youth, he was consistently described as "spiritual . . . moral . . . wise." Conversations with Tom Kelly, Dave Brown, J. K. McKay, Willie Brown, Jim Perry, John Vella, Rod McNeill, and, of course, Moore and Young, reveal a definite pattern: USC was racially divided in 1970 and 1971, probably over the Jimmy Jones–Mike Rae quarterback issue, but when the team joined together in Brown's Bible studies, they were victorious on the field.

Sam Cunningham, Craig Fertig, and the Alabama players, coaches, and staff were not the only people on the scene. The sportswriters were there, too, taking notes. Bryant could have kept them out, which was a common practice. But Bryant wanted them to see this.

At some point, another comment was made. Aside from Bear supposedly saying, to someone, "This here's what a football player looks like," another oft-quoted statement is remembered in connection with the game. The quote is this: "Sam Cunningham did more to integrate Alabama in sixty minutes than Martin Luther King had done in twenty years."

Jerry Claiborne, one of Bryant's assistant coaches, is credited with having said it. But Marv Goux also said it. He said Cunningham had done more to integrate the *South* in *three hours* than Martin Luther King had done in twenty years.

As for McKay, he repeated the "Cunningham did more than King" remark many times before his death in 2001. McKay normally did not qualify the remark, as in "Jerry Claiborne said it" or "Marv Goux said it"; he just repeated it, as have numerous others until it became a football article of faith.

Back in his own locker room, Cunningham is supposed to have told two other sophomores what Bryant said about him. The whole affair had by then taken on a religious tone, as if the words spoken and actions taken were Gospel, those who heard and saw witnesses. As for Tody Smith, he was all smiles. Nobody in the state was more relieved than he was.

Outside Legion Field, a throng of three thousand black fans greeted USC. Their cheers had swelled throughout the game as they listened on radios. They were cheering, singing, and crying. They had just witnessed, or at least heard, the turning of the Tide.

There was sustained cheering until long after the game. Clarence Davis introduced his teammates to his Alabama relatives, including his Uncle Claude. Most of the USC players said they had never seen so many people after a game. Black fans lined the road to cheer USC as they drove out. They held candles and sang songs.

One hundred and five years before that game, General Robert E. Lee had surrendered to Ulysses S. Grant's forces at the Appomattox Courthouse in Virginia. If that moment could have been endowed with one-fiftieth of the goodwill that, at least according to lore, existed in the Alabama locker room on this night, a great nation might have been spared an additional century of recriminations.

A race of people, brought over to a new world many hailed as the promised land, had been made to toil endlessly because of their physical power. Now, those same attributes, combined with a new pride honed out of a century of citizenship and struggle, had pushed open the last door to earthly salvation.

Hallelujah!

Something else had happened that day, although it had been happening for the better part of ten years. Bryant's Cage-driven game was replaced by the speed and skill game that McKay emphasized. Bryant would adopt the recruiting of not just black athletes but *athletes* instead of position players. Some coaches, such as Michigan's Bo Schembechler and Ohio State's Woody Hayes, would insist on their "three yards and a cloud of dust" offenses throughout the 1970s. They would consistently find themselves on the losing end of Rose Bowl games against a variety of fast-paced Pac 8 (later Pac 10) teams.

In 2003, a TV program called *Songs of Our Success*, hosted by Tony McEwing, said, "Thirty years ago, USC faced their toughest opponent ever, segregation. It was a game that changed the Deep South."

"It had the look and sounds of any ordinary football game, but this was no ordinary game," said McEwing. "If any game could be called the 'collegiate game of the century,' this was it. None of the players, the coaches, or the crowd could have predicted the profound impact it would have on history and on the Deep South."

"If at the time I'd known how significant it was going to be, I'd've paid a lot more attention," said Cunningham. "I was just a freshman riding on the plane to play my first football game, and from the game history was made."

"USC had the only all-black backfield in college football at the time," McEwing continued. "Big deal, you say? In 1970, it was a *very big deal.* . . . The Trojans were the first fully integrated team to play in Alabama, but Cunningham was oblivious to what would happen."

"It had a wide-ranging effect from that evening that is still being felt today," said Cunningham. "Coach Bryant wanted me to come to their locker room, and he said, 'This is what a football player looks like.' Which really probably didn't sit very well with me, because I'm a football player too, but what he was trying to impress was, 'I believe there's a change in the wind and this is how it's gonna be.'"

"Coach Bryant reportedly told his coaches that he would begin to recruit black players," said McEwing.

"You never would have thought it would happen," said Sam. "You think it would happen through protest, but we were just playing a simple game of football. From those sixty minutes of football, years and years of history had gone; and we changed it for the better."

"We exploded at the start of the game," said John Papadakis. "I was the defensive signal caller and middle linebacker, and we had predominantly black players on defense and the best black signal caller in the country.

"I knew when we went out to the bus and saw literally thousands of black people, carrying Bibles, thanking us and singing hymns, I knew something was up. I knew it in the third quarter, when Clarence Davis scored a touchdown, and there were cheers outside of the stadium, silence inside of the stadium. You could hear the black people on the outside yelling and screaming for the Trojans because they knew how important it was just for us to be there."

"It just made the opportunity that much more special for USC players to represent something that had happened in such great fashion years ago," said Pete Carroll regarding the 2003 opener at Auburn, in which he invited Cunningham and Papadakis to make the trip and speak to the team, "and we felt it was our responsibility as USC to live up to it, to the standards that Sam had set that night."

Carroll, who hails from the San Francisco Bay Area, was quoted in the 1980s in the *Marin Independent Journal*: "I didn't follow Cal or Stanford. I grew up rooting for John McKay and USC. I loved USC after Sam 'Bam' Cunningham ended segregation in the 1970 USC-Alabama game."

"You know, I keep hearing and I explain to kids," said Sam, "because none of them were born when I played that game. I try to explain to them that for the little time that you're out there, to do the best you can because you never know what's going to come up."

Papadakis and Cunningham shed further light (or confusion, depending on your point of view) on the subject in the 2003 interview with the *Mobile Press-Register*'s Neal McCready.

"Gentlemen, this ol' boy, I mean, this man and his Trojan brothers, just ran [you] right out of your own house," Bryant is quoted as saying by Papadakis in the story. "Raise your heads and open your eyes. This is what a football player looks like."

In the September 5, 2000, edition of *USC Report*, McKay told senior writer Loel Schrader that the story is true. "To his players, Paul pointed to Cunningham and said, 'Gentlemen, this is what a football player looks like.'"

"I already told you I don't remember a lot," Cunningham said, appearing to McCready to backtrack. "I don't remember clearly. I'm trying to think back and remember. Coach Bryant was very polite and very, very strong in his belief that we did something special that evening. For the sake of history, I was taken in. I kind of think it didn't happen. I think I would remember, but I don't want to be the guy who said it didn't happen."

"There were so many people I couldn't count them [after the game]," Papadakis said in the story. "It was late at night and all of the black people from the neighborhood were outside the stadium. By the time we left, they had gathered and they were singing hymns and beating on the bus. They were hitting Tody Smith with a Bible, saying, 'Thank you. Thank you for coming here.' They were cheering outside the stadium when USC made a touchdown in the third or fourth quarter. We could hear them."

"It was a very strong domination in that game by Southern Cal, and it was a great game by Cunningham" is all that current Alabama athletic director, and then assistant coach, Mal Moore (who did not grant an interview request for this book) said in the same story. "It was evident that Coach Bryant already planned to integrate his team. This helped him."

"I'm proud of being a part of the team that had a hand in it," Cunningham said. "It was going to happen eventually. I'm comfortable with it."

While the Trojans were showering and celebrating, *L.A. Times* sports columnist Jim Murray and beat writer Jeff Prugh were working. They were under deadline pressure but were able to deliver stories worthy of the occasion.

The September 13, 1970, *L.A. Times* sports page featured a photo of quarterback Jimmy Jones throwing a pass, next to the headline "Trojans Fall on Alabama; Bruins' Rally Defeats OSU." Dwight Chapin had missed history covering UCLA quarterback Dennis Dummit's performance in leading his team to a 14–9 win at Oregon State.

Prugh wrote, "It was a night when stars of Cardinal and Gold fell on Alabama. And the brightest star of them all—as USC's Trojans blasted once mighty Alabama, 42–21, Saturday night—was Sam Cunningham, a towering rookie fullback who runs like a locomotive."

Jim Murray is the finest sportswriter of all time. Of all the columns he ever wrote, however, the one printed on the entire top of the September 13, 1970, *L.A. Times* sports page remains the best of his career. Whether Murray came up with the headline is not known. Whoever did deserves the Congressional Medal of Freedom. It stated, "Hatred Shut Out as Alabama Finally Joins the Union."

The article read, in part:

BIRMINGHAM—OK, you can put another star in the Flag.

On a warm and sultry night when you could hear train whistles hooting through the piney woods half a county away, the state of

Alabama joined the Union. They ratified the Constitution, signed the Bill of Rights. They have struck the Stars and Bars. They now hold these truths to be self-evident, that all men are created equal in the eyes of the Creator.

Our newest state took the field against a mixed bag of hostile black and white American citizens without police dogs, tear gas, rubber hoses or fire hoses. They struggled fairly without the aid of their formidable ally, Jim Crow.

Bigotry wasn't suited up for a change. Prejudice got cut from the squad. Will you all please stand and welcome the sovereign state of Alabama to the United States of America? It was a long time coming, but we always knew we'd be 50 states strong some day, didn't we? Now, we can get on with it. So chew a carpet, George Wallace. . . . Get out of our way. We're trying to build a country to form a democracy.

The game? Shucks, it was just a game. You've seen one, you've seen 'em all. . . . Hatred got shut out, that's the point. Ignorance got shut out, that's the point. Ignorance fumbled on the goal line. Stupidity never got to the line of scrimmage. The big lie got tackled in the end zone.

Murray would go on to write that the previous time he had been in Alabama, the only black man in the stadium was carrying towels. But "a man named Martin Luther King" thought that if you paid for a seat on the bus, you ought to be able to sit in it. The only thing white folks in the state cared about was "beating Georgia Tech."

Murray pointed out that the citizens of Alabama took their football so seriously that they realized if they wanted to play in the big time, it would require integration. Otherwise, instead of invites to all the best bowl games, they would continue to be relegated to the Bluebonnet Bowl.

"And," wrote Murray, "if I know football coaches, you won't be able to tell Alabama by the color of their skin much longer. You'll need a program just like the Big 10."

He was prescient, but remarkably few others were. In the mid-1960s, Murray had written scathing columns about Alabama. He disputed their "national" championships, stating that for a team to attain such status, they not only had to win their bowl game (which 'Bama had failed to do after finishing number one in the AP poll prior to an Orange Bowl loss to Texas in 1965), they also had to play a "national" schedule that included games against integrated teams north of the Mason-Dixon

Line, not merely segregated college programs in segregated portions of America.

In his September 13, 1970, column, however, Murray recognized what Coach Bryant was now trying to do, something even the likes of McKay, Marv Goux, Sam Cunningham, and the fans in the stands did not fully understand.

CHAPTER **Twenty-Four**

Orange Countification

> Bill, I've just handed the South to the Republicans for fifty years.
> —*President Lyndon Johnson, talking with aide Bill Moyers*
> *right after the Voting Rights Act*

In 1964, the Democratic Party dominated U.S. politics. Lyndon Johnson defeated Barry Goldwater with 64 percent of the vote. He had enormous filibuster-proof majorities in the House and Senate. The imprimatur of John Kennedy's legacy hung solidly on LBJ. A majority of America's governors and state legislatures were Democratic. The Civil Rights Act and the Great Society were ongoing accomplishments of massive impact on American life, on a scale that experts felt would approach FDR's New Deal. LBJ had effectively erased the Democrats' "soft on Communism" label, still resonant from the McCarthy era, by launching a bold war to stop the scourge of Red advance in Vietnam. This was a war that surely would be won in massive victorious fashion by the Hitler-conquering U.S. forces.

Goldwater and his party were out of the mainstream, a fringe element of the "extreme Right." Furthermore, Goldwater's refusal to back the Civil Rights Act had swung the black vote, already leaning toward the Democrats after JFK's charismatic intervention in Dr. King's 1960 Birmingham jailing, solidly into the Democratic column.

If politics could be explained through the metaphor of baseball, the Democrats were the 1964 world champion St. Louis Cardinals—young, hip, urban, mixed races, aggressive. The Republicans were the New York Yankees, so yesterday in their pinstripes, so token in their African American representation—country club Wall Street elites.

An attempt to make a similar metaphorical comparison to the USC and Alabama football teams of 1970 is not as easy. However, the aftermath of the games, as viewed through the prism of sports as a metaphor for a changing America, offers the opportunity for some comparison.

The Trojans could be seen as a successful coalition, like those of Nixon and Reagan, who had risen in the Golden State and were prominent in 1970. They were conservative, in that the school, the alumni, and the coaching staff were conservative, but their "new breed" of black athletes was something different. Alabama represented the elephant in the corner of the Democratic Party. For years, the party had tolerated the Jim Crow South because they reliably voted Democratic. But their ways, just like 'Bama's old-style football, had no future.

Lost in the expert punditry of the time was the hopeful fact of Western political influence in confluence with growing migration to the wide-open spaces of Arizona, California, Nevada, Wyoming, Montana, Colorado, and other states that had for so many years been looked upon as the frontier.

It was Richard Nixon who understood the power of the new West; he manipulated it, improvised with it, and benefited from it. He had tapped into a seminal hatred of Communism that thrived in southern California. His constituency there was more conservative, more Christian, and, depending on one's point of view, arguably more patriotic than the population of the San Francisco Bay Area, where the labor unions were being radicalized and the universities turned into hotbeds of anarchist dissent. His opponent in the 1946 Congressional race (covering an area ranging from Orange County into Whittier, Artesia, and parts of the city of Los Angeles proper) was the New Dealer Jerry Voorhis. In the 1950 Senate campaign, Nixon squared off against Helen Gahagan Douglas, the Hollywood wife of actor Melvyn Douglas. Nixon painted Voorhis and Douglas as so radically liberal as to be virtually sympathetic to Communism. He was one of the first Republican politicians, if not the first, to successfully paint Hollywood as being left of the mainstream, unpatriotic, and far too influential. He won both elections.

Nixon's role in the House Un-American Activities Committee gave him this platform. He and the Republicans dragged Hollywood actors, directors, and producers before Congress, exposing and embarrassing many of them into detailing their flirtations with and sometimes even commitment to Communism and even Soviet espionage.

In 1952, anti-Communist fervor was at an all-time high. The Korean War was going badly in the wake of President Harry Truman's firing of General Douglas MacArthur. Wisconsin Senator Joseph McCarthy was one of the nation's most popular figures, based on his attacks and investigations of American Communists. But it was not McCarthy whom Republican presidential candidate Dwight Eisenhower tapped as his vice presidential running mate. It was Nixon.

Aside from his anti-Communist credentials, Nixon represented that great new bastion of influence, postwar social change, and electoral votes—California, and with it the other growing, influential states. The Republicans had briefly captured the House in 1946 but were branded by Truman as the "do nothing" Congress during their losing 1948 elections. The victory by Eisenhower and Nixon (and for a few years Republican Congressional control) had revived a political party that some thought might splinter into some lesser version of itself.

Nixon actually defeated John Kennedy in 1960, but a cabal led by JFK's father, Joseph P. Kennedy, stole the election from him. This cabal consisted mainly of the Chicago Democratic machine of Cook County, Illinois, controlled by Mayor William Daley and Johnson's cronies in Texas. The main tactic of the Kennedy campaign was to register millions of dead citizens in Illinois and Chicago, having them vote for JFK "early and often." It was a replay of Lyndon Johnson's 1948 Texas Senate victory, which he had stolen using dead voters still on the rolls. In what was the tightest campaign in history until the 2000 George Bush–Al Gore race, however, Nixon still might have pulled it out had he not lost the black vote. The South was still solidly Jim Crow Democratic. Even Eisenhower had not been able to win there.

However, the black vote was migrating north. Blacks in Illinois, in particular, might have made the difference for Nixon. But Nixon's decision not to interfere in Dr. King's Birmingham jailing had killed him. When JFK stepped in, he secured the support of first a skeptical Coretta Scott King, then her grateful husband, and perhaps even more disastrously for Nixon, baseball great Jackie Robinson. The official "black leadership" became solidly Democratic, and now African Americans were a bloc constituency.

The conundrum of the 1960 and 1964 elections was that the Democrats had the solid Jim Crow South *and* the black vote. Much changed between 1964 and 1968, however. Under the radar screen of actual voting patterns was the emergence of conservatism, embodied less by Nixon and more by Goldwater and actor-turned-political-figure Ronald Reagan. Goldwater's support was strongest, at least in a publicly identified way, in Orange County, California, just south of L.A.

Orange County, the home of Disneyland, was mostly white, mostly Christian, very capitalistic, completely suburban, totally anti-Communist, yet strangely *moderate*. It was a bastion of conservative Republicans, yes. The John Birch Society was strong there. But racism was strongly looked down upon. There was a substantial Latino population. Just a few miles to the north was the large black population of South L.A. Easy freeway access meant commingling in the new car-crazy commuter generation. People there were too beautiful, too tanned, too athletic, too laid back in a surfer kind of way; the women too pretty; and the weather too perfect to appeal to virulent racism, which seemed to emanate like rising hell in the sticky, humid muck of the angry South.

The man who embodied Orange County politics was Reagan. If Goldwater angered some black voters by playing to what he perceived as his constituency in not backing the Civil Rights Act (odd, since the solid antiblack Democratic South was off-limits, especially against Johnson), Reagan's easygoing charm made him palatable to a wider audience. It was this palatability that sowed the seeds of marriage between the South and what Orange County represented. This was, in essence, a "third way." The liberals were pounding the Southerners over the head with incessant charges of racism, accusing the proud denizens of Dixie of activities tantamount to those of the hated Nazis so many of them had fought against in World War II. Reagan and the new conservatives wanted change and racial equality, but they recognized the contributions of the South. They respected its symbols, its rich heritage, its fight for freedom on the fields of military strife. Reagan and the Western conservatives noted Southern literature, instead of denigrating the area as incessantly downtrodden, rural, ignorant, and backward. It was a simple approach, based on the old maxim that "it is easier to catch a fly with honey than vinegar." The protesters and shouters of the Left, many funded by Communist front groups, used only vinegar.

Waiting his turn (again) was Nixon. Goldwater had stirred a movement whose time would come. Reagan, after endorsing Goldwater at the 1964 Republican National Convention in San Francisco (while also making a televised performance revered by history simply as "the Speech"), was statesmanlike, while sound bites only seemed to repeat Goldwater's "extremism in the name of liberty is no vice" comment. But Reagan was not yet tested.

In 1966, the Right was organized. They ran Reagan for governor of California against the incumbent, Edmund "Pat" Brown. Two things drove conservative politics in California and, by reflection, nationally. These were the increasingly violent protests of free speech, civil rights, and, especially, anti–Vietnam War protesters. No place was more angry than the University of California, Berkeley, a state school funded by taxpayer dollars. The California citizenry wanted law 'n' order. Reagan ran on this premise.

The other event that stirred the soul of America was the disturbing 1965 Watts riot in South Central L.A. This, combined with the rise (and assassination) of Malcolm X and the Black Muslim "nation," along with the formation of the militant Black Panthers in Oakland, created fear in whites. They found comfort in Reagan's promise to deal with these elements in a stern manner instead of the "wishy-washy psychobabble" offered by the likes of Brown and his party. The Left, for the first time, began to see that its solid black voting bloc could be an albatross around its neck. Brown, who had defeated former vice president Nixon in 1962, was beaten soundly by Reagan. Reagan now had his hands full reforming California, and suddenly Nixon emerged as a viable figure once more.

The Republicans outflanked LBJ's Democrats in the 1966 midterms. They demanded a Douglas MacArthur-like resolution to the ongoing Vietnam conflict while expressing backlash against the Great Society. Nixon's legendary work ethic paid off. He crisscrossed the country campaigning for Republicans, who were beginning to knock a few chinks in the Democrats' Southern armor. Nixon then cashed in the chits he had earned with Republican elected officials and committeemen in 1966. In 1968, he outshone Nelson Rockefeller and the rest of the Republican field to earn the nomination.

What happened in 1968 will be debated forever. From a philosophical point of view, it was a year of irony, tragedy, karma, and horror, all wrapped up in nothing less than Shakespearean, maybe even Biblical, dimensions.

The year began in turmoil—race riots in Chicago, Newark, and other cities had continued from 1967 into the new year. The Tet Offensive turned the liberal media squarely against the Vietnam War, creating paradigms of confusing patriotism in a brave new world. The campuses were ablaze with hatred and protest. Democratic Senator Eugene McCarthy entered the New Hampshire primary as an antiwar candidate and took more than one-third of Johnson's vote. LBJ then announced he would not run. Robert Kennedy announced that he would. So did George Wallace.

In April, a white man assassinated Dr. King in Memphis. Black rage exploded throughout the country. Kennedy assumed the mantle of sainthood, and the Left willingly anointed him. He forged a giant shadow, as large as his martyred brother and the slain civil rights leader. He created a coalition of antiwar zealots and black and Chicano civil rights activists, along with traditional Democrats.

In June, after winning the California primary, RFK appeared unstoppable. A Nixon-Kennedy rematch had all the trappings of major political theater, but every indication, then and now, is that Nixon would have lost again; perhaps this defeat would have been too unbearable for him to overcome his dark inner demons. Then Sirhan Sirhan murdered RFK at the Ambassador Hotel in Los Angeles.

To say that Nixon benefited (in the short run) from this event is one of the great understatements of the twentieth century. When one examines the fourteen years between 1960 and 1974, it becomes hard to imagine that there is no God, or no devil, and that they do not interfere in the affairs of man, as Charle' Young likes to point out. The implications of all the "what might have beens" that surround Nixon and the Kennedys—John, Robert, and Teddy—conjure wild imaginings of evil and goodness pulling the strings of historical irony. An entire book could be written about all the scenarios that connect in a spiderweb of possibilities.

Kennedy stole the 1960 election from Nixon. Had Nixon been president, there probably never would have been a Cuban Missile Crisis and very likely either no Vietnam War or the conflict would have been concluded in a show of force resulting in American victory and Southeast Asian hegemony. The Communists, led by Soviet premier Nikita Khrushchev, concluded that JFK was a "rookie," and therefore they were emboldened to test him in Cuba, Indochina, Africa, and Latin America. It may be revisionist at this point, but it is also not a stretch to determine that they feared Nixon and would not have tried any of this had he been in the White House.

First, Nixon was the former vice president of the respected Dwight Eisenhower, a man nobody had wanted to challenge in his eight years as president. When the Communists defeated the French at Dien Bien Phu in 1954, Nixon had very seriously recommended the use of "battlefield nuclear weapons." This may sound crazy, but it frightened the Communists into halting major operations until JFK assumed office.

JFK either ordered or at least allowed a CIA-inspired coup to over-throw South Vietnamese president Ngo Dinh Diem in 1963. How much blood was on Kennedy's hands is debatable. A little over a month later he was dead himself. His plans to de-escalate in Vietnam were completely destabilized by these events.

(In retrospect, JFK might have achieved success in Vietnam by orches-trating elections in South Vietnam in 1963–1964. Instead he "allowed" the assassination of an ally. The lesson of this event was seemingly learned by the George W. Bush administration, which used the election option in Iraq. However, elections held in South Vietnam after LBJ took office did not quell disaster. Iraqi elections did not lead to immediate freedom and democracy, either.)

Had JFK lived, Bobby might have succeeded him in 1968. Nixon might never have been a major player on the national stage. Of course, that means Watergate never would have occurred. Teddy Kennedy might not have been driving drunk at Martha's Vineyard in 1969, and his viability as a presi-dential figure likely would have resulted in the family becoming what their father wanted them to be. They never got there. Almost as if to spite the Kennedy Left, the Bush family has assumed all the heights of power and prestige that seemed so destined for the so-called American royal family.

As it was, all the soaring rhetoric of King and RFK was replaced by naked political maneuverings. Wallace threatened to take not only the South but also a fair share of the West. But the Californian Nixon, who thwarted a native-son bid from Reagan and picked up Goldwater's con-stituency, cleaned up the region. In addition, he had in his Wall Street years made himself attractive to the East Coast establishment, once known as "Rockefeller Republicans."

The Democrats were hamstrung. First Vice President Hubert Humphrey divided the party by waiting too long to distance himself from President Johnson's Vietnam policy. Then, almost as if by karmic irony after the events of 1960, Mayor Daley's heavy-handed response to protests during their convention turned the event into a war zone. Riots in Chicago doomed their chances.

Humphrey never looked like a winner. He appeared to have won the Democratic nomination by drawing straws. He never really rose above the other second-rate post-Kennedy candidates.

But the key to 1968 was not really Vietnam or Kennedy's assassination. It was Wallace. Wallace, who was turned down by former USC-football-player-turned-actor John "Duke" Wayne for the running-mate slot (Air

Force general Curtis LeMay accepted the role), ran a wide swath through the South. For the first time since the Civil War, the South was not solidly Democratic. Nixon played it like the political genius he was. It was called the "Southern strategy."

Nixon did not run a particularly strong campaign in Dixie, but he saw to it that Humphrey, a Minnesota liberal who was now fully willing to cut and run against the Communists in Southeast Asia, was weak there. Nixon never campaigned against Wallace, instead associating himself with the policies that they could find common ground on. Call it the "Orange Countification" of Southern politics.

Nixon had attended Duke University Law School in North Carolina. During his time at Duke, he had engaged in long, friendly arguments with his Southern classmates regarding racial issues. Nixon (like Eisenhower before him) understood the Southern mind-set. He admired their traits of loyalty, aristocracy, gentlemanly manners, chivalry toward women, military valor, and patriotism. He contrasted that with his disdain for the "elitism" of Harvard and Ivy League intellectuals. Unfortunately his somewhat negative attitude toward Jews was perhaps reinforced by the experience.

All in all, Nixon's persona among the Southern electorate was a gentle agreement to disagree, but he refused to let the racial question overshadow his other traits, which were popular in the region. Nixon was a bona fide Commie hunter, a traditionalist, a huge football fan, and a believing Christian who had befriended the great Southern evangelist Billy Graham.

Over time, the "Southern strategy" has become vilified by blacks, who see in it a manipulation of white racism on the part of Nixon. In 2005, the Republicans themselves went so far as to apologize for engaging in such blatantly political maneuverings. However, this apology is much more about the attempt to swing modern twenty-first-century black voters into the Republican column than it is an honest historical appraisal of the strategy itself. The fact is that it swung Wallace voters away from Wallace and into a moderate political philosophy. The ensuing years, if one wishes to apply cause and effect, certainly indicate that it was successful not just for the GOP but also for blacks. Opportunities *did* open up. Racism *did* subside. Blacks *did* gain political power.

The Republicans have been frustrated in the succeeding decades by black refusal to vote their way. Blacks somehow have forgiven Democrats their Jim Crow legacy while allowing the "Southern strategy" to be defined as veiled Republican racism. What they have not understood in adopting this attitude is that the strategy was, like Bear Bryant's approach to desegregation and the USC game, an incremental approach to a problem that, in the end, needed just such Lincolnian leadership.

After Nixon's inauguration in 1969, oddly enough, many of his most popular achievements were unpopular in the South. Conversely, his most unpopular were popular down there. His handling of Vietnam, which included an escalation of bombing and aggressive action against Viet Cong sanctuaries, resulted in protests at Berkeley, Columbia, the Lincoln Memorial. . . .

In Birmingham, Oxford, Nashville, he was cheered.

Nixon's decision to open talks with Red China had the Left in a euphoric tizzy. Southern businessmen could not believe it. They saw Nixon as "going soft" on Communism, they thought NSC advisor Henry Kissinger was just another East Coast Jew, and they were infuriated by activist judges ordering enforced busing, EPA regulations, and abortion on demand. They had no choice but to back him, however. If the South and, in a larger sense, the conservative movement were to throw their hats in with Wallace full bore, America would find itself helmed by the likes of George McGovern and Teddy Kennedy. All of this went for naught when Watergate hit.

When Democrat Jimmy Carter was elected president in 1976, the Left felt almost an "end of history" sense of victory—not just victory in the latest national campaign, but a feeling they were the winners of twentieth-century political theory. This attitude is rich with hubris and reminiscent of Caesar after he crossed the Rubicon, reunifying Rome in his image. Modern-day Republicans have predicted the demise of the Democratic party as we know it, an event "planned" by Karl Rove to begin in 2008 and be in place by 2012. When the Iraq War did not result in easy victory followed by parades and speeches, the GOP watched their carefully nurtured Congressional majorities eliminated in the 2006 midterms. The 2008 presidential campaign promises to either fulfill the Rove strategy or reverse years of political groundlaying.

The Democrats of 1974–1976 and the Republicans of 2004–2006 would both have been wise to recall that Roman conquerors did understand the nature of hubris, at least to some limited extent. They employed slaves to walk in their shadows, at all times whispering in their ears, "You are mortal. All glory is fleeting."

The modern Republicans were planning to rule the world as Alexander did, blithely ignoring unseen future events that could spin them off their axis: terrorist mega-attacks, economic disasters, scandal, Armageddon in the Middle East . . .

The Nixon lesson, which emanated on a much smaller scale (a third-rate burglary), seemingly set the GOP back twenty years. George W. Bush's Texas cowboy image and Christianity seem to engender a similar loathing toward him. The liberal media tainted Nixon's Vietnam record. The pullout of U.S. forces, followed by the slaughter of anti-Communist resistance, was depicted as a refutation of American militarism and exceptionalism.

The period from 1974 to 1976 remains a dark one in American history, but as the saying goes, all dark clouds have a silver lining. The American and world Left felt they had achieved "victory." First, the hated Nixon, the slayer of Alger Hiss, had supposedly been brought down in a mountain of irony involving the "avenged" memories of the Kennedys and all the abused liberals in Nixon's wake. It was a tale that made *Macbeth* look tame. The Democrats on the Watergate Committee; Archibald Cox; and Bob Woodward and Carl Bernstein, *they* were portrayed as Moseses leading *their* people out of bondage from the "Pharaoh" Nixon.

One by one, Nixon and conservatism were deconstructed. The Soviet Union was now thought to be a nation we had to respect as an equal. The term Cold War was made passé. Enormous shifts in attitude toward race, sex, religion, drugs, morality, and patriotism took place, seemingly taking on a liberal image. In the late 1970s, Sam Cunningham's performance would have been given little credence in comparison with the protest movements. It has only been the sands of time that have allowed us to correctly judge the true sweep of history.

However, Nixon's own words still had resonance, in a phrase he had invented in 1968: the silent majority. Herein lies the effect of Sam Cunningham and the 1970 USC-Alabama game on America. It is inter twined with Ronald Reagan and the Orange Countification of the South, the husbanding of a region into the mainstream via Nixon and the GOP. It helps explain the backlash against liberalism that gained its foothold in the Goldwater run and its power in Nixon's presidency. In the wake of Gerald Ford's loss, its voice was found in the Reagan revolution. After Reagan, the road to George W. Bush was paved by the Contract with America. Even Bill Clinton's successes are attributed to Southern politics embodied by the post-Cunningham period.

One of Nixon's closest friends and advisors was Billy Graham, who invited the president to speak at one of his outdoor sermons before a sell-out football stadium crowd. The mainstream media treated the event in one of two ways. Either they ignored it as insignificant pandering to a no-longer-significant constituency, or they criticized it as a violation of the separation of church and state.

But Nixon's Christianity and his relationship with Graham are telling. This was Orange Countification. Nixon, despite his failure to come to King's aid in 1960, had significant black support. There was still a semi-conservative black minority. Basketball star Wilt Chamberlain was a Nixon man. So, too, were Sammy Davis Jr. and Frank Sinatra's "rat pack." Nixon was as stiff as a board, but a fair number of "cool" Hollywood and entertainment types, such as Elvis Presley, rallied to him.

Presley, born in Mississippi and raised in Tennessee, was overtly paranoid about Communists in the entertainment industry, offering his services to the president to help root these elements out, not unlike the way Reagan had in early 1950s Hollywood. Southerners like Presley were emerging as the image of the New South. In the wake of the Civil Rights Act of 1965, blacks now had the vote in Dixie. The Atlanta Falcons and Houston Oilers were two of several top pro football squads that operated totally integrated operations, as did the Houston Astros and Atlanta Braves baseball teams. Orange Countification was silently taking place. White racial moderates, conservative politically, Christian by religion, patriotic and respectful of Confederate Civil War valor, pro-family traditionalists who hated Communism and knew the way a military was supposed to be used. They were rugged Western individualists representing California's electoral juggernaut. A marriage was being made, if not in Heaven then in the South. This was a region that had been marginalized and taken for granted by its uneasy Democratic sponsors. They now saw a chance to attain its rightful place via a new partnership, first with conservatism and eventually in official alliance with the Republican Party. This was not an uneasy "understanding" between Huey Long and Franklin Roosevelt, but rather trust and respect between Southern politicians and their constituencies with Nixon, Reagan, and their growing followings. Amazingly, the American punditry either did not see it coming or mistook it for something else.

One reason for this was Jimmy Carter, the moderately conservative (liberal by Georgia standards) Southerner who succeeded the racist Lester Maddox as governor on the strength of the new black votes the 1965 legislation helped usher in. Carter was a hybrid of time and opportunity. He filled the Democratic vacuum still left open by Teddy Kennedy's Chappaquiddick. His squeaky-clean evangelical Christianity was palatable to the South and seen not in religious terms but rather as a sign of honesty by the liberals and the electorate, begging for accountability after Watergate. Carter's ascendancy was part of a trend, embodied by numerous national essays detailing how the "New South will rise again." Included in this development were strange tales of a "new" Ku Klux Klan, led by an educated, telegenic man named David Duke. Even racism understood the growing dynamics of public relations.

From 1964 to 1980, every election cycle saw the Republicans slowly chipping away at the Southern Democratic base. This trend took evolving forms. First, there was the "Wallace factor," in which the influence of Alabama's maverick Democratic governor proved to hurt his own party and help the Republicans. This "revolt" against Democratic liberalism within the party was not limited to Wallace, and it resulted in growing GOP success through the 1960s and 1970s.

Second, emerging Republican enclaves took shape in the solid South. One of them was the wealthy Houston district represented by Congressman George H. W. Bush from 1967 to 1971 (the future president lost Senate races in 1964 and 1970).

Finally, there was the unkindest cut of all, the actual switching of parties by prominent Democrats to the Republicans. Trent Lott made his switch in 1972. Senator Strom Thurmond, who had splintered the "Dixiecrats" in 1948, also switched. But conservative Democrats, the likes of which in later years included Georgia senator Zell Miller, undercut the party's base for years without actually leaving.

In 1980, America needed a change. Jimmy Carter had been bamboozled by the Communists, had allowed Islamo-Fascism to take root in Iran (with American hostages fueling the effort), and had created an economic "malaise" that allowed interest rates to climb to 25 percent, making home ownership extremely difficult to attain. Out of the Republican Party emerged Reagan. His detractors saw only an aging actor. His devoted followers remembered "the Speech" he made in 1964 and the way he righted California for eight years. They recalled the way he had almost nabbed the nomination from a sitting president in 1976, and now he was "the right man in the right place at the right time" (not unlike Cunningham ten years prior).

Reagan sent a message by starting his campaign, symbolically, in Mississippi. It was another example of the Orange Countification of the South. The Mississippians who supported Reagan had been supporting nearly a decade of integrated Ole Miss football. By 1980 the sight of black football players—not to mention basketball players, baseball players, cheerleaders, even fraternity brothers and professors—was, if not entirely commonplace, certainly no longer out of the question.

Reagan's critics naturally tried to paint him as racist for making his announcement in Mississippi. They totally missed the point that Reagan was *not* racist, and he was *still popular* in that state.

George Wallace called civil rights leader John Lewis, asking if he could apologize for his segregationist past. He went to a black church and apologized to a roomful of African Americans. They told him that what he had done "was forgiven, but not forgotten."

It should never be forgotten, but the power of Christianity is the power to forgive. It is not a power merely exercised by Christ, who sheds grace on sinful wretches. It is a power endowed to humans, who use this power to forge a better world. The mainstream of African American citizenry has, over time, forgiven the South for its sins. They have not forgotten, although too many young black people do not know the stories. They do not know about the sacrifices of Jackie Robinson or the accomplishments of Sam Cunningham.

Charles Scott, a close friend of baseball star Barry Bonds and a fellow African American, once said that being black in America meant "hearing the stories handed down, from aunts and uncles, grandfathers." While this is generally true, too often millionaire black superstar athletes take their success for granted. They too often fail to recognize not just that their paths were paved for them by black pioneers but also that a generous, hopeful America gave them opportunities unavailable anywhere else in the world.

Reagan's eight years in the White House are generally regarded by a circle of historians, who now have had time to assess his legacy, as the best presidency of the twentieth century, and one of the best in American history. Had Reagan failed, much of the conservative revolution would have faltered. The connection between the 1970 USC-Alabama game and the husbanding of the American South into the mainstream, thus setting the stage for Republican electoral hegemony, could not be drawn, at least in such startling terms, had Reagan not achieved what he did.

The success of the 1970 USC-Alabama game; the near-seamless transition of blacks not only into the SEC but also into Southern society; the continual economic, cultural, and political advancement of blacks in America—much of this can be attributed to the conditions that embody this game.

Bryant and his team succeeded in large measure because white hearts softened. On a larger scale, America succeeded because white hearts (and not just in Dixie) softened. Considering what the streets of Birmingham, Selma, and Montgomery looked like from 1963 to 1965, and what Legion Field looked like in 1970 and beyond, the prospect that a Christian miracle is responsible must be considered a valid possibility. From a more earthly perspective, it appears to be the success, in large measure, of a political philosophy espoused by Ronald Reagan, given the moniker conservatism, and embodied by a more succinct phrase herein called Orange Countification. The philosophies of Orange County adapted by the formerly hard-line South. Somehow, a football team just north of Orange County helps symbolize, thirty-seven years after the fact, how it all came about.

The region was officially Democratic but conservative to the extreme. Conservatism found its conscience, which moderated its extremist tendencies to more fittingly adapt to its natural Christian instincts. In so doing, conservatism moderated to better fit the Western model of Reagan, of California, and of Orange County. Instead of racism and resentment, rugged individualism, entrepreneurial spirit, and religious morality inculcated conservatism in the South. Its white citizens began to see as plain as day that Christianity did not mean white supremacy or separatism.

Herein lies a conundrum for liberals. Whites came to see that the Christian phraseology of Dr. Martin Luther King Jr. was as right as rain. Dr. King was a liberal, at least by standards of the 1960s. It always seemed that, to the extent a "winner" would emerge from the civil rights struggle, it would be the "liberals," the Democrats, the Left. Not so. It was the conservatives and the Republicans.

This fact has caused more than a little bit of angst among modern black leaders and Democrats, who instead of accepting the tenets of this self-evident truth often try to deny it, call it something else, accuse it of being a cynical ploy by the Right. In the meantime, as the old song says, "the truth is marching on."

This has a familiar ring to it, though. Some call this political phenomenon the "Nixon goes to China" syndrome. Nixon was the most vehement of all anti-Communists, yet he went against his own constituency to open diplomatic relations with Red China, which history judges to have been a smart move. "Only Nixon," it was said, could do this. A liberal would have been excoriated as being "soft on Communism."

Similarly, the Democrat Bill Clinton reformed welfare. A conservative would have been burned had he tried such a thing. These are just two examples of the "Nixon goes to China" theory.

Reagan's vice president, George Herbert Walker Bush, succeeded him. In theory, he was a Southerner. It was just a theory. Bush was a Northeast Rockefeller Republican. It was true that he earned his spurs wildcatting the Texas oil patch in the 1950s, but his Yale frat image was too ingrained. He was old money. A blue blood.

Reagan had taken major hits from the Democrats and the media. They pounded him during the failed Robert Bork nomination to the Supreme Court and the Iran-Contra scandal. What the liberals failed to realize was that the Bork and Iran-Contra events were viewed differently by conservatives, particularly in the South. Bork had argued against the constitutional legitimacy of *Roe v. Wade*. Southerners were just itching to overturn the questionable 1973 abortion ruling.

Marine lieutenant colonel Oliver North became a star defending Reagan during the Iran-Contra hearings. Southern anti-Communists were all for backing the rebels fighting an illegitimate Marxist cabal in Nicaragua.

Bush came on promising a "kinder, gentler" presidency. Bush tried to make friends with Democrats, to cut deals with them, to reach out. These efforts left him vulnerable to the campaigns of not one but two Southerners who, while not members of the Republican Party, had some conservative credentials.

Ross Perot ran as an independent. He was a billionaire Texas business mogul who had graduated from the Naval Academy. Bill Clinton claimed to be Baptist, and in an effort to right a floundering Democratic Party, he had helped found the Southern Democratic Leadership Council. These were moderately conservative Southern Democrats who recognized that the South was the key to electoral success.

Perot took an enormous bloc of votes away from Bush. Clinton painted a moderate downturn as "the worst economy of the twentieth century" and slickly got away with it. Bush lost because he did not appeal to the blue-collar, conservative, and Christian elements not only in the South but also throughout Republican heartlands.

His defeat was not lost on his son, who had had an epiphany leading to sobriety, had become a born-again Christian, and already had made contacts with the Christian Right. That Bush was a different kind of conservative. He does not fit the mold of Orange Countification reflected by Nixon and Reagan, but he is certainly closer to it than his father.

Bush, despite sporting the same blue-blood credentials as his father, was all Midland, Texas. He serves as a perfect example of the New South. The man does not have a racist bone in his body. Two of his top aides are African Americans. Secretary of State Colin Powell and his successor, former NSC advisor Condoleezza Rice, were (and in Rice's case, still is) two of his most trusted advisors. Their jobs are the furthest possible jobs in America from "token."

Rice is particularly symbolic in reflecting upon the 1970 USC-Alabama game. She grew up in segregated Birmingham and knew some of the little black girls killed when the KKK blew up a church there in the early 1960s.

Bush rode to success on the heels of successful Republican Congressional strategies and Clinton's personal immorality. The Contract with America was orchestrated in 1994 by Georgia's Newt Gingrich, the Speaker of the House. It was a brilliant campaign that completely devastated the Democratic Party.

Bush's presidency, beginning in 2001, benefited from the Republican majorities birthed by the Contract with America. After some party switching that briefly gave the Senate to the Democrats, Bush presided over historic Republican midterm victories in 2002, and in 2004 he won reelection with the largest vote count in history, in the election with the highest turnout ever. The Republicans dominated every level of U.S. politics—the House, the Senate, governors' races, and state legislatures. The key was "moral values" in the heartland, and the South was solidly behind Bush and his party. No American president, with the possible exception of Abraham Lincoln's Northern backers during the Civil War, has been more popular in a region than Bush in the South.

Republican hegemony in the twenty-first-century South has given rise to some telling observations. After the 2004 elections, Democrats in the "blue states" complained that "banjo pickers" and "crossbreeders" had decided the White House. This unfortunate statement, made en masse by a huge portion of the Left, is not only a lie but also the height of hypocrisy. Using the legal "but for" method of proximate causation, an examination of the facts reveals just how hypocritical. In so doing, it demonstrates almost as scientific fact the superiority of conservatism over liberalism, Republicans over Democrats. This is the kind of thing Plato would have made use of, since he sought not political advantage, or the majority opinion, but rather scientific truths to guide public administration. This is the birth of the phrase "political *science*."

For many decades, the South was backward. Their rural counties often lacked running water, electricity, and indoor plumbing, much less cable TV or computers. For all the decades in which a large swath of the South actually *was* ignorant, two constants remained:

1. They were racist.
2. They were Democrats.

After the Tennessee Valley Authority was established, federal works projects brought modernity. Over time, these modernities effectuated an educated, informed populace that was *no longer* ignorant. Along came cable TV, the Internet, talk radio. The following came about as a direct result:

1. They are no longer racists.
2. They are now Republicans.

Conservatism and Christianity, working hand in hand in America, have proven themselves to be the winning ideology of 2000 years of history. In the immediate here and now, there are variations on the theme. Had the United States gotten the same results in Iraq from 2003 to 2007 as they did in 1991, the Karl Rove strategy of a "permanent" GOP majority may well have been realized. The Democratic Party might not have survived such a thing, splintering into something else, possibly two parties independent of the traditional party of FDR and JFK.

The blame the Bush Administration received—much of it well deserved—when Iraq 2003 did not resemble Iraq 1991 emboldened the Democrats to midterm wins in 2006. Behind the likely banner of Hillary Clinton, they enter the 2008 presidential year with high hopes. However, this is a smokescreen diverting attention from the ultimate historic success of conservatism over liberalism.

"When I got started in the movement," columnist William F. Buckley, considered by some not to have been *part* of the movement but the *founder* of it, told *Human Events* magazine, "the Republican Party was a Northeast liberal party. Our ideas were considered to be fringe elements of society. But today I look about the political landscape and I see international Soviet Communism on the 'ash heap of history.' I see old-style socialism to be a thing of the past in this country; the New Deal and the Great Society discredited. I see conservatives proudly wearing their banner while nobody calls themselves liberal and expects to win elections under that moniker. I see a refutation of Keynesian economic theory in favor of that of Hayek or Friedman. I see losses but many more victories. Sure we won."

Indeed, even the 2006 congressional victories were achieved in large part by conservative Democrats taking advantage of an electorate, much of it in the South, frustrated that the Republicans were *not conservative enough*!

The prospects of a Northeastern liberal such as Hillary are not good. Her husband, Bill Clinton, ran as a Southern moderate-to-conservative Democrat. He was raked over the coals when, beholden to liberal money interests, he veered to the Left. He achieved success when the Republican Congress came in, held his feet to the fire, and "helped" him enact relatively conservative policies. The South continues to be the rock of Republican electoral prospects for years to come.

The world currently faces a new crisis in the form of Islamo-Fascist terror. Any long-term hopes the Democrats have will not reach fruition as a result of their response to terror. When they were elected by surly voters, frustrated by lack of progress in Iraq, they had the unique opportunity to join the fight and, with victory attained, share in the plaudits, just as history tells us the Cold War was won not just by Richard Nixon and Ronald Reagan but also by Harry Truman, John Kennedy, and Lyndon Johnson. So far, no Democrat has appeared on the horizon to do now what Truman or JFK clearly saw needed to be done in their day. Instead, the party has for all practical purposes assumed the role of de facto public relations wing for Al Qaeda, just as UC Berkeley once allowed its campus to be the staging ground of American Communism.

There are people on the Left—elected Democrats, media commentators, columnists, Hollywood actors, entertainers, "comics"—who are so unpatriotic that it appears they are on Osama bin Laden's payroll.

Conservatism is far from perfect, but to paraphrase Winston Churchill, it may be "the worst political philosophy known to man, with the exception of all other political philosophies known to man." The Republicans have consistently shot themselves in the foot. Their biggest mistake has been, despite being given the bully pulpit of the winning ideology of conservatism, trying to make friends with Democrats by adopting pseudo-Democratic ideas. The result: Democrats stab them in the back anyway, and the ideas are bad.

Whether conservatism's ultimate victory will manifest itself in Republican sweeps in 2008, resulting in Karl Rove actually getting his wish—the breakup of the Democrats in 2012, not unlike that experienced by the nineteenth-century Whigs—is immaterial to the movement's place in history. Individual candidates, public opinion, and external political factors—war, the economy, scandal—will swing individual elections to one side or the other based on peculiarities of the moment. There have been times when conservatism had the mandate, the votes, the majority; other times it has not. For the most part, even when it wins elections, it will always be a minority because to be a conservative requires courage, historical knowledge, and a willingness to buck easy public opinion.

Therefore, adherents of conservatism, even when a minority in number, shall remain in an evil world the "thin red line" separating civilization from anarchy; right from wrong; order from chaos. George Washington standing up to the British Empire; Abraham Lincoln standing up to slavery; Winston Churchill standing up to Nazism; Ronald Reagan standing up to Communism; and George W. Bush standing up to terrorism.

A recent documentary called *In the Face of Evil* outlines the lonely, brave role of conservatism in a world of unimpressives. It tells the story of Reagan's often lonely fight against Soviet expansion and influence. Although Reagan saw the Cold War won, the documentary does not declare "victory" as such. It describes "the Beast," a metaphor for the devil, Satan, evil, which simply changes form over generations: religious intolerance, despotism, racism, slavery, nationalism, Nazism, Communism, terrorism . . . and the seeming inability of supposedly well-meaning people to see what is placed before their eyes.

The Left has either failed to see evil in the past or, worse, been part and parcel of it (Communism most obviously). Communism may be dead, but it is still alive as an *idea*—something that is against religion, especially Judeo-Christianity; against family values, tradition, manly courage, military valor, and other things that mark America. Communism is, therefore, against America, and it manifests itself in the form of—take your pick—Leftism or liberalism. The worst part about it is that it camouflages itself as something righteous, something for the environment, the planet, the children, the poor.

In 1972–1973, Republican president Richard Nixon and Secretary of State Henry Kissinger crafted a hard-won peace with the North Vietnamese Communists. It was based on Kissinger's realpolitik, a European concept outlined in post-Napoleonic peace treaties, using the interests of rival

Communist states (the USSR and China) against each other in favor of American global interests.

Then Watergate hit. The Democrats, after having suffered a massive loss in the 1972 blowout to Nixon, saw political opportunity. They challenged Nixon on the issue. The Communists, seeing American military will weakened by Democratic gains, attacked South Vietnam, which had been maintained as a sanctuary not unlike South Korea. With Democrats in power after the 1974 midterms, Nixon weakened, then resigned. Gerald Ford, unable to get the Democrats to oppose the Communists, was thus unable to stop the North Vietnamese Army from invading the south.

It would be moral relativism to blame it all on Ted Kennedy, who led the Democrats at that time. After all, it was Communist leaders and soldiers who ordered and carried out the killings. Nevertheless, Kennedy, being an intelligent man, could reasonably have seen it coming, yet still he did not oppose it. None in his party did. The result? Estimates vary, but the results of all this add up to about 1 million South Vietnamese dead, 1.5 million Cambodians dead, multiple thousands of Laotians and others dead, and millions of refugees.

Democrats, as if having made a deal with the devil, won the White House in 1976. By 1980, these and other events were no longer murky, hidden behind Democratic allies in the liberal media. Millions by now had seen and understood what occurred. The result? Ronald Reagan in two landslides.

When faced with the "the Beast" in its 1980s form—nuclear weapons, threats against western Europe, Soviet invasion of Afghanistan, adventurism in Africa and Latin America—Reagan chose not the Kennedy strategy but victory.

"Reagan won the Cold War without firing a shot," declared British prime minister Margaret Thatcher.

Today, "the Beast" is Islamo-Fascist terror. The Democrats find themselves between a rock and a hard place. If a repeat of the Kennedy strategy—now outlined by House Speaker Nancy Pelosi (D.-California) and Senate majority leader Harry Reid (D.-Nevada)—is implemented, with the result a repeat of Cambodia's "killing fields," at some point Democratic responsibility for the carnage will again seep through the liberal media (which is now countered by conservative talk radio, meaning it will happen much faster). The electorate will react against the Democrats as it did in 1980, and the Republicans will go on another winning streak.

If, however, George Bush and his backers succeed first in fending off Democratic cowardice, then win, all credit will go to the Republicans. There will be no sharing of the credit, as in the Cold War. It will be the end of the Democratic Party, not merely another Republican winning streak. It will be that "permanent majority" Karl Rove is seeking.

This great nation is built on a two-party system. "Power corrupts, and absolute power corrupts absolutely." Pure Republican hegemony would not be good for the world. Despite its inherent ideological advantages, the party is run by human beings and therefore subject to human flaw. A "loyal opposition" is needed. At this point, however, only the Democrats can save themselves, and there do not appear to be any modern Lancelots on white steeds riding to their rescue.

It might seem incongruous that the cherished liberal view of racial equality somehow sparked the political fire that led to liberal failure and conservative triumph. It would also be a mistake to assume that the opinions expressed in this book advocate a "liberalism is all bad" philosophy. America *needs* liberalism. Conservatism, left to run amok, would screw up too. Liberalism is the bulwark of Western civilization. Many of its best tenets are found in Greek philosophy, Christian teachings, the Renaissance, the Age of Enlightenment, and the American Revolution.

It was liberalism that sparked the civil rights movement, and thank God for it. But it was only when conservatism met it halfway that the movement succeeded. Embodied by the modern South, symbolized by the 1970 USC-Alabama football game, it has been the impetus for monumental political change favoring the Right.

But the prospect of a Republican recovery's resulting in the ultimate demise of the Democratic Party foretells potential doom, too. Not just political doom, but a larger kind of Doom, with a capital "D."

"Pride goeth before the fall," as former USC All-American tight end Charles "Tree" Young likes to quote from Scripture. There are preachers, many on the radio, who believe the world is in the End Times. Call it what you like—the Great Tribulation, Apocalypse, Armageddon—but polls show that in America a remarkable 30 to 40 percent of the population holds to the evangelical Christian view that the Lord Jesus Christ is coming . . . soon!

The Bible describes the fall of great empires: Babylon, Persia, Greece, and Rome. Today, America is the greatest world empire in the history of human existence. Beyond our military, American dominance manifests itself in the form of pop culture, Hollywood, music, fashion, sports, and most important, the spread of Christianity through the freedoms advanced by this great nation.

Since great empires have all fallen in Biblical times, followed by the rise and fall of Spain, France, Great Britain, Germany, and the Soviet Union, if one takes Revelations to its logical conclusion, would it not make sense that the "last empire," its strongest and most righteous—America—be at its most impregnable when He returns in judgment?

Furthermore, would it not make sense that the truly *good* empire that is America be in place to free the most people, allowing the most souls to hear the Gospel, at a time of the world's greatest population explosion (roughly 2 billion to 6 billion in 50 years)?

And is it not logical (at least as far as such things go) that the last great political philosophy—the uniquely American form of conservatism astride evangelical Christianity—would be standing alone fighting "the Beast" in its death throes in the Last Days? And finally that Republican hubris, vanity, and pride would be man's final insult against God before the return of the Lord Jesus Christ?

Of course, if all this is to happen in our time, an Antichrist is required. An American political figure? Somebody out of the Middle East? The Bible tell us that all of this shall happen like "a thief in the night," except for those who are standing in metaphorical watchtowers, waiting.

CHAPTER Twenty-Five

"Mine Eyes Have Seen the Glory of the Coming of the Lord"

> Mine eyes have seen the glory of the coming of the Lord;
> He is trampling out the vintage where the grapes of wrath are stored;
> He hath loosed the fateful lightning of His terrible swift sword;
> His truth is marching on.
>
> —*"Battle Hymn of the Republic," written by Julia Ward Howe*

American politics in the South mirrored the 1970 USC-Alabama game. The game had accomplished a symbolic victory for African Americans, but it was so much more than that. It had opened the door for real change, and it had done it athletically the way Nixon and Reagan's theoretical Orange Countification had done it in politics: quietly.

The civil rights struggle had plodded along, loud, noisy, sometimes dangerous. King had attracted crowds, fomented protest, defied the law. Malcolm X was in the white man's face. The Black Panthers were openly militaristic and increasingly violent. An elemental staple of politics, diplomacy, and human psychology had seemingly died with Lincoln in 1865.

Lessons that would be learned and made instructive to any State Department desk chief studying China and its obsession with "saving face" or Russia's respect for toughness were (seemingly) not taught, learned, or implemented by the well-meaning civil rights crowd.

It took a Southerner, Bear Bryant, who was really a sly fox, to schedule a game with his duck-hunting friend John McKay. From there it took the hand of God, guiding a naïve, beautiful young black man named Sam Cunningham to his destiny on the field of athletic strife, thus embodying the best way to effectuate change.

Truth is what happened on that field.

When King spoke, his words could be misconstrued. He had Communists in his organization, or he was a degenerate womanizer. Nobody trusted the federal government. The courts, the laws, the judges, all of them could be viewed as corrupt. But Cunningham and the Trojans had done it in the purest form imaginable.

The pro athletes on the Falcons, Oilers, Braves, and Astros? They were mercenaries, subject to professional lifestyles, gambling interests, and other corruptions. Texas Western's basketball team? That was the "black man's" game, wasn't it? Black baseball players in the Southern minor leagues? That was the minor leagues, barnstormers, clown acts, minstrel shows.

No, this was the citadel of college football, the University of Alabama, in the very heart of Dixie. This was Bear Bryant, walking on water while drinking Coca-Cola. These were the new aristocrats of the South, its best and brightest football talent. And, yes, this was USC and its multitalented, multifaceted, integrated squad, coming in full of esprit de corps, kept together by the Socratic Greek linebacker Papadakis, led by coaches McKay and Goux, who *insisted* they do it the right way. With class, with honor, with jubilation but not overt celebration.

A school located half an hour north of Orange County had come to Birmingham, and a form of Orange Countification had taken place. What the Alabama football fans saw, in the esteemed McKay, the well-regarded Goux, the talented Jimmy Jones, the explosive Clarence Davis, and the spectacular Sam Cunningham, was the future. A way in which it *could* be done, with class and dignity. It was *palatable* to them, just as Nixon and Reagan were palatable to them.

Thus the merging of political and athletic theater, explaining so much about the next thirty-seven years of American history.

Black athletes did not desegregate just Southern football rosters after that game; they began to desegregate Southern political staffs, government office buildings, law firms, schoolhouses, grocery stores, and all other forms of society and commerce.

It did not happen because of court orders or protests. No National Guardsmen accompanied these people. It happened because the truth had been witnessed and understood.

"The truth will set you free," as it says in the Gospel according to John, and herein is the true answer to the civil rights question in the South. The answer is Christianity. Here was the most Christian region of this great nation, yet these same people had been inculcated by Satan's influence. The devil had fed them defeat, war, famine, and all their stepchildren: mistrust, hatred, vengeance. But Christianity *had* taken hold here. In the 1920s, a major revival had spread the religion throughout the region even more. For years, preachers had scoured the Bible, both Old and New Testaments, to justify slavery and racial separation. Arcane language was cited. Even Plato's Greece was demonstrated as "justification" for the practice, since Athens had been, like every other major population, a slave state.

But true Christians are required to look within their own beating hearts. The life of Jesus Christ was so far from an endorsement of slavery and racial hatred as to be beyond the ken. Christianity, hand in glove with a new country, blessed by God, a nation literally shining with God's grace, where freedom and justice were not words but sacred truths; no, people were *not* unequal. We are *all* God's children, and every one of us deserves the chance to roam unfettered in God's delightful path.

The politicians and educational administrators who made up the American South at the time of Sam Cunningham's remarkable football performance in 1970 had all ridden to their high places of public esteem at least in part because they adhered to the demand that they be churchgoing men of Jesus Christ.

"Mine eyes have seen the glory of the coming of the Lord."

No man can truly believe those words, instill their meaning in his own heart, live life adhering to what they really mean, and then turn around and enslave his fellow man. Man sees the coming of the Lord, and he knows too that the Lord sees him, into the bottom of his heart and soul.

The lie had to die.

The work of Dr. King had been done. The work of millions of well-meaning American citizens had taken place. It would not go for naught. The men and women who had traveled South during the Freedom Rides, to "teach the Southerners a lesson," had been frustrated in their efforts, but their work, like God's, would succeed in unforeseen, mysterious ways.

Quietly, just as Bear Bryant liked it. Like a thief in the night, as Christ told his followers, their time would come. Seemingly, a convergence took place, and a new "feeling was in the air." Many years of improvements would lie ahead. Hatred never dies, and it did not die that day at Legion Field. But one of its allies, the "prejudiced South," was on the way out. Cunningham and USC, with Bryant's "help," had put a chink in the armor.

King's dream has been realized. What he started was advanced as much by Sam Cunningham and the 1970 USC-Alabama game as by any event that occurred following King's death. But the game and its aftermath have had a profound effect on America that could not have been predicted at the time. Not only has black America seen a vast expansion of its rights, but the political landscape of the country has changed dramatically as well. What would have been most unpredictable, and what is most ironic, is that the beneficiaries of civil rights advances are not just the blacks in the South but also the whites in the South, the conservative movement, and the Republican Party.

Mahatma Gandhi said that the righteous elevation of a group of human beings is the elevation of all human beings. The Southern whites who saw a future of race mixing as equal to the lowering of standards—and there are still many who hold racist views, to be sure—instead found themselves elevated by the advancement of their region. Bear Bryant reiterated the sentiment that Cunningham had done more than King, John McKay agreed with it, and over the years these words have become almost apocryphal. But Cunningham himself was never comfortable with them. He is a humble man, and while John Papadakis tacitly felt Marv Goux's comment was true, building Sam up as an "American hero," Sam himself did not quite see it that way.

Sam may not have seen himself as a man of destiny, but he always knew he was a vessel of God. It could have been C. R. Roberts. It could have been Jack Johnson. But Sam and Jackie Robinson, more than any athletes in the American civil rights struggle, were in precisely the right places at the right times. The real credit they deserve is that they were the right *men*. It is instructive to consider that the "quiet revolution" gentle Sam started (or ended, depending on the way one looks at it) was more effective than the orations of the loudmouth Muhammad Ali.

The "wrong" man would have either tipped the scales of racial justice too much or not enough. Ali would have danced about, getting in people's faces, telling anybody who listened that "I am the greatest of *ALL*

TIMES!!!" He would have set the whole thing back for years. Sam did it just right.

"Later, with Vietnam and everything, Sam and the Trojans found themselves the right men in the right place at the right time," was Marv Goux's assessment. "But to be honest, and not to take away from Sam, C.R. Roberts had a better game against the Longhorns than Cunningham did against Alabama."

As for doing "more" than Dr. King, neither Sam nor any serious student of this era of American history would agree. What did happen was that King and his movement had built up the dominoes. They were poised, ready to fall. It was Sam who did the tipping. What is really not in dispute—and *Sports Illustrated* gave credence to this notion by ranking the event number six in its "20 Greatest Tipping Points"—is that there is a truly defined demarcation line, and that line is September 12, 1970. There is America and race relations before that date, the game played on that date, and America's race relations after the event.

The forces of societal evolution that came about when Sam "sparked" this beautiful, quiet revolution have been nothing less than cataclysmic, and they explain much of our political landscape. Black civil rights advancements had always seemed to be the province of liberal America, and if the dream was ever realized, it would be liberals who profited from it politically. The fact that they have not, at least not the way one might have predicted in 1970, is a matter of great frustration for the Left.

CHAPTER Twenty-Six

The South Rises Again

It ain't how things start that's important. It's how they finish up.

—*Paul "Bear" Bryant*

A labama finished the 1970 season with a 6–5–1 record. USC, despite their great start and obvious talent, went on to a disappointing 6–4–1 season. They lost to Jim Plunkett's Stanford team, who upset Ohio State in the Rose Bowl. Observers and players close to the team all agree that the Trojans failed to live up to their potential because they were not together, racially or otherwise—an ironic twist considering the good work they did on behalf of historical civil rights.

Also, while no team could possibly have been more ready to win than the Trojans of September 12, 1970, the letdown after such an intense physical and cultural test was too difficult to handle. Mere college football games, filling out a schedule against the likes of Stanford, California, and Washington, did not match up to the expectations they had in Birmingham. The result was upset defeats at the hands of lesser teams. When challenges were presented, USC lived up to their talent. Nebraska won the 1970 national championship. Their only blemish was a tie against Southern California. Notre Dame and Joe Theismann would have finished number one that season, except they lost to the Trojans, 38–28, despite Theismann passing for more than five hundred yards in a driving L.A. rainstorm.

Virtually every USC player and person associated with the program, black and white, who played on the 1970–1971 squads and also the 1972 national championship team, mentioned Dave Brown and the Fellowship of Christian Athletes. They all said the 1970–1971 squads were as good, but it was religious togetherness that created the greatness of 1972.

John Mitchell turned down USC and went to Alabama. Allen Barra has enjoyed for years recalling how McKay was "bragging" to Bryant about Mitchell, whereupon Bear rushed to the clubhouse, got Mitchell on the phone, and put a "sell job" on him, getting him to stay in the state instead of heading to the West Coast.

"I think we can be fairly certain that McKay never boasted again to Bryant about a prospect before he signed him," said Barra.

The University of Alabama football program, after several years of mediocrity, certainly rose again. Mitchell debuted in the Coliseum in 1971.

"John McKay saw Mitchell running down the field on the opening kickoff," recalled Craig Fertig. "He just turned to me with a funny look on his face and said, 'Well, that's what you get.'"

'Bama gained a measure of revenge and won 17–10 in that early-season night game at the Coliseum. Spurred on by this victory, Alabama ran the table in an undefeated regular season before losing to Nebraska in the Orange Bowl. They entered the Sugar Bowl undefeated in 1973 but were beaten by Notre Dame.

In 1977, Alabama ventured west again, upsetting the undefeated, number one ranked Trojans, 21–20. USC returned the favor in 1978 behind running back Charles White in a 24–14 victory at Legion Field. That was Alabama's only loss of the year. USC faltered once, to Arizona State. Alabama knocked off Penn State in the Sugar Bowl, and USC handled Michigan in the Rose Bowl. Despite the fact that the two contenders for the national championship had played each other (a fairly rare occurrence that gives the voters the opportunity to judge the winner to be better than the loser), and USC had soundly beaten the Tide on their home turf, the two wire services split the national championship vote. USC captured the UPI version, 'Bama the AP version.

This is a very telling development. John Robinson's Trojans beat Bryant's Crimson Tide and were deserving of an undisputed title, but many voters went with Alabama out of respect for Bryant. In 1966, they had lost a close "election" when the "Catholic vote" carried Notre Dame ahead of them. The segregated 1966 Alabama team was, to use a 1990s phrase, too politically incorrect. The more "diversified" Irish won.

Only eight years after the groundbreaking 1970 game, a totally desegregated Alabama team got the nod. The world had changed. Nobody can argue that Alabama in 1978 was paradise for African Americans, but one can argue that in those eight years the state, the region, and its university had made as swift and sure a social change for the better as any place, perhaps ever.

"What I recall about 1978," said Jim Perry, who covered the 1970 game for the *Long Beach Press-Telegram* and was USC's sports information director in 1978, "was that, while this was a really, really big game, there was absolutely no big deal associated with the fact that Alabama had a lot of black players."

Perry now found himself dealing with a school and a region that routinely employed and educated, and was even beginning to *elect*, its black citizens, who were gaining equality and power by leaps and bounds.

'Bama went on to a 103–16–1 record in the 1970s, one of the greatest decades in college football history. The only team better was USC. The Trojans captured three national championships that same decade. In the four games the two schools played against each other in the 1970s, the record was 2–2, with the visiting team winning each game.

The elderly Bryant never won another national championship after 1979, retiring a few years later having passed Amos Alonzo Stagg as the winningest coach in college history (Penn State's Joe Paterno passed Bryant in 2000, and a few years later Bobby Bowden passed Paterno). Under Gene Stallings, the Tide won the 1992 national championship, but overall the program slumped. Following the 2002 season, they hired Mike Price to take over, but he was fired for cavorting with strippers in an Alabama hotel room.

McKay coached his son J.K. and Pat Haden, winning two national championships in five years, before leaving for the NFL and the Tampa Bay Buccaneers. After McKay's departure in 1975, Robinson led USC to the 1977 Rose Bowl and the 1978 national championship. USC was the 1979 preseason favorite for a repeat national title. Only a tie against Stanford marred their season. Alabama finished number one. The two teams that had met on September 12, 1970, to start a relatively mediocre season for both were at the apex of the college football world.

In seven years at USC, Robinson would win one national championship, claim three Rose Bowl titles (without a loss), and mentor two Heisman Trophy winners, Charles White (1979) and Marcus Allen (1981). But after 1982, something changed.

Marv Goux would coach at USC, under McKay and Robinson, until 1982, when he left with Robinson to coach on his staff with the Los Angeles Rams. Goux's departure was not merely the symbolic end of an era. In his last year, 1982, USC fielded a strong 8-3 team. They mounted a stirring last-minute drive to beat Notre Dame at home, 17-13. But Goux's exit ushered in an era of, certainly by USC standards, mediocrity.

Coach Ted Tollner (1983-1986) was supposed to be a guru of the passing game. But instead he installed little in the way of offensive genius and ushered in a period of underperforming running backs. He did win the 1985 Rose Bowl but was fired after Notre Dame scored an enormous comeback victory over USC in 1986. USC lost to Notre Dame from 1983 to 1993, tied them in 1994, and lost again in 1995. They lost to UCLA in 1983 and 1984, then fell to the Bruins for eight straight years from 1991 to 1998.

Larry Smith took over in 1987 and led USC to three straight Rose Bowls. In 1988, he had Troy at 10-0, ranked second heading into the game versus number one Notre Dame in L.A. The Irish prevailed, 27-10. In many ways it was a "close but no cigar" moment for USC. They lost to Michigan in the Rose Bowl but thought they had regained their form with heralded prep recruit Todd Marinovich (Craig Fertig's nephew) quarterbacking the 1989 team. Marinovich showed signs of brilliance, along with linebacker Junior Seau, in a 9-2-1 season that included a victory over Michigan in the Rose Bowl but also a disheartening close loss at South Bend and an inexplicable tie versus underdog UCLA. In 1990, the team was expected to challenge for the top ranking, but Marinovich unraveled. He argued with Smith, got involved with drugs, and played erratically.

USC's two decades of struggle included NCAA probation. They occasionally fielded a strong team—five Rose Bowl appearances (three of them victories)—but like Alabama they yielded their kingdom to the likes of Notre Dame, Florida State, Nebraska, and Miami.

The 1990s were the worst years in USC football history and saw the firing of Smith, the rehiring and firing of Robinson, and the lackluster Paul Hackett years. There were bright spots, however. In 1994 Robinson led Troy to a 55-14 win over Texas Tech in the Cotton Bowl, and the next season they defeated a strong Northwestern team, 41-32, in the Rose Bowl. They finally ended the winless streak against Notre Dame in 1996, but Robinson failed to beat UCLA in his second go-around. Over the 1997 Christmas holidays, athletic director Mike Garrett fired the legendary coach by voice mail. Paul Hackett (1998–2000) never even went to the Rose Bowl, but he did recruit quarterback Carson Palmer.

Over the years, USC had worked hard to erase its academic image as a "football school." By 2000, the school was attracting an incoming freshman class with 4.0 grade point averages. USC was named the "College of the Year" and the "Hot School" by the *Princeton Review*. It was generally accepted that the higher academic standards were a necessary trade-off and that great football teams such as those in the past were just that—in the past.

In December 2000, Hackett was unceremoniously dumped. USC went after heralded coaches Dennis Erickson (Oregon State), Mike Bellotti (Oregon), and pro coach Mike Riley. All of them turned athletic director Mike Garrett down. By that point, Garrett's own job was very tenuous. Pete Carroll, twice fired in the NFL, applied for the job almost as an after-thought because his daughter was playing volleyball for the Women of Troy, which he figured was "cool." To no great fanfare, he was hired.

The Trojans went twenty-five years without winning the national championship, and they had such lackluster running attacks that their Tailback U. moniker became the joke "Yesterday U." By normal college football standards, they were still a marginal power. They went to their fair share of bowl games and finished in the Top 25 rankings somewhat often. But the mystique was gone. Could it have been because Goux was gone?

Goux passed away at the age of 69 in 2002. He barely missed seeing Pete Carroll's second year, which was his first real year of "resurrection." Carroll ushered in a new dynasty period, possibly more dominant than any in their past. The 2002 Trojans were home to the Heisman winner (Palmer); won the Orange Bowl in a rout over a 10–1 Iowa team; and were considered by most experts to be the best team in the nation at season's end, when they finished with an eight-game winning streak. Palmer was the number one NFL draft choice in 2003.

In 2003 the Trojans captured the national championship behind sophomore All-American Matt Leinart, dismantling Michigan 28–14 in the Rose Bowl. In 2004, USC fielded an undefeated team that many feel is one of the best of all time. Their back-to-back national championships featured Leinart winning the 2004 Heisman (running back Reggie Bush was a New York finalist for the award) and a demolition derby at the BCS Orange Bowl, 55–19 over previously 12–0 Oklahoma in a game that was supposed to be the best matchup ever. They were only the sixth team in history to be ranked number one every week of the season.

In 2005 USC just missed becoming the only team to accomplish this feat three times (the 1972 team having done it as well). The Trojans fell short of a first-ever third straight AP national title by virtue of a nine-yard Vince Young touchdown run with nineteen seconds left in a Rose Bowl classic that likely will go down as the greatest collegiate football game ever played. Reggie Bush became their third Heisman winner in four years. They surpassed Miami (2001–2002), who held the previous record for being ranked number one at twenty straight weeks, by holding that spot for thirty-three weeks going back to 2003. Texas's victory over Troy in the 2006 BCS title game ended their thirty-four-game winning streak.

Pete Carroll is in the middle of what could be the strongest dynasty ever. In 2006 USC won the Rose Bowl, and early prognostications for the 2007 season predicted that Southern California would be ranked number one, with quarterback John David Booty a Heisman Trophy favorite.

Carroll has had as much success in his first six years as any coach. Bud Wilkinson (1940s–1950s), Notre Dame's Knute Rockne (1918–1920s), and Frank Leahy (1940s) are in this elite group. Bear Bryant (1961–1966) had one of the greatest runs. But if Carroll's 2007 Trojans win his third national championship, then his 2001–2007 record breaks new ground.

By the mid-2000s, historians were beginning to acknowledge that overall, Notre Dame's ranking as the greatest college football program of all time has to take a backseat to their biggest rivals from the West Coast. USC now has eleven national championships. The Irish have eleven, but most have come in the archaic era of leather helmets and segregation. USC, Notre Dame, and Ohio State all have seven Heisman Trophy winners, but USC's are much more modern than those of the other two schools.

The Trojans have produced the most professionals (along with Notre Dame), the most first round draft picks, the most Hall of Famers, and the most Pro Bowlers, and they are second only to Notre Dame for the most All-Americans. They are, undisputedly, a football factory. The empirical evidence cannot be argued against. Did it take Goux's passing to restore order at University Park?

* * *

Since Bear Bryant's departure from Alabama, the legacy of Sam Cunningham's game in 1970 has reverberated not just in Birmingham and in "red state" politics but also in Southern football. In 1970, the dominant conferences were the Pacific 8 and the Big 10. Not surprisingly, these were the conferences that had opened their gates to African American athletes in the greatest numbers and with the most welcoming enthusiasm. The Big 10 became a "safe haven" for Southern blacks.

USC and the Pac 8 already had huge black populations in their backyards. Los Angeles prep sports had always been highly integrated. USC, however, had traditionally gone beyond L.A. and California, recruiting white and black stars from every geographical area in the United States. The slight weakening of the Big 10 and the Pac 8 (Pac 10 beginning in 1978 when Arizona and Arizona State came on board) can in part be attributed to integration in the South, particularly in the Southeastern Conference. The rise of the Florida schools—Miami, Florida, and Florida State—is directly linked to their taking on the enormous numbers of highly talented black athletes who populate their state. For the better part of ten years, the SEC has maintained its arguable perch as the strongest football conference in the nation.

Since Cunningham's performance helped open doors to blacks in the SEC, the conference has become far more than a football league. Black athletes of both genders have turned the conference into one of the most, if not *the* most, competitive football, basketball, baseball, track, and women's sports leagues in the nation. Women's sports are extremely popular now. The Tennessee Lady Vols are probably the greatest women's hoops program in history.

USC dominated college baseball and track at the time of Cunningham's breakthrough. They were so good in these sports it was as if there were two sets of rules: one for the Trojans and one for everybody else. After integration, USC's dominance diminished. Today, the SEC and the Southwest Conference are every bit as strong as the Pac 10. LSU under coach Skip Bertman won four baseball national championships in the 1990s. Texas coach Cliff Gustafson passed USC's Rod Dedeaux as the winningest in college baseball history. Track was once all USC. The Trojans have not won the NCAA title since 1976, ceding superiority to crosstown rival UCLA and a host of often-Southern teams from the SEC, the Big 12, and smaller conferences.

UCLA's basketball program, which from 1963 to 1975 probably dominated as thoroughly as any sports team in history (with the possible exception of Concord, California's De La Salle High School football program, which won 157 straight games from 1991 to 2003), became just another contender after John Wooden left in 1975. The reason was not just the departure of Wooden; the new egalitarianism of the South also very much played a part. In Wooden's day, when he fielded integrated squads, entire sections of the college landscape were virtually "not in his league," unable to compete with the Bruins because of the racial advantage they enjoyed.

In 1970, basketball was totally secondary in the South. Kentucky was an also-ran by that time, its power ceded to integrated UCLA and other similar programs. At Louisiana State, floppy-socked Pete Maravich began a resurgence in basketball interest, but the all-white nature of his team and league reduced their impact compared with John Wooden's Bruins and the real power teams of the era.

Today, while football is still king, the best college basketball is played in the South, namely at Florida, North Carolina, and Duke, and in the Atlantic Coast Conference. Advances among minorities in coaching and executive administrative jobs have not come as fast as most would like, but it cannot be argued that, although the current scene may not be a sea change, it would have been unheard of to predict the modern influx of black coaches in 1970. Today, black coaches dot the landscape in almost every sport and at every level throughout the South—high school, college, and professional.

CHAPTER Twenty-Seven

Legacy

Bryant was not just a football coach but a
personification of the idea of America.

—*Bryant biographer Keith Dunnavant*

USC opened the 2003 season at Auburn. USC Coach Pete Carroll
invited Sam Cunningham and John Papadakis to make the trip
and to speak to the team about the 1970 game in the state they
were now playing in—a state that had been changed by the events of that
day and by the men speaking to the team now. Southern California then
smoked the Tigers, 23–0.

Over the course of the next few years, the legacy of the 1970 USC-
Alabama football game began to take on new historical dimensions. With
the rise of Carroll's dynasty at Southern California, new interest in all
things USC took shape across a Trojan Nation.

USC ascended to a place in which its football past could finally be said
to have passed Notre Dame as the greatest collegiate tradition of all time.
Books, documentaries, and numerous retrospectives from the L.A. and
national media recaptured past glories Of all the glories—national championships, Heisman Trophy winners—Cunningham and Troy changing
the "complexion" of America, as Craig Fertig quoting John McKay called
it, proved to be its finest moment.

The game had not simply changed football. It had changed America.
The 2004 George W. Bush victory over John Kerry symbolized the new
power of the South, culturally and politically. It was the South's ability to

find "the better angels of our nature" that gave the region the chance to move forward. While Bush may have been a symbol of newfound Southern pride, it was the ghost of Paul "Bear" Bryant that hovered above him. For all of Cunningham's greatness on the field, for all of John McKay's progressivism and Marv Goux's spirit, it was Bryant who had been confronted with integration; thought it over; and like a salmon swimming against the stream, turned a federal law into an acceptable practice. He did it all by force of his personality.

Whether he said, "This here's what a football player looks like"; whether he should have or even could have done it earlier; whether he did it out of true altruism or to make his football program regain its lost footing, why, none of that matters. He stands like a Colossus over this event and the rise of the American South. Other figures—Huey Long, George Wallace, Jimmy Carter—pale in comparison to Bryant and his place in history, on and off the field. Among post–Civil War Southerners, only Lyndon Johnson and George W. Bush affected American history to the same extent.

"And we went down and our backfield was all black players, our wide receivers were both black, our tight end was black," recalled Fertig on *The History of USC Football* DVD (2005). "Alabama had no black players. Bear Bryant by design, these two had worked on this so that black players would be able to stay in the South and play for Coach Bryant.

"Now our guys, people ask us now, was that a big deal? It wasn't a big deal, the black-white thing with our players. We were scared to death because it was our first football game, and Alabama was *good*. Our guys knew how good Alabama was, but it was not a big racial thing, it was no racial thing whatsoever. It was a football game, and that's what I think is great about football whether you're pink, blue, or green; everybody has the same chance, and usually the best players'll win. We went down there and beat the devil out of 'em, and I was walking with Coach over to Coach Bryant, and like I say they're great friends off the field, they played golf together. Coach McKay even went huntin' with him, even though he didn't know which end of the gun to use, and I was expecting Coach Bryant to be really upset, and he says, 'John, I just want to thank you for what you've done for me and the University of Alabama.'"

"Martin Luther King Jr. preached equality," said Ozzie Newsome, who in the aftermath of that game became a black All-American and 'Bama legend under Bryant. "Coach Bryant practiced it. I'm not saying he couldn't have done more to integrate the football team faster, but when I was there, there were no complaints from black players about unfairness from Coach Bryant. I can tell you that the man practiced what he preached."

"Nothing changed over the weekend of the 1971 Alabama–Southern California game," said Professor Wayne Flint of the University of Auburn, "but you could see it start to change. As Churchill said of Dunkirk, it wasn't 'the beginning of the end, but it was the end of the beginning.'"

USC honored Cunningham in 2005, the thirty-fifth anniversary of the game, with a Sam "Bam" Cunningham Commemoration Day. "Bam's impact not forgotten" was the headline of an accompanying story by Bob Keisser in the *Long Beach Press-Telegram* on September 12, 2005. The continuing page headline read, "Bryant changed ways quickly," accompanied by a photo of Bear with the caption "Initially opposed to recruiting black players, Alabama coach Bear Bryant changed his tune after Sam Cunningham ran for 135 yards on 12 carries in a 42–21 USC victory."

This indicates that Bryant was opposed to the recruitment of blacks, despite the evidence to the contrary, and that it was Cunningham's performance that made him "change his tune." Not true. Wilbur Jackson was already recruited; the game was set up for this purpose.

"Bryant briefly met with Cunningham on the field, and although recollections on what exactly transpired are inconsistent, the upshot is that Bryant reiterated, time and time again—to his players, to the media, to Alabama fans—that 'This is what a football player looks like,'" wrote Keisser.

"I by no means think I did more than Dr. King or any social activist, because I didn't," Cunningham said. "Those people lost their lives for what they did.

"I just played a football game, and the outcome effected great change. Sometimes in that naïve manner, that's the best way. . . . By what he said, Bryant was impressing on his players that there's going to be change, and that it would be tough for all of them, not just the players coming in but the players already there, and the whole community. But it would be a change for the better.

"It had to be hard for people there to see that because it had been just one way [all white] for so long. We put a whipping on them. They couldn't put a spin on it. Their team got beat and no matter how you wrote it up, you couldn't change that fact."

"The reality is that football, and sports, is about excellence, and winning results from that, and black kids have historically excelled in sports," said Dr. Maulana Karenga, professor of black studies at Long Beach State. "So [Bryant] would have been making a mistake not to choose from all of the best players. He wanted to win. It was important to him.

"It provided much collateral benefit. By not practicing in sports the kind of early-man segregation that was unjust and immoral, his excellent decision also became an excellent moral choice."

"It was a pretty bold step," said Cunningham. "Bryant was the only one who could guarantee our safety, and Coach McKay had to have faith in Bear that he could bring his players, fans, and boosters in for a football game at a time when it probably wasn't conducive.

"They both took a very big step. But it was the easiest way to get it done. Back then, coaches were icons and could do whatever they wanted to do. It wouldn't have ever happened any other way."

Wilbur Jackson (1971–1973), John Mitchell (1971–1972), All-American center Sylvester Croom (1972–1974), linebacker Woody Lowe (1972–1975), cornerback Mike Washington (1972–1974), tight end Ozzie Newsome (1974–1977), center Dwight Stephenson (1978–1979), and defensive stars Thomas Boyd (1978–1981), Jeremiah Castille (1979–1982), E. J. Junior (1977–1980), and Don McNeal (1977–1979) followed at the University of Alabama.

"It's pretty simple," said Cunningham. "We flew in, played and won a football game, and left. We only had to deal with the South for two nights, and then we were gone.

"The people who actually had to work and deal with the change were the ones they recruited and played. Because nothing had changed other than allowing blacks to play football. The way people felt probably didn't change overnight. The difference was that blacks now had the opportunity to be part of the organization.

"They had to work in that atmosphere, and there's a lot of pressure to be the first, or second, or third player to come into a culture they've never visited before. I applaud them. What I did was easy. They had the pressure of the whole culture riding on them."

"What all of those athletes and other African American athletes in similar situations, from Jackie Robinson to Jack Johnson to Muhammad Ali, did was create free space for everyone by demonstrating their excellence without penalty," said Dr. Karenga.

Sam cast himself as a man trying to keep the memory alive, not as a noble person, "a black man in decidedly the wrong place at the right time," wrote Keisser.

"Sam is like so many others, an ordinary person who did an extraordinary thing and met the invitation of history," said Dr. Karenga. "He seized a moment at a time when the last thing the people in that crowd probably wanted to see was a black man excel."

* * *

John McKay said he had no idea what it was about, but he was a "poker player," always holding his cards close to the vest. He knew what it was all about. When Bryant proposed the game, it took USC's coach all of two seconds to accept, then counteroffer with an invitation to Alabama to play at the Coliseum in 1971 for more money. Since Bryant was the athletic director (McKay would become USC's AD in 1972, but he already had the authority to schedule the game) and the eleventh-game opponent had not been chosen by either school, he had an "inkling" of what to expect. The fact that Alabama was segregated and USC was integrated was like the proverbial elephant standing in the corner of the Horizon Room of Western Airlines when Bryant arrived for their meeting. USC carried star black players from New Jersey, Connecticut, Pennsylvania, and California. The best black athletes in the world were from the Golden State. One of the first black quarterbacks in the NFL, Doug Williams, had grown up a Trojan fan because McKay had used a black quarterback, Jimmy Jones.

"I told [assistant coach] Marv Goux that I didn't know what Bear was up to, but the whole thing had the feel of a spy novel," McKay recalled in 2000. "Bear asked if the Trojans would like to travel to Birmingham to open the following season. The NCAA had just granted an eleventh game, and Bear wanted that game to be against us on their home turf. I agreed to the matchup. What I didn't realize was that it was all part of Bryant's own plan to desegregate his program. Despite his popularity, he'd never been able to do it before, despite his desire to. He'd expressed to me that he'd wanted to do it for years. I can't say that I knew Bear's intentions fully at the time, but I did suspect it. It was a delicate situation and required just the right timing; but if any man understands how to do something like that, it was Bear Bryant."

"I can say with absolute certainty that Bear Bryant wanted to integrate his football program long before that game," said longtime college football broadcaster Keith Jackson.

McKay and Fertig were on their second or fourth round of drinks when Bryant arrived. A martini and history followed. Fertig later asked McKay why Bear wanted USC for the first game. McKay told Fertig that

Bear chose his Trojans to help "change the complexion," as Fertig later recalled it, of college football.

"Bryant 'walked on water' in Alabama," McKay said. "He could have been governor had he chosen to run. He could have been king."

Bear Bryant suspected that USC would blow them out. Beyond that, the game proved to be a seismic shift in American sports, politics, society, and Southern sensibilities. It was the Magna Carta of civil rights, encapsulating in one evening the hopes and dreams of African Americans. It gave life to the struggles of Selma, Montgomery, and Birmingham. It might as well have been John Hancock's signature giving imprimatur to the then five-year-old Civil Rights Act.

What made the game successful not just for McKay, Sam Cunningham, and the Trojans, however, was the fact that the trip was peaceful, the team was well treated, and fan reaction went from visibly semihostile to outwardly docile.

"Bryant had talked the game up," said assistant coach Marv Goux, in what may have been the last interview he granted prior to his passing. "It was his baby. And if Bear was for it, the state of Alabama was willing to accept change.

"After Sam's game, Alabama was able to use [recent black recruit] Wilbur Jackson." By the mid-1970s, "the Southeastern and Southwest Conferences were desegregated," continued Goux. "Earl Campbell at Texas, Billy Sims at Oklahoma—the whole region changed dramatically overnight. It was great, even though we found recruiting to be harder after that."

(Oklahoma had begun desegregation in the late 1950s; Texas was in the process of changing its practices around the time of Cunningham's game.)

"Oh, my, recruiting changed, yes," McKay recalled. "There was a time in which we could pluck black athletes from anywhere in the country. They wanted to play for the Trojans. Jimmy Jones from back East. O. J. Simpson from San Francisco. Tody Smith from Texas. It was a combination of things. They heard that USC accommodated blacks, that life there was pleasant in every way—the school, their classmates, the press and fans, everything—and they were right. It provided an urban environment, nightlife, and pretty girls of different races. Plus, they knew that the coaches were fair, and if they measured up, they would play and get all the recognition they earned. If their goal was to play in the NFL, USC was a place that showcased their talents.

"Over the next ten years, USC and other West Coast teams no longer could pick black stars who were turned away in the South," McKay noted. "You saw not only Alabama's resurgence after a down period, but the rise of teams like Georgia, LSU, and all those Florida schools. USC eventually went into a down period of their own, as did the whole conference, and one of the reasons for this is because the talent pool became limited."

"What people forget about Sam when they talk about this game," Goux said, "is that he was a sophomore battling for a starting job. He was a big recruit, yes. He was built like a brick you-know-what. But we were loaded, and John McKay was not promising starting jobs to sophomores. It was his first game, and considering the environment, McKay wanted to play it close to the vest. Look at the highlights of that game. Off-tackle, *boom*—breaking tackles, running over guys. Sam just made an outstanding contribution on his own.

"Plus, Sam was from Santa Barbara. I grew up in that area too. It's a very low-key area. He didn't have any idea, really, about what was happening in places like Selma. He was still a kid, barely away from home for the first time when that game was played."

Defensive standout Tody Smith, the brother of Bubba Smith, had grown up in Texas. He was extremely worried about the Alabama game. Many of the California blacks, unaware of race relations in the South, were less concerned.

Running back Clarence Davis was born in Birmingham. Bear Bryant knew all about him. The black press in Birmingham made a big deal of him. McKay had needled Bryant about how he had managed to go right under his nose and recruit a player like that.

"Davis was a typical example of our advantage at that time," said McKay. "Today he'd've finished school in Alabama and been up for grabs, probably in the SEC. His family left that environment, and we just got him to succeed O.J."

When the 42–21 blowout was over, nobody in the state of Alabama could deny any longer that in order to compete for a national championship, black players would have to play in the SEC. 'Bama fans knew that the many black high schools in the South produced great athletes. They had seen them go to Big 10 and Pac 8 schools. They had seen many of them go on to stardom in the NFL, the NBA, Major League Baseball, and the Olympics. They knew that Grambling was a traditional all-black college football powerhouse, but in the 1970s, their already legendary head coach

Eddie Robinson would be facing some stiff recruiting competition right in his backyard.

They knew all these things, but confronted with the proverbial elephant in the corner, they had chosen silence. Silence was now replaced by buzz, argument, and change.

Cunningham's performance in the face of pressure and adversity convinced many that blacks possessed not only the physical ability for the game but the mental acuity as well. This was accentuated by the fact that USC was led by a black quarterback, further negating the myth that African Americans could not play this position because of its leadership requirements.

The actions of Bryant immediately after the game were the most telling. He did enter USC's locker room and ask a surprised McKay if he could "borrow" Cunningham. What happened next is up for debate. Whether the rest is truth or lore may never really be known. Whether it happened as some say it happened, or as the storytellers say it happened, is immaterial. The rest was history.

* * *

In the years after the game, Bear elevated his program back to the top of the college football world.

"Alabama came out to the Coliseum the next year," recalled McKay, "and they gave us a big surprise. They had a terrific team that year."

Bryant's 1971 squad played through an undefeated regular season before losing to Nebraska, considered one of the best teams ever, in the Orange Bowl. His 1978–1979 national champions, by then fully integrated, are considered to be one of the great football dynasties of all time, marred only by a 1978 loss in Birmingham to Charlie White and USC.

Cunningham had propelled his team to victory in a contest that changed the minds, attitudes, hopes, dreams, and expectations of a new generation of Americans, white and black. In Dixie, there is the world before and then the world after this game. The results of this game are clear: goodness, decency, and justice prevailed. After this game, hatred was benched, and a nation lived up to its creed.

"That's what Jim Murray wrote in the *Times*," recalled Goux. "You know, at the time, I had my hands full. So did Coach McKay. We were talented but unable to build on that game. Our season was disappointing. The team was not as together as others were, although talentwise we were close. But it was only over time, the media bringing it up, old friends talking about it and asking about it, that I've come to see just what an incredible event it was. I made some strong statements about it at the time, but remember, right after we won that game, we had to fly back to L.A. and get ready for the next one, and the one after that. Sports are hard to be involved in and see the big picture."

What had happened, whether Goux was too busy to see it or not, was that a region looked into its collective Christian conscience and knew they could no longer interpret the Bible from a racist perspective. For Greek American USC linebacker John Papadakis, who found himself as the liaison bridging the volatile black-white world that still divided the Trojans, it fulfilled the Platonic ideals that shaped his life and gave it meaning.

Schools in the South, from kindergarten to law school, became diverse centers of learning. Politicians who had practiced race baiting integrated their staffs and courted black votes from newly enfranchised citizens. The Democratic Party, unable to completely shed itself of its Jim Crow past, lost the South to the Republicans, who rode their conservative, anti-Communist agenda to sweeping victories for Richard Nixon, Ronald Reagan, George H. W. Bush, and George W. Bush.

Today, the South is part of America. Its college and pro teams are as diverse as anybody's, with hardly any notice. It can be argued that the American South, by its own will (with some prompting, to be sure), has made a more positive change for the better, in less time, than any geographical region on the face of the earth. If such change could happen there, hope springs eternal everywhere. As the world deals with the problems of religious hatred, intolerance, and terrorism, this is a worthy thought.

On December 7, 2003, the day after number-one-ranked USC assured themselves of a spot in the Rose Bowl against Michigan (and with it, a chance at the national championship), influential African American sports columnist William Rhoden of the *New York Times* wrote that one of the reasons he wanted the Trojans to win the national title was

> so the nation can be reintroduced to Sam Cunningham. He is my favorite Trojan and an important player in the social evolution of college football.
>
> He and his former teammate John Papadakis joined the team on a charter flight last August when the Trojans traveled to Alabama to play Auburn in the season opener. Cunningham said he addressed the team.

"I told them I'd never lost a game in Alabama," he said. "I don't want this to be the first."

"I tell them, 'I'm a warrior just like you—just old and broke up now—but when I was playing, this is how I approached the game. Football is more entertainment now. There's more money. But in the trenches, it's still just a football game.

"I'm really connected to this team. This is a little more personal because I know them. None of them knew me when I played; they weren't even born. They just see my picture on the wall. They walk past it going out. They walk past it coming in. I get a chance to share with them.

*   *   *

The South did "rise again." Today, it is a cultural, economic, and political juggernaut. This rise, in keeping with the sporting nature of the region, often had an athletic component. In 1996, Atlanta hosted the most multicultural event ever devised, the Olympic Games that the ancient Greeks placed so much reverence in.

In observing the sweep of history, one makes note of social change. There is, of course, the rise of Christianity, the granting of civil liberties to English commoners, the Protestant Reformation, and the Renaissance, to name a few highlights. Most of these changes took place over decades, sometimes centuries.

In America, change occurred by comparable warp speed. For thousands of years, slavery was a thriving economic institution. Four score and seven years after the creation of America, it was a memory. While it is true that England and other nations abolished slavery prior to the United States, none did it at such great cost. Therefore, the actions of these other countries pale in comparison to the impact of America's abolition.

The lesson of all this is that for whatever reason—whether it be God, or a superior political system, or very smart, hardworking, well-meaning people of faith and charitable hearts—when the United States decides to do something, it does it better than any other country could. Other countries have taken centuries to overcome angst, bitterness, and hatred. How is it possible that a little group of agrarian colonies, separated by oceans, isolated from the world's centers of commerce, politics, and intellectualism, could in 200 years have risen to become the most powerful, most influential, most successful nation—indeed *empire*—this planet has ever seen? Is it possible this is just coincidence, or is this truly the promised land, God's country?

Nobody can claim that Alabama in 1978 was paradise for African Americans, but one can argue that in the eight years since the USC-Alabama game at Legion Field, the state, the region, and its university had made as swift and sure a social change for the better as any place, perhaps ever.

This change, when one considers the scope and power of its magnitude and then makes note of the swiftness of its time frame, can only be considered an American miracle—the kind we increasingly have come to rely on!

This change, in light of the memory of Bull Connor, firehouses, and German shepherds just fifteen years before, was cataclysmic. It is the kind of change that makes men and women find religion. It was deep, personal, and real.

Jeff Prugh, who had written the 1970 game story for the *L.A. Times*, discovered that night at Legion Field that "there's more to write about than sports." He moved into news reporting and transferred to his paper's Atlanta bureau. Whereas eight years before he was observing blacks barely edging their way into a slightly open door, he now found himself dealing with blacks in control of many of the levers of power. Prugh, who possessed a Californian's liberalism, now found himself at odds with Andrew Young and the new black leadership in Atlanta. When Prugh's quest for truth led to his criticism of that black power structure, he was assailed. Blacks no longer needed the "protection" of a "friendly" white journalist like Jeff Prugh to prop them up with fake self-esteem. The blacks were now discovering that they were part of the competition that makes America hum right along.

Black advancement in politics has surpassed demographic expectations. Today, blacks are mayors, congressmen, congresswomen, police chiefs, university presidents, and Fortune 500 executives. No blacks have ascended to the White House yet, and they have made few gains in the Senate, but it is now considered standard form to include a number of blacks—as well as other minorities—in presidential cabinets and judgeships. A black man, Barack Obama, is considered a leading Democratic presidential contender for 2008. A black Republican woman, Condoleezza Rice, has denied interest in the White House, but (her role in the Iraq War aside) if she did run, she would be a contender at the very least. A black Republican man, Colin Powell, has probably seen his time come and go, but had he run in 1996 or 2000, he would have been a very strong contender.

In surveying American culture, one might even conclude that there is a distinct *advantage*, at least in some professions, to being black. Blacks complain that they too often do not get the juicy hero roles in Hollywood. There is some truth to that. Denzel Washington has broken through in a big way, but he is, for now, an exception to the norm. However, commercials and character roles sometimes seem to favor the black persona. A typical recurring example is the high-strung, high-wire white cop who is shown the steady course by a tough yet fair black police chief or partner (think of Nick Nolte and Eddie Murphy in *48 Hours* or Mel Gibson and Danny Glover in the *Lethal Weapon* franchise).

Blacks and other minorities often fill commercials and "sidekick" roles. A scene of social friends is often not considered complete without a black face. A common trend, especially in TV ads, is to pair a white Dumbellionite subordinate with an all-knowing black colleague, who usually is computer-wired to the nth degree.

There is no doubt that it is a major advantage to be a *black conservative* in politics, business, talk radio, and a number of other professions. White people have come to open themselves up to black success, black intelligence, and black congeniality.

Observing America and the world in 2006–2007, it would be Pollyannaish to say that racial prejudice has been defeated, any more than terrorism or drugs have been defeated. But the world is a vastly different place today, and it might be difficult to find any place like the American South in the thirty-seven years that span 1970 to 2007.

America has its detractors. When searching for evidence that the United States is not as great as I claim it to be, people often point to slavery and our troubled civil rights history, claiming that "America is a racist nation."

At first glance, the history of slavery and Jim Crow would appear to justify the notion that America actually is racist.

However, there is one overriding fact disputing this notion more thoroughly than any other. To explore this premise, one must ask, "Who are the one thousand most famous and successful black people in the history of humankind?" *Famous* is a subjective term, but think broadly: athletes, musicians, actors, educators, politicians, military leaders, civil rights advocates, educators, authors, writers, broadcasters, pastors, entrepreneurs, and so on.

Most of these black people are probably American citizens.

Think of Muhammad Ali, George Washington Carver, Frederick Douglass, Booker T. Washington, Colin Powell, Jim Brown, Tony Dungy, Toni Morrison, Bryant Gumbel, Bernard Shaw, Denzel Washington, W. E. B. Du Bois, Armstrong Williams, and Beyoncé, just to name a few.

Is it possible for a racist nation to produce so many great people? The facts make this an impertinent question.

* * *

Southern sportswriters have their own take on the game, whether it be Allen Barra, Keith Dunnavant, or the *Birmingham Post-Herald*'s Bill Lumpkin, who in response to recent talk about books and movies depicting the event wrote, "I'm sure the abundance of Alabama fans in the Legion Field crowd of 72,157 left the game that night saying to themselves: We've got to have a Sam Cunningham. I'm sure Bryant had the same thoughts. Who wouldn't?

"Did Bryant schedule the game years in advance, hoping a positive impact by USC black players might hasten integration of his football team?

"Preposterous."

Lumpkin went on to state, truthfully, that the game was scheduled because of the McKay-Bryant friendship, and he correctly pointed out that Bryant had no way of knowing that a black Trojan running back would dominate his team. But Lumpkin also did not realize what had happened in some of those California high school coaching clinics, when McKay and Bryant, out of the earshot of others, sharing a late-night drink, confided in each other their most secret hopes and desires.

Lumpkin attempted in his commentary to state that because black athletes played professionally in the NFL, in the minor leagues, and by 1970 with the Atlanta Braves and Atlanta Hawks, for example, that segregation was over.

"An ironic twist to the Cunningham premise is that a month earlier the New York Jets and Buffalo Bills played an exhibition game at Legion Field," he wrote. "A player on the Bills team was one of the greatest running backs in USC history by the name of O. J. Simpson.

"The year before, another former USC running back played Legion Field with the Kansas City Chiefs. Mike Garrett. In 1968, the Chicago Bears brought a fellow named Gale Sayers to town."

Yes, Reggie Jackson had played for the Birmingham Barons, where Bryant's own son was a club executive. The point, however, is not that segregation was over. It was ending, but it was not over. The 1970 USC-Alabama game was the final nail in its coffin.

Sam Cunningham was embarrassed to hear Marx Goux say on that September day in Birmingham that he had done more for civil rights in the past three hours than Martin Luther King Jr. had done in twenty years. He is still embarrassed to hear the phrase repeated, as it has been by many people over the decades. But Sam knows that the current racial climate he lives in is markedly better than it was then, and Dr. King's legacy is the one most responsible for this climate. He also knows that he deserves to feel proud of his role in the scheme of things. He knows what he did was exceptional; and he understands now, after years of searching, that what he did is deserving of a special place in American history.

"Once you get people together, once they're sweatin' and workin' together, whether they're black or white, that falls down," said Taylor Watson, curator of the Paul W. Bryant Museum, in the 2006 CSTV documentary *Tackling Segregation*. "That's one of the great things about sports. It has done that. It has taken an obstacle and just smashed it to the ground."

"Even the most ignorant and bigoted individual *has* to respect talent," stated Sylvester Croom. "He *has* to respect courage. He *has* to respect discipline. All the lies, all the myths, on both sides, go away. It's all erased, except for what's inside of you."

"Did it radically change things overnight for black people?" asked Allen Barra rhetorically. "No, but it was the beginning. It changed for the fans, for the mind-set of the people, in Alabama and all over the South."

"We played eight linebackers, looking for someone who could tackle [Cunningham]," recalled former assistant coach Pat Dye, laughing. "We never found one who could tackle him." Dye reflected on Bryant's legacy, smiled, and added: "Coach Bryant is to the South what Martin Luther King is to the world."

"This game affected all of the South," said Charles Young. "This game affected the North. This game affected the East. This game—some people call it a shift, a paradigm shift. It was philosophies being challenged. That's what this game is."

"I think the ending was perfect," said Craig Fertig. "Coach Bryant won one, Coach McKay won one. They shook hands."

On the night when Papadakis and Cunningham arrived in Alabama for the 2003 USC-Auburn game, they were stunned to discover that Sam was a well-known hero to the local black populace. Their first hint was when an African American cab driver refused to take their money. Waiters stared at him as if he was "*the* Sam Cunningham," according to sportswriter Don Yaeger.

William Wagstaff, the headwaiter at the Sahara that night, told Yaeger, "I remember it . . . and everyone I know remembers it. . . . I had to say thank you. I wanted to thank him for what he did that night for us."

One by one, employees of the Sahara came out to shake Sam's hand.

"[Bryant] told me about how he'd read that stuff in the paper about me," said Clarence Davis, recalling Bryant's postgame graciousness, in the *Los Angeles Times*, "about how I used to live in Birmingham and how I thought about what it would be like to be one of the first black players at Alabama. He said to me, 'If only I had known about you two years ago. I was hoping you might not be very good, but now I'm a believer.'"

"This was the game that changed *the* game," said U. W. Clemon, who had filed the lawsuit against Bryant for failing to integrate his program. He did not attend the game, but his African American friends described the attitude of white 'Bama fans as "a Damascus Road experience for many of them."

In Jeff Prugh's September 14, 1970, postgame report for the *L.A. Times*, he reported overhearing a conversation at a Birmingham hotel coffee shop.

"You know," said a man in a plaid shirt, "I sure bet the Bear wishes he had two or three of them Nigra boys on his team *now*. They were huge!"

"The hospitable folks of Alabama began to leave Legion Field with 11 minutes to play between the Crimson Tide and USC Saturday night," wrote Bud Furillo in the *L.A. Herald-Examiner*. "And some may have been wondering if it might not be a good idea to search for some black running backs.

"It would appear at this stage in the evolution of man that the darkest people run fastest. Heck, they should. They have more practice."

No Alabama media outlet had made mention of race in the immediate aftermath of the game. There were no editorials suggesting that integration might just help the Tide roll faster. But if they were hoping to "sweep it under the rug," they would not be able to, since, to use another cliché, the "horse was out of the barn." Perhaps the best example of the new thinking came in Bryant's 1974 autobiography, *Bear: The Hard Life and Good Times of Alabama's Coach*. Bryant's view of black athletes seemed to mirror his view of his own hardscrabble life: "The ones who will consistently suck their guts up and stick by you now are the blacks, because they don't have anything to go back to. . . . Bo Schembechler of Michigan told me once, 'A black won't ever quit you,' and I got to thinking the way it had been for me, and he was right. Because I didn't have any place to go either."

"Birmingham will never be the same," wrote Jim Murray. "And brother, it's a good thing. The point of the game is not the score, the Bear, the Trojans; the point of the game will be reason, democracy, hope. The real winner will be Alabama. It'll be their first since the second day at Gettysburg, or maybe, The Wilderness."

The following Thursday, in a column titled "Language of Alabama," Murray wrote, "Time to time, when I visit a neighboring country to the South, I try to pass on to you some of the key phrases which will help you to get along in a strange tongue. . . . Alabama is a body of land separated from the main body of the United States by a century."

Murray continued with a "non-Berlitz course," but in a rare lack of eloquence the Pulitzer Prize–winning columnist appeared small and churlish, paying for it by virtue of a flood of angry letters to the *Times* over the next couple of weeks. In the years after he wrote that column, Murray was happy to discover that the South indeed had grown up, and he was more than pleased to eat his words.

Birmingham-born Florida State coach Bobby Bowden felt that Bryant used the game to "change the minds of Alabama fans."

"It is an honor to be a part of it," Sam Cunningham said in 2006. He was quoted by Don Yaeger as stating, "The thing about games is that if you go out and play really, really hard and play as well as you can and do the things you need to do, you never know when the hand of greatness is going to touch you. That night I had no clue that anything was going to happen because of my play. . . . My motivation was to play well enough so that I could play the next week. That was it. It had nothing to do with changing color lines, doing anything like that. But you never know when you will get the chance to do something special."

"Cunningham could not have spoken out against segregation any more forcefully if he had been preaching from a pulpit," *Sports Illustrated* wrote in assessing the game to be one of the "20 Greatest Tipping Points" in twentieth-century sports annals. "Alabama football, the Southeastern Conference and the South in general would never be the same. Even those 'Bama fans who didn't find the football program's racist policy to be hateful now saw that it was impractical."

For years, the myths surrounding the game outweighed the truths. The *Atlanta Journal-Constitution* reported incorrectly in 1992 that the night of the loss, Bryant told his staff to "begin recruiting black players." Of course, he had already begun doing that.

Warren Koon of the *Tuscaloosa News* actually reported that as USC left the field, they had a stash of Confederate money, which they threw around the field like confetti, all the while "whooping and carrying on like it was Gettysburg or something."

This is completely untrue. There was absolutely no Confederate money, and the Trojans departed the field quietly, with the usual class and dignity of a team that coaches like to say act as if they've "done this before," because they had.

"I think there were coaches at that time who wanted to integrate because it was right," recalled Grambling's legendary former coach, Eddie Robinson. "There were people like that. But I think most coaches, especially at big Southern state schools, integrated out of necessity. They realized there were many black players who were future All-Pros with great speed, size, quickness and intelligence. If they couldn't get them at Alabama or Mississippi, then those guys could end up playing against them, just like Nebraska [with Johnny Rodgers] and USC beat Alabama.

"So it wasn't so much a matter of what they felt about integration; it was mostly about wanting to win. If they could convince the alumni that their school could win with this black student-athlete, then the alumni might understand what it would mean to their program for this person to play."

"Having a black head coach at Mississippi State University is in many ways the final nail in the coffin of the kind of segregation for which the state and the region have been known for so long," wrote William Ferris, the senior associate director at the Center for the Study of the American South (and coeditor of *The Encyclopedia of Southern Culture*) at the University of North Carolina, in a December 12, 2003, editorial heralding the hiring of Sylvester Croom.

"Through the history of the last sixty years of our country, the state of Alabama has been a spot where a tremendous amount of significant cultural, social, and spiritual events have occurred," Pete Carroll told his USC team before introducing Papadakis and Cunningham prior to the momentous 2003 opener at Auburn. "For whatever reason, in this small rural state, there have just been significant things that have happened. I'm not going to stand here and try to recount them all because I can't.

"Sometimes people think about football as just a game. Sometimes it is more than that. We all have our own little chance at making a statement in our lifetimes, and for our football team at this time, if you haven't realized it, this is an extraordinary opportunity for us right now."

Carroll went on to describe to his players how Bryant wanted to bring "the University of Southern California to the South, to the Deep South," to make "a social statement. Anything could have happened that night. It could have been volatile, it could have been . . . Anything could have happened."

Cunningham was given the floor and said he was merely an older version of the young men in the room. Later, Carroll pulled a surprise from his pocket: a grainy video of the actual 1970 game. It was not a televised game; the feed was from the coaches' scouting film. But absent the sounds of the crowd or a droning announcer, the impact of Cunningham running over and through the Tide was even more powerful.

* * *

Making sense of what happened is easier said than done. In many ways, the Greek ideals of Socrates, Plato, and Aristotle were as alive on this day as they had been in the Parthenon some three thousand years before. The argument that Christian love propelled great change is easily accepted by some, less so by others. The forces of capitalism and democracy are attractive theories depending on whom they are being presented to. Perhaps placing the event into an easily understood niche is not possible, and instead we are left with the immortal words of William Shakespeare, who once wrote, "There are more things in heaven and earth, Horatio, than can be dreamt of in your philosophy."

What *is* known is that the United States was already a shining example of liberty and freedom to the world—despite prejudice, despite Vietnam—when in September 1970, liberalism and conservatism met at the fifty-yard line at Legion Field, in some ways for the last time. The winner was America.

Bibliography

The 1993–94 National Directory of College Athletics. Cleveland: Collegiate Directories, Inc., 1993

2006 USC Football Media Guide. Los Angeles: University of Southern California, 2006.

Adams, Bruce. "Cal sees the old USC swagger." *San Francisco Chronicle,* November 13, 2005.

Adande, J. A. "L.A. gets a double treat with Bush and James." *Los Angeles Times,* December 4, 2005.

———. "Return could mean back-to-back-to-back." *Los Angeles Times,* January 5, 2005.

Alabama Media Guide 2006. Tuscaloosa: University of Alabama, 2006.

Albee, Dave. "Keeping his lust for life." *Marin Independent Journal,* August 25, 2004.

———. "Coach T handed Carroll first gig." *Marin Independent Journal,* November 11, 2005.

Associated Press. "#1 USC 63, Hawaii 17." September 4, 2005.

———. "USC gets back to normal—scores 51 points." October 23, 2005.

———. "USC defense finally flexes its muscle." October 30, 2005.

Athlon Sports College Football. "Best of 2005." September 9, 2005.

Barra, Allen. *The Last Coach: A Life of Paul "Bear" Bryant.* New York: Norton, 2005.

Baum, Bob. "Trojans turn the tide on second-half surge." Associated Press, October 2, 2005.

Bisheff, Steve, and Loel Schrader. *Fight On! The Colorful Story of USC Football.* Nashville: Cumberland, 2006.

Bolch, Ben. "Leinart will take his time." *Los Angeles Times,* January 6, 2005.

———. "For Carroll, Dai is a family affair." *Los Angeles Times*, December 4, 2005.

Boyles, Bob, and Paul Guido. *Fifty Years of College Football*. Wilmington, Del.: Sideline Communications, 2005.

Brennan, Christine. "Trojans render Sugar Bowl meaningless." *USA Today*, January 2, 2004.

———. "No need for playoff this time." *USA Today*, January 5, 2005.

Carey, Jack. "Trojans don't horse around." *USA Today*, January 5, 2005.

Chavez, Kevin. "No need for nostalgia for Troy." *San Gabriel Valley News*, January 6, 2005.

Chengelis, Angelique. "USC defense overwhelms Michigan." *Detroit News*, January 2, 2004.

Chronicle News Services. "Arizona makes USC work for its fifth victory." *San Francisco Chronicle*, October 9, 2005.

Clary, Jack. *College Football's Great Dynasties: USC*. Popular Culture Ink, 1991.

Cole, Gary. *"Playboy's* 2004 pigskin preview." *Playboy*, September 2004.

———. "'05 *Playboy's* pigskin preview." *Playboy*, September 2005.

Collier, Gene. "Mitchell's tale still twisting." *Pittsburgh Post-Gazette*, September 2, 2004.

Collin, Phil. "Trojans go Carrolling." *Daily Breeze*, December 20, 2000.

Coyne, Tom. "Notre Dame hopes to rewrite the plot against USC." Associated Press, October 15, 2005.

Curtis, Jake. "These teams pass—or fail." *San Francisco Chronicle*, September 1, 2005.

———. "USC has offense, schedule to pull off unprecedented feat." *San Francisco Chronicle*, September 1, 2005.

———. "Pluck, luck benefit lion-hearted Leinart." *San Francisco Chronicle*, October 17, 2005.

———. "Diverse Trojan offense arguably the best ever." *San Francisco Chronicle*, November 3, 2005.

Dalton, Dennis. *Power Over People: Classical and Modern Political Theory*. Recorded course from Barnard College at Columbia University, New York. Available at www.teach12.com.

Dettlinger, Chet, and Jeff Prugh. *The List*. Atlanta: Philmay Enterprises, 1984.

Dilbeck, Steve. "Trojans' undefeated season leaves no doubt." *Los Angeles Daily News*, January 5, 2005.

Dohn, Brian. "Overshadowing Leinart?" *Long Beach Press-Telegram*, December 2, 2005.

DuFresne, Chris. "BCS obsessed." *Los Angeles Times*, January 5, 2005.

———. "Turnovers leave Sooners a shade of crimson." *Los Angeles Times*, January 5, 2005.

———. "With simple formula and fresh approach, Carroll builds a potential Trojan dynasty." *Los Angeles Times*, January 6, 2005.

———. "Weis leading a rivalry revival," *Los Angeles Times*, October 16, 2005.

———. "Getting to the point." *Los Angeles Times*, December 1, 2005.

———. "Putting the 'C' back in the BCS." *Los Angeles Times*, December 5, 2005.

———. "Rose Bowl hype balloon could burst on game day." *Los Angeles Times*, December 5, 2005.

Dunnavant, Keith. *Coach: Life of Paul "Bear" Bryant.* New York: Simon & Schuster, 1996.

———. *The Missing Ring.* New York: St. Martin's, 2006.

Dwyre, Bill. "More like powdered blue." *Los Angeles Times*, December 4, 2005.

Echoes of Notre Dame Football. Edited by John Heisler. Chicago: Triumph, 2006.

Elliott, Helene. "Trojans put up tough barricade to stop Sooners." *Los Angeles Times*, January 5, 2005.

ESPN College Football Encyclopedia. Edited by Michael MacCambridge. New York: ESPN, 2005.

Farmer, Sam. "49ers to go after Carroll." *Los Angeles Times*, January 6, 2005.

Feldman, Bruce. "Reaction time." *ESPN the Magazine*, August 30, 2004.

———. "Wanna see that again?" *ESPN the Magazine*, August 29, 2005.

Fighting Irish: The Might, the Magic, the Mystique of Notre Dame Football. St. Louis: The Sporting News, 2003.

Fittipaldo, Ray. "Experts: USC could be among greatest teams." *Pittsburgh Post-Gazette*, October 26, 2005.

Florence, Mal. *The Heritage of Troy.* JCP, 1980.

Friend, Tom. "Finishing school." *ESPN the Magazine*, July 18, 2005.

Game Day: Notre Dame Football. Foreword by Mike Golic. Chicago: Triumph, 2006.

Game Day: Southern California Football. Foreword by Manfred Moore. Chicago: Triumph, 2006.

Gardiner, Andy. "Tennessee, Nebraska top signing charts." *USA Today*, February 3, 2005.

Gigliotti, Jim. *Stadium Stories: USC Trojans.* Guilford, Conn.: Globe Pequot, 2005.

Gildea, William, and Christopher Jennison. *The Fighting Irish.* Englewood Cliffs, N.J.: Prentice-Hall, 1976.

Groom, Winston. *The Crimson Tide: An Illustrated History of Football at the University of Alabama.* Tuscaloosa: University of Alabama Press, 2000.

Hammerwold, Walter. "BCS finally delivers the goods." *Long Beach Press-Telegram*, December 5, 2005.

Harmonson, Todd. "Trojans run hog wild all night." *Orange County Register*, September 18, 2005.

———. "Two heads better for Trojans." *Orange County Register*, December 2, 2005.

———. "BCS will have its perfect game." *Orange County Register*, December 5, 2005.

Harris, Beth. "USC's focus: Limit mistakes." Associated Press, October 10, 2005.

Hayes, Matt. "Trouble for the Trojans." *The Sporting News*, October 21, 2005.

Himmelberg, Michele. "A workplace divided." *Orange County Register*, December 2, 2005.

Hisermam, Mike. "USC's win means a bit of a loss for business." *Los Angeles Times*, December 4, 2005.

Hoffarth, Tom. "L.A. deprived by early start." *Los Angeles Daily News*, January 5, 2005.

Jares, Joe, and John Robinson. *Conquest*, Neff, 1981.

———. *The USC Report*. October, 2006.

Katz, Fred. *The Glory of Notre Dame*. Bartholomey House, 1971.

Keisser, Bob. "Bam's impact not forgotten." *Long Beach Press-Telegram*, September 12, 2005.

———. "It's an old-school drubbing." *Long Beach Press-Telegram*, December 4, 2005.

Klein, Gary. "Cardinal and bold." *Los Angeles Times*, January 5, 2005.

———. "Conquest." *Los Angeles Times*, January 5, 2005.

———. "USC does the grunt work with ease." *Los Angeles Times*, September 18, 2005.

———. "Leinart's sneak peak." *Los Angeles Times*, October 16, 2005.

———. "Chart breakers." *Los Angeles Times*, December 2, 2005.

———. "Trojans go on a tear." *Los Angeles Times*, December 4, 2005.

Knapp, Gwen. "Finally, BCS gets its 'Magic' moment." *San Francisco Chronicle*, December 6, 2005.

Krikorian, Doug. "Pundits way off on USC." *Long Beach Press-Telegram*, January 6, 2005.

———. "Dennis waiting for his turn." *Long Beach Press-Telegram*, December 1, 2005.

———. "Trojans leave the Bruins Bushed." *Long Beach Press-Telegram*, December 4, 2005.

LeBatard, Dan. "The view from . . . Miami." *Miami Herald*, January 5, 2005.

LeBrock, Barry. *The Trojan Ten*. New York: New American Library, 2006.

Lumpkin, Bill. "USC back wasn't the real key to integration." *Birmingham Post-Herald*.

McCready, Neal. "Cunningham had impact on 'Bama football." *Mobile Press-Register*, August 2003.

McKay, John, with Jim Perry. *McKay: A Coach's Story*. New York: Atheneum, 1974.

Michaels, Vicki. "Southern Cal loaded for another shot." *USA Today*, January 2, 2004.

Modesti, Kevin. "Routing Oklahoma only the start for USC?" *Los Angeles Daily News*, January 5, 2005.

———. "Everything went right on this night." *Los Angeles Daily News*, January 6, 2005.

Moore, Leon. "Carroll re-energizes Trojans." *USA Today*, December 31, 2003.

———. "Senior Colbert turns in career day." *USA Today*, January 2, 2004.

———. "USC strikes first in title race." *USA Today*, January 2, 2004.

———. "Carroll's Trojans have talent to maintain prime position." *USA Today*, January 5, 2005.

———. "Junior Leinart easily junks Heisman jinx." *USA Today*, January 5, 2005.

Moran, Malcolm. "Dream season ends with nightmare." *USA Today*, January 5, 2005.

———. "Leinart cements legend with late heroics." *USA Today*, October 17, 2005.

Murphy, Austin. "Without a doubt." *Sports Illustrated*, January 10, 2005.

———. "College football 2005." *Sports Illustrated*, August 15, 2005.

———. "Danger is his game." *Sports Illustrated*, August 15, 2005.

———. "Can anyone beat USC?" *Sports Illustrated*, October 17, 2005.

———. "Fantastic finishes." *Sports Illustrated*, October 24, 2005.

Murray, Jim. "Hatred shut out as Alabama finally joins the Union." *Los Angeles Times*, September 13, 1970.

Nadel, John. "USC steamrolls Stanford." Associated Press, November 6, 2005.

Newhouse, Dave. "Leinart outshines Bears as USC cruises to victory." *Oakland Tribune*, November 13, 2005.

Norwood, Robyn. "Spotted fever." *Los Angeles Times*, December 3, 2005.

———. "Trojan defense gives the Bruins no shot." *Los Angeles Times*, December 4, 2005.

Nyiri, Alan. *The Heritage of USC*. Los Angeles: University of Southern California, 1999.

Parseghian, Ara. *What It Means to Be Fighting Irish*. Chicago: Triumph, 2004.

Penner, Mike. "There are no big winners in ABC booth." *Los Angeles Times*, January 5, 2005.

Perry, Jim. "Alabama goes black 'n' white." *Los Angeles Herald-Examiner*, September 11, 1971.

———. "USC loses one of its legends with the death of McKay." *Trojan Tail*, 2001.

Peterson, Anne M. "Oregon overwhelmed by USC in second half." Associated Press, September 25, 2005.

Pierson, Don. *The Trojans: Southern California Football*. Chicago: Regnery, 1974.

Plaschke, Bill. "It's crystal clear—no one can touch this USC team." *Los Angeles Times*, January 5, 2005.

———. "Good from the word 'go.'" *Los Angeles Times*, October 16, 2005.

———. "In run-up to a vote, Bush surely makes his case." *Los Angeles Times*, December 4, 2005.

Pool, Bob. "Rah, rah—boo, hiss." *Los Angeles Times*, December 3, 2005.

Prugh, Jeff. "Trojans fall on Alabama . . ." *Los Angeles Times*, September 13, 1970.

———. "Two black students had enrolled before Wallace showdown." *Los Angeles Times*, June 11, 1978.

———. *The Herschel Walker Story*. Fawcett, 1983.

———. "George Wallace was America's merchant of venom." *Marin Independent Journal*, September 15, 1998.

———. "Anger boiled within Gerald Ford before this football game." *Marin Independent Journal*, August 12, 1999.

Rappoport, Ken. *The Trojans: A Story of Southern California Football*. Huntsville, Ala.: Strode, 1974.

Ratto, Ray. "USC is the new Notre Dame, the new 'America's Team.'" *San Francisco Chronicle*, November 1, 2005.

Russo, Ralph. "Bush runs off with Heisman Trophy." Associated Press, December 11, 2005.

Schulman, Henry. "Astros win in time to watch USC." *San Francisco Chronicle*, October 16, 2005.

"Shake-up in college poll." *USA Today*, October 17, 2005.

Simers, T. J. "The Trojans owe it all to good ol' Uncle Pete." *Los Angeles Times*, January 5, 2005.

Sports Illustrated. "USC Trojans." 2005.

Springer, Steve, and Michael Arkush. *60 Years of USC-UCLA Football*. Stamford, Conn.: Longmeadow, 1991.

Steele, Michael R. *Knute Rockne: A Portrait of a Notre Dame Legend*. Champaign, Ill.: Sports Publishing, 1998.

Stewart, Larry. "Peete was looking for a special delivery." *Los Angeles Times*, December 1, 2005.

Taylor, Phil. "The Tide gets rolled." *Sports Illustrated*, September 27, 2004.

Thamel, Peter. "Leinart's goal-line dive gives No. 1 USC win in thriller." *New York Times*, October 16, 2005.

A Tradition Restored: Los Angeles Daily News. Champaign, Ill.: Sports Publishing, 2003.

Travers, Steven. "When legends played." *StreetZebra*, September 1999.

———. "Petros Papadakis: USC's player of the month." *StreetZebra*, October 1999.

———. "Is it too early to hype Palmer for the Heisman?" *StreetZebra*, September 2000.

———. "Villa Park wins rivalry game." *Los Angeles Times*, September 25, 2000.

———. "It wasn't a football game, it was a sighting." *StreetZebra*, November 2000.

———. "Legend: A conversation with John McKay." www.streetzebra.com, March 2000.

———. "Rich McKay." www.streetzebra.com, April 2000.

———. "The eternal Trojan." www.streetzebra.com, September 2000.

———. "The tradition of Troy." Unpublished book proposal, 1995.

———. "An unsung hero." *San Francisco Examiner*, May 1, 2001.

———. "He was a legend of the old school variety." Unpublished article, 2001.

———. *Barry Bonds: Baseball's Superman.* Champaign, Ill.: Sports Publishing, 2002.

———. "Orange Countification: The true story of how the GOP helped the South rise again." Unpublished article, 2005.

———. "Dynasty: The new centurions of Troy." Excerpted from *The USC Trojans: College Football's All-Time Greatest Dynasty.* Lanham, Md.: Taylor, 2006 (based on "2005 USC Trojans: Greatest college football dynasty ever?" available at www.american-reporter.com, July 4, 2005).

———. "The four horsemen of Southern California." Excerpted from *The USC Trojans: College Football's All-Time Greatest Dynasty.* Lanham, Md.: Taylor, 2006.

———. *The USC Trojans: College Football's All-Time Greatest Dynasty.* Lanham, Md.: Taylor, 2006.

———. *God's Country: A Conservative, Christian Worldview of How History Formed the United States Empire and America's Manifest Destiny for the Twenty-First Century.* Forthcoming.

Walsh, Bill. "Coaching Key to USC's Success." *Los Angeles Times*, January 5, 2005.

Wharton, David. "USC is better than OK for title win." *Los Angeles Times*, January 5, 2005.

———. "Leinart played conquest in clutch." *Los Angeles Times*, October 16, 2005.

———. "USC bowls over UCLA." *Los Angeles Times*, December 4, 2005.

Wharton, David, and Gary Klein. *Conquest: Pete Carroll and the Trojans' Climb to the Top of the College Football Mountain*. Chicago: Triumph, 2005.

Whicker, Mark. "Many questions abound about USC's defense, but does it matter?" *Orange County Register*, September 18, 2005.

———. "Perfect touch." *Orange County Register*, December 2, 2005.

White, Lonnie. *UCLA vs. USC: 75-Years of the Greatest Rivalry in Sports*. Los Angeles: Los Angeles Times Books, 2004.

———. "Bruins outgrow terrible twos." *Los Angeles Times*, December 1, 2005.

———. "Bush runs over Bruins' defense." *Los Angeles Times*, December 4, 2005.

Whiteside, Kelly. "Southern Cal could be just warming up." *USA Today*, January 5, 2005.

Wieberg, Steve. "What USA's top prep players are thinking." *USA Today*, December 31, 2003.

Witz, Billy. "Soon after early lead, OU fell apart." *Los Angeles Daily News*, January 5, 2005.

Wojciechowski, Gene. "USC setting standard for football dominance." ESPN.com (http://sports.espn.go.com/espn/columns/story?columnist =wojciechowski_gene&i%20d=2249925%3E%20&id=2249925), December 6, 2005.

Wolf, Scott. "It's unanimous: USC captures title in rout." *Los Angeles Daily News*, January 5, 2005.

———. "Leinart mum about his future." *Los Angeles Daily News*, January 5, 2005.

———. "Analysis: Can Trojans win a third title in a row?" *Long Beach Press-Telegram*, January 6, 2005.

———. "USC future is bright if Carroll stays." *Los Angeles Daily News*, January 6, 2005.

———. "Route 66 to Pasadena." *Long Beach Press-Telegram*, December 4, 2005.

Yaeger, Don, Sam Cunningham, and John Papadakis. *Turning of the Tide*. New York: Center Street, 2006.

Yaeger, Don, and Douglas S. Looney. *Under the Tarnished Dome*. New York: Simon & Schuster, 1993.

Zakaria, Fareed. *The Future of Freedom: Illiberal Democracy at Home and Abroad*. New York: Norton, 2003.

Websites

www.aaregistry.com.

www.cstv.com

www.rolltide.com.

www.trojanreport.com.

www.uscfootball.blogspot.com
www.usctrojans.com.
www.wearesc.com.

Additional DVD

Coach Paul "Bear" Bryant. New York: College Sports Television, 2005.
The History of Notre Dame Football. Burbank, Calif: Warner Home Video, 2006.
The History of USC Football. Produced and directed by Roger Springfield. Burbank, Calif.: Warner Home Video, 2005.*In Their Own Words: Marv Goux*. Los Angeles: Fox Sports, 2006.
Tackling Segregation. New York: College Sports Television, 2006.

Additional Video

Trojan Video Gold. Narrated by Tom Kelly. Los Angeles: University of Southern California, 1987.

Additional Websites

www.cfrc.com/Archives/Top_Programs_2004.htm
www.lhgames.com
www.msnbc.com

Additional Documentaries

Songs of Our Success. Hosted by Tony McEwen, 2003.
Sports Century. ESPN.

Miscellaneous

Around the Horn. ESPN.
Best Damn Sports Show Period. Fox Sports.
The Jim Rome Show. Premiere Radio Networks.
Pardon the Interruption. ESPN.
Rome Is Burning. ESPN.

Index